UNIVERSITY OF MEMPHIS LIBRARIES
3 2109 00876 8468

W9-CDO-901

CIVIL WAR BOOKS

A Critical Bibliography

II

VOLUME TWO

CIVIL WAR BOOKS

A Critical Bibliography

edited by

ALLAN NEVINS
JAMES I. ROBERTSON, JR.
BELL I. WILEY

Published for the U.S. Civil War Centennial Commission by

LOUISIANA STATE UNIVERSITY PRESS
BATON ROUGE

Library of Congress Catalog Card Number: 67-10687
SBN 8071-0310 1

PREFACE

This volume concludes a project begun five years ago by the U.S. Civil War Centennial Commission. Impetus for the first critical listing of principal Civil War titles came from the commission's chief officers: Allan Nevins, Chairman; James I. Robertson, Jr., Executive Director; and Bell I. Wiley, Chairman of the Executive Committee.

How this bibliography originated, and the procedures and restrictions involved in its preparation, are outlined in *Civil War Books*, I, v-vii, and need only be summarized here.

As the editors stated at the outset, the major objective of this work "was to analyze those volumes familiar and unfamiliar, general or limited, indispensable or useless, for the benefit of anyone delving into the literature of the Civil War." The seventeen historians involved in the compilation have never wavered from that goal. Section editors carefully examined every known bibliography—including the bibliographies in all books cited here, as well as some not included. The compilers visited numerous public and private depositories in search of relatively obscure titles. A majority of the editors made a meticulous, volume-by-volume examination of the unsurpassed holdings in the Library of Congress.

The result, of course, is not an exhaustive listing in the literal sense. To have itemized the estimated 60,000 books, pamphlets, and monographs treating of the Civil War would have been an impossibility for both editors and publisher. Yet this is undeniably the most comprehensive bibliography ever produced of the major and minor Civil War books.

Doubtless some omitted titles merited inclusion in this work. The editors repeat that omissions stemmed from one of several reasons: inadvertence, lack of Library of Congress cards, the unavailability to compilers of some titles—and the unimportance of others. This listing includes the best-known studies, and those most likely to be consulted by the student of the period. As such, this work should go far in remedying the greatest bibliographical deficiency that has heretofore confronted persons interested in the 1860–1865 period.

That Volume II falls 600 titles short of the 3,000 predicted in the beginning is attributable to one factor: the disappointingly few studies in the areas of government and politics, North and South. Obviously, much work remains to be done in those fields, especially on the Southern side. It is hoped that this bibliography will stimulate an increased study of Federal and Confederate politics.

One change in the roster of compilers occurred during the production of this bibliography. Owing to an unexpectedly heavy work load, Dr. Malcolm McMillan had to relinquish his editorship of the section, "The Confederacy—State and Local Studies." His colleague, Dr. Thomas A. Belser, Jr., volunteered to labor in his stead. That section reflects well the scholarship Professor Belser added to the overall project.

In this two-volume bibliography are more than

5,000 Civil War book titles. The cumulative index at the back of this volume lists each entry by title and author, and under one or more subject headings. Every effort has been made in its compilation to facilitate to the maximum degree the location of specific titles.

Once again the editors wish to express their deep appreciation to the following persons who contributed much in the preparation of this bibliography: the late Edmund C. Gass, James V. Murfin, the personnel of the Library of Congress's Card Division, the staff of the Louisiana State University Press, and—especially—the fifteen compilers who gave so unselfishly of their time and talents. Lastly, to David Walters and Robert T. Bell, graduate students at the University of Montana and Virginia Polytechnic Institute, respectively, Professor Robertson is indebted for assistance in the compilation of the index.

ALLAN NEVINS
JAMES I. ROBERTSON, JR.
BELL I. WILEY

COMPILERS

E. B. LONG was director of research for Bruce Catton's *Centennial History of the Civil War*. A research associate to Allan Nevins since 1965, he is the author or editor of a number of Civil War works.

ROBERT W. JOHANNSEN, author of *Frontier Politics and the Sectional Conflict* and now completing a biography of Stephen A. Douglas, is professor of history at the University of Illinois.

RODNEY C. LOEHR is professor of history at the University of Minnesota. He is currently at work on a history of military government in the Civil War.

JOHN T. HUBBELL is assistant professor of history at Kent State University, editor of *Civil War History*, and a doctoral candidate at the University of Illinois. He has published several articles on the pre-Civil War period.

WILLIAM E. PARRISH is professor and chairman of the history department at Westminster College. He is the author of three books on Missouri in the Civil War period.

MARTIN ABBOTT is professor and chairman of the History Department at the University of South Florida. His most recent work is *The Freedmen's Bureau in South Carolina, 1865–1872*.

MAY S. RINGOLD is professor of history at Mississippi State College for Women and the author of *The Role of the State Legislatures in the Confederacy*.

THOMAS A. BELSER, JR., is associate professor of history and university archivist at Auburn University. He is now at work on a military history of the Civil War in the Trans-Mississippi.

JAMES I. ROBERTSON, JR., the managing editor of this bibliography, is professor of history at Virginia Polytechnic Institute. He is currently preparing a volume on Civil War historiography.

CONTENTS

CIVIL WAR BOOKS

A Critical Bibliography

II

GENERAL WORKS

E. B. Long

Abbot, George Maurice.
Contributions towards a bibliography on the civil war in the United States. I. Regimental histories. By Geo. Maurice Abbot. Philadelphia [Collins, printer] 1886.

iii, [5]–34 p. 24cm.

Useful in its day, this bibliography for state and regimental participation has now been superseded by the Dornbusch compilation.

Abbott, John S[tevens] C[abot] 1805–1877.
The history of the civil war in America; comprising a full and impartial account of the origin and progress of the rebellion, of the various naval and military engagements, of the heroic deeds performed by armies and individuals, and of touching scenes in the field, the camp, the hospital, and the cabin. By John S. C. Abbott ... New York, H. Bill, 1866.

2 v. front., pl., port., maps. 24½cm.

Now archaic and mainly a period piece; strongly pro-Union; no annotation.

Adams, James Truslow, 1878–
America's tragedy, by James Truslow Adams ... New York, London, C. Scribner's sons, 1934.

vi p., 2 l., 415 p. illus. (maps) 23 cm.

Emphasizes pre-war, causative factors; war coverage is mainly political and social, with slavery stressed as a prime factor.

The **American** annual cyclopædia and **register of important events** ... Embracing political, civil, military, and social affairs; public documents; biography, statistics, commerce, finance, literature, science, agriculture, and mechanical industry. v. [1]–14; 1861–74. New York, D. Appleton and company, 1862–75.

14 v. illus., ports. 25½cm.

Encyclopedic yearbooks for each year of the war; excellent for congressional summaries, and still a most useful tool.

American heritage.
American heritage Civil War chronology, with notes on the leading participants. New York, American Heritage Pub. Co., ©1960.

[39] p. 28 cm.

A rather brief but usable pamphlet adequate for the very general reader.

American heritage.
The American heritage picture history of the Civil War, by the editors of American heritage. Editor in charge: Richard M. Ketchum. Narrative by Bruce Catton. New York, American Heritage Pub. Co.; book trade distribution by Doubleday [1960]

630 p. illus. (part col.) ports., maps (part col.) facsims. 29 cm.

By far the best of the modern general picture-book histories; unique maps complement Catton's tasteful text.

... The **American** soldier in the civil war. A pictorial history of the campaigns and conflicts of the war between the states, profusely illustrated with battle scenes, naval engagements and portraits, from sketches by Forbes, Taylor ... and other celebrated war artists. A complete history of the civil war and descriptive articles by Rossiter Johnson, General Fitzhugh Lee [and others] ... New York, Bryan, Taylor & co. [©1895]
1 p. l., xiii-xxix, [30]-528 p. front., illus. (incl. ports., maps) 42cm.

Typical of the several general texts by Johnson; this large volume, while making extensive use of Leslie's war sketches, is of little research value.

Angle, Paul McClelland, 1900–
A pictorial history of the Civil War years, by Paul M. Angle. Garden City, N. Y., Doubleday [1967]

242 p. illus., facsims., col. map (on lining papers), ports. 27 cm.

Hundreds of photographs and wartime sketches (most of them no more than one-fourth page size), bound together by a succinctly written summary of military events; more restricted than Donald's Divided We Fought.

Angle, Paul McClelland, 1900–
A shelf of Lincoln books; a critical, selective bibliography of Lincolniana, by Paul M. Angle. New Brunswick, Rutgers university press, in association with the Abraham Lincoln association of Springfield, Ill., 1946.

xvii, 142 p. 24 cm.

One of the better guides to the mass of Lincoln literature; more comprehensive but less detailed than Thomas' listing.

Angle, Paul McClelland, 1900–
Tragic years, 1860–1865; a documentary history of the American Civil War, by Paul M. Angle and Earl Schenck Miers. New York, Simon and Schuster, 1960.

2 v. (x, 1097 p.) maps. 25 cm.

One of several high quality "reader"-type sets; the excellently chosen material includes eye-witness and secondary sources.

Aptheker, Herbert, 1915–
The American Civil War. New York, International Publishers [©1961]

22 p. 20 cm.

Primarily propaganda masking as history, with very strong Marxist overtones and influences.

The **Army** & navy official gazette. Containing reports of battles; also, important orders of the War department, record of courts-martial, etc. Published by authority of the War department. v. 1–2; July 7, 1863–June 27, 1865. Washington city, Printed at the office of J. C. Rives [etc.] 1864–65.

2 v. pl., maps. 30cm. weekly.

One of the earliest sources for official sources; now recognized as inaccurate and full of gaps.

Barker, Alan.
The Civil War in America. London, A. & C. Black [1961]

182 p. 23 cm.

A concise "think piece" rather than a history of the war; written by an intelligent English historian.

Barstow, Charles Lester, 1867– *ed.*
...The civil war, ed. by Charles L. Barstow. New York, The Century co., 1912.

vii, 224 p. incl. front., illus., ports. 19½cm.

An older collection of military readings, gleaned largely from The Century and Battles and Leaders of the Civil War.

Bartlett, John Russell, 1805–1886.

The literature of the rebellion. A catalogue of books and pamphlets relating to the civil war in the United States, and on subjects growing out of that event, together with works on American slavery, and essays from reviews and magazines on the same subjects. Comp. by John Russell Bartlett ... Boston, Draper and Halliday; Providence, S. S. Rider and bro., 1866.

iv, [5]–477 p. 25cm.

A non-appraising bibliography strong on speeches, sermons, reports, Lincoln eulogies and essays; now obviously outdated.

Basler, Roy Prentice, 1906–

A short history of the American Civil War [by] Roy P. Basler. New York, Basic Books [1967]

xix, 140 p. illus., facsims., ports. 22 cm.

An intriguing effort to cover the whole war in 124 pages; non-chronological, the book treats specific topics in some depth.

Battles of the Civil War, 1861–1865; a pictorial presentation. [Little Rock? Ark., 1960]

1 v. (unpaged) col. plates. 48 x 64 cm.

Full-size, clear reproductions of the famous Kurtz & Allison prints, with accompanying battle narratives written by modern historians.

Benardete, Doris, *ed.*

Civil War humor. With illus. by James Schwering. Mount Vernon, N. Y., Peter Pauper Press [©1963]

62 p. col. illus. 19 cm.

Brief excerpts that form an introduction to the writings of Josh Billings, Orpheus Kerr, Petroleum Nasby, Artemus Ward, and others.

Beyer, Walter Frederick, 1871– *ed.*

Deeds of valor; how America's heroes won the medal of honor; a history of our country's recent wars in personal reminiscences and records of officers and enlisted men who were rewarded by Congress for most conspicuous acts of bravery on the battle-field, on the high seas and in Arctic explorations ... Ed. by W. F. Beyer and O. F. Keydel. Introduction by Brig.-Gen'l H. M. Duffield ... Detroit, Mich., The Perrien-Keydel company, 1903.

2 v. illus., col. plates. 29 cm.

More reliable than Rodenbough's compilation on the same subject; however, possessed of some inaccuracies.

Beymer, William Gilmore, 1881–

On hazardous service; scouts and spies of the North and South, by William Gilmore Beymer; illustrated by Howard Pyle and others. New York and London, Harper & brothers, 1912.

xii, [1] p., 1 l., 286, [1] p. col. front., 1 illus., plates (part col.) ports. 22½ cm.

A typical adventure-spy book, although some effort was made to collect original data; the style is spritely neo-Victorian.

Bill, Ledyard, 1836–1907, *comp.*

Pen-pictures of the war. Lyrics, incidents, and sketches of the rebellion; comprising a choice selection of pieces by our best poets, also, current and well authenticated anecdotes and incidents of the war. Together with a full account of many of the great battles, also, a complete historical record of all events, both civil and military, from the commencement of the rebellion. Comp. by Ledyard Bill. New York, 1864.

x, [11]–344 p. front. 20½cm.

Typical of wartime publications, with emphasis on adventure, poor poetry and dubious facts.

Bishop, John Soast, 1834–1915.

A concise history of the war. Designed to accompany Perrine's new war map of the southern states ... By Lt.-Col. John S. Bishop ... Indianapolis, Ind., C. O. Perrine [1865]

1 p. l., v–x, 11–213, vi [*i. e.* v] p. fold. map. 15cm.

Interesting only as a Northern imprint and possible collector's item.

Blay, John S

The Civil War; a pictorial profile. New York, Crowell [1958]

342 p. illus., ports., maps, facsims. 29 cm.

One of many average picture-books; most of the illustrations are from Harper's and Leslie's--and therefore familiar.

Blythe, Vernon, 1876–

A history of the civil war in the United States, by Vernon Blythe ... New York, The Neale publishing company, 1914.

411 p. front., maps. 21cm.

Mainly a general military history; well-balanced, though the author had strong Southern roots.

Boatner, Mark Mayo, 1921–
The Civil War dictionary. Maps and diagrs. by Allen C. Northrop and Lowell I. Miller. New York, D. McKay Co. [1959]

xvi, 974 p. illus., maps. 22 cm.

Fulfills a large need; although conscientiously prepared, the work contains a number of omissions and errors.

Boston athenæum.
Confederate literature; a list of books and newspapers, maps, music and miscellaneous matter printed in the South during the Confederacy, now in the Boston athenæum. Prepared by Charles N. Baxter and James M. Dearborn, with an introduction by James Ford Rhodes ... [Boston] The Boston athenæum, 1917.

3 p. l., iii–x, 213, [1] p. 23½ cm.

An early and still-valuable catalogue, in spite of its many gaps; the starting point for any study of Confederate bibliography.

Botkin, Benjamin Albert, 1901– *ed.*
A Civil War treasury of tales, legends, and folklore; illustrated by Warren Chappell. New York, Random House [1960]

625 p. illus. 25 cm.

A seriously researched study of Civil War folklore; selective rather than comprehensive, but void of much analysis.

Botts, John Minor, 1802–1869.
The great rebellion: its secret history, rise, progress, and disastrous failure. By John Minor Botts, of Virginia. The political life of the author vindicated ... New York, Harper & brothers, 1866.

xxviii, [29]–402 p. incl. front. (port.) 19 cm.

A highly slanted and opinionated "history" by an outspoken Virginian who remained loyal to the Union.

Brady, Mathew B., 1823 (*ca.*)–1896.
National photographic collection of war views, and portraits of representative men, New York and Washington, D. C. [Catalogue] New York, C. A. Alvord, printer, 1869.

139 p. 19 cm.

A guidebook to the public exhibitions of Brady's photographs; not illustrated.

Bridges, Leonard Hal, 1918–
Civil War and reconstruction. Washington, Service Center for Teachers of History [©1957]

22 p. 23 cm.

An intriguing historiographical essay that deplores "quickie" books, assesses the influence of the Centennial, and calls for more social history.

[**Brockett, Linus Pierpont**] 1820–1893.
Scouts, spies, and heroes of the great civil war. Including thrilling adventures, daring deeds, heroic exploits, wonderful escapes of spies, scouts, and detectives, with songs, ballads, anecdotes, witty sayings, watchwords, battle-cries, and humorous and pathetic incidents of the war. By Captain Joseph Powers Hazelton [*pseud.*] ... Jersey City, Star publishing company, 1892.
6, 4, 11–512 p. front., plates, ports. 23cm.

A "heroics" volume full of daring-do escapes, espionage agents and "true stories"; of modest historical value.

Buchanan, Lamont, 1919–
A pictorial history of the Confederacy. New York, Crown Publishers [1951]

288 p. illus., ports. 29 cm.

Photographs, lithographs and art work all connected by a shallow text; in places the reproductions are extremely poor.

Buhoup, Jonathan W
The rebellion, or History of the late Civil War in the United States. [Part first] Chicago, Abdill [1884]

40 p. 29 cm.

A serialized history of the war; incomplete and of no value to historians.

Campbell, Robert Allen, *comp.*
The rebellion register: a history of the principal persons and places, important dates, documents and statistics, military and political, connected with the civil war in America. To which is added a citizen's manual: containing national documents, proclamations, and statistics, political platforms, Grant's report, parliamentary rules, &c., alphabetically arranged. Comp. from official and other authentic sources, by Robert A. Campbell. Kalamazoo, Mich., R. A. Campbell, 1866.
378, [1] p. 2 port. (incl. front.) 19½cm.

This outdated work contains an alphabetical dictionary of engagements and people, plus some official documents.

Carnahan, J Worth.
Manual of the civil war and key to the Grand army of the republic and kindred societies, by J. Worth Carnahan. Rev. ed. ... Chicago, The Easel monument association, 1897.
255 p. incl. illus., pl. 22½ cm.

A complete listing of battles and engagements, alphabetically arranged, with dates and losses included.

Catton, Bruce, 1899-
America goes to war. [1st ed.] Middletown, Conn., Wesleyan University Press [1958]
126 p. illus. 21 cm.

Thoughtful, authoritative and well-written lectures that delve into the inner meaning of the Civil War today.

Catton, Bruce, 1899-
The centennial history of the Civil War. E. B. Long, director of research. [1st ed.] Garden City, N. Y., Doubleday, 1961-65.
3 v. col. illus., col. maps. 25 cm.

One of the outstanding literary achievements of the Centennial years; Catton here demonstrates his prodigious ability to tell a story well without neglecting detail.

Catton, Bruce, 1899-
This hallowed ground; the story of the Union side of the Civil War. [1st ed.] Garden City, N. Y., Doubleday, 1956.
ix, 437 p. maps. 25 cm.

A movingly written, general history of the war, with heavy emphasis on the Northern side; contains some of Catton's best analyses.

Catton, Bruce, 1899-
The meaning of the Civil War; an address delivered at the Chicago Historical Society, April 12, 1961. [Chicago] Chicago Historical Society, 1961.
13 p. 22 cm.

This thought-provoking address points out that from the war came real rather than limited freedom.

Chanal, François Victor Adolphe de, 1811-1882.
The American army in the war of secession. By General de Chanal ... Tr. by First Lieut. M. J. O'Brien ... Leavenworth, Kan., G. A. Spooner, 1894.
245 p. 23½cm.

In this French officer's observations of the Union army are comments on such things as organization, personnel and logistics.

Channing, Edward, 1856-1931.
A history of the United States, by Edward Channing. New York, The Macmillan company, 1905-25.
6 v. illus., maps (part fold.) 22½ cm.

In Vol. VI, which covers the war period, Channing relied too much on episodic narrative and too little on needed interpretation.

Chicago. Public Library.
A nation divided; a representative, annotated selection of books on the Civil War period and Abraham Lincoln. [Chicago, 195-]
37 p. 22 cm.

A concise reading list beneficial to the beginning student.

Churchill, *Sir* Winston Leonard Spencer, 1874-
The American Civil War. **New York, Dodd, Mead, 1961** [©1958]
145 p. illus. 22 cm.

Lifted entirely from the author's History of the English Speaking Peoples; of interest mainly for the Churchill viewpoint.

The **Civil War.** New York, Grosset & Dunlap [1956]
2 v. illus., ports., maps, facsims. 24 cm.

The first of the modern "readers;" eyewitness accounts are carefully woven to tell the story of the war; Vol. II contains a month-by-month chronology, plus capsule biographies.

Civil War history. v. 1–
Mar. 1955–
[Iowa City]

v. illus., maps, facsims. 24 cm.

An outstanding, learned journal indispensable to any serious student of the Civil War.

The Civil war through the camera, hundreds of vivid photographs actually taken in Civil war times, together with Elson's new history, by Henry W. Elson ... [New York, Trow directory printing and bookbinding co.] ©1912.

16 pt. in 1 v. illus., col. plates. 27½ cm.

The best of the early one-volume picture books; sixteen paintings are included with the photos, most of which were made by Brady.

Civil War times illustrated. v. 1–
Apr. 1962–
Gettysburg, Pa., Historical Times, inc.

v. illus. (part col.) maps, ports. 30 cm.

A well-edited periodical containing many informative articles mainly on military topics; unannotated but of importance.

Clark (Arthur H.) company, *publishers, Glendale, Calif.*

A catalogue of books relating to the American civil war ... The Arthur H. Clark company, Cleveland, Ohio. [Cleveland, 1917]

cover-title, 120 p. 18½cm.

Contains 1, 849 entries, none of which are annotated; now painfully outdated.

Clogston, William.

Catalogue of Mr. William Clogston's collection of reminders of the war of 1861–65. Comprising medals of union officers, metallic and paper currency, U. S. fractional currency, war posters, tickets, etc. of sanitary fairs, revenue stamps, and an unsurpassed collection of union and secession envelopes. Also, a collection of mound and Indian pottery, and stone implements, also, a variety of ancient coins, all to be sold by auction, by Messrs. Bangs & co. ... Catalogue by W. Elliot Woodward ... Boston, T. R. Marvin & son, numismatic printers, 1881.

1 p. l., [5]–59 p. fold. pl. 24cm.

Of interest only to those who collect or admire Civil War decorations.

Cochrane, John, 1813–1898.

American civil war. Memories of incidents connected with the origin and culmination of the rebellion that threatened the existence of the national government:—including reminiscences of the course of the rebel leaders in Congress and in the National Democratic convention which immediately preceded the outburst of rebellion; together with movement in and concerning the Army of the Potomac during the first two years of the war;—including the proposition made in a speech at the Astor House, in New York, in November, 1861, when, in company with Simon Cameron ... General John Cochrane ... first publicly advocated the arming of the slaves in the war for the union ... From writings on those subjects (printed for private use) by John Cochrane ... collated by Henry O'Rielly ... (Designed as an appendix to O'Rielly's "Brief history of the organization of colored troops in the state of New York"—deposited among his donations to the New York historical society) New York, Rogers & Sherwood, printers, 1879.

7, 12 p. 22½cm.

A mistitled pamphlet that throws much light on Northern political-military relations in the war's first years.

Cole, Arthur Charles, 1886–

... The irrepressible conflict, 1850–1865, by Arthur Charles Cole ... New York, The Macmillan company, 1938.

xv p., 1 l., 468 p. front., plates, ports., map, facsim. 22 cm.

Sound material on social history, customs, economics, agriculture, slavery, and religion.

Columbia University. *Libraries.*

The Townsend library of National, State, and individual Civil War records at Columbia University, New York City. [New York, 1899]

15 p. front. 22 cm.

This small bibliography shows its age badly.

Commager, Henry Steele, 1902– *ed.*

The Blue and the Gray; the story of the Civil War as told by participants. [1st ed.] Indianapolis, Bobbs-Merrill [1950]

2 v. (1201 p.) illus., maps. 25 cm.

Another "reader;" well organized, with subject matter carefully chosen.

Commager, Henry Steele, 1902– *ed.*

The defeat of the Confederacy, a documentary survey. Princeton, N. J., Van Nostrand [1964]

192 p. 19 cm.

The selections in this "reader" are largely nonmilitary and written primarily by leading historians; Commager himself emphasizes the failure of Confederate leadership.

Confederate memorial literary society, *Richmond, Va. Southern historical manuscripts commission.*

A calendar of Confederate papers, with a bibliography of some Confederate publications; preliminary report of the Southern historical manuscripts commission, prepared under the direction of the Confederate memorial literary society, by Douglas Southall Freeman. Richmond, Va., The Confederate museum, 1908.

620 p., 1 l. 24½ cm.

A very useful research guide to the papers in the Confederate White House; mostly chronological, with full comments.

Congdon, Don.

Combat; the Civil War, edited and with commentary by Don Congdon. Introd. by Bruce Catton. New York, Delacorte Press [1967]

x, 564 p. fold. illus., maps. 25 cm.

Another "reader" utilizing familiar eyewitness and modern accounts; surpassed by better balanced works.

Coulter, Ellis Merton, 1890–

The Confederate States of America, 1861–1865. [Baton Rouge] Louisiana State University Press, 1950.

x, 644 p. illus., ports., fold. map. 25 cm.

Decidedly the best non-military study of the Confederacy; a scholarly, readable, comprehensive coverage of homefront life.

Coulter, Ellis Merton, 1890–

Travels in the Confederate States, a bibliography. [1st ed.] Norman, University of Oklahoma Press, 1948.

xiv, 289 p. 24 cm.

An outstanding, essential bibliographical tool; describes the merits of 493 works by soldiers and foreign observers.

Crafts, William Augustus, 1819–1906.

The southern rebellion; being a history of the United States from the commencement of President Buchanan's administration to the inauguration of General Ulysses S. Grant as president. By William A. Crafts ... Boston, S. Walker and co., 1869–70.

2 v. front., pl., port. 28½cm.

One of many, similar narratives written shortly after the war; of small use today.

Crandall, Marjorie Lyle, 1900–

Confederate imprints; a check list based principally on the collection of the Boston Athenæum. With an introd. by Walter Muir Whitehill. [Boston] Boston Athenæum, 1955.

2 v. (xxxv, 910 p.) facsims. 24 cm.

The most complete listing of Confederate publications, although the contents were limited mainly to the collection in the Boston Athenaeum.

Craven, Avery Odelle, 1886–

An historian and the Civil War, by Avery Craven. Chicago, University of Chicago Press [1964]

v, 233 p. 25 cm.

The title is misleading; this study treats exclusively of causative factors leading to war.

Cremer, Henry.

Available sources for the study of American history, written from the southern point of view, by Henry Cremer ... Indiana, Pa., Printed by R. S. Grosse print shop, 1931.

11 p. 23½cm.

More concerned with causative factors and secession than with the war itself; inadequate by any standard.

Cromie, Alice Hamilton.

A tour guide to the Civil War. Introd. by Bell Irvin Wiley. Chicago, Quadrangle Books, 1965 [c1964]

xxv, 372 p. illus., maps. 22 cm.

A "must" volume for anyone touring Civil War sites; carefully compiled; covers not only battlefields but other important points.

Cussons, John, 1838–

A glance at current history, by John Cussons ... Glen Allen, Va., Cussons, May & company, inc., 1899.

172 p. front. (port.) 18 x 15cm.

Interesting essays by a former Confederate soldier who opposed disunion but believed in states' rights.

Dannett, Sylvia G L 1909–
A treasury of Civil War humor. New York T. Yoseloff [1964, ©1963]

184 p. facsims. 29 cm.

This tall volume contains a sampling of the humor of the period; most of the text and illustrations came from periodicals of the day.

Davis, Burke.
Our incredible Civil War. Drawings by Raymond Houhlihan. [1st ed.] New York, Holt, Rinehart and Winston [1960]

249 p. illus. 24 cm.

An entertaining collection of facts and anecdotes; although the work as a whole is a compilation of the unusual, it suffers from lack of organization.

Davis, Washington.
Camp-fire chats of the civil war; being the incident, adventure and wayside exploit of the bivouac and battle field, as related by members of the Grand army of the republic. Embracing the tragedy, romance, comedy, humor and pathos in the varied experience of army life. By Washington Davis. Containing a history and other valuable information for members of the G. A. R. Chicago, The Coburn publishing company, 1884.

xiii, [1], 15–346, [1] p. incl. front., illus. 20cm.

Highly romanticized yarns and legends presented in an old-boiling style; the whole must be handled with care.

Deering, John Richard, 1842–
Lee and his cause; or, The why and the how of the war between the states, by John R. Deering ... New York and Washington, The Neale publishing company, 1907.

183 p. 2 port. (incl. front.) 20cm.

Deering believes that for the South the war was justifiable, great, and hopeless.

[Devens, Richard Miller]
The pictorial book of anecdotes and incidents of the war of the rebellion, civil, military, naval and domestic ... from the time of the memorable toast of Andrew Jackson—"The federal union; it must be preserved!" ... to the assassination of President Lincoln, and the end of the war. With famous words and deeds of woman, sanitary and hospital scenes, prison experiences, &c. By Frazar Kirkland [*pseud.*] ... Hartford, Hartford publishing co.; Philadelphia, National publishing co.; [etc., etc.] 1867.

705 p. incl. front., illus., pl., port. 25cm.

An antiquated general collection of anecdotes: some true, some exaggerated, some false; of little historical use.

Divided we fought; a pictorial history of the war, 1861–1865. Picture editors: Hirst D. Milhollen and Milton Kaplan. Caption editors: Hirst D. Milhollen, Milton Kaplan, and Hulen Stuart. Author of the text and general editor: David Donald. New York, Macmillan [©1956]

viii, 454 p. illus., ports. 29 cm.

One of the best modern picture books; includes photographs, pencil sketches and a skillfully written text.

Dodd, William Edward, 1869–1940.
Expansion and conflict, by William E. Dodd ... Boston, New York [etc.] Houghton Mifflin company [©1915]

xii p., 1 l., 329, xxiv p. front. (port.) maps (part double) 18 cm.

An old but classic study written from a decided Southern viewpoint; the emphasis is on the causative factors of the war.

Dodge, Theodore Ayrault, 1842–1909.
A bird's-eye view of our civil war, by Theodore Ayrault Dodge ... Boston, J. R. Osgood and co., 1883.

xi, 346 p. illus., maps (part fold.) 23½ cm.

Primarily military, this volume remains a satisfactory outline of the war.

Donald, David Herbert, 1920–
An excess of democracy; the American Civil War and the social process. An inaugural lecture delivered before the University of Oxford on 2 May 1960. Oxford, Clarendon Press, 1960.

22 p. 22 cm.

A very thought-provoking essay; Donald suggests that the war may have been the result of too much freedom among a democratic people.

Donald, David Herbert, 1920–
Lincoln reconsidered; essays on the Civil War era. [1st ed.] New York, Knopf, 1956.

200 p. 20 cm.

Poignant essays on political issues, with emphasis on Lincoln's role; Donald's defenses of the Radicals is particularly stimulating.

Donald, David Herbert, 1920– *ed.*
Why the North won the Civil War. Essays by Richard N. Current [and others. Baton Rouge] Louisiana State University Press [1960]

128 p. 23 cm.

Five essays by a like number of prominent historians attribute Union victory to everything from superior resources to Confederate internal weaknesses.

Dornbusch, Charles Emil, 1907–
Regimental publications & personal narratives of the Civil War; a checklist. New York, New York Public Library, 1961–

v. in 26 cm.

Two volumes now comprise this valuable bibliography listing; the bulk of the subject matter is arranged by state.

Dowdey, Clifford, 1904–
Experiment in rebellion, by Clifford Dowdey. Garden City, N. Y., Doubleday & company, inc., 1946.

xxi p., 1 l., 455 p. illus. (maps) plates, ports. 23½ cm.

Mainly the story of embattled Richmond; a vigorous narrative but of limited value because of a strong pro-Southern bias.

Dowdey, Clifford, 1904–
The land they fought for; the story of the South as the Confederacy, 1832–1865. [1st ed.] Garden City, N. Y., Doubleday, 1955.

viii, 438 p. map (on lining papers) 24 cm.

Political, military, and social history blended to portray the rise and fall of the South; a highly readable narrative with strong pro-Confederate views.

Draper, John William, 1811–1882.
History of the American Civil War. New York, Harper [c1896–98]

3 v. maps. 24 cm.

One of the better, lengthy, immediate postwar histories, but not of important use today.

[**Dudley, Dean**] 1823–1906, *ed.*
Officers of our Union army and navy. Their lives, their portraits. Vol. 1. Boston, Washington, L. Prang & co., c1862.

viii, [9] 148 p. incl. ports. port. 14cm.

Brief biographies of Union leaders; no use now except in collections.

Duncan, Louis Caspar, 1869–
The Medical department of the United States army in the civil war, by Captain Louis C. Duncan, Medical corps, U. S. Army. [Washington? 19—?]

[327] p. illus. (incl. ports., maps, diagrs.) 23½cm.

A series of magazine articles reprinted in book form; concentrates solely on conditions within the Army of the Potomac.

Dunning, William Archibald, 1857–1922.
Essays on the civil war and reconstruction and related topics, by William Archibald Dunning ... New York, The Macmillan company; London, Macmillan & co., ltd., 1898.

ix, 376 p. 19½ cm.

Dunning was one of Columbia University's most distinguished professors; these essays (all originally printed in various journals) treat largely of constitutional questions and reflect his Southern sympathies.

Dupuy, Richard Ernest, 1887–
The compact history of the Civil War [by] R. Ernest Dupuy [and] Trevor N. Dupuy. With battlefield maps designed by T. N. Dupuy and C. G. Dupuy. [1st ed.] New York, Hawthorn Books [1960]

445 p. illus. 24 cm.

Well-told and conventional military history, admittedly limited in research.

Duyckinck, Evert Augustus, 1816–1878.
National history of the war for the union, civil, military and naval. Founded on official and other authentic documents. By Everet A. Duyckinck ... Illustrated ... from original paintings by Alonzo Chappel and Thomas Nast ... New York, Johnson, Fry and company [1861–65]

3 v. fronts., plates, ports. 28½cm.

This typical, old-style narrative is of value only as a wartime imprint.

Dyer, Frederick Henry, 1849–
A compendium of the War of the Rebellion. With a new introd. by Bell Irvin Wiley. New York, T. Yoseloff [1959]

3 v. (1796 p.) illus., ports., maps, facsims., tables. 29 cm.

A reprinting of the 1908 edition cited in I, 6; one of the indispensable "fact" volumes, enhanced by Wiley's long introduction.

Eaton, Clement, 1898–
A history of the Southern Confederacy. New York, Macmillan, 1954.

351 p. 22 cm.

Scholarly, accurate, impartial; one of the best brief accounts; weaker on military events than on social and political.

Eaton, Edward Bailey.
Original photographs taken on the battlefields during the civil war of the United States, by Mathew B. Brady and Alexander Gardner, who operated under the authority of the War department and the protection of the Secret service. Rare reproductions from photographs selected from seven thousand original negatives ... now the private collection of Edward Bailey Eaton. Valued at $150,000 ... Hartford, Conn. [E. B. Eaton] 1907.

1 p. l., 5–126 p., 1 l. illus. 28½ x 38½ cm.

A useful collection of Brady photographs at the time of publication; the extended captions still possess some value.

Egan, Joseph Burke, 1879– *ed.*
The civil war, its photographic history ... compiled from actual photographs taken at the time of action by Mathew B. Brady and others, edited by Joseph B. Egan, LL. D. and Arthur W. Desmond ... Processing of plates and studio work, John D. Payne. Wellesley Hills, Mass., Character building publications [c1941]

2 v. fronts., illus. (incl. ports., maps) 27½ cm.

Another of the usual type of general picture histories; contains many well-known prints.

Eisenschiml, Otto, 1880– *ed.*
The American Iliad; the epic story of the Civil War as narrated by eyewitnesses and contemporaries, by Otto Eisenschiml and Ralph Newman. Indianapolis, Bobbs-Merrill Co. [1947]

720 p. ports., maps, facsims. 25 cm.

One of the first of the modern "readers;" composed largely of eyewitness accounts of military events; later republished under the title Eyewitness.

Eisenschiml, Otto, 1880–
As luck would have it, chance and coincidence in the Civil War, by Otto Eisenschiml and E. B. Long; maps by Barbara Long. [1st ed.] Indianapolis, Bobbs-Merrill [1948]

285 p. maps, facsim. 23 cm.

How some minor events led to major consequences; authentic but popularly written on the "if" theme.

Eisenschiml, Otto, 1880–
The hidden face of the Civil War. [1st ed.] Indianapolis, Bobbs-Merrill [1961]

319 p. illus. 24 cm.

A potpourri of unorthodox viewpoints on the war, its generals and strategy.

Eisenschiml, Otto, 1880–
O. E.: historian without an armchair. Indianapolis, Bobbs-Merrill [c1963]

224 p. 22 cm.

The adventures of an indefatigable student of the war; provocative because of the author's theory of possible Northern involvement in Lincoln's assassination.

Eisenschiml, Otto, 1880–
Why the Civil War? [1st ed.] Indianapolis, Bobbs-Merrill [1958]

208 p. 23 cm.

An iconoclastic historian presents a new and provocative explanation for 1861 Union strategy at Fort Sumter.

Evans, Clement Anselm, 1833–1911, *ed.*
Confederate military history; a library of Confederate States history ... written by distinguished men of the South, and ed. by Gen. Clement A. Evans ... Atlanta, Ga., Confederate publishing company, 1899.

12 v. front., plates (1 col.) ports., maps (part fold.) double plan. 24 cm.

A still-excellent reference work for the embattled Confederacy; each volume treats of a separate state, and each was written by a different Southern notable.

Fish, Carl Russell, 1876–1932.

The American civil war; an interpretation by Carl Russell Fish ... edited by William Ernest Smith ... London, New York [etc.] Longmans, Green and co., 1937.

xi, 531 p. front., plates, ports., facsim. 22½ cm.

Wide coverage in a good standard text; constitutional issues, politics, foreign relations, economics and finance all receive proper attention.

Fisher, Richard Swainson.

A chronological history of the civil war in America. Illustrated with A. J. Johnson's and J. H. Colton's steel plate maps and plans of the southern states and harbors ... By Richard Swainson Fisher ... New York, Johnson and Ward, 1863.

iv, [5]–160 p. maps (part fold.) 22cm.

The chronology stops with January, 1863; many so-called minor events are included; of limited usefulness today.

Fletcher, Henry Charles.

History of the American war, by Lieut.-Colonel Fletcher ... London, R. Bentley, 1865–66.

3 v. fronts. (v. 2, 3) maps (1 fold.) 22½cm.

An immediate postwar military history by an officer of the Scots Guards; the author's observations are unusual.

Foote, Shelby.

The Civil War, a narrative. New York, Random House [1958–

v. maps. 26 cm,

Two volumes in this projected trilogy are now in print; this panoramic military study is written in a sweeping style.

Forbes, Edwin, 1839–1895.

A Civil War artist at the front; Edwin Forbes' Life studies of the great army. Edited by William Forrest Dawson. New York, Oxford University Press, 1957.

[94] p. illus. 21 x 27 cm.

Well-produced life studies of the war by one of the outstanding sketch-artists of the period.

Forbes, Edwin, 1839–1895.

Life studies of the great army, by Edwin Forbes ... A historical art work, in copper-plate etching, containing forty plates, illustrating the life of the Union armies during the late rebellion. New York, E. Forbes [c1876]

1 p. l., 40 pl. 61cm.

A superb reproduction of the best of Forbes' drawings of army life; contains no text.

Forbes, Edwin, 1839–1895.

Thirty years after. An artist's story of the great war, told, and illustrated with nearly 300 relief-etchings after sketches in the field, and 20 half-tone equestrian portraits from original oil paintings, by Edwin Forbes ... New York, Fords, Howard & Hulbert [c1890]

2 v. fronts., illus., plates, ports. 41cm.

Excellent reproductions of Forbes' sketches of soldier life; extensive enough to cover many personal subjects.

Formby, John.

The American civil war, a concise history of its causes, progress, and results, by John Formby ... New York, Charles Scribner's sons, 1910.

xiii p., 1 l., [xv]–xvii, 520 p. *and* atlas of 2 pl., 66 maps on 50 fold. pl. 22½ cm.

A chronological general history by a British author; useful in its day, but now showing age.

Frank Leslie's illustrated history of the Civil War. The most important events of the conflict between the States graphically pictured. Stirring battle scenes and grand naval engagements ... portraits of principal participants ... By such well-known artists as Becker ... A concise history of the Civil War, being official data secured from the war records. Edited by Louis Shepheard Moat. With an introd. by Joseph B. Carr. New York, Mrs. F. Leslie [c1895]

512 p. (chiefly illus., maps, ports.) 42 cm.

A highly useful collection of the best wartime illustrations from this popular newspaper; the narrative is painfully outdated and biased.

Frank Leslie's scenes and portraits of the civil war ... by such well-known artists as Becker, Crane, Beard ... and others. With an introduction by Joseph B. Carr, Major-general. pts. 1–10. New York, Mrs. F. Leslie [c1894]

10 pts. in 1 v. illus. (incl. ports.) 41 cm.

Another of the numerous reproductions of soldier scenes by battlefield artists; this one is incomplete.

Freeman, Douglas Southall, 1886–1953.

The last parade; an editorial by Douglas S. Freeman from "Richmond news leader" of Friday, June twenty-fourth, nineteen hundred and thirty-two, the last day of the forty-second annual reunion of the United confederate veterans. Richmond, Va., Whittet & Shepperson, 1932.

20 l. incl. mounted front., mounted plates. 33 x 25 cm.

An immensely moving essay that honors Southern soldiers and leaders and at the same time shows a broad understanding of the whole war.

Freeman, Douglas Southall, 1886–

The South to posterity; an introduction to the writings of Confederate history, by Douglas Southall Freeman ... New York, C. Scribner's sons, 1939.

xii p., 2 l., 235 p. 21 cm.

The pre-eminent study of Confederate historical writing by a great practitioner in the field; invaluable as a guide to printed literature of the wartime South.

Frost, *Mrs.* **Jennett Blakeslee.**

The rebellion in the United States; or, The war of 1861; being a complete history of its rise and progress, commencing with the presidential election ... Taken from government documents and other reliable sources. Carefully comp. by Mrs. J. Blakeslee Frost. Hartford [Boston, G. C. Rand & Avery, printers (v. 1)] 1862–63.

2 v. 3 port. (incl. fronts.) $23\frac{1}{2}^{cm}$.

A Union imprint in chronological form; now of little value.

Fry, James Barnet, 1827–1894.

Military miscellanies. By James B. Fry ... New York, Brentano's, 1889.

528 p. $23\frac{1}{2}^{cm}$.

A strange mixture, but one useful in appraising many books and articles on the war; predominately military in content.

Gardner, Alexander, 1821–1882.

Catalogue of photographic incidents of the war, from the gallery of Alexander Gardner, photographer to the Army of the Potomac ... September, 1863 ... Washington, H. Polkinhorn, printer, 1863.

28 p. $16\frac{1}{2}^{cm}$.

An early, wartime guidebook to the Gardner exhibition of Civil War photographs.

Gardner, Alexander, 1821–1882.

Gardner's photographic sketch book of the war. Washington, D. C., Philp & Solomons [1865]

2 v. plates. $32\frac{1}{2} \times 44^{cm}$.

The remarkable photographs of Gardner and associates with a succinct, but well-conceived text; reprinted in 1959.

Garrett, William Robertson, 1839–1904.

... The civil war from a southern standpoint, by the late William Robertson Garrett ... and Robert Ambrose Halley ... Philadelphia, Printed for subscribers only by G. Barrie & sons [1905]

xxv, 553 p. col. front., plates, ports., maps, facsims. 23 cm.

As its title implies, this thick but superficial study is strongly biased--fatally so to be of usable value.

Gates, Paul Wallace, 1901–

Agriculture and the Civil War, by Paul W. Gates. [1st ed.] New York, Knopf, 1965.

x, 383, xiii p. illus., facsims., maps (1 fold.) ports. 25 cm.

An extremely sound, thoroughly researched, and skillfully presented volume that fills a great void; covers both North and South.

Gerrish, Theodore, 1846–

The blue and the gray; a graphic history of the Army of the Potomac and that of northern Virginia, including the brilliant engagements of these forces from 1861 to 1865. The campaigns of the Shenandoah valley and the Army of the James, together with reminiscences of tent and field ... and a complete roster of the two great armies ... By Rev. Theodore Gerrish ... and Rev. John S. Hutchinson ... With introductions by Colonel Augustus C. Hamlin, Maine, and Gen. Fitzhugh Lee, Virginia. Portland, Hoyt, Fogg & Donham, 1883.

816 p. incl. maps. $23\frac{1}{2}^{cm}$.

Still moderately useful for an older history; covers the Eastern campaigns only; several reminiscences are included.

Giddings, Joshua Reed, 1795–1864.

History of the rebellion: its authors and causes. By Joshua R. Giddings. New York, Follet, Foster & co., 1864.

viii, 9–498 p. 23^{cm}.

An incomplete treatment by an active abolitionist; must be handled with great care.

Goodhue, Benjamin W
Incidents of the civil war, by Benjamin W. Goodhue. Chicago, J. D. Tallmadge, 1890.

158 p. front. (port.) illus. (ports.) 19½ cm.

Stories, poems, incidents and adventures, some semi-fictional and others dubiously factual.

Greeley, Horace, 1811–1872.
The American conflict: a history of the great rebellion in the United States of America, 1860–'65: its causes, incidents, and results: intended to exhibit especially its moral and political phases, with the draft and progress of American opinion respecting human slavery, from 1776 to the close of the war for the Union. By Horace Greeley ... Hartford, O. D. Case & company, 1879, '77.

2 v. fronts., illus., plates, ports., maps. 24½ cm.

The great editor's account of the war--with all of his emotionalism, errors and distortions; yet still a primary source.

Greg, Percy, 1836–1889.
History of the United States from the foundation of Virginia to the reconstruction of the Union, by Percy Greg ... London, W. H. Allen & co., 1887.

2 v. maps. 22½ cm.

An error-filled study by an Englishman who was hostile to the North; Vol. II treats of the Civil War.

Guernsey, Alfred Hudson, 1824–1902.
Harper's pictorial history of the great rebellion. By Alfred H. Guernsey and Henry M. Alden ... New York, Harper & bro^s. [1866–68]

2 v. illus., port., maps (part fold.) facsim. 41 x 29½^cm.

One of the old standbys, with sketches from Harper's Weekly and a lengthy text.

Hansen, Harry, 1884–
The Civil War; a new one-volume history. [New York] New American Library [1961]

663 p. illus. 19 cm.

Designed for popular consumption from limited research; primarily military in content.

Harper's weekly; a journal of civilization. v. 1–62; Jan. 3, 1857–Apr. 29, 1916. New York, Harper & brothers [etc.] 1857–1916.

62 v. in 78. illus. (part col.) plates (part col.) ports., maps. 34–41 cm.

The most popular periodical of its day and valuable for a study of any aspect of the war; the illustrations are unsurpassed.

Harper's weekly; a journal of civilization. v. 4– (no. 209–); Dec. 29, 1860–
New York [Shenandoah, Iowa, Living History, 1960–

facsim: v. illus., ports., maps. 42 cm.

An above-average reprinting of the issues for the war years; accompanying the 1861 numbers were informative supplements written by James Robertson.

Hart, Albert Bushnell, 1854–1943, *ed.*
... The romance of the Civil war; selected and annotated by Albert Bushnell Hart ... with the collaboration of Elizabeth Stevens ... New York, The Macmillan company; London, Macmillan & co., ltd., 1903.

xiv p., 1 l., 418 p. front., illus. (incl. ports.) 19½^cm.

Selections from fictional and non-fictional sources cover army life, slavery, women, and naval aspects; useful as supplementary reading to a text.

Harwell, Richard Barksdale, *ed.*
The Confederate reader. [1st ed.] New York, Longmans, Green, 1957.

389 p. illus. 24 cm.

A literary miscellany that captures much of the flavor of life and society in the embattled South.

Harwell, Richard Barksdale.
Cornerstones of Confederate collecting. 2d ed., with an introd. by Clifford Dowdey. Charlottesville, University of Virginia Press for the Bibliographical Society of the University of Virginia, 1953.

35 p. facsims. 24 cm.

Describes twenty Confederate imprints around which a collection might be built.

Harwell, Richard Barksdale.
More Confederate imprints. Richmond, Virginia State Library, 1957.
2 v. (xxxvi, 345 p.) facsims. 24 cm.

An addenda to the Crandall publication; compiled by an expert in the field.

Harwell, Richard Barksdale, ***ed.***
The Union reader. [1st ed.] New York, Longmans, Green, 1958.
362 p. illus. 24 cm.

Well-chosen selections from Federal wartime literature; includes both military and civilian topics.

Harwell, Richard Barksdale, ***ed.***
The war they fought. [1st ed.] New York, Longmans, Green, 1960.
389, 362 p. illus. 24 cm.

The Confederate Reader and The Union Reader in one volume and under a different title.

Headley, Joel Tyler, 1813–1897.
The great rebellion; a history of the civil war in the United States. By J. T. Headley ... Hartford, American publishing co.; Chicago, R. C. Treat, 1866.
2 v. fronts., plates, ports. 24cm.

An immediate postwar history by an expert popularizer of military events; readable but now badly outdated.

Headley, Joel Tyler, 1813–1897.
Our army in the great rebellion. Heroes and battles of the war 1861–65. By Hon. J. T. Headley ... Comprising an authentic account of battles and sieges, adventures and incidents, including biographies of the prominent generals who were instrumental in bringing the civil war to a triumphant close ... New York, E. B. Treat; Chicago, Patriotic publishing co., 1891.
11, [2], [13]–637 p. incl. front., illus., plates, maps. plates, ports., maps. 23cm.

A newer edition of Grant and Sherman; contains several badly dated military biographies.

Heaps, Willard Allison, 1909–
The singing sixties; the spirit of Civil War days drawn from the music of the times, by Willard A. and Porter W. Heaps. [1st ed.] Norman, University of Oklahoma Press [1960]
xiv, 423 p. illus., facsims. 25 cm.

In spite of its several shortcomings, this volume remains the best general history of Civil War music.

Heartman, Charles Frederick, 1883–
What constitutes a Confederate imprint? Preliminary suggestions for bibliographers and catalogers, by Charles F. Heartman. Hattiesburg, Miss., The Book farm, 1939.
8 p. 24cm.

Written by a collector-dealer in the field, this scarce pamphlet presents basic guidelines for determining imprints.

Hedrick, Mary A ***comp.***
1861–1865. Incidents of the civil war during the four years of its progress, by Mary A. Hedrick. Lowell, Mass., Vox populi press, S. W. Huse & co., 1888.
179 p. incl. front. 4 facsim. 30cm.

A collection of newspaper clippings with no sources; rather interesting material but of little modern value.

Henderson, George Francis Robert, 1854–1903.
The Civil War: a soldier's view; a collection of Civil War writings. Edited by Jay Luvaas. [Chicago] University of Chicago Press [1958]
xi, 322 p. maps (1 fold.) plans. 25 cm.

Major war studies by an eminent English military critic; editor Luvaas adds a discerning and scholarly analysis of Henderson himself.

Henry, Robert Selph, 1889–
The story of the confederacy, by Robert Selph Henry. New and rev. ed. and with a foreword by Douglas Southall Freeman. Indianapolis, The Bobbs-Merrill company [c1936]
8 p. l., 11–514 p. front., illus. (maps) plates, ports. 23½ cm.

An old standby and still one of the most widely recommended books for the beginning student.

Herbert, George B
The popular history of the civil war in America (1861-1865.) A complete narrative of events, military, naval, political and congressional, that occurred during the war for the union, with full information as to the causes which brought on the rebellion. By Capt. George B. Herbert ... With portraits and numerous other illustrations. New York, F. M. Lupton, 1884.

1 p. l., [xi]-xx, [21]-415 p. illus. (incl. ports.) 17 cm.

Outdated, completely military, and padded with anecdotes; published under at least three different titles.

Hergesheimer, Joseph, 1880-
Swords & roses [by] Joseph Hergesheimer. New York, London, A. A. Knopf, 1929.

5 p. l., 3-327 p., 1 l. 22½ cm.

Highly romanticized but readable segments of Confederate history; semi-fictional in places.

Hesseltine, William Best, 1902- *ed.*
The tragic conflict; the Civil War and reconstruction. Selected and edited with introd and notes by William B. Hesseltine. New York, G. Braziller, 1962.

528 p. 25 cm.

Excellent collateral material on disunion, armies, Confederate politics, economic impact and Reconstruction.

Hitchcock, Benjamin W.
Hitchcock's chronological record of the American civil war, giving every event in the order of its occurrence from November 8th. 1860, to June 3d, 1865; also a complete list of vessels captured by the Confederate navy. New York, B. W. Hitchcock, 1866.

1 p. l., 106, [561]-566 p. front. (port.) 23cm.

This day-by-day chronology contains many errors but is still useful for a coverage of lesser known events.

Hosmer, James Kendall, 1834-1927.
... The appeal to arms, 1861-1863, by James Kendall Hosmer ... New York and London, Harper & brothers, 1907.

xvi, 354 p. front. (port.) 12 maps (3 double) 21½ cm.

A sound general text, but now aged; treats of military events during the first half of the war.

Hosmer, James Kendall, 1834-1927.
Outcome of the Civil war, 1863-1865, by James Kendall Hosmer ... New York and London, Harper & brothers, 1907.

xvi, 352 p. front. (port.) 9 maps. 21½ cm.

Covers adequately the second half of the war; a product of moderately thorough research.

Hosmer, James Kendall, 1834-1927.
The American civil war, by James Kendall Hosmer ... New York and London, Harper & brothers, 1913.

2 v. fronts. (ports.) maps. 21½cm.

A combination of the two above titles, with no changes in text.

Hume, John Ferguson, 1830-
The abolitionists; together with personal memories of the struggle for human rights, 1830-1864, by John F. Hume. New York and London, G. P. Putnam's sons, 1905.

vi p., 1 l., 224 p. 19½cm.

Now outdated, Hume's study nevertheless is useful because it carried the story of the abolitionists into wartime.

Joel, Joseph A.
Rifle shots and bugle notes; or, The national military albun of sketches of the principal battles, marches, picket duty, camp fires, love adventures, and poems connected with the late war. By Joseph A. Joel ... and Lewis R. Stegman ... Illustrations by Darley, Leslie, and other well-known artists. New York, Grand army gazette publishing co., 1884.

x, [11]-564 p. front., plates, ports. 27cm.

A typical volume of anecdotes and "love adventures," plus poems; an anthology of the true and the exaggerated.

Johannsen, Robert W *ed.*
The Union in crisis, 1850-1877, edited by Robert W. Johannsen. New York, Free Press [c1965]

x, 294 p. 21 cm.

A modern group of selections suitable for classroom use in a generalized course.

Johnson, James Ralph.
Horsemen, blue and gray: a pictorial history. Pictures by Hirst Dillon Milhollen. Text by James Ralph Johnson and Alfred Hoyt Bill. New York, Oxford University Press, 1960.

vii, 236 p. illus., ports., maps, facsims. 29 cm.

This pictorial history contains well-chosen illustrations and a text that provides a reasonable summation of the subject.

Johnson, Rossiter, 1840–1931.
The fight for the republic; a narrative of the more noteworthy events in the war of secession, presenting the great contest in its dramatic aspects, by Rossiter Johnson; with maps and battle plans ... New York and London, G. G. Putnam's sons, 1917.

xii p., 1 l., 404 p. front., plates, ports., maps (part fold.) plans (part fold.) 23½ cm.

The best of Johnson's several general histories; based on the thesis that the Emancipation Proclamation changed the war from the search for a temporary peace to that for a permanent peace.

Johnson, Rossiter, 1840–1931.
A short history of the war of secession, 1861–1865, by Rossiter Johnson ... Boston, Ticknor and company, 1888.

xiv, 552 p. incl. maps. 23½cm.

Editions of this popular work were still being issued as late as 1910; military in content, with considerable judgement displayed by the author.

Joinville, François Ferdinand Philippe Louis Marie d'Orléans, ***prince*** **de,** 1818–1900.
A Civil War album of paintings, by the Prince de Joinville. Pref. by the Comte de Paris. Texts by André Maurois and General James M. Gavin. New York, Atheneum, 1964.

33 p., 20 col. plates. 25 x 33 cm.

Beautiful and revealing, Joinville's sketches rank on a par with those of Edwin Forbes.

Kane, Harnett Thomas, 1910–
Spies for the Blue and Gray. [1st ed.] Garden City, N. Y., Hanover House [1954]

311 p. 22 cm.

Biographies covering the exploits of all the better-known spies North and South, plus some coverage of less known operators; lacks studious analyses.

Kelly, James, 1829–1907.
The American catalogue of books, (original and reprints,) published in the United States from Jan., 1861, to Jan. ... [1871], with date of publication, size, price, and publisher's name ... Compiled and arranged by James Kelly. New York, P. Smith, 1938.

2 v. 25½ cm.

Volume I covers 1861-1866; Vol. II, 1866-1871; useful as a checklist only.

Kettell, Thomas Prentice.
History of the great rebellion, from its commencement to its close, giving an account of its origin, the secession of the southern states, and the formation of the Confederate government, the concentration of the military and financial resources of the federal government ... together with sketches of the lives of all the eminent statesmen and military and naval commanders, with a full and complete index. From official sources. By Thomas P. Kettell ... Hartford, Conn., L. Stebbins; Cincinnati, F. A. Howe, 1865.

iv, [5]–778, [4] p. incl. maps. front., pl., port. 22 cm.

A wartime general history emphasizing the development of America into a world giant.

Kibby, Leo P
Book review reference for a decade of Civil War books, 1950–1960. San Jose, Calif., Spartan Bookstore, 1961.

64 p. 28 cm.

A sometimes useful guide for authors, titles, publishers, reviews and reviewers of approximately 450 books issued during an over-productive decade.

King, William C 1853– *comp.*
Camp-fire sketches and battle-field echoes of the rebellion. Comp. by W. C. King and W. P. Derby ... Springfield, Mass., W. C. King & co., 1887.

624 p. front., illus. 24 cm.

One of the better books of adventure and sometimes-true sketches of life in camp and on the battlefield; suffers from the usual exaggeration found in such volumes.

Kirwan, Albert Dennis, ***ed.***
The Confederacy. New York, Meridian Books [1959]

320 p. 19 cm.

Carefully chosen excerpts from contemporary material describing life on the Southern homefront.

Knowles, David, *father*, 1896–
The American civil war; a brief sketch by David Knowles. Oxford, The Clarendon press, 1926.
v, [2], 223 p. incl. front., illus. (maps) 19 cm.

Brief, rather elementary coverage; of use as a preliminary text.

Korn, Bertram Wallace.
American Jewry and the Civil War. With an introd. by Allan Nevins. Philadelphia, Jewish Publication Society of America, 1951.
xii, 331 p. illus., ports. 25 cm.

The best treatment of the subject, but restricted largely to the Northern side; reprinted in 1961.

Lambert, William Harrison, 1842–1912.
Library of the late Major William H. Lambert of Philadelphia ... to be sold ... at the Anderson galleries. New York, Metropolitan art association [1914]
5 v. fronts. (v. 1–4) plates, ports., facsims. 23½ cm.

An outstanding collection of manuscripts, pamphlets and books offered for sale in 1914; heavy on Lincoln items.

Lawrence, Samuel Crocker, 1832–1911.
Catalogue of the masonic library, masonic medals, Washingtoniana, Ancient and honorable artillery company's sermons, regimental histories, and other literature relating to the late civil war, belonging to Samuel C. Lawrence, Medford, Mass. Boston, Printed by C. H. Heintzemann, 1891.
320 p. 24½cm.

Another listing of a private collection; although larger than most catalogues of that day, this one too shows age.

Lee, Guy Carleton, 1862–1936.
The true history of the civil war, by Guy Carleton Lee ... with twenty-four illustrations and maps ... Philadelphia & London, J. B. Lippincott company, 1903.
421 p. front., plates, ports., maps, facsims. 20½cm.

One-third of this superficial study treats of causation; the remainder is too pro-Southern to be accepted at face value.

Leslie's illustrated weekly newspaper. v. 1–134; Dec. 15, 1855–June 17, 1922. New York, F. Leslie [etc.] 1855–1922.
134 v. in 127. illus., plates. 29–41 cm.

Ranks second only to Harper's Weekly as the most important periodical printed during the war; the 1861-1865 issues have been qualitatively reprinted.

Leslie's weekly.
At the front with the army and navy; a pictorial history of the civil and subsequent wars as seen by the correspondents of Leslie's weekly. New York city, Leslie-Judge company [©1912]
[141] p. illus. (1 col.) 41½cm.

Photographs and line drawings, with emphasis on the Civil War; contains enlarged captions rather than text.

Lewis, Lloyd, 1891–
It takes all kinds. [Newspaper and magazine articles. 1st ed.] New York, Harcourt, Brace [1947]
ix, 276 p. 21 cm.

Half of the brief essays in this volume of newspaper columns pertain to the war; intriguing on such subjects as "The Battle of Kilpatrick's Pants."

Lincoln herald.
[Harrogate, Tenn., Lincoln Memorial University]
v. in illus. 22–26 cm.

The oldest of those Civil War periodicals still in existence; respected and comprehensive.

Lively, Robert A
Fiction fights the Civil War; an unfinished chapter in the literary history of the American people. Chapel Hill, University of North Carolina Press [1957]
230 p. 23 cm.

By far the outstanding study of Civil War fiction; lists the best novels and contains a worthy bibliography.

Logan, John Alexander, 1826–1886.
The great conspiracy: its origin and history. By John A. Logan. New York, A. R. Hart & co., 1886.

xxiii p., 1 l., 810 p. front., port., maps (part fold.) 23 cm.

Sen. -Gen. Logan gives his own highly personalized viewpoints on the war; predominately political.

Lord, Francis Alfred, 1911–
Bands and drummer boys of the Civil War [by] Francis A. Lord and Arthur Wise. New York, T. Yoseloff [1966]

237 p. illus., ports. 29 cm.

An abundantly illustrated summary of music and musicians near the front lines.

Lord, Francis Alfred, 1911–
They fought for the Union. [1st ed.] Harrisburg, Pa., Stackpole Co. [1960]

375 p. illus., ports., map, facsims., tables. 29 cm.

A very useful volume on the Northern soldier; contains chapters on training, arms, flags, uniforms, equipment, etc.

Lossing, Benson John, 1813–1891.
Pictorial history of the civil war in the United States of America. By Benson J. Lossing. Illustrated by ... engravings on wood, by Lossing and Barritt, from sketches by the author and others. Philadelphia, G. W. Childs, 1866–68.

3 v. front., illus., port., maps, facsim. 24 cm.

Since Lossing was both an eyewitness and an historian, his study has value in the extent of his coverage and in his unusual first-hand impressions.

Lossing, Benson John, 1813–1891.
A history of the civil war, 1861–65, and the causes that led up to the great conflict, by Benson J. Lossing, LL. D., and a chronological summary and record of every engagement ... showing the total losses and casualties together with war maps of localities, comp. from the official records of the War department. Illustrated with facsimile photographic reproductions of the official war photographs, taken at the time by Matthew B. Brady, under the authority of President Lincoln and now in the possession of the War department, Washington, D. C. ... New York, The War memorial association, [c1912]

512 p. col. front., illus. (incl. ports., maps, facsims.) col. plates. 31 cm.

With a large number of Brady photographs included, Lossing's text forms an interesting volume for general persual; now of little historical value.

The **Lost** cause; a Confederate war record. v. 1–10; June 1898–Apr. 1904. Louisville, Ky., 1898–1904.
10 v. in 3. illus. (incl. ports.) 30cm.

One of several Confederate veterans' publications; contains romantic folklore as well as a goodly number of reminiscences.

Luvaas, Jay.
The military legacy of the Civil War. [Chicago] University of Chicago Press [1959]

v. illus., group ports. 24 cm.

A thorough and valuable study of how English, French and German observers viewed the war; Luvaas concludes that most Europeans rejected American battlefield tactics.

Macartney, Clarence Edward Noble, 1879–1957.
Grant and his generals. [1st ed.] New York, McBride Co. [1953]

352 p. illus. 22 cm.

Standard interpretations of Grant's relations with thirteen of his leading generals; the author, a prolific writer of Civil War studies, paints Sheridan in unfavorable colors.

Macartney, Clarence Edward Noble, 1879–
Lincoln and his generals, by Clarence Edward Macartney, D. D., illustrated with official photographs from the War department, Washington. Philadelphia, Dorrance and company [c1925]

5 p. l., [ix]–xi p., 1 l., 15–226 p. front., ports. 21 cm.

An inferior work to that of the same title by T. Harry Williams; McCartney discusses Lincoln's relations with ten generals, notably Scott, Fremont and Butler.

Mackenzie, Robert, 1823–1881.
America and her army. By Robert Mackenzie. London, New York [etc.] T. Nelson and sons, 1865.

iv, [5]–60 p. 19cm.

The limited story of the Union army, its officers and agencies, soldier life, and other associated subjects.

McMaster, John Bach, 1852–1932.

A history of the people of the United States during Lincoln's administration, by John Bach McMaster ... New York and London, D. Appleton and company, 1927.

xxxi, 693 p. maps (part fold.) 22½ cm.

Even though outdated, this study still remains a solid source for all aspects of the war; reprinted in 1961 under the title Our House Divided.

McPherson, Edward, 1830–1895.

The political history of the United States of America, during the great rebellion, from November 6, 1860, to July 4, 1864; including a classified summary of the legislation of the second session of the Thirty-sixth Congress, the three sessions of the Thirty-seventh Congress, the first session of the Thirty-eighth Congress, with the votes thereon, and the important executive, judicial and politico-military facts of that eventful period; together with the organization, legislation, and general proceedings of the rebel administration. By Edward McPherson ... Washington, D. C., Philp & Solomons; [etc., etc.] 1864.

viii, 440 p. 24cm.

Though haphazardly organized, this remains a valuable source for Northern political documents and records of political conventions; McPherson was clerk of the U. S. House of Representatives.

McWhiney, Grady, *ed.*

Grant, Lee, Lincoln and the radicals; essays on Civil War leadership. [Evanston, Ill.] Northwestern University Press, 1964.

vi, 117 p. 22 cm.

Contains four comparative essays; one pair is a comparison between Lee and Grant; the other --and more stimulating--pair views from opposite poles Lincoln's relations with the radicals.

Malone, Dumas, 1892–

Crisis of the Union, 1841–1877 [by] Dumas Malone [and] Basil Rauch. New York, Appleton-Century-Crofts [1964, ©1960]

xii, 429 p. maps (1 fold.) 24 cm.

A broad, general history of the entire period; for beginning students only.

Marx, Karl, 1818–1883.

The civil war in the United States, by Karl Marx and Frederick Engels. London, Lawrence and Wishart [1938]

xxv, 325 p. 22½cm.

A purely Communistic interpretation of the war; most of the text appeared originally as articles in New York and Vienna newspapers.

Massey, Mary Elizabeth.

Bonnet brigades. [1st ed.] New York, Knopf, 1966.

xxi, 371 p. illus. 25 cm.

A poor title for a splendid book; all important facets of women in wartime have been covered in a scholarly and colorful manner.

Meredith, Roy, 1908–

Mr. Lincoln's contemporaries; an album of portraits by Mathew B. Brady. New York, Scribner, 1951.

xii, 233 p. illus., ports. 29 cm.

A collection of Brady photographs of generals and politicians close to Lincoln; the accompanying text is minimal in length and content.

[Meriwether, Elizabeth (Avery)] 1824–

Facts and falsehoods concerning the war on the South, 1861–1865, by George Edmonds [*pseud.*] ... Memphis, Tenn., A. R. Taylor & co. [©1904]

1 p. l., vii, [1], 271 p. 22cm.

An anti-radical approach, with a pro-Southern viewpoint; largely a setting forth of opinions in "factual form."

Meserve, Frederick Hill.

Historical portraits and Lincolniana; index of a part of the collection of Americana of Frederick Hill Meserve. New York, Priv. print., 1915.

xii, 143 p. incl. mounted photos. front. 32cm.

A listing of nearly 8,000 photographs, mainly portraits; includes many lesser known figures.

Miers, Earl Schenck, 1910–

The American Civil War: a popular illustrated history of the years 1861–1865 as seen by the artist-correspondents who were there. New York, Golden Press [1961]

319 p. illus. (part col.) ports., maps, facsims. (part col.) 35 cm.

One of the most attractive and well-arranged of the modern picture books.

Miers, Earl Schenck, 1910–
The Great Rebellion; the emergence of the American conscience. [1st ed.] Cleveland, World Pub. Co. [1958]
369 p. 24 cm.

A thought-provoking discussion of the events of December, 1860, April, 1861, and April, 1865; Miers hammers the point that slavery was the primary causative factor for war.

Milhollen, Hirst Dillon, 1906–
Best photos of the Civil War. [Authors: Hirst Dillon Milhollen and James Ralph Johnson] New York, Arco Pub. Co. [1961]
144 p. illus. 24 cm.

A paperback compilation in which the photographs are far superior to the text.

Miller, Francis Trevelyan, 1877– *ed.*
... The photographic history of the civil war ... Francis Trevelyan Miller, editor-in-chief; Robert S. Lanier, managing editor. Thousands of scenes photographed, 1861–65, with text by many special authorities. New York, The Review of reviews co., 1911.
10 v. fronts, illus. (incl. ports.) maps. 28½ cm.

Still remains the major source for photographs; the greatest single collection of Brady illustrations.

Milton, George Fort, 1894–
... Conflict; the American civil war. New York, Coward-McCann, inc. [©1941]
xii, 433 p. incl. maps. 22 cm.

A one-volume military history for the general reader; intentionally simplified, with limited detail.

Moat, Louis Shepheard, *ed.*
Frank Leslie's illustrated famous leaders and battle scenes of the Civil War ... by such well-known artists as Becker [and others] A concise history of the Civil War, being official data secured from the war records. With an introd. by Joseph B. Carr. New York, Mrs. F. Leslie [1896]
544 p. illus., ports., maps. 44 cm.

A typical early picture-book reprinting many Leslie's sketches with captions but no text.

Moore, Frank, 1828–1904, *ed.*
Anecdotes, poetry, and incidents of the war: North and South. 1860–1865. Collected and arranged by Frank Moore ... New York, Publication office, Bible house, J. Porteus, agent, 1867.
560 p. front., port. 25cm.

Mainly of a fictional or semi-fictional nature; old but still useful for delving into the humor incidents of the day.

Moore, Frank, 1828–1904.
The Civil war in song and story. 1860–1865. Collected and arranged by Frank Moore ... [New York] P. F. Collier, 1889.
560 p. front., plates. 26½ cm.

The best-known and most easily obtainable old collection of anecdotes, songs, etc.; many of the incidents related are of doubtful authenticity.

Moore, Frank, 1828–1904, *ed.*
Heroes and martyrs: notable men of the time. Biographical sketches of military and naval heroes, statesmen and orators, distinguished in the American crisis of 1861–62. Ed. by Frank Moore ... New York, G. P. Putnam [1862]
iv, [3]–253 p. front., ports. 27½ x 23½ cm.

An early collection of biographies, including subjects more notable in the war's first stages than today; the sketches suffer from errors of fact.

Moore, Frank, 1828–1904, *ed.*
The portrait gallery of the war, civil, military, and naval: a biographical record. Ed. by Frank Moore ... New York, G. P. Putnam for Derby & Miller, 1864.
iv, 353 p. front., ports. 25½cm.

Wartime biographies of leaders both civil and military, with many not now considered major; contains numerous errors.

Moore, Frank, 1828–1904.
Women of the war; their heroism and self-sacrifice. By Frank Moore ... Hartford, Conn., S. S. Scranton & co.; Chicago, R. C. Treat; [etc., etc.] 1866.
xvi, 17–596 p. 2 pl., 8 port. (incl. front.) 23 cm.

Idealistic biographies of then-famous women; antiquated in treatment.

Morgan, Matthew Somerville, 1839–1890.
The American war. Cartoons by Matt Morgan and other English artists. With illustrative notes. London, Chatto and Windus, 1874.

[224] p. incl. 55 pl. 28 x 23cm.

A scarce volume of considerable historic value; strongly critical particularly of Lincoln.

Morris, Richard Brandon, 1904– *ed.*
A house divided; the Civil War, 1850–1865. Edited by Richard B. Morris [and] James Woodress. St. Louis, Webster Pub. Co. [1961]

58 p. illus. 23 cm.

A short source book for use as a supplement to a college text; better compilations are available.

Morton, Joseph W *jr., ed.*
... Sparks from the camp fire; or Tales of the old veterans. Thrilling stories of heroic deeds ... as re-told today around the modern camp fire. New and rev. ed. ... Ed. by Joseph W. Morton, jr. ... Philadelphia, Keystone publishing co., 1893.
13 p. l., 15–648 p. incl. illus., plates, ports., maps, plans, fold. facsim. front., col. plates, ports. 24½cm.

Supposedly true veterans' tales, anecdotes, adventures, and accounts of camp and battle; must be handled with extreme caution.

Mottelay, Paul Fleury, *b.* 1841, *ed.*
The soldier in our Civil war: a pictorial history of the conflict, 1861–1865, illustrating the valor of the soldier as displayed on the battle-field. From sketches drawn by Forbes, Waud, Taylor, Beard, Becker, Lovie, Schell, Crane and ... other eye-witnesses ... Edited by Paul F. Mottelay ... With an introduction by Robert B. Beath ... History of the Grand army of the republic by Paul Vandervoort ... History of the Sons of veterans by A. P. Davis ... and Frank P. Merrill ... New York, The J. H. Brown publishing company, 1884–85.

2 v. front., illus., ports., maps. 41½ cm.

Liberally illustrated with familiar battle sketches, these volumes also contain a lengthy text with several eyewitness accounts.

Munden, Kenneth White.
Guide to Federal archives relating to the Civil War, by Kenneth W. Munden and Henry Putney Beers. Washington, National Archives, National Archives and Records Service, General Services Administration, 1962.

x, 721 p. facsim. 23 cm.

A descriptive guide to Federal sources in the National Archives; a long-needed tool that will make difficult tasks easier; a similar guide to Confederate records is in preparation.

Nalty, Bernard C
The United States Marines in the Civil War. Rev. Washington, Historical Branch, G–3 Division, Headquarters, U. S. Marine Corps, 1962.

16 p. 26 cm.

A cursory summary of a subject still awaiting full study.

The **National** almanac and annual record for ... 1863–64. Philadelphia, G. W. Childs; [etc., etc.] 1863–64.

2 v. 18½ cm.

Similar to modern alamanacs; very valuable for census reports and endless facts and figures; the best and most complete of several such works.

Nevins, Allan, 1890–
The statesmanship of the Civil War. New York, Macmillan, 1953.

82 p. 22 cm.

A brilliant evaluation of Northern and Southern leadership; especially good for analyses of Lincoln as a statesman and the dilemma of Southern leaders.

Nevins, Allan, 1890–
The War for the Union. New York, Scribner [1959–

v. illus., ports., maps. 24 cm.

Two deeply analytical volumes that carry the war to May, 1863; marked by such thorough research and scholarship that the volumes will stand for years at the peak of Civil War history.

New York & Pennsylvania Company, inc., *New York.*
A bibliography of the American Civil War. [New York, 1962]

18 p. illus., ports. 23 x 31 cm.

A brief bibliography of current books, arranged by subject; includes prices.

Newman, Ralph G 1911–
A basic Civil War library; a bibliographical essay, by Ralph G. Newman and E. B. Long. Springfield, Civil War Centennial Commission of Illinois, 1964.

23 p. 23 cm.

A basic bibliography divided into subject sections; intended as a guide to essential, fundamental volumes.

Newman, Ralph G 1911– *ed.*
The Civil War digest, by Ralph Newman and E. B. Long. Introd. by Allan Nevins. Maps by Barbara Long. New York, Grosset & Dunlap [1960]

xiii, 274 p. illus., ports., maps, facsims. 21 cm.

A useful handbook with a month-to-month chronology, biographies and photographs of leading figures, maps and bibliography.

Nichols, Roy Franklin, 1896–
The stakes of power, 1845–1877. New York, Hill and Wang [1961]

246 p. illus. 22 cm.

Provocative and stimulating; a detailed interpretation by a recognized scholar in the field.

Nicholson, John Page, 1842–1922.
Catalogue of library of Brevet Lieutenant-Colonel John Page Nicholson ... relating to the war of the rebellion, 1861–1866. Philadelphia [Priv. print. by J. T. Palmer co.] 1914.

3 p. l., 5–1022 p., 1 l. front. 25cm.

A listing of one of the most important Civil War collections (now deposited in the Huntington Library); Lincolniana and naval works are not included.

Nicolay, John George, 1832–1901.
... The outbreak of rebellion, by John G. Nicolay ... New York, C. Scribner's sons, 1881.

viii p., 1 l., 220 p. incl. maps. 19 cm.

An able outline of the early military and political events; written from the vantage point of the author's White House post; still a worthwhile volume.

Niven, Alexander C
Civil War day-by-day: 1861; a chronology of the principal events of the war's first year. Edited by Arthur W. Monks. [1st ed.] Cambridge, Mass., Berkshire Pub. Co. [1961]

64 p. illus. 21 cm.

An accurate, simple and reliable chronology for 1861; no more published.

Officers of the Army and Navy (regular and volunteer) who served in the civil war. Philadelphia, Pa., L. R. Hamersly & co., 1894.

2 p. l., 5–172 numb. l., 173–177 p. incl. 838 port. 32 cm.

Biographies with portraits of all major leaders; particularly useful for naval officers, but outdated for army figures.

Pakula, Marvin H
Centennial album of the Civil War, by Marvin H. Pakula, in collaboration with William J. Ryan and David K. Rothstein. New York, T. Yoseloff [1960]

299 p. 20 col. plates, ports. 37 cm.

This attractively printed compilation contains sections on generals, flags, uniforms, and equipment; useful for the beginner.

Paxson, Frederic Logan, 1877–
The civil war, by Frederic L. Paxson ... New York, H. Holt and company; [etc., etc., ©1911]

x, 11–256 p. illus. (maps) 18 cm.

A modest general account, somewhat outdated; strongly pro-Northern in tone.

Peck, George, 1797–1876.
Our country: its trial and its triumph. A series of discourses suggested by the varying events of the war for the union. By George Peck, D. D. New York, Carlton & Porter, 1865.

300 p. 19½cm.

A collection of strong anti-slavery essays and sermons; useful for the flavor of the times.

Peterson, Clarence Stewart, 1896–
Last Civil War veteran in each State. Baltimore, ©1951.
51 l. 28 cm.

An analysis of the last veteran in each of the fifty states, with brief biographies of each.

A Portion of that field; the centennial of the burial of Lincoln [by] Gwendolyn Brooks [and others] Urbana, University of Illinois Press, 1967.
97 p. 21 cm.

A collection of poems, tributes and short speeches delivered in conjunction with the closing convention of the U. S. Civil War Centennial Commission.

Powell, William Henry, 1838–1901.
Officers of the army and navy (regular) who served in the civil war. Ed. by Major William H. Powell ... and Medical-Director Edward Shippen ... Philadelphia, Pa., L. R. Hamersly & co., 1892.
487 p. illus. (ports.) 32 x 25½ᶜᵐ.

Early but helpful biographies of regular army and navy officers; inaccurate in places and now outdated.

Powell, William Henry, 1838–1901, *ed.*
Officers of the army and navy (volunteer) who served in the civil war. Ed. by Lieutenant-Colonel William H. Powell, U. S. army. Philadelphia, Pa., L. R. Hamersly & co., 1893.
419 p. illus. (ports.) 32ᶜᵐ.

A companion volume to the above; often referred to as "Hammersly."

Pratt, Fletcher, 1897–
Ordeal by fire; an informal history of the Civil War. Maps by Rafael Palacios. [Rev. ed.] New York, W. Sloane Associates [1948]
xvi, 426 p. maps. 22 cm.

With an awareness that this book contains errors and distortions, it is one of the more readable military histories.

Pratt, Fletcher, 1897–1956, *ed.*
Civil War in pictures. New York, Holt [1955]
256 p. illus. 29 cm.

Another modern volume featuring sketches from Harper's and Leslie's; the unconnected text appears to have been hastily written.

Pressly, Thomas J
Americans interpret their Civil War. With a new introd. by the author. New York, Collier Books [1962]
384 p. 18 cm.

This well-conceived but highly controversial study is a basic work in Civil War historiography; the volumes appraised are mainly those emphasizing causation and politics.

Price, William Hamilton, 1931–
The Civil War centennial handbook, 1861–1865, 1961–1965. [1st ed.] Arlington, Va., Civil War Research Associates, ©1961.
72 p. illus. 23 cm.

A collection of somewhat disassociated facts intended as a primer for the Centennial.

Pullen, John J
A shower of stars; the medal of honor and the 27th Maine, by John J. Pullen. [1st ed.] Philadelphia, Lippincott [1966]
269 p. illus., ports. 22 cm.

More valuable for a history of the Congressional Medal than for a chronicle of the 27th Maine, every member of which received the medal.

Randall, James Garfield, 1881–1953.
The Civil War and Reconstruction [by] J. G. Randall [and] David Donald. 2d ed. Boston, Heath [1961]
820 p. illus. 25 cm.

A skillful revision by Donald of Randall's superb text; has marked improvements in the military sections, plus an updated bibliography; one of the most fundamental sources for any study of the war.

Randall, James Garfield, 1881–1953.
The Civil War and reconstruction; with supplementary bibliography. Boston, Heath [1953]

xvii, 971 p. illus., ports., maps. 23 cm.

Still the basic text for mid-century history, and deservedly so; strongest in political and economic coverage; weakest in military events.

Randall, James Garfield, 1881–1953.
The divided Union [by] J. G. Randall [and] David Donald. Boston, Little, Brown [1961]

xvi, 572 p. illus., ports., maps. 24 cm.

Identical to the Randall-Donald 1961 work, except that the chapters on Reconstruction have been omitted.

Rawley, James A
Turning points of the Civil War [by] James A. Rawley. Lincoln, University of Nebraska Press [1966]

ix, 230 p. map (on lining papers) 24 cm.

Seven essays on as many events recount the "highwater marks" of the war; based in large part on secondary sources.

The **Rebellion** record; a diary of American events, with documents, narratives, illustrative incidents, poetry, etc. Ed. by Frank Moore ... With an introductory address on the causes of the struggle, and the great issues before the country, by Edward Everett ... New York, G. P. Putnam, 1861–63; D. Van Nostrand, 1864–68.

11 v. fronts., ports., maps (part fold.) plans (part fold.) diagrs. 25 cm.

——— Supplement.—First volume. New York, G. P. Putnam; H. Holt, 1864.

1 p. l., vi, 759, iv p. front., port., fold. map, plans. 25 cm.

Still an excellent source for such material as newspaper accounts, eyewitness testimonies, anecdotes, poetry, and public documents; heavy on things military.

Reeder, Russell Potter.
The story of the Civil War, by Red Reeder. Illustrated by Frederick Chapman. [1st ed.] New York, Duell, Sloan and Pearce [1958]

212 p. illus. 22 cm.

While designed for younger readers, this volume has value as a basic military account.

Rhodes, James Ford, 1848–1927.
History of the civil war, 1861–1865, by James Ford Rhodes ... New York, The Macmillan company, 1917.

xxi, 454 p. fold. front., maps (part fold.) 23 cm.

A fresh study that Rhodes wrote after completion of his multi-volume history; this volume is predominately military and still of value; reprinted in 1961, with editorial notes by E. B. Long.

Rhodes, James Ford, 1848–1927.
History of the United States from the compromise of 1850 to the end of the Roosevelt administration, by James Ford Rhodes ... New ed. in nine volumes ... New York, The Macmillan company; London, Macmillan & co., ltd., 1928.

9 v. illus., ports., maps (part fold.) 21 cm.

Three volumes pertain to the war; carefully researched, this was one of the first works to present in detail reasoned viewpoints from both sides.

Rhodes, James Ford, 1848–1927.
Lectures on the American civil war, delivered before the University of Oxford in Easter and Trinity terms 1912, by James Ford Rhodes ... New York, The Macmillan company, 1913.

xi, 206 p. fold. map. 20½ cm.

Two of three lectures treat of the Civil War; somewhat simplified for English audiences.

Roberts, Allen E
House undivided, the story of Freemasonry and the Civil War. [n. p.] Missouri Lodge of Research, 1961.

356 p. 24 cm.

This thorough but unannotated history described the wartime relations between Northern and Southern masons.

Robertson, James I
The Civil War. Washington, U. S. Civil War Centennial Commission, 1963.

63 p. illus., map. 23 cm.

A capably prepared handbook in simple language; of good use to secondary school students and beginning readers.

Rodenbough, Theophilus Francis, 1838–1912, *ed.*
Uncle Sam's medal of honor; some of the noble deeds for which the medal has been awarded, described by those who have won it. 1861–1866. Collected and edited by Theo. F. Rodenbough ... New York & London, G. P. Putnam's sons [c1886]
xiv, [2], 424 p. incl. illus., port., facsim. front. 21½ cm.

An early but still useful compilation on Northern heroes in the field; three later editions appeared under as many different titles.

Roland, Charles P
The Confederacy. [Chicago] University of Chicago Press [1960]
218 p. illus. 21 cm.

The best brief introduction to Confederate history; within space limitation, it achieves admirable balance of military and non-military events.

Ropes, John Codman, 1836–1899.
The story of the civil war; a concise account of the war in the United States of America between 1861 and 1865. By John Codman Ropes ... New York, G. P. Putnam's sons, 1933.
3 v. in 4. maps (part fold.) plans (part fold.) 23½ cm.

Exclusively military, with Vicksburg and Gettysburg the centers of attention; a good side referance for military campaigns.

Sandburg, Carl, 1878–
Storm over the land, from Abraham Lincoln: the war years, 1861–1865, by Carl Sandburg. London, J. Cape [1943]
250 p. illus. (maps) 23cm.

A general history of the war, drawn from Sandburg's biography of Lincoln; colorfully written, but lacking in depth and analysis.

Schmucker, Samuel Mosheim, 1823–1863.
The history of the civil war in the United States: its cause, origin, progress and conclusion. Containing full, impartial and graphic descriptions of the various military and naval engagements, with the heroic deeds achieved by armies and individuals, touching scenes and incidents in the camp, the cabin, the field and the hospital. And biographical sketches of its heroes. By Samuel M. Schmucker ... Rev. and completed by Dr. L. P. Brockett ... Illustrated with over one hundred and fifty fine portraits of general, battle scenes, maps and diagrams. Philadelphia [etc.] Jones brothers & co.; Chicago [etc.] Zeigler, McCurdy & co. [1865]
1021 p. front., illus., plates, ports., maps, plans. 26½ cm.

Possibly the best of the contemporary general accounts; largely military; as with all such volumes, it contains errors and distortions.

Schouler, James, 1839–1920.
History of the United States of America under the Constitution. By James Schouler Washington, D. C., W. H. & O. H. Morrison, 1880–[c1913]
7 v. fronts. (double maps, v. 6–7) 19½ cm.

Volumes V-VII treat of the war period; yet the whole study is marred by inaccuracies of research and opinion--as well as by the passage of time.

Shotwell, Walter Gaston, 1856–
The civil war in America, by Walter Gaston Shotwell ... London, New York [etc.] Longmans, Green and co., 1923.
2 v. 23½cm.

A moderately successful re-telling of military events; Shotwell believed that the result justified the sacrifice.

Simmons, Henry Eugene, 1929–
A concise encyclopedia of the Civil War, compiled by Henry E. Simmons. New York, A. S. Barnes [1965]
221 p. 22 cm.

An overly concise fact book in dictionary form; much too superficial for use by any but the beginning student or youthful reader.

The **South** in the building of the nation; a history of the southern states designed to record the South's part in the making of the American nation; to portray the character and genius, to chronicle the achievements and progress and to illustrate the life and traditions of the southern people ... Richmond, Va., The Southern historical publication society [c1909–13]
13 v. col., front., plates (part col.) ports. (part col.) map, fascims. 24 cm.

A cooperative work on the economic, political and cultural life of the South; largely superseded by modern scholarship.

Southern historical society.
Southern historical society papers. v. 1–38, 1876–1910; new ser., no. 1– (whole no. 39–) 1914–
Richmond, Va. [1876]–19
v. illus., plates, ports. 23½ cm.

Other than the Official Records, this 52-volume set is the most important printed source for the Confederacy; an index is in preparation.

Squier, Ephraim George, 1821–1888, *ed.*

Frank Leslie's pictorial history of the American civil war. Ed. by the Hon. E. G. Squier ... New York, F. Leslie ⌊1861⌋–62.

2 v. illus., fold. pl., port., maps, plans. $58\frac{1}{2}$cm.

One of several such publications; most of the drawings are available in easier-to-find volumes.

Stacke, Henry.

The story of the American war. 1861–1865. By Henry Stacke. With a map illustrating the battle fields. London, F. Warne and co., 1866.

viii, 264 p. front. (fold. map) 16cm.

A collection of dramatic anecdotes and questionable adventures; reissued in 1867 under the title Heroism and Adventure in the Nineteenth Century.

Stephens, *Mrs.* **Ann Sophia (Winterbothom)** 1813–1886.

Pictorial history of the war for the union. A complete and reliable history of the war from its commencement to its close ... Together with a complete chronological analysis of the war. By Mrs. Ann S. Stephens. Embellished with over two hundred illustrations. New York, J. G. Wells, 1863–66.

2 v. illus., plates, ports. (incl. front.) maps. 23cm.

A wartime period piece of little use to historians today.

Stephenson, Nathaniel Wright, 1867–1935.

Abraham Lincoln and the union; a chronicle of the embattled North, by Nathaniel W. Stephenson. New Haven, Yale university press; ⌊etc., etc.⌋ 1921.

xiii, 272 p. col. front. 18 cm.

Inferior to the same author's volume on the Confederacy; in overpraising Lincoln, Stephenson too often over-condemns Lincoln's opponents.

Stephenson, Nathaniel Wright, 1867–1935.

The day of the confederacy; a chronicle of the embattled South, by Nathaniel W. Stephenson. New York, Yale university press; ⌊etc., etc.⌋ 1919.

xi, 214 p. front., pl., ports. 21 cm.

An older, general, brief history of the Confederacy.

Stern, Philip Van Doren, 1900– *ed.*

The Civil War Christmas album. ⌊1st ed.⌋ New York, Hawthorn Books ⌊1961⌋

125 p. illus. 26 cm.

Contains a series of eyewitness accounts of wartime holidays; of limited value because it was written more for the market than for history.

Stern, Philip Van Doren, 1900–

Secret missions of the Civil War; first-hand accounts by men and women who risked their lives in underground activities for the North and the South, woven into a continuous narrative. Chicago, Rand McNally ⌊1959⌋

320 p. illus. 22 cm.

Carefully chosen selections by and about secret service personnel; Stern furnishes lucid introductions and connecting passages.

Stern, Philip Van Doren, 1900–

They were there; the Civil War in action as seen by its combat artists. With 6 poems by Walt Whitman. New York, Crown Publishers ⌊1959⌋

166 p. (chiefly illus.) 31 cm.

A modern anthology of Civil War sketches, primarily from Harper's, Leslie's, and Illustrated London News; fair reproductions with full captions.

Stewart, Lucy Shelton, 1875–

The reward of patriotism; a refutation of the present-day defamations of the defenders and preservers of the Union in the civil war and an exposition of the cause which they overcame, by Lucy Shelton Stewart. New York, W. Neale, 1930.

484 p. front., ports., maps. $24\frac{1}{2}$cm.

A violent polemic against the South and all Confederate leaders, particularly R. E. Lee.

Storke, Elliot G 1811–1879 *or* 1880.

... A complete history of the great American rebellion, embracing its causes, events and consequences, with biographical sketches and portraits of its principal actors ... By Elliot G. Storke ... Auburn, N. Y., The Auburn publishing co. ⌊1863–65⌋

2 v. front., illus., pl., port., maps (part fold.) 23cm.

Written too close to the times to be either comprehensive or balanced; marked as well by too much sentimentalism.

Street, James Howell, 1903–
The Civil War; an unvarnished account of the late but still lively hostilities. Illustrated by John Alan Maxwell. New York, Dial Press [1953]

144 p. illus. 24 cm.

Obviously, a hastily prepared, debunking account; Street rambles amusingly and widely over many favorite subjects.

Strong's pictorial and biographical record of the great rebellion. Containing sketches of departed heroes, prominent personages of the past, facts, incidents and stories connected with that important epoch of the history of America. Illustrated with 265 portraits. Compiled and edited by Julian K. Larke ... New York, T. W. Strong [1866?]

1 p. l., 288 p. illus. (ports.) 34½cm.

Biographical sketches of war heroes, plus anecdotes and incidents; of no great importance today.

Swinton, William, 1833–1892.
... The war for the Union. By William Swinton ... The first, second, third and fourth years of the war. September 9, 1864. New York, Loyal publication society, 1864.

20 p. 22cm.

A brief pamphlet by one of the most controversial of wartime correspondents; writing in 1864, he saw no hope for the Confederacy.

Tenney, William Jewett, 1814–1883.
The military and naval history of the rebellion in the United States. With biographical sketches of deceased officers ... By W. J. Tenney ... New York, D. Appleton & company, 1865.

1 p. l., x, 843 p. front., illus., pl., ports., fold. map. 26 cm.

Typical of many hastily prepared and over-glamorized general histories issued immediately after the war.

Thompson, Charles Willis, 1871–1946.
The fiery epoch, 1830–1877, by Charles Willis Thompson ... Indianapolis, The Bobbs-Merrill company [©1931]

367 p. 22½ cm.

In this opinionated but well-written work, Thompson viewed the war as a conspiracy to abolish the nation of the Founding Fathers.

Thompson, William Fletcher, 1929–
The image of war; the pictorial reporting of the American Civil War. New York, T. Yoseloff [1960]

248 p. illus. 25 cm.

A sound study of Northern pictorial reporting and the use of sketches as propaganda; a study of image-makers, not a picture book.

Thorpe, Francis Newton, 1857–1926.
... The Civil war: the national view, by Francis Newton Thorpe ... Philadelphia, Printed for subscribers only by G. Barrie & sons [1906]

xxi, 535 p. col. front., plates, ports., facsims. 23 cm.

Written by the editor of the twenty-volume series of which this study was a part; strongly biased in favor of the North.

Tomes, Robert, 1817–1882.
The war with the South, a history of the late rebellion, with biographical sketches of leading statesmen and distinguished naval and military commanders, etc. By Robert Tomes, M. D. Continued from the beginning of the year 1864 to the end of the war, by Benjamin G. Smith ... New York, Virtue & Yorston [1862–67]

3 v. fronts., plates, ports., maps. 29 cm.

A wartime publication, this set presents a purely Northern viewpoint; rather heavy on politics.

Townsend, Edward Davis, 1817–1893.
Anecdotes of the civil war in the United States. By Brevet Major-General E. D. Townsend ... New York, D. Appleton and co., 1884 [1883]

xii, 287 p. illus. 19½cm.

A well-known potpourri of unrelated material, some of it of doubtful accuracy and all of it of little interest.

Tredwell, Daniel M, 1826–
A catalogue of books and pamphlets, belonging to Daniel M. Tredwell, relating to the great civil war ... with about 500 portraits of military men and civilians who were participators in the ... strife. Brooklyn, N. Y., E. F. Deselding [pref. 1874]

iv, 220 p. 25cm.

An uncritical list of 1,268 books and pamphlets in a private collection; a number of obscure items are included.

The **Union** army; a history of military affairs in the loyal states, 1861–65—records of the regiments in the Union army—cyclopedia of battles—memoirs of commanders and soldiers ... Madison, Wis., Federal publishing company, 1908.

8 v. front. (v. 8) ports. 24cm.

Includes four volumes of brief regimental histories (state by state), a two-volume encyclopedia of battles, one volume on the navy and one biographical.

U. S. *Census Office. 8th census, 1860.*
The United States on the eve of the Civil War, as described in the 1860 census [edited by the Bureau of the Census] Washington, U. S. Civil War Centennial Commission [for sale by the Superintendent of Documents, U. S. Govt. Print. Off.] 1963.

viii, 73 p. illus., map, port. 24 cm.

A valuable starting point for population statistics at war's outset.

U. S. *Civil War Centennial Commission.*
Facts about the Civil War. Washington, 1959.

20 p. illus. 22 cm.

A very brief chronology, with random facts added; of some interest to a general public.

U. S. *Dept. of the Army. Army Library.*
The Civil War; a catalog of books in the Army Library, pertinent to the American Civil War. Prepared by the Catalog Unit. [Washington] 1961.

1 l., 51 p. 27 cm.

Mainly a general and campaign bibliography, but useful for material on arms and special services.

U. S. *Library of Congress.*
The American Civil War; a centennial exhibition. Washington, 1961.

v, 88 p. illus., ports. 27 cm.

A guide to lithographs, drawings, photographs, broadsides, music etc., displayed at the Library of Congress; full annotations.

U. S. *Library of Congress. General Reference and Bibliography Division.*
The American Civil War; a selected reading list, compiled by Donald H. Mugridge. [Washington, 1960]

24 p. 27 cm.

A brief, useful reading list broken into twenty categories.

U. S. *Library of Congress. General Reference and Bibliography Division.*
The Civil War in pictures, 1861–1961; a chronological list of selected pictorial works, compiled by Donald H. Mugridge. Washington, 1961.

30 p. 24 x 30 cm.

A needed bibliography of pictorial works; perceptive, critical evaluations clearly indicate the quality of the volumes cited.

U. S. *Library of Congress. Map Division.*
Civil War maps; an annotated list of maps and atlases in map collections of the Library of Congress, compiled by Richard W. Stephenson. Washington, 1961.

v, 138 p. map (on cover) 26 cm.

A well-documented listing of 700 maps; fully indexed.

U. S. *Library of Congress. Map Division.*
The Hotchkiss map collection; a list of manuscript maps, many of the Civil War period, prepared by Major Jed. Hotchkiss, and other manuscript and annotated maps in his possession, compiled by Clara Egli LeGear, with a foreword by Willard Webb. Washington, 1951.

67 p. 23 cm.

The useful guide to 341 maps in this excellent collection; indexed; excellent for Jackson's campaigns.

U. S. *Library of Congress. Prints and Photographs Division.*
Civil War photographs, 1861–1865; a catalog of copy negatives made from originals selected from the Mathew B. Brady Collection in the Prints and Photographs Division of the Library of Congress. Compiled by Hirst D. Milhollen and Donald H. Mugridge. Washington, Reference Dept., Library of Congress, 1961.

x, 74 p. front. 24 cm.

A useful catalogue of important Brady photographs; 1,047 negatives are listed by place, engagement and person.

U. S. *Library of Congress. Stack and Reader Division.*
The Civil War in motion pictures; a bibliography of films produced in the United States since 1897. Compiled by Paul C. Spehr, and the staff of the Motion Picture Section. Washington, 1961.

vi, 109 p. 27 cm.

A helpful bibliography for both schools and the treatment of the war in movies.

U. S. *Military Academy, West Point. Dept. of Military Art and Engineering.*
The West Point atlas of the Civil War. Chief editor: Vincent J. Esposito. New York, Praeger [1962]

1 v. (various pagings) 154 col. maps. 27 x 37 cm.

By far the best modern atlas for the major military campaigns; indispensable when touring the battlefields.

U. S. *National Archives.*
Civil War maps in the National Archives. Washington, National Archives and Records Service, General Services Administration; [for sale by the Superintendent of Documents, U. S. Govt. Print. Off.] 1964.

xi, 127 p. illus., maps. 26 cm.

This handy tool lists about 8,000 maps, charts and plans, mostly Federal; well-indexed.

U. S. *National Archives.*
Preliminary inventory of the War Department collection of Confederate records (Record group 109) Compiled by Elizabeth Bethel. Washington, 1957.

ix, 310 p. 26 cm.

A synopsis of, and introduction to, one of the most valuable manuscript collections in existence.

U. S. *National Gallery of Art.*
The Civil War: a centennial exhibition of eyewitness drawings. Washington, 1961.

153 p. illus. 26 cm.

Well-reproduced Civil War drawings by famous artists; each is fully annotated and described.

U. S. *National Museum.*
Uniform regulations for the Army of the United States, 1861. Illustrated with contemporary official War Dept. photos. Washington, Smithsonian Institution, 1961.

61 p. (p. 7–[23] reprint) illus. 28 cm.

Another reprint of a wartime work that vividly illustrated what the well-dressed soldier of that era wore.

U. S. *War Dept.*
The official atlas of the Civil War. Introd. by Henry Steele Commager. New York, T. Yoseloff [1958]

[8] p., facsim.: 29 p., 175 plates (incl. illus. (part col.) maps (part col.) plans) 45 cm.

A qualitative reprint of the Atlas to Accompany the Official Records; in spite of some fuzzy reproductions and the unwieldly size of the work, it is still highly useful.

U. S. *War dept.*
The war of the rebellion: a compilation of the official records of the Union and Confederate armies. Pub. under the direction of the ... secretary of war ... Washington, Govt. print. off., 1880–1901.

70 v. in 128. 23½ cm.

The major source of Civil War research material and absolutely indispensable to the serious student; contains all the major reports and correspondence available to the time of publication; commonly referred to as the Official Records or OR.

U. S. *War dept. Library.*
... Bibliography of state participation in the civil war 1861–1866 ... [3d ed.] Washington, Govt. print. off., 1913.
x, 1140 p. 25cm.

This guide is still an important starting point for regimental and state studies; reprinted without updating in 1961, but now rendered obsolete by the Dornbusch compilation.

U. S. *War dept. Library.*
... List of the photographs and photographic negatives relating to the war for the union, now in the War department library ... Washington, Govt. print. off., 1897.

219 p. 23cm.

An outdated listing of available photographs in the War Department; the breakdown by place, subject and person is useful.

U. S. *War dept. Library.*
... Military literature in the War department library relating chiefly to the participation of the individual states in the war for the union ... 2d ed. ... Washington, Govt. print. off., 1899.

266 p. 23 cm.

—— Appendix to Subject catalogue no. 6, containing accessions in state and regimental literature of the war for the union for four years ending April 9, 1904 ... Washington, Govt. print. off., 1904.

103 p. 23 cm.

A list of state and local participation sources; far surpassed by the publication later of Bibliography of State Participation.

Vandiver, Frank Everson, 1925–
Basic history of the Confederacy. Princeton, N. J., Van Nostrand [1962]

186 p. 19 cm.

A brief survey equally divided between a descriptive summary and selected documents illustrating Confederate history.

Victor, Orville James, 1827–1910.
The history, civil, political and military, of the southern rebellion, from its incipient stages to its close. Comprehending, also, all important state papers, ordinances of secession, proclamations, proceedings of Congress, official reports of commanders, etc., etc. By Orville J. Victor ... New York, J. D. Torrey [c1861–68?]

4 v. fronts., plates, ports., maps (part fold.) 26cm.

While antiquated and outdated, this extensive set remains one of the best of the semi-contemporary general histories that came out during and shortly after the war.

... The **war** for the union. Boston, Old South meeting house, 1885.
cover-title, [71] p. 18½cm.

A wide variety of addresses, including several by Lincoln and leading abolitionists; useful for the works of Lowell, Garrison and Beecher.

Warren, Robert Penn, 1905–
The legacy of the Civil War; meditations on the centennial. New York, Random House [1961]

109 p. 21 cm.

A modern novelist thoughtfully and provocatively meditates on the Civil War Centennial.

Webb, Willard, 1903– *ed.*
Crucial moments of the Civil War. With an introd. by Bruce Catton. New York, Fountainhead Publishers [1961]

356 p. illus. 21 cm.

Eighteen selections on major military engagements by leading critics, mostly eyewitnesses; adroitly and wisely chosen.

Werstein, Irving.
1861–1865: the adventure of the Civil War told with pictures. [1st ed.] Paterson, N. J., Pageant Books, 1960.

128 p. illus. 28 cm.

Sketches depicting the major events of the war; of value to a new reader, despite superficiality in much of the text.

[**Westcott, Thompson,** 1820–1888.
Chronicles of the great rebellion against the United States of America. Being a concise record and digest of the events connected with the struggle—civil, political, military and naval—with the dates, victories, losses and results—embracing the period between April 23, 1860, and October 31, 1865. Philadelphia, A. Winch [c1867]

136 p. 24cm.

An early, detailed chronology, abounding in errors of date and fact.

Williams, George Forrester, 1837–
The memorial war book, as drawn from historical records and personal narratives of the men who served in the great struggle, by Major George F. Williams ... Illustrated by two thousand magnificent engravings reproduced largely from photographs taken by the U. S. government photographers, M. B. Brady and Alexander Gardner, being the only original photographs taken during the war of the rebellion; making a complete panorama of this greatest event in history, including portraits of the leaders and commanders of both the federal and Confederate armies and navies, giving, for the first time, a complete pictorial representation of the scenes, battles, and incidents, the whole forming a fitting memorial of the greatest event of the century, the most momentous of the age. New York, Lovell brothers company, c1894.

610, [2] p., 1 l. incl. front., illus. (incl. ports.) 31½cm.

Another picture book, primarily of Brady and Gardner photographs.

Williams, Hermann Warner, 1908–
The Civil War: the artists' record. [Washington] Corcoran Gallery of Art [c1961]

251, [17] p. illus., col. plates. 26 cm.

Catalogues an important exhibition of Civil War art work, with a good many reproductions emphasizing camp and soldier life.

Williams, Thomas Harry, 1909–
Americans at war; the development of the American military system. [1st ed. Baton Rouge] Louisiana State University Press [1960]
138 p. illus. 23 cm.

An excellent starting point for viewing the Civil War as a part of American military history; the bibliography is especially useful.

Williams, Thomas Harry, 1909–
Lincoln and his generals. [1st ed.] New York, Knopf, 1952.
viii, 363, iv p. ports., map. 22 cm.

A superb study of Lincoln's relations with the dozen leading Union field commanders; interpretive as well as factual.

Wilson, Edmund, 1895–
Patriotic gore; studies in the literature of the American Civil War. New York, Oxford University Press, 1962.
816 p. 20 cm.

A prominent literary critic re-examines intellectual history and assesses the writings of Grant, Sherman and others; a work with which many will disagree, but which no one can ignore.

Wilson, John Laird, 1832–1896.
Story of the war. Pictorial history of the great civil war: embracing full and authentic accounts of battles by land and sea ... Containing carefully prepared biographies of the leading generals and naval commanders. By John Laird Wilson ... With numerous ... steel-plate engravings of battle-scenes, and with portraits of leading generals. [Philadelphia? 19—]
3 p. l., iii–iv, 5–976 p. front., plates, ports., maps. 26cm.

Another of the endless postwar general histories; this one was also issued as Vol. III of Robert Tomes' Battles of America.

Wilson, William Bender.
A few acts and actors in the tragedy of the civil war in the United States. By William Bender Wilson ... Philadelphia, By the author, 1892.
114 p. 19½cm.

Twelve chapters treat of subjects ranging from Governors Curtin and Andrew to telegraphy and military railroads; interesting but hardly authoritative.

Wilson, Woodrow, *pres. U. S.*, 1856–1924.
... Division and reunion, 1829–1889, by Woodrow Wilson ... with five maps. New ed. New York [etc.] Longmans, Green and co., 1926.
xxv, 336 p. 5 fold. maps (incl. front.) 16½ cm.

A general account extending from causation through Reconstruction; mainly political in emphasis, with very little on war actions.

Wood, William Charles Henry, 1864–
... In defense of liberty, by William Wood [and] Ralph Henry Gabriel. New Haven, Yale university press; [etc., etc.] 1928.
3 p. l., 370 p. col. front., illus. (incl. ports., maps, facsims.) col. plates. 26 cm.

A fine set for the young or beginning reader; generously illustrated; the text concentrates on things military.

Woodward, William E 1874–1950.
Years of madness. New York, Putnam [1951]
viii, 311 p. 22 cm.

The original "debunker" roams widely in presenting views on the entire war; argumentative and colorful; not recommended for the beginning reader.

Wright, Marcus Joseph, 1831–1922, *ed.*
Official portfolio of war and nation; a graphic and pictorial history prepared directly from the government records in the departments of war and statistics ... accompanied by the complete, superb collection of the Leslie's famous war pictures ... Narrative and descriptive by John Clark Ridpath, Rossiter Johnson, General Fitzhugh Lee, General John T. Morgan, George L. Kilmer and General Joseph B. Carr. Carefully ed. by General Marcus J. Wright ... [Philadelphia, ©1904–05]
2 p. l., ix–xxvii, [2], 24–584 (*i. e.* 612) p. front., illus. 44 x 32½ cm.

An oversized period piece more attractive than useful; padded with portraits, biographies, and battle scenes from Leslie's.

BIBLIOGRAPHIES, MEMOIRS AND COLLECTED WORKS

Robert W. Johannsen

Abbott, Lyman, 1835–1922, *ed.*

Henry Ward Beecher. A sketch of his career: with analyses of his power as a preacher, lecturer, orator, and journalist, and incidents and reminiscences of his life. Commemorative of his entrance upon his seventieth year. Edited by Lyman Abbott, D. D. New York, Funk & Wagnalls, 1883.

xi p., 2 l., [13]–604 p. front., plates, ports. 24cm.

An admiring biography by the man who succeeded Beecher at Plymouth Church in Brooklyn.

[Addey, Markinfield]

Life of Jefferson Davis, with an authentic account of his private and public career, and his death and burial; together with The life of Stonewall Jackson ... including his glorious military career and his tragic death on the battlefield. Philadelphia, Keystone Pub. Co., 1890.

197, 300 p. illus., ports. 20 cm.

A eulogistic tribute to the Confederate president, together with the biography of Jackson cited in the next entry.

Adams, Charles Francis, 1835–1915.

... Charles Francis Adams, by his son, Charles Francis Adams ... Boston and New York, Houghton, Mifflin and company, 1900.

3 p. l., [v]–vii p., 2 l., 426 p., 1 l. 4 port. (incl. front.) fold. facsim. 22½ cm.

Focuses principally on Adam's diplomatic service; the author regarded this work as only "a preliminary study" of his father's life.

Addey, Markinfield.

"Stonewall Jackson." The life and military career of Thomas Jonathan Jackson, lieutenant-general in the Confederate army. By Markinfield Addey ... New York, C. T. Evans; Chicago, J. R. Walker; [etc., etc.] 1863.

240 p. front. (port.) 19cm.

This laudatory account of Jackson's military achievements was published a few months after the General's death.

Alderman, Edwin Anderson, 1861–1931.
J. L. M. Curry; a biography, by Edwin Anderson, Alderman and Armistead Churchill Gordon. New York, The Macmillan company; London, Macmillan & co., ltd., 1911.
xx p., 1 l., 468 p. front. (port.) 20cm.

A complete, balanced study of the Alabama politician and congressman; based on Curry's papers, including many of his letters.

Alexander, Thomas Benjamin, 1918–
Thomas A. R. Nelson of east Tennessee. Nashville, Tennessee Historical Commission [1956]
x, 186 p. illus., ports., fold. map, facsims. 25 cm.

Well researched though brief, this study emphasizes the public career of an East Tennessee Unionist during the war.

Alfriend, Frank H
The life of Jefferson Davis. By Frank H. Alfriend ... Cincinnati, Caxton publishing house; Philadelphia, National publishing co.; [etc., etc.] 1868.
xvii, [13]–645 p. front. (port.) 22½ cm.

A eulogistic attempt to vindicate the motives and conduct of the Southern leader; includes extensive quotations from Davis's letters and speeches.

Ambler, Charles Henry, 1876–
Francis H. Pierpont, Union war governor of Virginia and father of West Virginia, by Charles H. Ambler ... Chapel Hill, The University of North Carolina press, 1937.
xiii, 483 p. front., illus. (incl. facsims.) plates, ports., maps (1 fold.) 24cm.

Thoroughly researched and quite readable, this is the somewhat favorable biography of the man who pioneered West Virginia's statehood.

Ambrose, Stephen E
Halleck: Lincoln's Chief of Staff. Baton Rouge, Louisiana State University Press [1962]
226 p. illus. 24 cm.

A sound, scholarly study of the figure whose contributions to the Union effort were primarily administrative in character.

The **American** civil war book and Grant album, "art immortelles"; a portfolio of half-tone reproductions from rare and costly photographs designed to perpetuate the memory of General Ulysses S. Grant, depicting scenes and incidents in connection with the civil war ... Boston, New York, W. H. Allen, ©1894.
2 p. l., [202] p. of illus. 27½ x 35½cm.

Well-presented pictures of Grant, his family, and the scenes connected with his career and death.

Ames, Blanche (Ames)
Adelbert Ames, 1835–1933, general, senator, Governor; the story of his life and times and his integrity as a soldier and statesman in the service of the United States of America throughout the Civil War and in Mississippi in the years of Reconstruction. [1st ed.] North Easton, Mass., 1964.
xviii, 625 p. illus., ports., plans (part col., 1 fold.) 26 cm.

An attempt to rectify "errors" of interpretation surrounding one who was a military governor, U. S. Senator, and Reconstruction governor of Mississippi.

Anderson, Mabel Washbourne.
The life of General Stand Watie, the only Indian brigadier general of the Confederate army and the last general to surrender, by Mabel Washbourne Anderson. 2d ed. (rev.) Pryor, Okl., Mrs. Mabel W. Anderson, 1931.
85 p. incl. plates, port. 22½ cm.

A brief, superficial account by the grandniece of Gen. Watie.

Andrews, Byron, 1852–
... A biography of Gen. John A. Logan, with an account of his public services in peace and in war. By Byron Andrews. Illustrated. New York and Chicago, H. S. Goodspeed & co., 1884.
x, [352] p. incl. plates, ports. front., pl. 21cm.

A political biography, published when Logan was a candidate for the vice-presidency.

Angle, Paul McClelland, 1900– *ed.*
The Lincoln reader, edited, with an introduction, by Paul M. Angle. New Brunswick, Rutgers university press, 1947.
xii, 564 p. plates, ports., facsims. 22½ cm.

Selections from the writings of sixty-five authors; skillfully arranged so as to provide a complete and continuous story of Lincoln's life.

Arnold, Isaac Newton, 1815–1884.
The life of Abraham Lincoln. By Isaac N. Arnold ... Chicago, Jansen, McClurg, & company, 1885.
462 p. front. (port.) 21½ cm.

A friend's eulogy; contains much contemporary material of value, but overstresses Lincoln's role as the "Great Emancipator."

Arnold, Thomas Jackson.
Early life and letters of General Thomas J. Jackson, "Stonewall" Jackson, by his nephew, Thomas Jackson Arnold ... New York, Chicago [etc.] Fleming H. Revell company [c1916]
379 p. front., plates, ports., facsims. 21½ cm.

Of value chiefly for Jackson's letters in the 1843-1861 period; the author, a nephew of the General, added some connecting material.

Ashby, Thomas Almond, 1848–1916.
Life of Turner Ashby, by Thomas A. Ashby ... New York, The Neale publishing co., 1914.
275 p. front. (port.) 21 cm.

A partisan and superficial account of Ashby's "manly character and heroic deeds, his knightly bearing and chivalric courage."

Auchampaugh, Philip Gerald.
Robert Tyler, southern rights champion, 1847–1866: a documentary study chiefly of antebellum politics, by Philip Gerald Auchampaugh. Duluth, Minn., H. Stein, printer, 1934.
ix p., 1 l., 387 p. front. (port.) 23½cm.

The best study of the Virginian who served as register of the Confederate Treasury; unfortunately, only 150 copies of this book were printed.

Austin, George Lowell, 1849–1893.
The life and times of Wendell Phillips. By George Lowell Austin ... New ed. Boston, Lee and Shepard, 1888.
431 p. plates, port. 19cm.

Superficial, sympathetic and admiring; published the year Phillips died.

Bache, Richard Meade.
Life of General George Gordon Meade, commander of the Army of the Potomac, by Richard Meade Bache ... Philadelphia, H. T. Coates & co., 1897.
2 p. l., iii–xxii, 596 p. front., plates, ports., maps (part fold.) plans. 21½ cm.

A sympathetic, defensive study, based in part on the author's own recollections of Meade.

Bailey, Hugh C
Hinton Rowan Helper, abolitionist-racist [by] Hugh C. Bailey. University, University of Alabama Press [1965]
xi, 256 p. port. 22 cm.

The brief but scholarly study of one of the Civil War era's most paradoxical persons.

Baker, La Fayette Charles, 1826–1868.
The United States secret service in the late war, comprising the author's introduction to the leading men at Washington, with the origin and organization of the United States secret service bureau, and a graphic history of rich and exciting experiences, North and South ... By General La Fayette C. Baker ... Philadelphia, J. E. Potter and company [c1889]
398 p. incl. pl. front. (port.) 8 chromolith. pl. 24 cm.

An exaggerated, totally unreliable memoir by one whose sanity in recent years has been increasingly challenged.

Ballard, Colin Robert, 1868–1941.
The military genius of Abraham Lincoln; an essay by Brigadier-General Colin R. Ballard ... London, Oxford university press, H. Milford, 1926.
4 p. l., 246 p. front., illus., maps. 23cm.

Praises the President as a military strategist at least equal in ability to his early generals

Baltz, John D.
Hon. Edward D. Baker, U. S. senator from Oregon ... Colonel E. D. Baker's defense in the battle of Ball's Bluff, fought October 21st, 1861, in Virginia, and slight biographical sketches of Colonel Baker and Generals Wistar and Stone. By John D. Baltz ... Lancaster, Pa., Pub. for the author, Inquirer printing company, 1888.
248 p. front., pl., port., fold. plan. 19½cm.

An early biography of practically no use because of the author's adoration for his subject.

Bancroft, Frederic, 1860–
The life of William H. Seward, by Frederic Bancroft ... New York & London, Harper and brothers, 1900.

2 v. fronts. (ports.) 21½cm.

A well-balanced study that is pointedly critical when it is not sympathetic to the subject; the work is now quite outdated.

Barrows, Chester Leonard, 1891–
William M. Evarts, lawyer, diplomat, statesman, by Chester L. Barrows. Chapel Hill, The University of North Carolina press, 1941.

x p., 1 l., 587 p. front. (port.) 23½ cm.

A scholarly, critical appraisal, with some emphasis on Evarts' legal career; based principally on published sources.

Barrows, John Henry, 1847–1902.
Henry Ward Beecher; the Shakespeare of the pulpit, by John Henry Barrows ... New York [etc.] Funk & Wagnalls company, 1893.

xvi, 541 p. front. (port.) 19½ cm.

Superficial and eulogistic; the author termed Beecher "a richly-gifted, heroic, and much-suffering servant of Christ . . ."

Bartlett, Irving H
Wendell Phillips, Brahmin radical. Boston, Beacon Press [1961]

438 p. 21 cm.

A comprehensive study, sound in its execution and judicious in its interpretation; carefully documented.

Bartlett, Ruhl Jacob, 1897–
John C. Frémont and the Republican party, by Ruhl Jacob Bartlett ... Columbus, O., The Ohio state university [©1930]

viii p., 1 l., 146 p. 23 cm.

An older monograph of some value for data on both Fremont and the Republican party; yet now outdated in almost every respect by the Nevins biography.

Barton, William Eleazar, 1861–1930.
The life of Clara Barton, founder of the American red cross, by William E. Barton ... Boston and New York, Houghton Mifflin company, 1922.

2 v. fronts., plates, ports., facsims. 22½ cm.

Written by a cousin of Miss Barton and based on primary material not available to Epler; many of Miss Barton's wartime letters and statements are included in Vol. I.

Barton, William Eleazar, 1861–1930.
The life of Abraham Lincoln, by William E. Barton ... Indianapolis, The Bobbs Merrill company [©1925]

2 v. fronts., plates, ports., facsims. 24½ cm.

Undistinguished and generally superficial, even though Barton explored some areas more thoroughly than earlier writers.

Basler, Roy Prentice, 1906–
The Lincoln legend; a study in changing conceptions [by] Roy P. Basler. Boston and New York, Houghton Mifflin company, 1935.

viii, [1] p., 3 l., 3–335, [1] p. front., plates, ports. 21 cm.

An important and successful study of the national legend that has been created about Lincoln in literature (historical, biographical or otherwise).

Basso, Hamilton, 1904–
Beauregard, the great Creole, by Hamilton Basso. New York, London, C. Scribner's sons, 1933.

xiv, 333 p. front., illus., plates, ports. 23cm.

An attempt to capture "the feeling of a time and the spirit of a man;" written in the breezy style of one of the South's noted novelists.

Bates, Edward, 1793–1869.
The diary of Edward Bates, 1859–1866, edited by Howard K. Beale. Washington, U. S. Govt. print. off., 1933.

xvi, 685 p. 23½ cm.

A significant source for insights into the political history of the war by a member of Lincoln's cabinet; fully and carefully edited.

Baxter, Maurice Glen, 1920–
Orville H. Browning, Lincoln's friend and critic. Bloomington, Indiana University Press, 1957.
vii, 351 p. 23 cm.

One-third of this biography treats of Browning's wartime services as an Illinois senator; the best study, though the subject lacks for life.

Bean, William Gleason, 1891–
Stonewall's man: Sandie Pendleton. Chapel Hill, University of North Carolina Press [1959]
252 p. illus. 24 cm.

Richly documented by the young staff officer's private letters, this is an intimate and detailed biography.

Beaty, John Owen, 1890–
John Esten Cooke, Virginian, by John O. Beaty ... New York, Columbia university press, 1922.
viii p., 1 l., 173 p. 21cm.

This effective, critical biography of the Confederacy's most famous writer incorporates much manuscript material.

Belmont, August, 1816–1889.
Letters, speeches and addresses of August Belmont ... [New York] Priv. print., 1890.
4 p. l., 3–236 p. 26½cm.

Valuable and revealing correspondence by a strong Unionist whose constant contacts with influential Europeans did much on behalf of Northern diplomacy.

Beveridge, Albert Jeremiah, 1862–1927.
Abraham Lincoln, 1809–1858, by Albert J. Beveridge ... Boston and New York, Houghton Mifflin company, 1928.
2 v. fronts., pl., ports., map. 24½ cm.

This carefully researched, soundly documented study of Lincoln and his times carries the story to 1858; the work reflects modern scholarship at its best.

Binney, Charles Chauncey, 1855–1913.
The life of Horace Binney, with selections from his letters, by Charles Chauncey Binney. Philadelphia and London, J. B. Lippincott company, 1903.
xi, 460 p. 3 port. (incl. front.) 24½ cm.

Throws some light on a leader of the Pennsylvania bar whose defense of Lincoln's suspensions of writs of habeas corpus helped stem the storm.

Black, Jeremiah Sullivan, 1810–1883.
Essays and speeches of Jeremiah S. Black. With a biographical sketch. By Chauncey F. Black. New York, D. Appleton and company, 1885.
vi, 621 p. front. (port.) 24 cm.

Of some use for a better understanding of Northern politics; Black served as Attorney-General and Secretary of State under Buchanan.

Blackmar, Frank Wilson, 1854–1931.
... Charles Robinson, the first free-state governor of Kansas, by Frank W. Blackmar ... Topeka, Kan., Crane & company, 1900.
115 p. 19cm.

The standard biography of Kansas's first governor under statehood.

Blackwell, Sarah Ellen, 1828–
A military genius. Life of Anna Ella Carroll, of Maryland, ("the great unrecognized member of Lincoln's cabinet.") Comp. from family records and congressional documents, by Sarah Ellen Blackwell ... Washington, D. C., Judd & Detweiler, printers, 1891–95.
2 v. 2 pl. (incl. front., v. 2) 3 port. (incl. front., v. 1) 17½ cm.

A renewal of the unauthenticated claim that Miss Carroll was responsible for the 1862 Tennessee River campaign, plus a new plea that the lady be compensated for her patriotic efforts.

Blaine, James Gillespie, 1830–1893.
Twenty years of Congress: from Lincoln to Garfield. With a review of the events which led to the political revolution of 1860. By James G. Blaine ... Norwich, Conn., The Henry Bill publishing company, 1884–86.
2 v. fronts., ports., fold. map. 25 cm.

Four chapters treat of this famous Maine senator's Civil War service; surprisingly objective and even-tempered.

Blair, Harry C

The life of Colonel Edward D. Baker, Lincoln's constant ally, together with four of his great orations, by Harry C. Blair and Rebecca Tarshis. [Portland, Or.] 1960.

xiii, 233 p. illus., ports., maps, facsims. 24 cm.

This choppy, disappointing biography does little credit to the Oregon senator who lost his life at Ball's Bluff.

Blake, Nelson Morehouse.

William Mahone of Virginia, soldier and political insurgent, by Nelson Morehouse Blake, PH. D. Richmond, Garrett & Massie, 1935.

xv, [1], 323 p. incl. geneal. tab. front., plates, ports., maps, facsims. 23½cm.

Only one chapter of this scholarly, documented biography treats of Mahone's Confederate service.

Boney, F. N.

John Letcher of Virginia; the story of Virginia's Civil War Governor, by F. N. Boney. University, Ala., University of Alabama Press [1966]

319 p. port. 21 cm.

The only thorough study of the strange executive from Lexington; thoroughly researched and ably presented.

Boutwell, George Sewall, 1818–1905.

Reminiscences of sixty years in public affairs, by George S. Boutwell ... New York, McClure, Phillips & co., 1902.

2 v. front. (port.) 23½ cm.

Reliable recollections by Lincoln's capable commissioner for internal revenue; includes articles, letters and other documents by Boutwell.

Bowman, Samuel Millard, 1815–1885.

Sherman and his campaigns; a military biography, by S. M. Bowman and R. B. Irwin. New York, C. B. Richardson, 1865.

520 p. ports., maps. 24 cm.

A defense and vindication of Sherman against those (notably Stanton) who criticized his truce agreement with J. E. Johnston in 1865.

Boyd, Belle, 1844–1900.

Belle Boyd in camp and prison, written by herself. With an introduction, by George Augusta [!] Sala. New York, Blelock & company, 1865.

1 p. l., [5]–464 p. 18½ cm.

A highly dramatic and somewhat sketchy autobiographical statement of the famed Civil War spy; written in England in the final stages of the war.

Boyd, James Penny, 1836–1910.

The life of General William T. Sherman, by James P. Boyd ... [Philadelphia] Publishers' union, 1891.

608 p. incl. front., plates, ports., maps. 20 cm.

A fairly well-balanced study, except for a lack of attention to Sherman's postwar career.

Boykin, Samuel, 1829–1899, *ed.*

A memorial volume of the Hon. Howell Cobb, of Georgia, Edited by Samuel Boykin. Philadelphia, J. B. Lippincott & co., 1870.

280 p. 2 port. (incl. front.) 21½cm.

Mainly speeches and tributes offered at Cobb's death, along with a brief, laudatory biography.

Bradford, Gamaliel, 1863–1932.

Confederate portraits, by Gamaliel Bradford. Boston and New York, Houghton Mifflin company, 1914.

xviii p., 1 l., 291, [1] p. 8 port. (incl. front.) 22½ cm.

"Psychographs" that attempt to study the souls of J. E. Johnston, Stuart, Longstreet, Beauregard, Benjamin, Stephens, Toombs and Semmes.

Bradford, Gamaliel, 1863–1932.

Lee the American, by Gamaliel Bradford. Rev. ed. Boston and New York, Houghton Mifflin company, 1927.

xxvi, 324 p. front., ports., facsim. 21½ cm.

The author has succeeded in his purpose--to give a clear, consistently sympathetic portrait of a great soul.

Bradford, Gamaliel, 1863–1932.
Union portraits, by Gamaliel Bradford. Boston and New York, Houghton Mifflin company, 1916.
xvi p., 2 l., ₍3₎–330 p., 1 l. 4 port. (incl. front.) 19½ cm.

Another set of "soul-searchers" by the famed psychographer; included here are chapters on McClellan, Hooker, Meade, Thomas, Sherman, Stanton, Seward, Sumner and Samuel Bowles.

Bradford, Gamaliel, 1863–1932.
Wives, by Gamaliel Bradford ... New York and London, Harper & brothers ₍©1925₎
xiii, 298 p. front., ports. 22½ cm.

Psychographic essays on seven prominent women, including Varina Davis, Mary Lincoln and Mrs. B. F. Butler.

Bradley, Erwin Stanley.
Simon Cameron, Lincoln's Secretary of War; a political biography. Philadelphia, University of Pennsylvania Press ₍1966₎
451 p. illus., ports. 22 cm.

Scholarly and well-documented; the author seeks to correct what he believes to be the commonly accepted, though distorted, picture of Cameron.

Bridges, Leonard Hal, 1918–
Lee's maverick general, Daniel Harvey Hill. ₍1st ed.₎ New York, McGraw-Hill ₍1961₎
323 p. illus. 22 cm.

This study of a caustic North Carolinian is well-researched, sympathetic, but controversial because of the author's opinionated text.

Brigance, William Norwood, 1896–
Jeremiah Sullivan Black, a defender of the Constitution and the Ten commandments, by William Norwood Brigance ... Philadelphia, University of Pennsylvania press; London, H. Milford, Oxford university press, 1934.
ix, ₍2₎, 303 p. front., ports., facsims. 24 cm.

A rather uncritical study, which generally avoids judgment of Black's legal role and contributions.

Brigham, Johnson, 1846–1936.
... James Harlan, by Johnson Brigham. Iowa City, Ia., The State historical society of Iowa, 1913.
xvi, 398 p. front. (port.) 21½ cm.

The best study of the Iowan who left a highly respected U. S. Senate post and proved a failure as Lincoln's Secretary of the Interior.

Brinkerhoff, Roeliff, 1828–1911.
Recollections of a lifetime, by General Roeliff Brinkerhoff. Cincinnati, The Robert Clarke company, 1900.
xiii, 448 p. front. (port.) pl. 22cm.

An incisive commentary on men and events by a newspaperman, army quartermaster, and postwar politician.

Brock, Robert Alonzo, 1839–1914, *ed.*
Gen. Robert Edward Lee; soldier, citizen, and Christian patriot, by Mrs. Roger A. Pryor, Dr. Edmund Jenings Lee, Col. John J. Garnett, Mrs. Sally Nelson Robins, General T. L. Rosser and others. Also an interesting early history of the Lee family in England and America ... Ed. by R. A. Brock ... Richmond, Va., B. F. Johnson publishing co. ₍1897₎
1 p. l., 586 p. incl. illus., ports., map, facsims. 24cm.

A conglomeration of official reports and other military material, most of it having little relationship to Lee; a good example of using a hallowed name to sell a hodgepodge of minutiae.

Brockett, Linus Pierpont, 1820–1893.
Men of our day; or, Biographical sketches of patriots, orators, statesmen, generals, reformers, financiers and merchants, now on the stage of action: including those who in military, political, business and social life, are the prominent leaders of the time in this country. By L. P. Brockett ... Elegantly illustrated with forty-two portraits from life. Philadelphia, Penn'a, Cincinnati, O. ₍etc.₎ Zeigler, McCurdy & co., 1868.
xxiv, 17–653 p. front., ports. 22½ cm.

Brief biographical sketches of fifty individuals; valuable, in some cases, for the comments of a contemporary on leading figures in his own time.

₍**Brockett, Linus Pierpont**₎ 1820–1893.
Our great captains. Grant, Sherman, Thomas, Sheridan, and Farragut ... New York, C. B. Richardson, 1865.
6, ₍9₎–251 p. 5 port. (incl. front.) 19cm.

Short, highly laudatory sketches that sought to present the men "as they were;" now degenerated by time.

Brodie, Fawn (McKay) 1915–
Thaddeus Stevens, scourge of the South. ⌊1st ed.⌋ New York, Norton ⌊1959⌋
448 p. illus. 24 cm.

This documented but sympathetic biography attempts to employ psychological techniques in assessing Stevens's personality.

Brown, Ernest Francis, 1903–
Raymond of the Times. ⌊1st ed.⌋ New York, Norton ⌊1951⌋
viii, 345 p. illus., ports. 25 cm.

This solid biography of a prominent editor is also useful for insights into Republican campaign tactics during the war.

Brown, R Shepard.
Stringfellow of the Fourth. New York, Crown Publishers ⌊1960⌋
307 p. illus. 22 cm.

A popularly written account of the adventures of a Confederate cavalry scout; based on Stringfellow's own postwar recollections, family tradition and some records.

⌊**Browne, Albert Gallatin**⌋ 1835–1891.
Sketch of the official life of John A. Andrew, as governor of Massachusetts, to which is added the valedictory address of Governor Andrew, delivered upon retiring from office, January 5, 1866, on the subject of reconstruction of the states recently in rebellion. New York, Hurd and Houghton, 1868.
xii, 211 p. front. (port.) 18cm.

A highly personal biography by Andrew's military secretary; based on records and observations.

Browning, Orville Hickman, 1806–1881.
... The diary of Orville Hickman Browning ... edited with introduction and notes by Theodore Calvin Pease ... and James G. Randall ... Springfield, Ill., The Trustees of the Illinois state historical library, 1925–⌊33⌋
2 v. 22½ cm.

Voluminous and revealing diary by one of Lincoln's close friends; the journal as a whole makes for wearisome reading.

Bruce, Philip Alexander, 1856–1933.
... Robert E. Lee, by Philip Alexander Bruce ... Philadelphia, G. W. Jacobs & company ⌊1907⌋
380 p. front. (port.) 19½ cm.

A concise, sometimes superficial, and highly laudatory study.

Buckingham, Samuel Giles.
The life of William A. Buckingham, the war governor of Connecticut, with a review of his public acts, and especially the distinguished services he rendered his country during the war of the rebellion; with which is incorporated, a condensed account of the more important campaigns of the war, and information from private sources and family and official documents. By Rev. Samuel G. Buckingham, D. D. Springfield, Mass., The W. F. Adams company, 1894.
xii, 537 p. front. (port.) plates. 23½cm.

More a general history of the participation of Connecticut troops in the Civil War than a biography of Buckingham; generally unreliable.

Bullard, Frederic Lauriston, 1866–1952.
Famous war correspondents, by F. Lauriston Bullard ... Boston, Little, Brown and company, 1914.
xii p., 3 l., 437 p. front., pl., ports. 21 cm.

Contains weak chapters on W. H. Russell, Vizetelly, and reporters in general during the Civil War.

Burger, Nash Kerr.
South of Appomattox ⌊by⌋ Nash K. Burger ⌊and⌋ John K. Bettersworth. ⌊1st ed.⌋ New York, Harcourt, Brace ⌊1959⌋
376 p. illus. 23 cm.

Dramatically written and well-researched, this work recounts the postwar careers of several of the Confederacy's most noted leaders.

Burnett, Alfred, *b.* 1823 *or* 4.
Incidents of the war: humorous, pathetic, and descriptive. By Alf Burnett ... Cincinnati, Rickey & Carroll, 1863.
x p., 1 l., 13–310 p. front. (port.) plates. 18½cm.

Poignant observations on 1862 military affairs in Kentucky; by a reporter for the Cincinnati Times.

Burtis, Mary Elizabeth.
Moncure Conway, 1832–1907. New Brunswick, Rutgers University Press, 1952.
xii, 260 p. port. 21 cm.

An effective study of the prominent but little-remembered reformer and abolitionist.

Bushong, Millard Kessler.
Old Jube, a biography of General Jubal A. Early. Illus. and maps by Timothy T. Pohmer. Boyce, Va., Carr Pub. Co. ₍1955₎
343 p. illus. 24 cm.

Eulogistic, with a heavy concentration on battles; the wide variety of sources do not show to advantage.

Butler, Benjamin Franklin, 1818–1893.
Autobiography and personal reminiscences of Major-General Benj. F. Butler; Butler's book. By Benj. F. Butler. A review of his legal, political, and military career ... Boston, A. M. Thayer & co., 1892.
1037, 95, 1135–1154 p. incl. front., illus., plates (part double) ports., double map, facsims. (1 fold.) 25 cm.

A large and ponderous "apologia;" Butler's defensive attitude throughout reduces the value of his story.

Butler, Benjamin Franklin, 1818–1893.
Private and official correspondence of Gen. Benjamin F. Butler, during the period of the civil war. ... Privately issued. ₍Norwood, Mass., The Plimpton press₎ 1917.
5 v. illus. (map) 24 cm.

Members of the family compiled this mass of correspondence to counteract the popular criticism of Butler's wartime actions.

Butler, Pierce, 1873–
... Judah P. Benjamin, by Pierce Butler. Philadelphia, G. W. Jacobs & company ₍1907₎
459 p. front. (port.) 19½ cm.

A comprehensive, judicious and sympathetic biography, although hampered by a lack of primary source material.

Cain, Marvin R
Lincoln's Attorney General: Edward Bates of Missouri, by Marvin R. Cain. Columbia, University of Missouri Press ₍1965₎
x, 361 p. ports. 23 cm.

A well-researched and detailed study of the colorless attorney-general; Bates appears as a transition figure in 19th century politics.

Callender, Edward Belcher, 1851–1917.
Thaddeus Stevens: commoner. By E. B. Callender. Boston. A. Williams and company. 1882.
iv p., 1 l., ₍7₎–210 p. front. (port.) 20cm.

A partial, sympathetic account that strives to restore the reputation of the "stalwarts;" contains many long quotations from Stevens' speeches.

Campbell, James Havelock.
McClellan; a vindication of the military career of General George B. McClellan; a lawyer's brief, by James Havelock Campbell ... New York, The Neale publishing company, 1916.
458 p. front. (port.) 22½cm.

The first of several detailed assertions that McClellan was "the man who saved the Union;" now outdated but a necessary handbook for McClellan's friends.

Canby, Courtlandt, *ed.*
Lincoln and the Civil War; a profile and a history. New York, G. Braziller, 1960.
416 p. 22 cm.

A collection of selections from the more important works published on the subject.

Capers, Henry Dickson, 1835–1910.
The life and times of C. G. Memminger. By Henry D. Capers ... Richmond, Va., Everett Waddey co., 1893.
604 p. front. (port.) plates (incl. ports.) 24 cm.

A sympathetic appraisal of the Confederacy's first Secretary of the Treasury; quotes extensively from many useful documents; Capers was Memminger's chief clerk.

Carpenter, Francis Bicknell, 1830–1900.
Six months at the White House with Abraham Lincoln. The story of a picture. By F. B. Carpenter. New York, Hurd and Houghton, 1866.
vii, ⌊9⌋–359 p. 18 cm.

Learned observations on Washington politics in general and Mr. Lincoln in particular.

Carpenter, John Alcott, 1921–
Sword and olive branch; **Oliver Otis Howard, by John A.** Carpenter. Pittsburgh, **University of Pittsburgh Press** ⌊1964⌋
viii, 379 p. illus., ports. 22 cm.

A successful attempt at a scholarly study of a long-neglected figure; based on wide research and well-documented.

Cary, Edward, 1840–1917.
... George William Curtis, by Edward Cary. Boston and New York, Houghton, Mifflin and company, 1894.
ix, 343 p. front. (port.) 18 cm.

A study of Curtis as a man of public affairs as well as a man of letters; published two years after his death.

Caskie, Jaquelin Ambler.
Life and letters of Matthew Fontaine Maury, by Jaquelin Ambler Caskie ... Richmond, Va., Richmond press, inc., 1928.
191 p. 2 port. (incl. front.) $20\frac{1}{2}$cm.

A brief, laudatory and superficial account; includes many passages from Maury's letters.

Cassidy, Vincent H
Henry Watkins Allen of **Louisiana** ⌊by⌋ **Vincent H.** Cassidy and Amos E. Simpson. **Baton Rouge, Louisiana** State University Press ⌊1964⌋
vii, 201 p. port. 24 cm.

The best treatment of Louisiana's last war governor; more human and alive than the average biography.

Castel, Albert E
William Clarke Quantrill: his life and times. New York, F. Fell ⌊1962⌋
250 p. illus. 21 cm.

Largely impartial, but contains insufficient annotations; Castel made exhaustive use of known manuscript materials.

Cate, Wirt Armistead, 1900–
Lucius Q. C. Lamar, secession and reunion, by Wirt Armistead Cate. Chapel Hill, The University of North Carolina press ⌊©1935⌋
xiii p., 1 l., 594 p. front., plates, ports. $24\frac{1}{2}$cm

The best study of a Mississippian who, whether serving as a soldier, statesman or European envoy, never wavered in his support of Pres. Davis.

Catton, Bruce, 1899–
Grant moves south. With maps by Samuel H. Bryant. ⌊1st ed.⌋ Boston, Little, Brown ⌊1960⌋
x, 564 p. port., maps. 22 cm.

A continuation of Lloyd Lewis's Captain Sam Grant; carries Grant to the fall of Vicksburg; detailed and judicious.

Catton, Bruce, 1899–
U. S. Grant and the American military tradition. ⌊**1st ed.**⌋ **Boston, Little, Brown** ⌊**1954**⌋
x, 201 p. 22 cm.

A convenient, very brief synthesis of Grant's life and career.

Chambers, Lenoir.
Stonewall Jackson. New York, W. Morrow, 1959.
2 v. ports., maps. 25 cm.

A comprehensive, definitive biography of Jackson; well-written and based upon careful use of a wide array of source material.

Chandler, Peleg Whitman, 1816–1889.
Memoir of Governor Andrew, with personal reminiscences. By Peleg W. Chandler. To which are added two hitherto unpublished literary discourses, and the Valedictory address. Boston, Roberts brothers, 1880.
298 p. front. (port.) 2 pl., facsim. 18 cm.

Highly laudatory; prepared at the instigation of the Massachusetts Historical Society; supplemented by personal reminscences of the author and two addresses by Andrew.

Chaplin, Jeremiah, 1813–1886.
The life of Charles Sumner. By Jeremiah Chaplin and J. D. Chaplin. With an introduction by Hon. William Claflin. Boston, D. Lothrop & co.: Dover, N. H., G. T. Day & co., 1874.
x p., 1 l., 17–504 p. plates, 2 port. (incl. front.) facsims. (1 double) 19½ cm.

An uncritical survey, published in the year of Sumner's death; includes extracts from many of his speeches.

Chapman, John Jay, 1862–1933.
William Lloyd Garrison, by John Jay Chapman ... New York, Moffat, Yard and company, 1913.
3 p. l., 278 p. front. (port.) 19½ cm.

Limited to Garrison's pre-Civil War career.

Charnwood, Godfrey Rathbone Benson, *1st baron*, 1864–
... Abraham Lincoln, by Lord Charnwood. London, Constable & company, ltd., 1916.
viii, 479 p. front. (port.) fold. map. 23cm.

A balanced and thorough one-volume biography; still an excellent work in spite of its age.

Chase, Salmon Portland, 1808–1873.
Diary and correspondence of Salmon P. Chase ...
(*In* American historical association. Annual report ... for the year 1902. Washington, 1903. 23 cm.

Contains a fragment of Chase's diary, plus many letters to and by him in the period 1846-1870; published with virtually no editorial comment.

Chase, Salmon Portland, 1808–1873.
Inside Lincoln's Cabinet; the Civil War diaries of Salmon P. Chase, edited by David Donald. ⌜1st ed.⌝ New York, Longmans, Green, 1954.
ix, 342 p. port. 24 cm.

Brought together and published for the first time, these carefully edited diaries are a valuable source for the politics of the Lincoln administration.

Chesnutt, Charles Waddell, 1858–1932.
Frederick Douglass, by Charles W. Chesnutt. Boston, Small, Maynard & company, 1899.
4 p. l., ⌜vii⌝–xix p., 1 l., 141 p. front. (port.) 14½ cm.

A brief and superficial sketch of Douglass's life.

Chidsey, Donald Barr, 1902–
The gentleman from New York: a life of Roscoe Conkling, by Donald Barr Chidsey. New Haven, Yale university press, 1935.
viii, 438 p. front. (port.) illus., plates. 24cm.

Chidsey relied heavily on public documents and periodicals for this study that is necessarily slanted toward the postwar years.

Chittenden, Lucius Eugene, 1824–1900.
Recollections of President Lincoln and his administration, by L. E. Chittenden ... New York and London, Harper & brothers, 1901.
viii, 470 p. front. (port.) 22½cm.

Rather shallow reminiscences of Washington politics by a minor Treasury official; Chittenden had unconcealed affection for Lincoln.

Church, William Conant, 1836–1917.
The life of John Ericsson, by William Conant Church ... New York, C. Scribner's sons, 1890.
2 v. fronts., ilus., plates, ports., facsims. 23 cm.

An effective study of Ericsson's life as well as his science; authorized by Ericsson and based on papers made available by the executors of Ericsson's estate.

Clapp, Margaret Antoinette, 1910–
Forgotten first citizen: John Bigelow. [1st ed.] Boston, Little, Brown, 1947.
x, 390 p. port. 23 cm.

The author used a wealth of material in producing this full but sympathetic biography; Bigelow was a prominent Republican who served as consul to Paris during the war.

Clark, Dan Elbert, 1884–
... Samuel Jordan Kirkwood, by Dan Elbert Clark. Iowa City, Ia., The State historical society of Iowa, 1917.
xiv, 464 p. front. (port.) 21½cm.

A generally objective account of Iowa's war governor, with approximately one-third of the book treating of the war period.

Cleaves, Freeman, 1904–
Meade of Gettysburg. Norman, University of Oklahoma Press [1960]
xi, 384 p. illus., ports., maps. 24 cm.

Well-documented and judicious; one-third of the biography concentrates on the Gettysburg Campaign.

Cleaves, Freeman, 1904–
Rock of Chickamauga, the life of General George H. Thomas. [1st ed.] Norman, University of Oklahoma Press, 1948.
xi, 328 p. illus., ports., maps. 22 cm.

A scholarly study of Thomas, emphasizing particularly the battles of Mill Springs, Stone's River, Chickamauga, Missionary Ridge and Nashville.

Cleveland, Henry.
Alexander H. Stephens in public and private. With letters and speeches before, during, and since the war. By Henry Cleveland ... Philadelphia, Chicago, Ill. [etc.] National publishing company [c1866]
1 p. l., [7]–833 p. plates, 2 port. (incl. front.) facsims. 22½ cm.

A collection of Stephens's more important speeches, with a brief and general sketch of his life.

Clingman, Thomas Lanier, 1812–1897.
Selections from the speeches and writings of Hon. Thomas L. Clingman, of North Carolina, with additions and explanatory notes. Raleigh, J. Nichols, printer, 1877.
v, 623 p. 25cm.

A two volume, unorganized miscellany of talks, interviews and speeches by a North Carolinian who unenthusiastically supported secession.

Coleman, Ann Mary Butler (Crittenden) "*Mrs.* Chapman Coleman," 1813–1891.
The life of John J. Crittenden, with selections from his correspondence and speeches. Ed. by his daughter, Mrs. Chapman Coleman ... Philadelphia, J. B. Lippincott & co., 1871.
2 v. fronts. (ports.) 23½ cm.

This volume is valuable chiefly for the Crittenden letters which it contains.

Condon, William Henry.
Life of Major-General James Shields, hero of three wars and senator from three states. By Hon. William H. Condon ... Chicago, Press of the Blakely printing co. [c1900]
4, 387 p. illus. (incl. ports.) 24cm.

The only study of the soldier-senator who once challenged Lincoln to a duel; disappointing in content.

Connor, Henry Groves, 1852–1924.
John Archibald Campbell, associate justice of the United States Supreme court, 1853–1861, by Henry G. Connor ... Boston and New York, Houghton Mifflin company, 1920.
viii p., 1 l., 310 p., 1 l. front. (port.) 21cm.

Its age notwithstanding, this biography is still of value for an insight into the Virginia jurist remembered for his role in the abortive Hampton Roads Conference.

Conway, Moncure Daniel, 1832–1907.
Autobiography, memories and experiences of Moncure Daniel Conway ... Boston and New York, Houghton, Mifflin and company, 1904.
2 v. fronts., plates, ports., facsims. 22½ cm.

Balanced and revealing memoirs by an abolitionist publisher-minister who, in 1863, went to Europe to lecture on behalf of the Union.

Cook, Roy Bird, 1886–
The family and early life of Stonewall Jackson. 3d ed., rev. Charleston, W. Va., Charleston Print. Co., 1948.
ix, 198 p. illus., ports., facsims. 24 cm.

Written to fill the neglect of Jackson's early life, but highly anecdotal and antiquarian in nature.

Cooke, John Esten, 1830–1886.
A life of Gen. Robert E. Lee. By John Esten Cooke ... New York, D. Appleton and company, 1871.
vi, 577 p. plates, ports. (incl. front.) maps (1 fold.) 24 cm.

Published just after Lee's death, and described by the author as a "popular" rather than a full and elaborate account.

[**Cooke, John Esten**] 1830–1886.
The life of Stonewall Jackson. From official papers, contemporary narratives, and personal acquaintance. By a Virginian ... New York, C. B. Richardson, 1863.
305 p. 2 port. (incl. front.) 19 cm.

"Composed in bivouac" by an unconcealing admirer; based on personal observation and some official documents.

Cooke, John Esten, 1830–1886.
Stonewall Jackson: a military biography ... By John Esten Cooke ... New York, D. Appleton and company, 1866.
470 p. front. (port.) maps. 20cm.

An expansion of Cooke's 1863 biography of Jackson, with some new material.

Coolidge, Louis Arthur, 1861–1925.
Ulysses S. Grant, by Louis A. Coolidge, with portraits. Boston and New York, Houghton Mifflin company, 1917.
xi p., 1 l., 596 p., 1 l. front., ports. 20 cm.

Sympathetic yet detailed; half of the book treats of Grant's presidency and thereafter.

Coppée, Henry, 1821–1895.
... General Thomas, by Henry Coppée ... New York, D. Appleton and company, 1893.
x p., 1 l., [2], 332 p. front. (port.) 4 maps. 19½ cm.

That the author refers to Thomas's "shining record, unrivaled in the history of war," is sufficient to make objectivity here suspect.

Coppée, Henry, 1821–1895.
Grant and his campaigns: a military biography. By Henry Coppée... New York, C. B. Richardson; Cincinnati, C. F. Vent & co.; [etc., etc.] 1866.
521 p. front., illus., ports., maps (1 double) 24 cm.

A laudatory, superficial and episodic "military biography" of Grant; sanctioned by the General himself.

Corbin, *Mrs.* **Diana Fontaine (Maury)**
A life of Matthew Fontaine Maury ... Comp. by his daughter, Diana Fontaine Maury Corbin. London, S. Low, Marston, Searle, & Rivington, limited, 1888.
vi, 326 p. front. (port.) 22½cm.

This highly laudatory study of the great scientist gives disappointing attention to his Civil War years.

Cornell, William Mason, 1802–1895.
The life and public career of Hon. Horace Greeley. By William M. Cornell ... Boston, Lee & Shepard; New York, Lee, Shepard, & Dillingham; [etc., etc.] 1872.
312 p. front., ports. 19 cm.

A campaign biography designed to enhance Greeley's 1872 Candidacy for the presidency.

Coulson, Thomas, 1886–
Joseph Henry, his life and work. Princeton, Princeton University Press, 1950.
352 p. illus., ports. 24 cm.

A scholarly and informative study of the career and achievements of one of America's greatest 19th century scientists.

Coulter, Ellis Merton, 1890–

William G. Brownlow, fighting parson of the Southern highlands, by E. Merton Coulter. Chapel Hill, The University of North Carolina press, 1937.

vii p., 3 l., 432 p. illus., plates, 2 port. (incl. front.) fold. map. 24 cm.

The only reliable study of a militant editor-minister who resisted unceasingly all Confederate efforts to tame East Tennessee.

Cox, Jacob Dolson, 1828–1900.

Military reminiscences of the civil war, by Jacob Dolson Cox ... New York, C. Scribner's sons, 1900.

2 v. front. (ports.) illus. (maps) 22 cm.

This detailed account, by an Ohio general and veteran of many campaigns, gives a broader picture than the usual description of battle.

Cox, Samuel Sullivan, 1824–1889.

Eight years in Congress, from 1857 to 1865. Memoir and speeches. By Samuel S. Cox ... New York, D. Appleton and company, 1865.

viii, [5]–442 p. front. (port.) 23cm.

An extensive collection of speeches, with a brief introduction explaining Cox's basic position on the issues of the conflict.

Cox, Samuel Sullivan, 1824–1889.

Union—disunion—reunion. Three decades of federal legislation. 1855 to 1885. Personal and historical memories of events preceding, during and since the American civil war, involving slavery and secession, emancipation and reconstruction, with sketches of prominent actors during these periods. By Samuel S. Cox ... Illustrated with thirty-six portraits engraved on steel expressly for this work. Providence, R. I., J. A. and R. A. Reid, 1885.

1 p. l., 726 p. 35 port. on 7 pl. 24cm.

A long and rambling account by the Ohio congressman; treats principally of the Reconstruction period.

Cox, William Ruffin, 1832–

Address on the life and services of General James H. Lane, Army northern Virginia. By General William Ruffin Cox ... Delivered before R. E. Lee camp Confederate veterans, no. 1, Richmond, Va., December 4, 1908. [Richmond? 1908]

cover-title, 23 p. 23cm.

Another short tribute to one of those unheralded but indispensable generals in the second echelon of command.

Cox, William Ruffin, 1832–

Address on the life and services of General Marcus J. Wright, by General William Ruffin Cox; delivered before R. E. Lee camp no. 1 of Confederate veterans, Richmond, Va., February 26th, 1915. [Richmond? 1915]

1 p. l., 15, [2] p. port. 22cm.

Similar in tone to the above titles; a full biography of Wright is badly needed.

Cox, William Ruffin, 1832–1919.

Address on the life and character of Maj. Gen. Stephen D. Ramseur, before the Ladies' memorial association of Raleigh, N. C., May 10th 1891. By Hon. William R. Cox. Raleigh [N. C.] E. M. Uzzell, 1891.

54 p. front. (port.) 24 cm.

A eulogy to the North Carolina general who died in the Second Valley Campaign; contains some biographical data amid much praise.

Cox, William Van Zandt, 1852–1923.

Life of Samuel Sullivan Cox, by his nephew, William Van Zandt Cox, and his friend, Milton Harlow Northrup ... Syracuse, N. Y., M. H. Northrup, 1899.

280 p., 1 l. front., plates, ports. 23½cm.

An adulatory and superficial account; treats only slightly of the Civil War.

Craven, Avery Odelle, 1886–

Edmund Ruffin, southerner; a study in secession, by Avery Craven ... New York and London, D. Appleton and company, 1932.

ix p., 2 l., 283 p. front., plates, ports., facsims. 22½ cm.

A documented, sympathetic and balanced study of the eminent Virginia scientist, editor and secessionist.

Craven, John J.

Prison life of Jefferson Davis, embracing details and incidents in his captivity, particulars concerning his health and habits, together with many conversations on topics of great public interest. By Bvt. Lieut. Col. John J. Craven ... New York, G. W. Dillingham company [1905]

319, [1] p. incl. front. (port.) 19cm.

A sympathetic account of Davis's confinement at Fortress Monroe; by the physician assigned to attend him; includes several long conversations.

Croffut, William Augustus, 1835–1915.
An American procession, 1855–1914; a personal chronicle of famous men, by William A. Croffut; with reproductions of woodcuts from Frank Leslie's weekly. Boston, Little, Brown, and company, 1931.

viii p., 1 l., 321 p. front., plates, ports. 21½ cm.

While this compilation by a New York Herald reporter contains a number of personal insights into important Union officials, it also describes much action on the front.

Croly, David Goodman, 1829–1889.
Seymour and Blair, their lives and services with an appendix containing a history of reconstruction by David G. Croly ... New York, Richardson and company, 1868.

275 p. 2 port. (incl. front.) fold. facsim. 19½ cm.

A campaign biography, strongly oriented toward the issues of the 1868 election.

Crook, George, 1828–1890.
General George Crook, his autobiography; edited and annotated by Martin F. Schmitt. Norman, University of Oklahoma press, 1946.

xviii, 326 p. front., illus. (maps) plates, ports. 22cm.

Only 58 pages of this memoir treat of the famous Indian fighter's experiences as a cavalry general in the Civil War.

Crook, William Henry, 1839–1915.
Through five administrations; reminiscences of Colonel William H. Crook, body-guard to President Lincoln, comp. and ed. by Marguerita Spalding Gerry ... New York and London, Harper & brothers, 1910.

4 p. l., 279, [1] p. pl., 7 port. (incl. front.) 21½ cm.

Because Crook concentrated on the 1865-1900 period, his account of his associations with Lincoln in Washington is disappointingly thin.

Crosby, Ernest Howard, 1856–1907.
Garrison, the non-resistant, by Ernest Crosby ... Chicago, The Public publishing company [c1905]

141 p. front. (port.) 18cm.

A brief tract, drawing lessons from Garrison's career for reform in the author's day.

Cullum, George Washington, 1809–1892.
Biographical register of the officers and graduates of the U. S. military academy, at West Point, N. Y., from its establishment, March 16, 1802, to the army re-organization of 1866–67. By Bvt. Major-General George W. Cullum ... New York, D. Van Nostrand, 1868.

2 v. 23½cm.

A fundamental starting point for data on the war's leading commanders; provides full records of antebellum service.

Cunningham, Frank, 1911–
Knight of the Confederacy, Gen. Turner Ashby. San Antonio, Naylor [1960]

225 p. illus. 22 cm.

A rambling, undocumented, antiquarian study of a heroic Confederate cavalry commander.

Current, Richard Nelson.
The Lincoln nobody knows. [1st ed.] New York, McGraw-Hill [1958]

314 p. 22 cm.

A series of penetrating essays, each examining an aspect of Lincoln's life and career for which complete documentation is lacking.

Current, Richard Nelson.
Old Thad Stevens, a story of ambition, by Richard Nelson Current ... Madison, The University of Wisconsin press, 1942.

v, [1] p., 1 l., 344 p. front., illus. (map) plates, ports., facsim. 22½ cm.

A critical, scholarly and authentic study; the author sees a contradiction between Stevens' support of human equality and his contributions to the growth of big business.

Curtis, George Ticknor, 1811–1894.
McClellan's last service to the republic, together with a tribute to his memory. By George Ticknor Curtis. New York, D. Appleton and company, 1886.

150 p. front. (map) 19½ cm.

A defense of McClellan's military leadership, with a tribute to the general published after his death in 1885.

Curtis, George William, 1824–1892.
Orations and addresses of George William Curtis; edited by Charles Eliot Norton ... New York, Harper & brothers, 1894.

3 v. front. (port., v. 3) 23 cm.

Contains several addresses on Union politics and Southern slavery; Curtis was one of the leading orators of the day.

Custer, George Armstrong, 1839–1876.
The Custer story; the life and intimate letters of General George A. Custer and his wife Elizabeth. Edited by Marguerite Merington. New York, Devin-Adair, 1950.

xii, 339 p. illus., ports., maps. 24 cm.

Correspondence between George and Elizabeth Custer, with some additional source material added.

Cutler, Julia Perkins, *b.* 1815.
Life and times of Ephraim Cutler, prepared from his journals and correspondence, by his daughter Julia Perkins Cutler; with biographical sketches of Jervis Cutler and William Parker Cutler. Cincinnati, R. Clarke & co., 1890.

vi, 353 p. pl., 2 port. (incl. front.) 24 cm.

Contains the little-known but very quotable diary of Ohio Congressman William Cutler, whose observations were generally keen and pessimistic.

Cutting, Elisabeth Brown, 1871–
Jefferson Davis, political soldier, by Elisabeth Cutting ... New York, Dodd, Mead and company, 1930.

x p., 3 l., 361 p. front., plates, ports., facsims. 24½ cm.

A sympathetic biography; the author concluded that Davis "was a leader of a cause but not of men."

Dabney, Robert Lewis, 1820–1898.
Life and campaigns of Lieut.-Gen. Thomas J. Jackson, (Stonewall Jackson) By Prof. R. L. Dabney ... New York, Blelock & co., 1866.

x, [2], 742 p. front. (port.) maps. 21 cm.

Dabney, a Virginia clergyman, wrote this biography at the invitation of Jackson's family; while the work is polemical in its defense of the Southern cause, it contains much primary material

Davis, Burke.
Gray Fox: Robert E. Lee and the Civil War. New York, Rinehart [1956]

466 p. illus. 24 cm.

An attempt to reduce the Lee of myth to easily understood terms through a heavy reliance on eyewitness accounts; superficial in places.

Davis, Burke.
Jeb Stuart, the last cavalier. With maps by Rafael D. Palacios. New York, Rinehart [1957]

462 p. illus., ports., maps. 24 cm.

Sympathetic and personal, this study focuses on the man rather than cavalry operations; written in a fast-paced style.

Davis, Burke.
They called him Stonewall; a life of Lt. General T. J. Jackson, C. S. A. New York, Rinehart [1954]

470 p. illus. 22 cm.

A sympathetic portrait, attempting to replace "myth" with accuracy through a scrupulous use of contemporary sources.

Davis, Charles Henry, 1845–1921.
Life of Charles Henry Davis, rear admiral, 1807–1877; by his son, Captain Charles H. Davis, U. S. N. Boston and New York, Houghton, Mifflin and company, 1899.

2 p. l., 349, [1] p. front. (port.) 1 illus. 22½ cm.

Biography of a Civil War naval officer; includes extensive extracts from his private letters.

Davis, Charles Shepard, 1910–
Colin J. McRae; Confederate financial agent. [Lim. ed.] Tuscaloosa, Confederate Pub. Co., 1961.

101 p. illus. 22 cm.

A useful study of an ordnance and purchasing agent who promoted a unified purchasing system for the Confederacy.

Davis, Henry Winter, 1817–1865.

Speeches and addresses delivered in the Congress of the United States, and on several public occasions [1856–1865] by Henry Winter Davis, of Maryland. Preceded by a sketch of his life, public services, and character, being an oration by the Hon. J. A. J. Cresswell [!] ... With notes, introductory and explanatory. New York, Harper & brothers, 1867.

xxxv p., 1 l., [39]–596 p. front. (port.) 24cm.

The best source for material on an anti-administration Unionist who served as wartime chairman of the House Committee on Foreign Relations.

Davis, Jefferson, 1808–1889.

Jefferson Davis, constitutionalist, his letters, papers and speeches, collected and edited by Dunbar Rowland ... Jackson, Miss., Printed for the Mississippi department of archives and history, 1923.

10 v. fronts. (v. 1–6, 8–10, ports.) pl. 24½ cm.

For many years the best source for Davis's writings and utterances--in spite of its errors; now being superseded by the work of a Rice University-based foundation.

Davis, Jefferson, 1808–1889.

Private letters, 1823–1889. Selected and edited by Hudson Strode. [1st ed.] New York, Harcourt, Brace & World [1966]

xxi, 580 p. 24 cm.

A small collection of the Confederate president's private correspondence; the sum is rather unrevealing.

Davis, Jefferson, 1808–1889.

The rise and fall of the Confederate government. By Jefferson Davis ... New York, D. Appleton and co., 1881.

2 v. front., plates, ports., maps (part fold.) plans (part fold.) 23½ cm.

Conceals more than it reveals of the inner history of the Confederacy; mainly an argumentative dissertation on secession and states rights.

Davis, Jefferson, 1808–1889.

The rise and fall of the Confederate Government. Foreword by Bell I. Wiley. New York, T. Yoseloff [1958]

2 v. illus., ports., maps. 24 cm.

A new edition with a foreward summarizing strengths and weaknesses of Davis the man and the President.

Davis, Jefferson, 1808–1889.

Robert E. Lee. Edited and with an introd. and notes by Harold B. Simpson. [1st ed. Hillsboro, Tex.] Hill Junior College Press [1966]

xiii, 81 p. ports. 24 cm.

A eulogistic essay that originally appeared in the January, 1890, North American Review; this reprint is skillfully edited.

Davis, Julia.

Stonewall, by Julia Davis Adams ... with illustrations by Cameron Wright. New York, E. P. Dutton and company, inc. [©1931]

3 p. l., 9–255 p., 1 l. front., illus., ports. 21½ cm.

A sympathetic biography for older boys and girls.

Davis, Varina (Howell) 1826–1906.

Jefferson Davis, ex-president of the Confederate States of America; a memoir by his wife ... New York, Belford company [©1890]

2 v. plates, ports., fold. plans, facsims. 22½ cm.

A superficial, sometimes inaccurate and sentimentalized account, including parts which Davis dictated before his death.

Dawes, Anna Laurens, 1851–1938.

... Charles Sumner, by Anna Laurens Dawes ... New York, Dodd, Mead and company, 1892.

xii, 330 p. front. (port.) 18 cm.

So general that it only skims the surface--and then in a highly laudatory way.

Dawson, George Francis.

Life and services of Gen. John A. Logan, as soldier and statesman; by George Francis Dawson ... Pub. by subscription only. Chicago and New York, Belford, Clarke & company, 1887.

xx, 580 p. incl. pl., facsim. 8 pl., 2 port. (incl. front.) 24 cm.

Eulogistic; Logan himself furnished much of the material; very little of the book treats of Logan's wartime services.

Deming, Henry Champion, 1815–1872.
The life of Ulysses S. Grant, general United States army. By Henry C. Deming. Hartford [Conn.] S. S. Scranton & co.; Cincinnati, National pub. co.; [etc., etc.] 1868.

533 p. front. (port.) 22 cm.

A campaign biography of "the man who saved the nation's life."

Dennett, Tyler, 1883–
John Hay: from poetry to politics, by Tyler Dennett ... New York, Dodd, Mead & company, 1933.

xi p., 1 l., 476 p. front., plates, ports., facsim. 24½ cm.

Thorough and well-documented; yet only a small space is devoted to Hay's service as Lincoln's secretary.

De Peyster, John Watts, 1821–1907.
Personal and military history of Philip Kearny, major-general United States volunteers ... By John Watts De Peyster. New York, Rice and Gage; Newark, N. J., Bliss & co., 1869.

3 p. l., xii, [13]–516 p. plates, ports., map. 23½ cm.

An uncritical "memorial" to Kearney, written by his cousin; lavish in its praise but contains many exerpts from pertinent documents.

Detroit post and tribune.
Zachariah Chandler: an outline sketch of his life and public services. By the Detroit post and tribune. With an introductory letter from James G. Blaine ... Detroit, The Post and tribune company; New York, C. Drew; [etc., etc.] 1880.

xvii, [1], [19]–396, xxxvi p. front. (port.) illus. 23½cm.

Almost 100 pages of this laudatory study treat of Chandler's Civil War experiences.

Dickinson, Sally Bruce.
Confederate leaders [by] Sally Bruce Dickinson. Staunton, Va., Printed by McClure company [©1937]

198 p. port., facsim. 23½ cm.

Superficial sketches of some of the principal Southern generals; of no value except perhaps to the beginning reader.

Dix, Morgan, 1827–1908.
Memoirs of John Adams Dix; comp. by his son, Morgan Dix ... New York, Harper & brothers, 1883.

2 v. fronts., illus., plates, ports., facsims. 23 cm.

Rather uneven in courage, these memoirs of a New York politician contain only one chapter on the Civil War.

Dodd, William Edward, 1869–1940.
... Jefferson Davis, by William E. Dodd ... Philadelphia, G. W. Jacobs & company [1907]

396 p. front. (port.) 19½ cm.

Sympathetic in tone, yet judicious in judgment; still regarded as among the best Davis studies.

Dodge, Grenville Mellen, 1831–1916.
Personal recollections of President Abraham Lincoln, General Ulysses S. Grant and General William T. Sherman, by Major-General Grenville M. Dodge. Council Bluffs, Ia., The Monarch printing company, 1914.

2 p. l., [7]–237 p. plates, ports. 23½cm.

Brief recollections of Lincoln, Grant and Sherman, extending in the latter two instances through the postwar years.

Donald, David Herbert, 1920–
Charles Sumner and the coming of the Civil War. [1st ed.] New York, Knopf, 1960.

392 p. illus. 25 cm.

The first volume of what will prove to be a definitive study; based on wide research and carefully documented.

Dorsey, *Mrs.* **Sarah Anne (Ellis)** 1829–1879.
Recollections of Henry Watkins Allen, brigadier-general Confederate States army, ex-governor of Louisiana. By Sarah A. Dorsey. New York, M. Doolady; New Orleans, J. A. Gresham [©1866]

420 p. front. (port.) 19½cm.

A fiercely pro-Southern biography of Louisiana's wartime governor; includes letters written by Allen during his Mexican exile.

Douglass, Frederick, 1817–1895.
Life and times of Frederick Douglass, written by himself. His early life as a slave, his escape from bondage, and his complete history to the present time, including his connection with the anti slavery movement ... With an introduction, by Mr. George L. Ruffin ... Hartford, Conn., Park publishing co., 1881.

xii, xv–xxiii, 13–516 p. 12 pl., 6 port. (incl. front.) 21cm.

The last and most complete of many editions of Douglass' autobiography.

Douglass, Frederick, 1817?–1895.
The life and writings of Frederick Douglass [by] Philip S. Foner. New York, International Publishers [1950–55]

4 v. ports. 22 cm.

Although not a complete edition, this set contains extensive selections of Douglass' speeches, letters and editorials.

Dowd, Clement, 1832–1898.
Life of Zebulon B. Vance. By Clement Dowd. Charlotte, N. C., Observer printing and publishing house, 1897.

8 p. l., 493 p. front., plates, ports. 23cm.

Many chapters were written by various individuals who knew Vance; eulogistic in tone, the study was authorized by Vance's family.

Dowdey, Clifford, 1904–
Lee. With photos. and with maps by Samuel H. Bryant. [1st ed.] Boston, Little, Brown [1965]

xiv, 781 p. illus., maps, ports. 24 cm.

An outstanding study, well-balanced, analytical and, although without documentation, based on an intensive use of primary and secondary sources.

Duberman, Martin B
Charles Francis Adams, 1807–1886. Boston, Houghton Mifflin, 1961 [©1960]

525 p. illus. 22 cm.

A balanced, scholarly and definitive study of Adams' life; the author made effective use of the voluminous Adams Family Papers.

Du Bois, James T 1851–1920.
Galusha A. Grow, father of the homestead law, by James T. DuBois and Gertrude S. Mathews. Boston and New York, Houghton Mifflin company, 1917.

xi p., 1 l., 305, [1] p. front., plates, facsim. 20½ cm.

This eulogistic, "authorized" biography consists in large part of reminiscences by Grow himself.

Du Bose, John Witherspoon, 1836–1918.
The life and times of William Lowndes Yancey. A history of political parties in the United States, from 1834 to 1864; especially as to the origin of the Confederate States. By John Witherspoon Du Bose ... Birmingham [Ala.] Roberts & son, 1892.

xiv p., 1 l., 752 p. pl., 8 port. (incl. front.) 25 cm.

A well-researched study striving for objective treatment, though the author's pro-Southern bias shows.

Dufour, Charles L
Nine men in gray. [1st ed.] Garden City, N. Y., Doubleday, 1963.

364 p. illus. 24 cm.

Brief essays on nine lesser-known, perhaps "little remembered," Confederate military figures.

Duncan, Robert Lipscomb, 1927–
Reluctant general; the life and times of Albert Pike. [1st ed.] New York, Dutton [1961]

289 p. 22 cm.

In spite of some weaknesses, this remains the best biography of the prominent Mason who commanded Indian regiments in the West.

Durkin, Joseph Thomas, 1903–
Stephen R. Mallory: Confederate Navy chief. Chapel Hill, University of North Carolina Press, 1954.

xi, 446 p. 25 cm.

A sound, scholarly study of the "most neglected member of the Confederate Cabinet;" also an important discussion of Confederate naval policy and development.

Dyer, Brainerd, 1901–
The public career of William M. Evarts, by Brainerd Dyer. Berkeley, Calif., University of California press, 1933.
5 p. l., 297 p. 24 cm.

A brief but scholarly discussion of one aspect of Evarts' life.

Dyer, John Percy, 1902–
"Fightin' Joe" Wheeler, by John P. Dyer. University, La., Louisiana state university press, 1941.
viii p., 2 l., 417 p. front., ports., maps. 22½ cm.

A soundly documented and balanced study of a professional soldier who shone in the Civil and Spanish-American wars.

Dyer, John Percy, 1902–
The gallant Hood. [1st ed.] Indianapolis, Bobbs-Merrill [1950]
383 p. ports., maps. 23 cm.

A fine, well-balanced and critical study of the zealous and often impetuous Confederate commander; based on an imposing array of sources.

Early, Jubal Anderson, 1816–1894.
... Autobiographical sketch and narrative of the war between the states, with notes by R. H. Early. Philadelphia & London, J. B. Lippincott company, 1912.
xxv, [1], 496 p. front., plates, ports. 23½ cm.

A partisan but exciting account of the military activities of one of Lee's most prominent generals; reprinted in 1960, with an introductory essay by Frank E. Vandiver.

Easby-Smith, Mildred, *mother*, 1873–
William Russell Smith of Alabama, his life and works; including the entire text of The uses of solitude. By Anne Easby-Smith ... foreword by George H. Denny ... Philadelphia, The Dolphin press, 1931.
4 p. l., 5–298 p. front., pl., ports. 23 cm.

The only usable volume on a Southern soldier-congressman-educator.

Easum, Chester Verne.
The Americanization of Carl Schurz, by Chester Verne Easum. Chicago, Ill., The University of Chicago press [c1929]
xi, 374 p. 19½ cm.

A scholarly study of Schurz's first ten years in the United States; not a biography, the book stresses Schurz's adjustment to American life and problems.

Eckenrode, Hamilton James, 1881–
George B. McClellan, the man who saved the Union, by H. J. Eckenrode ... and Bryan Conrad ... Chapel Hill, The University of North Carolina press, 1941.
xi p., 1 l., 296 p. front. (port.) illus. (maps) 23½ cm.

A highly favorable defense of McClellan; the author blamed Lincoln's "lack of support" for some of the General's shortcomings.

Eckenrode, Hamilton James, 1881–
James Longstreet, Lee's war horse, by H. J. Eckenrode ... and Bryan Conrad ... Chapel Hill, The University of North Carolina press, 1936.
viii p., 3 l., 3–399 p. front. (port.) illus. (maps) 24 cm.

Emphasizing the relationship between Lee and Longstreet, the book is critical of the latter's role in the war.

Eckenrode, Hamilton James, 1881–
Jefferson Davis, president of the South, by H. J. Eckenrode. New York, The Macmillan company, 1923.
6 p. l., 371 p. 20½cm.

Of interest primarily for Eckenrode's racist interpretation of the Civil War; Davis was a "tropical Nordic;" the Confederacy "a Nordic protest against a leveling age."

Edmonds, Franklin Spencer, 1874–
... Ulysses S. Grant, by Franklin Spencer Edmonds ... Philadelphia, G. W. Jacobs & company [1915]
3 p. l., [3]–376 p. front. (port.) 19 cm.

A fairly objective "attempt to record a life that is full of significance for our own era."

Egle, William Henry, 1830–1901, *ed.*

Andrew Gregg Curtin: his life and services. Ed. by William H. Egle, M. D. Philadelphia, Avil printing company, 1895.

1 p. l., xi–xiv, 521 p. incl. plates, ports., facsim. front., pl. 22½cm.

A number of writers prepared this series of laudatory sketches, each devoted to a special aspect of the life of Pennsylvania's war governor.

Eliot, Ellsworth, 1864–

West Point in the Confederacy, by Ellsworth Eliot, jr. New York, G. A. Baker & co., inc., 1941.

xxxii, 491 p. incl. tables, 22½ cm.

A still-useful glossary on Confederate officers, though superseded to a great extent by Ezra Warner's Generals In Gray.

Elliott, Charles Winslow, 1887–

Winfield Scott, the soldier and the man [by] Charles Winslow Elliott ... illustrated with maps and photographs. New York, The Macmillan company, 1937.

xviii p., 2 l., 817 p. front., illus. (maps) ports. 24 cm.

The most scholarly study of "Old Fuss and Feathers;" likely to stand unchallenged for many years to come.

Epler, Percy Harold, 1872–

The life of Clara Barton, by Percy H. Epler. New York, The Macmillan company, 1915.

xvii, 438 p. front., plates, ports. 20½ cm.

A laudatory and rather superficial survey; the biography was authorized by the family of Clara Barton.

Fahrney, Ralph Ray.

Horace Greeley and the Tribune in the civil war, by Ralph Ray Fahrney ... Cedar Rapids, Ia., The Torch press, 1936.

5 p. l., 229 p. 20 cm.

A broad, thorough study that puts Greeley in a more favorable light than history has accorded him.

Fairman, Charles, 1897–

Mr. Justice Miller and the Supreme court, 1862–1890, by Charles Fairman. Cambridge, Mass., Harvard university press, 1939.

vii, [1] p., 3 l., 3–456 p. front., pl., ports. 23½cm.

A first-rate study of a Lincoln appointee whose vote often swung a court decision to the Republicans advantage.

Faulkner, Joseph.

The life of Philip Henry Sheridan, the dashing, brave and successful soldier, by Joseph Faulkner. New York, Hurst & co., c1888.

1 p. l., 149 p. front., plates, ports 19cm.

Brief, superficial and adulatory.

Fessenden, Francis, 1839–1906.

Life and public services of William Pitt Fessenden, United States senator from Maine 1854–1864; secretary of the Treasury 1864–1865; United States senator from Maine 1865–1869, by his son Francis Fessenden ... Boston and New York, Houghton, Mifflin and company, 1907.

2 v. fronts., pl., ports. 24½ cm.

A detailed study, with many of the Senator's letters included; treats principally of the war and postwar years.

Field, Maunsell Bradhurst, 1822–1875.

Memories of many men, and of some women: being personal recollections of emperors, kings, queens, princes, presidents, statesmen, authors, and artists, at home and abroad during the last thirty years. By Maunsell B. Field. London, Sampson Low, Marston, Low, & Searle, 1874.

2 p. l., x, [11]–339 p. 20½cm.

Another of those "memoirs" as unrevealing as they are unreliable.

Fielder, Herbert.

A sketch of the life and times and speeches of Joseph E. Brown. By Herbert Fielder. Springfield, Mass., Press of Springfield printing company, 1883.

2 p. l., 785 p. front. (port.) 24 cm.

Disorganized and eulogistic, this account contains some miscellaneous data on state politics.

Fields, Annie (Adams) 1834–1915.

Life and letters of Harriet Beecher Stowe, edited by Annie Fields. Boston, Houghton, Mifflin [1897]

406 p. port. 20 cm.

An admiring and sentimental study, consisting in large part of Mrs. Stowe's own statements.

[Fletcher, Thomas Clement] 1827–1899.

Life and reminiscences of General Wm. T. Sherman. By distinguished men of his time ... Baltimore, R. H. Woodward company, 1891.

2 p. l., ix–xvi, 479 p. incl. front., plates, 2 port. 20½ cm.

A very brief and highly superficial account of Sherman's life, with reminiscences and tributes added by men who knew him.

Flippin, Percy Scott, 1874–

Herschel V. Johnson of Georgia, state rights Unionist, by Percy Scott Flippin ... Richmond, Va., Press of the Dietz printing co., 1931.

xv p., 1 l., 336 p. front., plates, ports., 2 fold. facsim. 24 cm.

So complete a political study of this Georgia figure that it has stood unchallenged for over three decades; its one glaring weakness is the lack of a bibliography.

Flower, Frank Abial, 1854–1911.

Edwin McMasters Stanton, the autocrat of rebellion, emancipation, and reconstruction ... by Frank Abial Flower ... Akron, O., New York [etc.] The Saalfield publishing company, 1905.

6 p. l., [19]–425, [20] p. front., plates, ports., facsims. 24½cm.

An uncritical study, based on oral testimony as well as documentary materials.

Foote, Henry Stuart, 1804–1880.

Casket of reminiscences, by Henry S. Foote. Washington, D. C., Chronicle publishing company, 1874.

2 p. l., 498 p. 21½cm.

Rambling recollections that stretch as far back as the era of James Monroe; colored by highly opinionated judgements.

Foote, Henry Stuart, 1804–1880.

War of the rebellion; or, Scylla and Charybdis. Consisting of observations upon the causes, course, and consequences of the late civil war in the United States. By H. S. Foote ... New York, Harper & brothers, 1866.

1 p. l., xii, [13]–440 p. front. (port.) 19½ cm.

A disorganized memoir bitterly critical of Jefferson Davis; valuable only for author's experiences in the Confederacy.

Force, Manning Ferguson, 1824–1899.

... General Sherman, by General Manning F. Force. New York, D. Appleton and company, 1899.

ix, 353 p. front., 1 illus., pl., port. group, 8 maps, facsim. 19½cm.

An old but generally adequate study, focussing almost exclusively on the wartime years; parts of the book were written by J. D. Cox.

Ford, Worthington Chauncey, 1858–1941, *ed.*

A cycle of Adams letters, 1861–1865, ed. by Worthington Chauncey Ford ... Boston and New York, Houghton Mifflin company, 1920.

2 v. fronts., plates, ports. 22 cm.

A valuable collection of the letters of C. F. Adams and his two sons, Charles, Jr., and Henry; significant for their lucid comments on the economic, political and diplomatic developments of the war.

Forney, John Wien, 1817–1881.

Anecdotes of public men. By John W. Forney ... New York, Harper & brothers, 1873.

1 p. l., [vii]–viii, [9]–444 p. 19cm.

Shallow vignettes that originally appeared serially in two newspapers; the subjects are statesmen rather than militarists.

Forney, John Wien, 1817–1881.

Life and military career of Winfield Scott Hancock ... his early life, education and remarkable military career ... Also contains a succinct biographical sketch of Hon. Wm. H. English ... By Hon. John W. Forney ... Boston, W. H. Thompson & co. [1880]

3 p. l., 11–500 p. incl. front., illus., plates, ports., maps, plans. 19½cm

Disorganized and rambling; written as an 1880 campaign biography.

Foulke, William Dudley, 1848–1935.
Life of Oliver P. Morton, including his important speeches, by William Dudley Foulke ... Indianapolis-Kansas City, The Bowen-Merrill company 1899
2 v. front. (port.) 23½ cm.

Volume I of this highly favorable study treats of Morton's wartime governorship.

Fox, Gustavus Vasa, 1821–1883.
Confidential correspondence of Gustavus Vasa Fox, assistant secretary of the navy, 1861–1865, edited by Robert Means Thompson and Richard Wainwright ... New York, Printed for the Naval history society by the De Vinne press, 1918–19 [©1920]
2 v. front. (port) 24 cm.

Undocumented letters that reveal a great deal about Union naval operations during the war.

Freeman, Douglas Southall, 1886–1953.
Lee. New York, Scribner [1961]
xvii, 601 p. illus., ports., maps. 24 cm.

A superb condensation of Freeman's four-volumes on Lee; the text has been tightened and footnotes removed; prepared by Richard Harwell and approved by Mrs. Freeman.

Freeman, Douglas Southall, 1886–1953.
Lee of Virginia. New York, Scribner [1958]
243 p. illus. 24 cm.

A moving tribute by the biographer who knew Lee best; recommended for those who do not wish to delve into Freeman's monumental study.

Freeman, Douglas Southall, 1886–1953.
R. E. Lee, a biography, by Douglas Southall Freeman ... New York, London, C. Scribner's sons, 1934–35.
4 v. fronts., illus., plates, ports., maps, facsims. 24 cm.

A classic example of the biographical form; exhaustively researched, vividly written, balanced, judicious and definitive in its portrayal of the Confederacy's greatest soldier.

Freidel, Frank Burt.
Francis Lieber, nineteenth-century liberal. Baton Rouge, Louisiana State Univ. Press [1948, ©1947]
xiii, 445 p. ports. 24 cm.

Thorough and definitive; based on exhaustive research in the Lieber manuscripts.

French, William M.
Life, speeches, state papers and public services of Gov. Oliver P. Morton. Ed. by William M. French ... Cincinnati, Moore, Wilstach, & Baldwin, printers, 1864.
vii, [9]–406 p. front. (port.) 20cm.

Self-explanatory, and incomplete.

Frothingham, Paul Revere, 1864–1926.
Edward Everett, orator and statesman, by Paul Revere Frothingham ... Boston and New York, Houghton Mifflin company, 1925.
x p., 2 l., 495 p. front., plates, ports., facsims. 23 cm.

Everett's own journal and letters provided most of the material for this somewhat superficial study.

Fuess, Claude Moore, 1855–1963.
Carl Schurz, reformer; 1829–1906. Port Washington, N. Y., Kennikat Press [1963]
421 p. illus., ports. 22 cm.

A full, well-balanced account, based primarily on printed sources and lightly documented.

Fuess, Claude Moore, 1885–
The life of Caleb Cushing, by Claude M. Fuess ... New York, Harcourt, Brace and company [©1923]
2 v. fronts., plates, ports. 22½ cm.

Based largely on Cushing's collection of writings, this biography remains the standard work on the famed statesman.

Fuller, John Frederick Charles, 1878–
Grant & Lee, a study in personality and generalship, by Major-General J. F. C. Fuller ... London, Eyre and Spottiswoode, 1933.

2 p. l., 7–323 p. illus., 11 fold. maps. 22 cm.

An evaluation of the relative merits of the two commanders, with Grant coming out best; reprinted in 1957.

Garland, Hamlin, 1860–1940.
Ulysses S. Grant; his life and character, by Hamlin Garland ... New York, Doubleday & McClure co., 1898.

xix, 524 p. front., plates, ports., facsim. 23½cm.

Hamlin made no claim to thoroughness or analysis in this sympathetic, readable characterization.

[**Garrison, Wendell Phillips**] 1840–1907.
... William Lloyd Garrison, 1805–1879; the story of his life told by his children ... New-York, The Century co., 1885–1889,

4 v. fronts., illus., plates, ports., facsims. 23½cm.

A voluminous compendium that includes many of Garrison's letters, editorials, speeches and other statements.

Gilbertson, Catherine (Peebles) 1890–
Harriet Beecher Stowe, by Catherine Gilbertson. New York, London, D. Appleton-Century company, incorporated, 1937.

xii p., 3 l., 3–330 p. front., illus., ports. 21½ cm.

An interpretive study of Mrs. Stowe's personality and emotional reaction to the events of her time.

Gilmore, James Roberts, 1822–1903.
Personal recollections of Abraham Lincoln and the Civil War, by James R. Gilmore (Edmund Kirke) London, J. Macqueen, 1899 [c1898]

338 p. ports. 23 cm.

Too autobiographical to be of use for either Lincoln or the war; Gilmore wrote a series of wartime books under the pseudonym "Edmund Kirke."

Godkin, Edwin Lawrence, 1831–1902.
Life and letters of Edwin Lawrence Godkin; ed. by Rollo Ogden ... New York, The Macmillan company; London, Macmillan & co., ltd., 1907.

2 v. fronts., pl., ports. 21 cm.

Very little of this study treats of the famous editor's wartime activities.

Goode, John, 1829–1909.
Recollections of a lifetime, by John Goode, of Virginia. New York and Washington, The Neale publishing company, 1906.

x p., 1 l., [13]–266 p. front. (port.) 23 cm.

Interesting memoir by a member of the Virginia secession convention and the Confederate Congress.

Gordon, Armistead Churchill, 1855–1931.
... Jefferson Davis, by Armistead C. Gordon. New York, C. Scribner's sons, 1918.

viii p., 1 l., 329 p. 20 cm.

Somewhat sympathetic and superficial; Gordon was more concerned with Davis's character than with the issues and events to which Davis reacted.

Gorham, George Congdon, 1832–1909.
Life and public services of Edwin M. Stanton, by George C. Gorham, with portraits, maps, and facsimiles of important letters ... Boston and New York, Houghton, Mifflin and company, 1899.

2 v. fronts., plates, ports., maps, facsims. (part double) 24½ cm.

Less a balanced biography than a close and detailed study of Stanton's relation to the Civil War.

Govan, Gilbert Eaton, 1892–
A different valor, the story of General Joseph E. Johnston, C. S. A., by Gilbert E. Govan and James W. Livingood. New York, Bobbs-Merrill [1956]

470 p. illus. 24 cm.

A full and scholarly study; while sympathetic with Johnston, the authors failed to analyze completely his controversial career.

Graham, Shirley.
...There was once a slave ... The heroic story of Frederick Douglass. New York, J. Messner, inc. [1947]

ix, 310 p. 22 cm.

A popularly written, semi-fictional study of Douglass' life.

Grant, Ulysses Simpson, *Pres. U. S.*, 1822–1885.
The papers of Ulysses S. Grant. Edited by John Y. Simon. Carbondale, Southern Illinois University Press [1967–

v. illus., facsim., map, port. 26 cm.

Although still in preparation, this proposed fifteen volume work will be the primary source for the Federal commander; skillfully edited.

Grant, Ulysses Simpson, *Pres. U. S.*, 1822–1885.
Personal memoirs. Edited with notes and an introd. by E. B. Long. [1st ed.] Cleveland, World Pub. Co. [1952]

xxv, 608 p. ports., maps, facsim. 24 cm.

A condensation of the next work; the editor added useful introduction and explanatory notes.

Grant, Ulysses Simpson, *pres. U. S.*, 1822–1885.
Personal memoirs of U. S. Grant ... New York, C. L. Webster & co., 1885–86.

2 v. front. (ports.) plates, maps, facsims. 23½ cm.

Written frantically while in a race with death, these recollections rank with the best of the Civil War period.

Greeley, Horace, 1811–1872.
Recollections of a busy life, by Horace Greeley. New York, J. B. Ford and co., 1868.

xv, [17]–624 p. front. (port.) illus., plates, facsim. 22 cm.

Autobiographical reminiscences originally published as a series of newspaper articles; anecdotal and disjointed.

Green, Horace, 1885–
General Grant's last stand; a biography, by Horace Green; illustrated by facsimiles of letters and family portraits. New York, C. Scribner's sons; London, C. Scribner's sons ltd., 1936.

xvii, [1], 334 p. front., illus. (maps) plates, ports., facsims. 23 cm.

An unfolding of Grant's career as he recalled it while writing his Memoirs; Green relied on a host of unique sources, both primary and secondary.

Greenbie, Marjorie Latta (Barstow) 1891–
... My dear lady; the story of Anna Ella Carroll, the "great unrecognized member of Lincoln's cabinet" ... New York, London, Whittlesey house, McGraw-Hill book company, inc. [c1940]

xx, 316 p. front. (port.) illus. (maps) plates. 23½cm.

A sympathetic study of an unofficial--and questionable--adviser to Lincoln.

Greenbie, Sydney, 1889–
Anna Ella Carroll and Abraham Lincoln, a biography, by Sydney Greenbie and Marjorie Barstow Greenbie. [1st ed.] Manchester, Me., University of Tampa Press in cooperation with Falmouth Pub. House [1952]

xvi, 539 p. illus., ports., map. 22 cm.

An overdramatic defense of Miss Carroll; abounds with errors and unsupported conclusions.

Greenhow, Rose (O'Neal) 1814–1864.
My imprisonment and the first year of abolition rule at Washington. By Mrs. Greenhow. London, R. Bentley, 1863.

x, 352 p. front. (port.) 19½ cm.

A bitter, emotional account of her arrest and imprisonment by the famed Confederate spy.

Griffis, William Elliot, 1843–1928.
Charles Carleton Coffin, war correspondent, traveller, author, and statesman, by William Elliot Griffis ... Boston, Estes and Lauriat, 1898.

357 p. incl. front. port. 21cm.

The only biography of one of the few wartime newspaper reporters who remained on the job throughout the conflict; Coffin penned a number of weak books based on his observations.

Grimké, Archibald Henry, 1849–1930.

... Charles Sumner centenary, historical address, by Archibald H. Grimke ... Washington, D. C., The Academy, 1911.

18 p., 1 l. 23 cm.

Lavish in its praise of Sumner; emphasizes the political aspects of the struggle against slavery.

Grimké, Archibald Henry, 1849–1930.

William Lloyd Garrison, the abolitionist, by Archibald H. Grimke, M. A. New York [etc.] Funk & Wagnalls, 1891.

ix, [11]–405 p. front. (port.) 19 cm.

An uncritical narrative; only one chapter treats of the Civil War.

Hale, Edward Everett, 1863–1932.

... William H. Seward, by Edward Everett Hale, jr. Philadelphia, G. W. Jacobs & company [1910]

2 p. l., [3]–388 p. front. (port.) 19cm.

Half of this study treats of Seward's prewar career; the author also relied too heavily on other printed works.

Hale, William Harlan, 1910–

Horace Greeley, voice of the people. [1st ed.] New York, Harper [1950]

xiii, 377 p. port. 22 cm.

A detailed but readable study, based on Greeley manuscripts but not documented; somewhat narrow in perspective and interpretation.

[**Halpine, Charles Graham**] 1829–1868.

Baked meats of the funeral. A collection of essays, poems, speeches, histories, and banquets. By Private Miles O'Reilly [*pseud.*], late of the 47th reg't, New York volunteer infantry, 10th army corps. Collected, rev., and ed., with the requisite corrections of punctuation, spelling, and grammar. By an ex-colonel ... New York, Carleton, 1866.

viii, [3]–378 p. 18cm.

Poignant recollections and essays by the journalist-poet who created the humorous character, "Miles O'Reilly;" Halpine served early in the war with the 69th New York.

Hamersly, Thomas Holdup Stevens, *comp.*

Complete regular army register of the United States: for one hundred years (1779 to 1879) Together with the volunteer general staff during the war with Mexico, and a register of all appointments by the President of the United States in the volunteer service during the rebellion, with the official military record of each officer. Also, a military history of the Department of war, and of each staff department of the army. With various tables relating to the army and other important military information, comp. from the official records. Comp. ed. and pub. by Thomas H. S. Hamersly. Washington, T. H. S. Hamersly, 1880.

viii, 928, 381, xxxvi p. 24½ cm.

Useful for commanders and their assignments, but inferior to the compilations of Cullum and Heitman.

Hamilton, Charles, 1913–

Lincoln in photographs; an album of every known pose, by Charles Hamilton and Lloyd Ostendorf. [1st ed.] Norman, University of Oklahoma Press [©1963]

x, 409 p. illus., ports., facsims. 26 cm.

A collection of 119 photographs of Lincoln; also includes many pictures of Lincoln's family, friends and places identified with Lincoln's career.

Hamlin, Charles Eugene.

The life and times of Hannibal Hamlin; by his grandson, Charles Eugene Hamlin ... Cambridge, Printed at the Riverside press, 1899.

xi p., 1 l., 627 p. front., plates, ports., facsim. 25cm.

Inadequate and prejudiced, but the only usable study of Lincoln's first vice president.

Hamlin, Percy Gatling, 1894–

"Old Bald Head" (General R. S. Ewell) the portrait of a soldier, by Percy Gatling Hamlin. Strasburg, Va., Shenandoah publishing house, inc., 1940.

x p., 1 l., 216 p. maps. 23½ cm.

A sympathetic, appreciative account of Ewell's military career; Ewell, the author claims, possessed many qualities often lacking in our most celebrated heroes.

Hammond, James Henry, 1807–1864.

Selections from the letters and speeches of the Hon. James H. Hammond, of South Carolina. New York, J. F. Trow & co., printers, 1866.

iv, [5]–368 p. 24cm.

Contains the bulk of the South Carolinian's utterances; the correspondence reveals Hammond's strong pro-Confederate, anti-Davis views.

[Hancock, Almira (Russell)]
Reminiscences of Winfield Scott Hancock, by his wife. New York, C. L. Webster & company, 1887.
xiii, 340 p. incl. illus., ports. front., pl., ports. 23 cm.

Brief and sentimental; sheds disappointingly little light on Hancock's role in the war.

Harley, Lewis Reifsneider, 1866–
Francis Lieber; his life and political philosophy, by Lewis R. Harley, PH. D. New York, The Columbia university press, 1899.
x p., 1 l., 213 p. front. (port.) 23 cm.

Somewhat superficial; based on limited sources and emphasizes Lieber's political philosophy and writings.

Harrington, Fred Harvey, 1912–
Fighting politician, Major General N. P. Banks. Philadelphia, Univ. of Pennsylvania Press, 1948.
xi, 301 p. port., maps (on lining-papers) 23 cm.

A scholarly study, focusing on Banks' Civil War service and demonstrating, through Banks' career, the role of the political general in the conflict.

Harris, William Charles, 1933–
Leroy Pope Walker: Confederate Secretary of War. Tuscaloosa, Ala., Confederate Pub. Co., 1962 [c1961]
141 p. 22 cm.

A thoroughly researched, though brief study of the first and least-known of Davis' secretaries of war.

Harris, Wilmer Carlyle.
Public life of Zachariah Chandler, 1851–1875, by Wilmer C. Harris, PH. D. Lansing, Michigan historical commission, 1917.
5 p. l., [7]–152 p. ports. 23½cm.

A very unsatisfactory resume of Chandler's political career; the author attempted to study his subject "with reasonable impartiality."

Hart, Albert Bushnell, 1854–
... Salmon Portland Chase, by Albert Bushnell Hart. Boston and New York, Houghton, Mifflin and company [c1899]
ix p., 1 l., 465, [1] p. 18½ cm.

Based on an extensive collection of Chase papers, although without documentation; old but still a fine biographical study.

Hartje, Robert George, 1922–
Van Dorn, the life and times of a Confederate general [by] Robert G. Hartje. [Nashville] Vanderbilt University Press, 1967.
xiii, 359 p. maps, port. 25 cm.

An excellent biography of the enigmatic Southern general; the author made maximum use of the sparsity of source material on Van Dorn.

Hassard, John Rose Greene, 1836–1888.
Life of the Most Reverend John Hughes, D. D., first archbishop of New York. With extracts from his private correspondence. By John R. G. Hassard. New York, D. Appleton and company, 1866.
519 p. front. (port.) fold. facsim. 23 cm.

The only biography of the Catholic Archbishop of New York who labored unceasingly during the war for slave abolition and Union restoration.

Hassler, Warren W
General George B. McClellan, shield of the Union. [1st ed.] Baton Rouge, Louisiana State University Press [1957]
350 p. illus. 24 cm.

Not a full biography; devoted principally to McClellan's Civil War career; sympathetic and laudatory.

Hassler, William Woods.
A. P. Hill; Lee's forgotten general. Richmond, Garrett & Massie [1957]
249 p. illus. 24 cm.

A useful and documented study of one of the most neglected Confederate officers; the author was limited by a dearth of primary sources.

Hay, John, 1838–1905.
Lincoln and the civil war in the diaries and letters of John Hay; selected and with an introduction by Tyler Dennett ... New York, Dodd, Mead & company, 1939.
xii p., 1 l., 348 p. front. (port. group) 24 cm.

A highly useful abridgement of Hay's voluminous notes made during his career as a secretary to Lincoln; a basic source on the 16th President.

Hayes, Rutherford Birchard, *pres. U. S.*, 1822–1893.
Diary and letters of Rutherford Birchard Hayes, nineteenth president of the United States, edited by Charles Richard Williams ... ⌊Columbus, O.⌋ The Ohio state archæological and historical society, 1922–26.
5 v. fronts., plates, ports. 24½ cm.

Volume II contains the correspondence of the future president while he served as a general officer; the whole set is skillfully edited.

Haynes, George Henry, 1866–1947.
... Charles Sumner, by George H. Haynes ... Philadelphia, G. W. Jacobs & company ⌊1909⌋
469 p. front. (port.) 19 cm.

An adequate, balanced study that add little to previous biographies.

Headley, Joel Tyler, 1813–1897.
Grant and Sherman; their campaigns and generals. By Hon. J. T. Headley ... Comprising an authentic account of battles and sieges, adventures and incidents, including biographies of the prominent generals who brought to a triumphant close the great rebellion of 1861–1865 ... New York, E. B. Treat & co.; Chicago, C. W. Lilley; ⌊etc., etc.⌋ 1866.
608 p. front., plates, ports., maps. 22 cm.

More military than biographical--and very weak in both treatments.

Headley, Joel Tyler, 1813–1897.
The life of Ulysses S. Grant, ex-president of the United States and general of the United States Army, comprising his early training, military career, presidential administrations, travels round the world, sufferings and death. By Hon. J. T. Headley ... New York, E. B. Treat; Chicago, R. C. Treat, 1885.
xv, ⌊1⌋, ⌊17⌋–590, ⌊647⌋–656 p. front., illus., plates, ports., map. 21 cm.

Eulogistic; published in the year of Grant's death.

Headley, Phineas Camp, 1819–1903.
The patriot boy; or, The life and career of Major-General Ormsby M. Mitchel. By Rev. P. C. Headley ... New York, W. H. Appleton, 1865.
278 p. front., illus., plates, ports., map. 18cm.

Purposefully designed for younger readers; hence, lacking in scholarship.

Hebert, Walter H
Fighting Joe Hooker, by Walter H. Hebert. Indianapolis, New York, The Bobbs-Merrill company ⌊1944⌋
366 p. front., illus. (maps, plans) plates, ports., double facsim. 22cm.

A critical study, based on extensive research; contains a fine account of the Chancellorsville campaign.

Heitman, Francis Bernard, 1838–1926.
... Historical register and dictionary of the United States Army, from its organization, September 29, 1789, to March 2, 1903. By Francis B. Heitman. Pub. under an act of Congress approved March 2, 1903 ... Washington, Govt. print. off., 1903.
2 v. 26½ cm.

One of the most extensive coverages of Civil War officers; contains hundreds of brief biographies, many treating of now--obscure figures.

Henderson, George Francis Robert, 1854–1903.
Stonewall Jackson and the American civil war, by Lieut.-Col. G. F. R. Henderson ... London, New York ⌊etc.⌋ Longmans, Green and co., 1898.
2 v. 2 port. (incl. front.) 33 maps (part fold.) 23 cm.

In all, eighteen editions of this well-done study have appeared; while not achieving impartiality on Jackson, Henderson viewed the war with a detached objectivity.

Henry, Robert Selph, 1889–
"First with the most" Forrest, by Robert Selph Henry. Indianapolis, New York, The Bobbs-Merrill company ⌊1944⌋
558 p. front., illus., plates, ports., maps, facsims. 22 cm.

A carefully documented, detailed study of Forrest's wartime campaigns.

Hergesheimer, Joseph, 1880–
... Sheridan; a military narrative. Boston and New York, Houghton Mifflin company, 1931.

5 p. l., 3–381, [1] p. front. (port.) plates, maps (1 fold.) 23½ cm.

An inadequate biography that ends with the war; no analyses or evaluations were attempted.

Herndon, William Henry, 1818–1891.
Herndon's Lincoln; the true story of a great life ... The history and personal recollections of Abraham Lincoln, by William H. Herndon ... and Jesse William Weik ... Chicago, New York [etc.] Belford, Clarke & company; [etc., etc., ©1889]

3 v. front., plates, ports., facsims. (1 fold.) 20 cm.

Herndon, a devoted friend of Lincoln's, drew upon a multitude of sources for this study; in spite of exaggerations and erroneous conclusions, Herndon has contributed more than any other author to our knowledge of Lincoln.

Hesseltine, William Best, 1902–
Confederate leaders in the New South. Baton Rouge, Louisiana State University Press [1950]

xi, 146 p. 21 cm.

An excellent summary; more comprehensive and less specialized than Burger's study of the same subject.

Hesseltine, William Best, 1902–
Ulysses S. Grant, politician, by William B. Hesseltine. New York, Dodd, Mead & company, 1935.

xiii, 480 p. front., plates, ports., facsim. 24 cm.

This study of Grant's postwar career attempted to revise traditional views of the man as a politician.

Hibben, Paxton, 1880–1928.
Henry Ward Beecher: an American portrait, by Paxton Hibben. New York, George H. Doran company [©1927]

x p., 2 l., 15–390 p. front., plates, ports. 23½ cm.

A literary portrait, judicious in its presentation and based to some extent on original sources.

Higdon, Hal.
The Union vs. Dr. Mudd. Chicago, Follett Pub. Co., 1964.

235 p. illus., map, ports. 22 cm.

An exoneration of the physician who treated the broken leg of John Wilkes Booth; popularly written.

Higginson, Mary Potter (Thacher) 1844–1941.
Thomas Wentworth Higginson; the story of his life, by Mary Thacher Higginson; with portraits and other illustrations. Boston and New York, Houghton Mifflin company, 1914.

x p., 1 l., 435, [1] p. front., plates, ports. 22½cm.

A sensitive portrait written by Higginson's second wife; includes quotations from many of Higginson's letters and manuscripts.

Higginson, Thomas Wentworth, 1823–1911.
Letters and journals of Thomas Wentworth Higginson, 1846–1906, ed. by Mary Thacher Higginson. Boston and New York, Houghton Mifflin company, 1921.

4 p. l., 358 p., 1 l. front. (port.) 21 cm.

Topically, rather than chronologically, organized, this selection includes only one chapter on Higginson's service in the war.

Hill, Benjamin Harvey, *jr.*
Senator Benjamin H. Hill of Georgia; his life, speeches and writings, written and comp. by his son Benjamin H. Hill, jr. Also memorial addresses of eminent citizens of Georgia, senators and representatives in the Congress of the United States. Tributes of the press, north and south, and exercises attending the unveiling of the statue to his memory erected in the city of Atlanta by his grateful countrymen ... Atlanta, T. H. P. Bloodworth, 1893.

2 p. l., iii–ix, 11–823 p. front., plates, port. 24cm.

Partly biographical, partly documentary; includes speeches, letters, debates; worthwhile and useful in understanding Hill's life.

Hill, Louise Biles, 1891–
Joseph E. Brown and the Confederacy, by Louise Biles Hill, PH. D. Chapel Hill, The University of North Carolina press, 1939.

viii p., 2 l., 360 p. 23½ cm.

A well-documented and reliable study of Brown's wartime career as governor of Georgia; the author concluded that Brown was important in the failure of the South.

Hillard, George Stillman, 1808–1879.
Life and campaigns of George B. McClellan, major-general U. S. Army. By G. S. Hillard. Philadelphia, J. B. Lippincott & co., 1864.

396 p. front. (port.) 18½ cm.

An uncritical account written as a buttress for McClellan's presidential candidacy in 1864.

Hilliard, Henry Washington, 1808–1892.
Politics and pen pictures at home and abroad. By Henry W. Hilliard ... New York [etc.] G. P. Putnam's sons, 1892.

xi, 445 p. front. (port.) 23½ cm.

Eloquent memoirs by an Alabama Unionist remembered largely for his heated debates with William L. Yancey.

Hindes, Ruthanna.
George Alfred Townsend, one of Delaware's outstanding writers, by Ruthanna Hindes ... [Wilmington, Printed by Hambleton printing & publishing company, 1946]

72 p. incl. geneal. tab. front. (incl. ports.) 24cm.

This sole biography recaptures but part of the life and career of the famous war correspondent.

Hirshson, Stanley P 1928–
Grenville M. Dodge, soldier, politician, railroad pioneer [by] Stanley P. Hirshson. Bloomington, Indiana University Press [1967]

xiv, 334 p. illus., ports. 25 cm.

Error-filled and unconvincing, this study concentrates too heavily on but one facet of the life of the versatile Dodge.

Hoar, George Frisbie, 1826–1904.
Autobiography of seventy years, by George F. Hoar ... New York, C. Scribner's sons, 1903.

2 v. fronts. (ports.) 25 cm.

The oft-quoted memoirs of one of the Republican Party's most famous congressmen.

Holden, William Woods, 1818–1892.
... Memoirs of W. W. Holden. Durham, N. C., The Seeman printery, 1911.

viii, 199 p. 20cm.

Brief and superficial; only two of the five chapters cover Holden's involvement in North Carolina's wartime politics.

Holland, Cecil Fletcher, 1907–
Morgan and his raiders, a biography of the Confederate general, by Cecil Fletcher Holland. New York, The Macmillan company, 1942.

xiii, [2], 373 p. front., illus. (map) plates, ports., facsims. 22cm.

A sympathetic and fairly complete study of Morgan; based to a large extent on newly-discovered Morgan correspondence and papers.

Holland, Frederic May, 1836–1908.
Frederick Douglass: the colored orator. By Frederic May Holland ... New York [etc.] Funk & Wagnalls, 1891.

vi, [7]–423 p. front. (port.) 19 cm.

An admiring, sympathetic account, written during Douglass' lifetime and authorized by him.

Holland, Josiah Gilbert, 1819–1881.
Life of Abraham Lincoln, by J. G. Holland ... Springfield, Mass., G. Bill, 1866.

544 p. front., plates, port. 22 cm.

Interesting as the first full biography of Lincoln; the author eulogized him as a folk-hero whose life was shaped by God.

Hollister, Ovando James, 1834–1892.
Life of Schuyler Colfax. By O. J. Hollister ... New York [etc.] Funk & Wagnalls, 1886.

535 p. plates, 2 port. (incl. front.) facsim. 22½ cm.

An uncritical, laudatory biography by Colfax's brother-in-law.

Holzman, Robert S
Stormy Ben Butler. New York, Macmillan, 1954.
297 p. illus. 22 cm.

A relatively brief and sympathetic narrative of Butler's life and career; heavily documented but rarely penetrating.

Hood, John Bell, 1831–1879.
Advance and retreat. Personal experiences in the United States and Confederate States armies. By J. B. Hood ... New Orleans, Pub. for the Hood orphan memorial fund, 1880.
358 p. front., port., plans. 22½ cm.

The controversial, sometimes bitter, memoirs of a maimed Confederate general; reprinted in 1959.

[Hopley, Catherine Cooper]
"Stonewall" Jackson, late general of the Confederate States army. A biographical sketch, and an outline of his Virginian campaigns. By the author of "Life in the South." 2d ed. London, Chapman and Hall, 1863.
xiv, 178 p. front. (fold. map) 19cm.

One of the first tributes published to the Confederate general; as expected, the work is steeped in sentimentalism and short on scholarship.

Horan, James David, 1914–
Confederate agent, a discovery in history. New York, Crown Publishers [1954]
xxii, 326 p. illus., ports., maps, facsims. 25 cm.

Chiefly a biography of Thomas Hines, secret agent of the Confederacy; interesting but adds little of substance to Civil War history.

Horan, James David, 1914–
Mathew Brady, historian with a camera. Picture collation by Gertrude Horan. New York, Crown Publishers [1955]
xix, 244 p. illus., ports., map. 32 cm.

A praiseworthy attempt to present a complete biography of Brady, in spite of a lack of evidence; includes many Brady photographs not previously available to scholars.

Horan, James David, 1914–
Timothy O' Sullivan, America's forgotten photographer; the life and work of the brilliant photographer whose camera recorded the American scene from the battlefields of the Civil War to the frontiers of the West, by James D. Horan. [1st ed.] Garden City, N. Y., Doubleday, 1966.
xiv, 334 p. illus. 29 cm.

The best biography produced to date on a photographer who, during the war, ranked second only to Mathew Brady.

Horn, Stanley Fitzgerald, 1889– *ed.*
The Robert E. Lee reader. [1st ed.] Indianapolis, Bobbs-Merrill Co. [1949]
542 p. illus., ports. 23 cm.

A skillfully prepared "mosaic portrait" of Lee; composed of extracts from the writings of those who have studied him.

Horner, Harlan Hoyt, 1878–
Lincoln and Greeley. [Urbana] University of Illinois Press, 1953.
viii, 432 p. 26 cm.

An extremely weak study, sagging from long quotations, weak organization and--at times--the author's lack of understanding of the period.

Houston, Samuel, 1793–1863.
The writings of Sam Houston, 1813–1863; edited by Amelia W. Williams and Eugene C. Barker ... Austin, Tex., The University of Texas press, 1938–43.
8 v. 23cm.

Volume VIII covers adequately the small role the eminent Texan played in the war.

Howe, Mark De Wolfe, 1906–
Justice Oliver Wendell Holmes. Cambridge, Belknap Press of Harvard University Press, 1957–
v. illus., ports. 24 cm.

The first volume of a definitive biography of Holmes; covers his early years and includes his Civil War experiences; well-executed and soundly researched.

Howe, Samuel Gridley, 1801–1876.
Letters and journals of Samuel Gridley Howe, ed. by his daughter, Laura E. Richards ... with notes and a preface by F. B. Sanborn. Boston, D. Estes & company; [etc., etc., ©1906–©09]
2 v. fronts. (ports.) fold. map. 23½ cm.

A useful but rather poorly organized collection, with some connecting material by the editor, Howe's daughter.

Hoyt, Edwin Palmer.
Andrew Johnson, by Edwin P. Hoyt. Chicago, Reilly & Lee, 1965.
145 p. illus. 21 cm.

A brief survey written for young adults.

Hughes, Nathaniel Cheairs.
General William J. Hardee: Old Reliable. Baton Rouge, Louisiana State University Press [1965]
ix, 329 p. port. 24 cm.

An exceptionally thorough and well-written study of a long neglected military tactician and Confederate commander.

Hughes, Robert Morton, 1855–
... General Johnston, by Robert M. Hughes. New York, D. Appleton and company, 1893.
ix p., 2 l., 353 p. front. (port.) 6 maps. 19½ cm.

A rather brief, but defensive, summary of Johnston's life; Johnston personally selected Hughes as his biographer.

Hughes, William J
Rebellious ranger; Rip Ford and the old Southwest. [1st ed.] Norman, University of Oklahoma Press [1964]
xi, 300 p. illus., ports., map. 23 cm.

The best biography of James S. Ford, whose Civil War service was overclouded by his later more illustrious career as a Texas Ranger.

Humphreys, Henry Hollingsworth, 1840–
Andrew Atkinson Humphreys; a biography, by Henry H. Humphreys ... Philadelphia, The John C. Winston company, 1924.
xi, 335 p. front., plates, ports., facsim. 23cm.

Humphreys was a dependable but uninspiring division commander in the Army of the Potomac; this biography fits the subject.

Hunter, David, 1802–1886.
Report of the military services of Gen. David Hunter, U. S. A., during the war of the rebellion, made to the U. S. War department, 1873. New York, D. Van Nostrand, 1873.
55 p. front. (facsim.) 19cm.

This short autobiography is in essence an apologia by a controversial general whose wartime career matched his character.

Hunter, Martha T.
A memoir of Robert M. T. Hunter, by Martha T. Hunter ... with an address on his life (prepared for the Hunter monument association) by Col. L. Quinton Washington. Washington, The Neale publishing company, 1903.
166 p. front. (port.) 20cm.

A eulogistic compilation, far exceeded in value by Hunter's own correspondence and a later biography by Henry H. Simms.

Hunter, Robert Mercer Taliaferro, 1809–1887.
... Correspondence of Robert M. T. Hunter, 1826–1876; ed. by Charles Henry Ambler. Washington [Govt. print. off.] 1918.
383 p. 24½ cm.

A well-edited, extremely valuable collection of source material relating to the prominent Virginia political figure.

Hunton, Eppa, 1822–1908.
Autobiography of Eppa Hunton. Richmond, Va., The William Byrd press, inc., 1933.
xx, 268 p. front., ports. 22½cm.

Unfortunately, this memoir by a noted Virginia secessionist and postwar congressman concentrates on his service as colonel of the 8th Virginia Infantry.

[Hurlbert, William Henry] 1827–1895.
The life and services of Gen. Geo. B. McClellan ... [New York? Rand & Avery, 1864]
63 p. 24½cm.

A pamphlet designed to reinforce McClellan's candidacy in the 1864 election; totally eulogistic, partially factual.

Jackson, Mary Anna (Morrison) 1831–1915.
Memoirs of Stonewall Jackson by his widow, Mary Anna Jackson, with introductions by Lieut.-Gen. John B. Gordon and Rev. Henry M. Fields, and sketches by generals Fitzhugh Lee, S. G. French ... and Col. G. F. R. Henderson ... [2d ed.] Louisville, Ky., The Prentice press, Courier-Journal job printing company [1895]
xxiv, 647 p. front., illus. (incl. map) plates, ports. 26½ cm.

Written nearly thirty years after Jackson's death "expressly for his grandchildren;" includes many of Jackson's personal letters.

Jahns, Patricia.
Matthew Fontaine Maury & Joseph Henry, scientists of the Civil War. New York, Hastings House [1961]
308 p. 22 cm.

Brief biographies of two important 19th century scientists; interwoven, however, in such a manner as to reduce the impact of each.

Jellison, Charles Albert.
Fessenden of Maine, Civil War Senator. [Syracuse, N. Y.] Syracuse University Press [1962]
vi, 294 p. plates, ports. 24 cm.

A rather general study, primarily political but never probing deeply enough into the political problems with which Fessenden was identified.

Johnson, Bradley Tyler, 1829–1903, *ed.*
A memoir of the life and public service of Joseph E. Johnston, once the quartermaster general of the army of the United States, and a general in the army of the Confederate States of America ... Ed. by Bradley T. Johnson ... Baltimore, R. H. Woodward & company, 1891.
viii, 362 p. front. (port.) plates. 20 cm.

A highly sympathetic and strongly partisan account by a soldier who served with Johnston throughout the war.

Johnson, Richard W 1827–1897.
Memoir of Maj.-Gen. George H. Thomas, by Richard W. Johnson ... Philadelphia, J. B. Lippincott & co., 1881.
322 p. front., ports. 22 cm.

A brief, superficial and adulatory account of Thomas's military career; written by an associate.

Johnson, Thomas Cary, 1859–
The life and letters of Robert Lewis Dabney. By Thomas Cary Johnson. Richmond, Va., The Presbyterian committee of publication [1903]
xvi, 585 p. plates, 2 port. (incl. front.) geneal. tables. 24 cm.

The only study of merit of Jackson's chief of staff and wartime minister.

Johnson, Virginia Weisel.
The unregimented general; a biography of Nelson A. Miles. Illustrated with photos. and with maps prepared by Brigadier General W. M. Johnson. Boston, Houghton Mifflin, 1962.
401 p. illus., maps. 23 cm.

Barely thirty pages of this eulogistic study treat of Miles's unspectacular Civil War career.

Johnson, Willis Fletcher, 1857–1931.
Life of Wm. Tecumseh Sherman ... By W. Fletcher Johnson ... Carefully reviewed ... and with an introduction by Maj. Gen. O. O. Howard ... [Philadelphia] Edgewood publishing company, 1891.
607 p. incl. illus. (maps) plates, ports. front. 20cm.

An uncritical study, rather badly organized and containing testimonials to Sherman's greatness from many prominent individuals.

Johnson, Zachary Taylor.
The political policies of Howell Cobb, by Zachary Taylor Johnson ... Nashville, Tenn., George Peabody college for teachers, 1929.
187 p. illus. (maps) 22½ cm.

In keeping with its brevity, this volume makes a small contribution to both a knowledge and an understanding of Cobb.

Johnston, Joseph Eggleston, 1807–1891.
Narrative of military operations, directed, during the late war between the states, by Joseph E. Johnston, general, c. s. a. ... New York, D. Appleton and co., 1874.
602 p. front., ports., maps (1 fold.) 23 cm.

One of the earliest Confederate reminiscences; strongly partisan, anti-Davis, and defensive in tone; reprinted in 1960, with an incisive introduction by Frank E. Vandiver.

Johnston, Richard Malcolm, 1822–1898.
Autobiography of Col. Richard Malcolm Johnston. 2d ed. Washington, The Neale company, 1901.
190 p. front. (port.) 20 cm.

These memoirs by a prominent author-educator are especially revealing for insights into the character of Alexander H. Stephens.

Johnston, Richard Malcolm, 1822–1898.
Life of Alexander H. Stephens. By Richard Malcolm Johnston and William Hand Browne. Philadelphia, J. B. Lippincott & co., 1878.
619 p. front., port. 23cm.

An attempt to show Stephens' "inner nature;" written from materials supplied by Stephens and authorized by him before its publication.

Johnston, William Preston, 1831–1899.
The life of Gen. Albert Sidney Johnston, embracing his services in the armies of the United States, the republic of Texas, and the Confederate States. By William Preston Johnston ... New York, D. Appleton and company, 1878.
xviii, 755 p. incl. illus. (maps) front. (port.) plates. 23½cm.

An uncritical study by Johnston's son (himself a Confederate soldier); contains much quoted material.

Jones, Houston Gwynne, 1924–
Bedford Brown: state rights unionist. Carrollton, Ga., 1955.
54 p. illus. 24 cm.

A too-short study of a North Carolina statesman most remembered for several terms in the U. S. Senate.

Jones, James Sawyer, 1861–
Life of Andrew Johnson. Seventeenth president of the United States. By Rev. James S. Jones. Greeneville, Tenn., East Tennessee publishing company [1901]
400 p. front., plates, ports., facsim. 23 cm.

A superficial and uncritical study, authorized by Johnson's daughter and based on family materials.

Jones, John William, 1836–1909.
The Davis memorial volume; or, Our dead president, Jefferson Davis, and the world's tribute to his memory, by J. Wm. Jones ... Richmond, Va., B. F. Johnson & co., 1890.
xxiii p., 1 l., 27–672 p. incl. illus., plates, ports., facsims. plates, ports. 22 cm.

The best collection of eulogies to the Confederate president; some useful data will be found among the testimonials.

Jones, John William, 1836–1909.
Life and letters of Robert Edward Lee, soldier and man, by Rev. J. William Jones ... New York and Washington, The Neale publishing company, 1906.
9, [xi]–xii, [13]–486 p. front., ports. 23cm.

A tender, affectionate portrait by a former Washington College chaplain; contains many important Lee letters and dispatches.

Jones, John William, 1836–1909.
Personal reminiscences, anecdotes, and letters of Gen. Robert E. Lee. By Rev. J. William Jones ... ⟨Published by authority of the Lee family, and of the faculty of Washington and Lee university.⟩ New-York, D. Appleton and company, 1874.
xvi, 509 p. front., plates, ports. 23½ cm.

This potpourri of material is markedly inferior to Jones' later compilation on Lee; useful for those seeking minutae.

Jones, Virgil Carrington, 1906–
Ranger Mosby, by Virgil Carrington Jones. Chapel Hill, The University of North Carolina press, 1944.
xiii, 347 p. front., plates, ports. 23½ cm.

A popular study, conveying the romantic character of Mosby and his exploits; not fully documented but interestingly written.

Julian, George Washington, 1817–1899.
Political recollections, 1840 to 1872. By George W. Julian. Chicago, Jansen, McClurg & company, 1884.

384 p. 19½ cm.

Devoted principally to the facts and incidents of antislavery politics from 1840 to the "close of the work of Reconstruction."

Junkin, David Xavier, 1808–1888.
The life of Winfield Scott Hancock: personal, military, and political, by D. X. Junkin and Frank H. Norton. Illustrated on wood with battle-scenes by A. R. Waud, and steel portrait by Hall, from Sarony. New York, Appleton, 1880.

xiii, 398 p. illus., ports., maps. 20 cm.

A more than usually conscientious campaign biography; devotes considerable space to Hancock's Civil War campaigns.

Kamm, Samuel Richey.
... The civil war career of Thomas A. Scott ... ⌊by⌋ Samuel Richey Kamm. Philadelphia, 1940.

vi, 208 p. 23cm.

The only useful study of the man whose wartime activities as head of the Pennsylvania Railroad did much to preserve the Union.

Kearny, Thomas, 1878–
General Philip Kearny, battle soldier of five wars, including the conquest of the West by General Stephen Watts Kearny, by Thomas Kearny; with a preface by Frank Monaghan ... New York, G. P. Putnam's sons, 1937.

xv p., 1 l., 19–496 p. plates, 2 port. (incl. front.) plan. 24 cm.

A full but eulogistic study by Kearney's grandson; contains extensive quotations from contemporary sources and Kearney's letters.

Keyes, Erasmus Darwin, 1810–1895.
Fifty years' observations of men and events, civil and military. By E. D. Keyes ... New York, C. Scribner's sons, 1884.

vii, 515 p. 19½ cm.

Surprisingly void of material on Keyes, a second-line Union commander, but quite revealing for pen-pictures of such Union stalwarts as McClellan, Grant and Sherman.

Kibler, Lillian Adele, 1894–
Benjamin F. Perry, South Carolina unionist, by Lillian Adele Kibler. Durham, N. C., Duke university press, 1946.

xiii p., 2 l., 562 p. front., illus. (maps) plates, ports. 24cm.

A carefully researched, detailed and sympathetic study of an exemplar of Unionist and conservative thought in the antebellum and wartime South.

King, Charles, 1844–1933.
The true Ulysses S. Grant, by Charles King ... With twenty-eight illustrations. Philadelphia and London, J. B. Lippincott company, 1914.

6 p. l., 11–400 p. front., plates, ports., map. 20½ cm.

In this rather sentimental work, King sought to illuminate the virtues of the "true Grant," whom he felt earlier writers had neglected.

King, Willard Leroy, 1893–
Lincoln's manager, David Davis. Cambridge, Harvard University Press, 1960.

383 p. illus. 24 cm.

A scholarly and balanced account, based on the voluminous collection of Davis' manuscripts; includes many quotations from Davis' letters.

Kinsley, D A
Favor the bold; Custer: the Civil War years ⌊by⌋ D. A. Kinsley. ⌊1st ed.⌋ New York, Holt, Rinehart and Winston ⌊1967⌋–

v. map, ports. 22 cm.

Popularly written, this work treats only of Custer's Civil War career; lack of documentation and too much conversation make the whole suspect.

Kirwan, Albert Dennis.
John J. Crittenden; the struggle for the Union. ⌊Lexington⌋ University of Kentucky Press ⌊1962⌋

514 p. illus. 24 cm.

The definitive study of the career of Kentucky's eminent political leader.

Klein, Philip Shriver, 1909–
President James Buchanan, a biography. University Park, Pennsylvania State University Press [1962]
xviii, 506 p. illus., ports. 24 cm.

An impressively thorough study, based on sound and solid research; sympathetic to Buchanan and frequently defensive in its treatment.

Korngold, Ralph, 1886–
Thaddeus Stevens; a being darkly wise and rudely great. [1st ed.] New York, Harcourt, Brace [1955]
xiv, 460 p. 24 cm.

The author contended that Steven's great humanitarianism was a direct outgrowth of an unhappy childhood.

Korngold, Ralph, 1886–
Two friends of man; the story of William Lloyd Garrison and Wendell Phillips, and their relationship with Abraham Lincoln. [1st ed.] Boston, Little, Brown, 1950.
xii, 425 p. ports. 23 cm.

A popular, sympathetic study, emphasizing the antislavery movement before the Civil War.

Krug, Mark M 1915–
Lyman Trumbull, conservative radical [by] Mark M. Krug. New York, A. S. Barnes [1965]
370 p. ports. 22 cm.

An attempt to revise the standard picture of Trumbull as a radical; based on research in extensive Trumbull manuscripts.

Kunhardt, Dorothy (Meserve) 1901–
Twenty days; a narrative in text and pictures of the assassination of Abraham Lincoln and the twenty days and nights that followed—the Nation in mourning, the long trip home to Springfield, by Dorothy Meserve Kunhardt and Philip B. Kunhardt, Jr. Foreword by Bruce Catton. [1st ed.] New York, Harper & Row [1965]
312 p. illus., facsims., ports. 31 cm.

By far the best volume on the assassination of Lincoln; the illustrations alone are worth the cost of the book.

Lamers, William Mathias, 1900–
The edge of glory; a biography of General William S. Rosecrans, U. S. A. [1st ed.] New York, Harcourt, Brace [1961]
499 p. illus. 22 cm.

This scholarly biography is based largely on Rosecrans' papers; yet the author tends to exaggerate the General's talents and to minimize his shortcomings.

Lamon, Ward Hill, 1828–1893.
The life of Abraham Lincoln; from his birth to his inauguration as president. By Ward H. Lamon ... Boston, J. R. Osgood and company, 1872.
xiv p., 1 l., 547 p. front., plates, ports., plan, facsim. 23 cm.

Ghost-written by Chauncey F. Black; the study is unreliable and frequently displays Black's anti-Republican bias.

Langford, *Mrs.* Laura (Carter) Holloway, 1848–
Howard: the Christian hero, by Laura C. Holloway ... New York, London, Funk & Wagnalls, 1885.
iv, [5]–235 p. 19cm.

An early biography, now superseded in every respect by several recent, scholarly studies.

Larke, Julian K.
General Grant and his campaigns. By Julian K. Larke ... New York, J. C. Derby and N. C. Miller, 1864.
473, [3]–40 p. front. (port.) pl. 19cm.

An uncritical study of Grant, about whom the author concluded: "No military man of modern times has accomplished as much, with so little noise."

Larson, Henrietta Melia.
Jay Cooke, private banker, by Henrietta M. Larson ... Cambridge, Mass., Harvard university press, 1936.
xvii, 512 p. front., plates, ports., map, facsim. 22 cm.

An excellent biography of the well-known Union financier.

Lathers, Richard, 1820–1903.
Reminiscences of Richard Lathers; sixty years of a busy life in South Carolina, Massachusetts and New York; edited by Alvan F. Sanborn. New York, The Grafton press, 1907.
6 p. l., [3]–425 p. 4 pl., 9 port. (incl. front.) 24½ cm.

Lathers, a minor political figure, traveled from South to North to Europe during the war; his observations on political matters are often keen, but the memoir as a whole is overdone.

Lathrop, Henry Warren, 1819–
The life and times of Samuel J. Kirkwood, Iowa's war governor ... By H. W. Lathrop ... Iowa City, The author; [Chicago, Press of Regan printing house] 1893.
474, vi p. plates, ports. 22cm.

An early, authorized biography of Iowa's war governor; based on public documents and on correspondence furnished by Kirkwood.

Lawrence, Alexander A 1906–
James Moore Wayne, Southern unionist [by] Alexander A. Lawrence. Chapel Hill, The University of North Carolina press, 1943.
xiv, 250 p. pl., ports. 22 cm.

The best section of this definitive work recounts Wayne's career as a member of Roger Taney's Supreme Court.

Lee, Fitzhugh, 1835–1905.
... General Lee. By Fitzhugh Lee, his nephew ... New York, D. Appleton and company, 1894.
433 p. front. (port.) maps (2 fold.) 19½ cm.

An undistinguished study that includes copious extracts from Lee's private letters.

Lee, Robert Edward, 1807–1870.
Lee's dispatches; unpublished letters of General Robert E. Lee, C. S. A., to Jefferson Davis and the War department of the Confederate States of America, 1862–65, from the private collections of Wymberley Jones De Renne ... ed., with an introduction, by Douglas Southall Freeman. New York and London, G. P. Putnam's sons, 1915.
lxiii, 400 p. front. (port.) fold. map. 23½ cm.

Over 200 letters, expertly edited by Lee's definitive biographer; a newer edition, released in 1957 and edited by Grady McWhiney, contains ten dispatches omitted from the 1915 volume.

Lee, Robert Edward, 1807–1870.
"To Markie"; the letters of Robert E. Lee to Martha Custis Williams from the originals in the Huntington library, edited and with introduction by Avery Craven ... Cambridge, Harvard university press, 1933.
vii, 91 p. front. (port.) facsim. 20cm.

Thirty-nine letters written by Lee in the 1844-1870 period; the originals are in the Huntington Library.

Lee, Robert Edward, 1807–1870.
The wartime papers of R. E. Lee. Clifford Dowdey, editor; Louis H. Manarin, associate editor. With connective narratives by Clifford Dowdey and maps by Samuel H. Bryant. [1st ed.] Virginia Civil War Commission. Boston, Little, Brown [1961]
xiv, 994 p. facsim., maps. 24 cm.

Through Lee's correspondence, excellent editorial material, and fine maps, this volume presents a graphic history of the major Confederate army.

Lee, Robert Edward, 1843–1914.
Recollections and letters of General Robert E. Lee, by his son, Captain Robert E. Lee ... New York, Doubleday, Page & company, 1904.
xii p., 1 l., 461 p. 4 port. (incl. front.) 23½ cm.

Rather disjointed and sentimental; over half of the book treats of the postwar years; includes many of Lee's letters.

Lester, Charles Edwards, 1815–1890.
Life and public services of Charles Sumner. By C. Edwards Lester ... New York, United States publishing company, 1874.
3 p. l., 596 p. plates (1 double) 2 port. (incl. front.) 23½ cm.

A superficial, eulogistic statement published in the year of Sumner's death.

Lewis, Charles Lee, 1886–
Matthew Fontaine Maury, the pathfinder of the seas, by Charles Lee Lewis ... Annapolis, The United States naval institute, 1927.
xvii, 264 p. plates, ports. 24½ cm.

A general account that delves but lightly into the Civil War; based on Maury's papers, but lacks documentation.

Lewis, Lloyd, 1891–1949.
Captain Sam Grant. [1st ed.] Boston, Little, Brown, 1950.

viii, 512 p. port. 23 cm.

A sympathetic and absorbing portrayal of Grant's youth and service in the Mexican War; the book concludes with the outbreak of civil war.

Lewis, Lloyd, 1891–
Myths after Lincoln [by] Lloyd Lewis. New York, Harcourt, Brace and company [c1940]

x, 422 p. 22½ cm.

A provocative series of conjectures, facts and suppositions that concentrates on Lincoln's death; written in journalistic fashion and still rather controversial.

Lewis, Lloyd, 1891–
Sherman, fighting prophet, by Lloyd Lewis; illustrated with reproductions of maps, engravings and photographs. New York, Harcourt, Brace and company [c1932]

xii p., 1 l., 690 p. front., illus. (maps, facsim.) plates, ports. 24 cm.

An interesting, sympathetic (even defensive) study of Sherman; written with the flair of a journalist but historically sound.

Lewis, Walker.
Without fear or favor; a biography of Chief Justice Roger Brooke Taney. Boston, Houghton Mifflin, 1965.

viii, 556 p. port. 22 cm.

A sympathetic portrait; the book lacks analysis and falls short of relating Taney to wartime legal and constitutional issues.

Liddell Hart, Basil Henry, 1895–
Sherman; soldier, realist, American, by B. H. Liddell Hart ... with maps. New York, Dodd, Mead & company, 1929.

viii p., 2 l., 456 p. front. (port.) maps (part fold.) 24½ cm.

A sound, scholarly study of "the most original genius of the American Civil War."

Lieber, Francis, 1800–1872.
The life and letters of Francis Lieber; ed. by Thomas Sergeant Perry ... Boston, J. R. Osgood and company, 1882.

iv, 439 p. front. (port.) 23½cm.

Excerpts from Lieber's letters and journals, compiled under the direction of Lieber's widow; poorly balanced and frequently inaccurate.

Lincoln, Abraham, *Pres. U. S.*, 1809–1865.
Abraham Lincoln: his speeches and writings. Edited with critical and analytical notes by Roy P. Basler. Pref. by Carl Sandburg. New York, Grosset & Dunlap [1962, c1946]

xxx, 843 p. 21 cm.

The editor believes this selection to be most important from the standpoint of historical significance, literary quality, and human interest.

Lincoln, Abraham, *Pres. U. S.*, 1809–1865.
Collected works. The Abraham Lincoln Association, Springfield, Illinois. Roy P. Basler, editor; Marion Dolores Pratt and Lloyd A. Dunlap, assistant editors. New Brunswick, N. J., Rutgers University Press, 1953–55.

9 v. ports., facsims. 24 cm.

A complete collection of Lincoln's works, including letters, speeches, endorsements, etc.; the editor has provided both valuable textual criticism and full editorial annotation.

Lindsey, David.
"Sunset" Cox, irrepressible Democrat. Detroit, Wayne State University Press, 1959.

xx, 323 p. port. 21 cm.

A rather brief, though scholarly, study of a long political career; only a small portion of the book covers the Civil War years.

Linn, William Alexander, 1846–1917.
Horace Greeley, founder and editor of the New York tribune, by William Alexander Linn ... New York, D. Appleton and company, 1903.

xiii, 267 p. front. (port.) plates, facsims. 19½cm.

An adulatory account, based on limited research; the author devoted only one chapter to the Civil War.

... The **lives** of General U. S. Grant, and Henry Wilson. This work is a complete history of the lives of General Ulysses S. Grant, and of the Hon. Henry Wilson, from their birth up to the present time. With portraits of General U. S. Grant, Hon. Henry Wilson and other illustrative engravings. Philadelphia, T. B. Peterson & brothers [©1872]

1 p. l., 11–373 p. front., plates, port. 19cm.

Propaganda literature for the 1872 presidential race; as such, totally unreliable and unbelievably slanted.

Long, Armistead Lindsay, 1827–1891.

Memoirs of Robert E. Lee; his military and personal history, embracing a large amount of information hitherto unpublished, by A. L. Long ... together with incidents relating to his private life subsequent to the war, collected and edited with the assistance of Marcus J. Wright ... New York, Philadelphia [etc.] J. M. Stoddart & company, 1886.

1 p. l., 707 p. front., illus., plates, ports., maps (3 fold.) facsim. 25 cm.

Uncritical and superficial, with heavy emphasis on the military campaigns; by a former Confederate officer who served on Lee's staff.

Lothrop, Thornton Kirkland, 1830–1913.

... William Henry Seward, by Thornton Kirkland Lothrop. Boston and New York, Houghton, Mifflin and company, 1896.

vi, 446 p. 18 cm.

A general and, on the whole, balanced treatment; devotes considerable space to Seward's Civil War career.

Luthin, Reinhard Henry, 1905–

The real Abraham Lincoln; a complete one volume history of his life and times. Englewood Cliffs, N. J., Prentice-Hall [1960]

778 p. 24 cm.

A thorough, highly factual study, with emphasis on Lincoln's development as a politician.

Lytle, Andrew Nelson, 1902–

Bedford Forrest and his critter company, by Andrew Nelson Lytle ... New York, Minton, Balch & company, 1931.

ix, 402 p. front., illus. (maps) plates, ports. 24½ cm.

This highly sympathetic and partisan account concentrates on Forrest's wartime career; the author makes strong claims for the military genius of his subject.

McCabe, James Dabney, 1842–1883.

Life and campaigns of General Robert E. Lee. By James D. McCabe, jr. ... New York [etc.] Blelock & co.; Richmond, Va. [etc.] National publishing company, 1867.

717 p. front. (port.) fold. maps. 21cm.

More campaigns than life; the author attempted to present the events of the war in a fair and dispassionate manner.

McCabe, James Dabney, 1842–1883.

The life and public services of Horatio Seymour: together with a complete and authentic life of Francis P. Blair, jr. By James D. McCabe, jr. New York, United States publishing company; Cincinnati, O., Jones brothers & co.; [etc., etc.] 1868.

xiv p., 1 l., [17]–511 p. 2 front. (ports.) 23cm.

Designed to achieve the election of the Democratic ticket in 1868; contains extensive quotations from the utterances of Seymour and Blair.

McCall, Samuel Walker, 1851–1923.

... Thaddeus Stevens, by Samuel W. McCall. Boston and New York, Houghton, Mifflin and company, 1899.

vi p., 1 l., 369, [1] p. 18 cm.

A balanced, readable and fairly objective study; old, but in some ways still useful.

McClellan, George Brinton, 1826–1885.

McClellan's own story: the war for the Union, the soldiers who fought it, the civilians who directed it and his relations to it and to them; by George B. McClellan ... New York, C. L. Webster & company, 1887 [1886]

xiv, 678 p. incl. illus., pl., maps, facsim. front. (port.) 23½ cm.

Defensive in tone, the volume covers only the period of McClellan's generalship.

McClellan, Henry Brainerd, 1840–1904.

The life and campaigns of Major-General J. E. B. Stuart, commander of the cavalry of the Army of northern Virginia. H. B. McClellan ... Boston [etc.] Houghton, Mifflin and company; Richmond, Va., J. W. Randolph and English, 1885.

xv p., 1 l., 468 p. front. (port.) 7 fold. maps. 23½ cm.

Written by one who served with Stuart; its authenticity is enhanced by McClellan's eyewitness accounts; reprinted in 1958.

McClure, Alexander Kelly, 1828–1909.
Abraham Lincoln and men of war-times. Some personal recollections of war and politics during the Lincoln administration. With introduction by Dr. A. C. Lambdin. By A. K. McClure, LL. D. 2d ed. Philadelphia, The Times publishing company, 1892.

2 p. l., 3–462 p. front., illus., plates, ports., facsims. 23 cm.

A trustworthy study of Lincoln's relations with high-ranking members of his administration; the author relied on both memory and published works.

McClure, Alexander Kelly, 1828–1909.
The life and services of Andrew G. Curtin. An address by A. K. McClure, delivered in the House of representatives at Harrisburg, Pa., January 20, 1895. [Harrisburg] C. M. Busch, state printer of Pennsylvania, 1895.

35 p. front. (port.) 24½cm.

An eulogistic address on Pennsylvania's war governor.

McCormick, Robert Rutherford, 1880–
Ulysses S. Grant, the great soldier of America, by Robert R. McCormick. New York, London, D. Appleton-Century company, incorporated, 1934.

xviii, 343 p. front. (port.) maps (part fold.) 23½ cm.

As critical of Grant's subordinates as it is laudatory of Grant himself; the book covers only the Civil War years.

McCulloch, Hugh, 1808–1895.
Men and measures of half a century; sketches and comments, by Hugh McCulloch ... New York, C. Scribner's sons, 1888.

xxv, 542 p. 24 cm.

Relatively little of this huge autobiography treats of the author's service in the Treasury during Lincoln's administration.

MacDonald, Rose Mortimer Ellzey.
Mrs. Robert E. Lee, by Rose Mortimer Ellzey MacDonald ... Boston, New York [etc.] Ginn and company [©1939]

xxvi, 309, [1] p. incl. front., illus., ports. 20½cm.

A highly sympathetic study, too often marked by a displacement of fact with sentimentalism.

McElroy, Robert McNutt, 1872–
Jefferson Davis; the unreal and the real, by Robert McElroy ... New York and London, Harper & brothers, 1937.

2 v. fronts., illus. (facsim.) ports. 24½ cm.

McElory rather consciously attempted to vindicate Davis from the hostile accusations of the war period; somewhat superficial but easy to read.

McKee, Irving, 1909–
"Ben-Hur" Wallace, the life of General Lew Wallace. Berkeley, University of California Press, 1947.

301 p. illus., ports. 22 cm.

A sympathetic and well-written biography, but falls short in its discussion of the events in which Wallace participated.

McKinney, Francis F 1891–
Education in violence; the life of George H. Thomas and the history of the Army of the Cumberland. Detroit, Wayne State University Press, 1961.

530 p. illus. 25 cm.

Contains good accounts and analyses of Thomas's military operations, but based too much on printed sources.

McLaughlin, Andrew Cunningham, 1861–1947.
... Lewis Cass, by Andrew C. McLaughlin ... Boston and New York, Houghton, Mifflin and company, 1891.

vii p., 1 l., 363 p. 18 cm.

A study of Cass as representative of the growth and development of the Old Northwest; only the last chapter treats of the Civil War.

Macartney, Clarence Edward Noble, 1879–
Little Mac; the life of General George B. McClellan, by Clarence Edward Macartney ... Philadelphia, Dorrance and company [©1940]

ix p., 4 l., 19–363 p. front., illus. (maps) plates, ports. 23½cm.

Sympathetic and favorably disposed toward McClellan and hard on McClellan's superiors and critics.

Mansfield, Edward Deering, 1801–1880.

A popular and authentic life of Ulysses S. Grant. By Edward D. Mansfield. Cincinnati, R. W. Carroll & co., 1868.

377 p. front. (port.) illus. (maps) 20cm.

A campaign biography; treats almost wholly of the war years.

Marshall, Helen E.

Dorothea Dix, forgotten samaritan, by Helen E. Marshall. Chapel Hill, The University of North Carolina press, 1937.

xi, 298 p. plates, 2 port. (incl. front.) 23½ cm.

A critical, scholarly study of the famous humanitarian reformer who served during the war as Superintendent of U. S. Army Nurses.

Martyn, Carlos, 1841–1917.

Wendell Phillips: the agitator. By Carlos Martyn ... With an appendix containing three of the orator's masterpieces, never before published in book form, viz.: "The lost arts." "Daniel O'Connell." "The scholar in a republic" ... New York [etc.] Funk & Wagnalls, 1890.

xi p., 1 l., [15]–600 p. front. (port.) 19 cm.

A highly sympathetic treatment, with copious quotations from Phillips' utterances; three of Phillips' lectures are printed in the appendix.

[**Mason, Virginia**] 1833–1920, *ed. and comp.*

The public life and diplomatic correspondence of James M. Mason, with some personal history, by his daughter ... Roanoke, Va., The Stone printing and manufacturing co., 1903.

ix, 603 p. incl. front. (port.) 24cm.

Rather disjointed and unsatisfactory as a biography, but includes many of Mason's letters, speeches and documents.

Mathes, James Harvey.

... General Forrest, by Capt. J. Harvey Mathes ... New York, D. Appleton and co., 1902.

ix, 395 p. front., pl., port., maps, facsim. 19½cm.

An attempt to portray Forrest's life from early youth to his death, but with almost sole emphasis on his military service.

Maurice, *Sir* **Frederick Barton,** 1871–

Robert E. Lee, the soldier, by Major-General Sir Frederick Maurice; with portrait, maps, and plans. Boston and New York, Houghton Mifflin company, 1925.

vii p., 2 l., 313 p. front. (paper) maps (part fold.) facsim. 22½ cm.

"An appreciation of Lee's generalship;" Maurice judged Lee's actions against standards suggested by World War I.

Maurice, *Sir* **Frederick Barton,** 1871–

Statesmen and soldiers of the civil war; a study of the conduct of war, by Major General Sir Frederick Maurice ... Boston, Little, Brown, and company, 1926.

xi p., 2 l., [3]–173 p. front., plates, ports. 22 cm.

Widely used and quoted in spite of its age; poignant essays on such subjects as Lincoln, Davis, McClellan and J. E. Johnston.

Meade, George Gordon, 1815–1872.

The life and letters of George Gordon Meade, major-general United States Army, by George Meade ... ed. by George Gordon Meade. New York, C. Scribner's sons, 1913.

2 v. fronts. (v. 1, port.) fold. maps. 23½ cm.

Excerpts from Meade's letters, with a brief and general connecting narrative written by his son.

Meade, Robert Douthat, 1903–

... Judah P. Benjamin and the American civil war ... by Robert Douthat Meade. Chicago, Ill., 1944.

1 p. l., 34 p. 23cm.

A balanced, well-documented study, emphasizing Benjamin's role as a statesman in the Confederate government.

Mearns, David Chambers, 1899–

The Lincoln papers; the story of the collection, with selections to July 4, 1861; introd. by Carl Sandburg. [1st ed.] Garden City, N. Y., Doubleday, 1948.

2 v. (xvii, 681 p.) illus., ports. 22 cm.

A relatively small sampling of the extensive Robert Todd Lincoln Collection of Lincoln manuscripts (first opened to investigators in July, 1947).

Mercer, Philip.
The life of the gallant Pelham, by Philip Mercer. Macon, Ga., The J. W. Burke company [©1929]
180 p. front., plates, ports., map. 21 cm.

A brief, uncritical and somewhat romanticized study.

Meredith, Roy, 1908–
Mr. Lincoln's camera man, Mathew B. Brady, by Roy Meredith ... New York, C. Scribner's sons, 1946.
xiii, [2], 368 p. illus. (incl. ports., maps, facsims.) 31 cm.

A fine collection of Brady photographs, accompanied by a brief and general outline of Brady's life.

Merrill, Walter McIntosh.
Against wind and tide, a biography of Wm. Lloyd Garrison. Cambridge, Harvard University Press, 1963.
xvi, 391 p. illus., ports. 24 cm.

A thorough, scholarly study, based on extensive research in manuscript collections and carefully documented; good balance between Garrison and his times.

Merritt, Elizabeth, 1890–
James Henry Hammond, 1807–1864, by Elizabeth Merritt ... Baltimore, 1923.
viii, 9–151, [1] p. 24½cm.

The only biography of the South Carolina statesman who rested his faith in the belief that "cotton is king;" well-researched but lacking depth in presentation.

Meserve, Frederick Hill, 1865–
The photographs of Abraham Lincoln [by] Frederick Hill Meserve [and] Carl Sandburg. New York, Harcourt, Brace and company [1944]
1 p. l., 30 p. 95 pl. (incl. ports.) on 48 l. 24 cm.

A collection of the known photographs of Lincoln, with illuminating introductory essays by Carl Sandburg.

Meyer, Howard N.
Colonel of the black regiment; the life of Thomas Wentworth Higginson [by] Howard N. Meyer. Illustrated with photos. and engravings. [1st ed.] New York, Norton [1967]
xix, 346 p. illus., ports. 24 cm.

Undocumented, and filled with countless lengthy quotations, this study of the famed abolitionist colonel suffers as well from the author's over-fondness for his subject.

Michie, Peter Smith, 1839–1901.
... General McClellan, by General Peter S. Michie ... New York, D. Appleton and company, 1901.
ix, 489 p. 2 port. (incl. front.) plans (1 fold.) 19½ cm.

Although laudatory in many respects, the author's appraisal of McClellan's military qualifications is both thoughtful and balanced.

Miers, Earl Schenck, 1910–
Robert E. Lee, a great life in brief. [1st ed.] New York, Knopf, 1956.
203 p. 19 cm.

A delightful synthesis, brief yet capturing much of Lee's character.

Milham, Charles G
Gallant Pelham, American extraordinary. Introd. by U. S. Grant, 3rd. Washington, Public Affairs Press [1959]
250 p. illus. 24 cm.

This biography of the young artillerist whose life was cut short by the war is well-written but very dramatic.

Miller, Alphonse Bertram.
Thaddeus Stevens, by Alphonse B. Miller. New York and London, Harper & brothers, 1939.
xi p., 1 l., 440 p. front. (port.) 24½cm.

An undocumented, journalistic study, defensive in its treatment of Stevens; includes lengthy extracts from Stevens' speeches.

[Miller, E V D] *ed.*
A soldier's honor with reminiscences of Major-General Earl Van Dorn; by his comrades. New York, London [etc.] The Abbey press [c1902]

369 p. front. (port.) plates. 20½ cm.

This early, eulogistic study has now been interred by Hartje's more balanced and detailed biography.

Milne, Gordon.
George William Curtis & the genteel tradition. Bloomington, Indiana University Press, 1956.

294 p. illus. 24 cm.

A literary and intellectual biography of the antislavery reformer and columnist for <u>Harper's</u> during the war.

Mitchell, Stewart, 1892–
Horatio Seymour of New York [by] Stewart Mitchell. Cambridge, Mass., Harvard university press, 1938.

xx, 623 p. front., plates, ports., fold. maps, fold. geneal. tab. 24½ cm.

A sympathetic, thoroughly researched and documented study; provides excellent background for the political struggles in which Seymour was involved.

Mogelever, Jacob.
Death to traitors; the story of General Lafayette C. Baker, Lincoln's forgotten Secret service chief. [1st ed.] Garden City, N. Y., Doubleday, 1960.

429 p. illus. 22 cm.

Over-dramatic; while based on original sources, the work is lacking in documentation.

Monaghan, James, 1891–
Custer; the life of General George Armstrong Custer, by Jay Monaghan. [1st ed.] Boston, Little, Brown [1959]

469 p. illus. 22 cm.

Lively and comprehensive; treats of Custer both during and after the Civil War.

Monaghan, James, 1891–
... Lincoln bibliography, 1839–1939 ... Compiled by Jay Monaghan ... with a foreword by James Randall ... Springfield, Ill., Illinois state historical library, 1943–45.

2 v. x pl. on 5 l. 23 cm.

The basic listing for books on Lincoln, though the bibliography is now in need of revision; some omissions are evident.

Monaghan, James, 1891–
Swamp Fox of the Confederacy; the life and military services of M. Jeff Thompson. [Limited ed.] Tuscaloosa, Ala., Confederate Pub. Co., 1956.

123 p. illus. 22 cm.

An adequate study of a little-known figure whose service was primarily in the West.

Montgomery, Horace, 1906–
Howell Cobb's confederate career. [Limited ed.] Tuscaloosa, Ala., Confederate Pub. Co., 1959.

144 p. port. 22 cm.

A brief but excellent study of the eminent Georgian who chose to serve the Confederacy in a military capacity.

Moore, Ambrose Yoemans.
The life of Schuyler Colfax. By Rev. A. Y. Moore ... Philadelphia, T. B. Peterson & brothers [c1868]

2 p. l., 25-394 p. front. (port.) 19 cm.

Designed to promote Colfax's 1868 candidacy for vice president, this campaign biography includes a few of his letters and speeches.

Moore, Avery C
Destiny's soldier. San Francisco, Fearon Publishers [1958]

197 p. illus. 23 cm.

A superficial biography of Albert Sidney Johnston; inferior in every respect to Charles P. Roland's study of the same subject.

Morse, John Torrey, 1840–1937.
... Abraham Lincoln, by John T. Morse, jr. ... Boston and New York, Houghton Mifflin and company, 1893.

2 v. front. (port.) fold. map. 18 cm.

According to Basler, "the first account that dealt with Lincoln's entire life in an approximately unbiased manner."

Mosby, John Singleton, 1833–1916.
The memoirs of Colonel John S. Mosby, ed. by Charles Wells Russell ... Boston, Little, Brown, and company, 1917.

xxi, 414 p. front., pl., ports., fold. map. 22½ cm.

Written late in life with the assistance of his brother-in-law; includes some of Mosby's letters; reprinted in 1959.

Mosby, John Singleton, 1833–1916.
Mosby's war reminiscences, and Stuart's cavalry campaigns. By John S. Mosby ... New York, Dodd, Mead & company [1887]

256 p. 18½cm.

Originally a series of lectures printed first in newspapers and later in book form; reprinted without change in 1958.

Myers, Raymond E
The Zollie tree [by] Raymond E. Myers. With a foreword by Robert Emmett McDowell. [1st ed.] Louisville, Ky., Filson Club Press [1964]

xiii, 200 p. illus., maps, ports. 24 cm.

A successful study, based on extensive research, of Felix Zollicoffer, the Tennessee political figure and Confederate general.

Myers, William Starr, 1877–
A study in personality, General George Brinton McClellan, by William Starr Myers ... New York, London, D. Appleton-Century company, incorporated, 1934.

xiii, [1], 520 p. front., ports., maps, facsim. 23 cm.

A sympathetic analysis of McClellan's personality as the key to the problems he faced; contains little on his Civil War actions.

Nash, Charles Edward.
Biographical sketches of Gen. Pat Cleburne and Gen. T. C. Hindman; together with humorous anecdotes and reminiscences of the late civil war. By Charles Edward Nash ... Little Rock, Ark., Tunnah & Pittard, printers, 1898.

300 p. front., illus. 19½cm.

Of value because of the scarcity of data on either of these prominent Confederate generals in the West; full of gaps and badly dated.

Nason, Elias, 1811–1887.
The life and public services of Henry Wilson, late vice-president of the United States. By Rev. Elias Nason ... and Hon. Thomas Russell ... Boston, B. B. Russell; Philadelphia, Quaker city publishing house; [etc., etc.] 1876.

452 p. front. (port.) illus., pl. 19cm.

Eulogistic, with long quotations from Wilson's speeches and letters; written "to inspire working-men with confidence in themselves."

Neiman, Simon I 1904–
Judah Benjamin. With a foreword by Otto Eisenschiml. Indianapolis, Bobbs-Merrill [1963]

220 p. 22 cm.

This undocumented attempt to examine Benjamin's inner self adds little to an understanding of the man's role in the war crisis.

Nevins, Allan, 1890–
Frémont, the West's greatest adventurer; being a biography from certain hitherto unpublished sources of General John C. Frémont, together with his wife, Jessie Benton Frémont, and some account of the period of expansion which found a brilliant leader in the Pathfinder, by Allan Nevins ... New York and London, Harper & brothers, 1928.

2 v. fronts., plates, ports., maps (1 double) facsims. 24½ cm.

A critical, definitive and thoughtful account of a remarkably varied and controversial career.

Nevins, Allan, 1890– *ed.*
Lincoln: a contemporary portrait, edited by Allan Nevins and Irving Stone. [1st ed.] Garden City, N. Y., Doubleday, 1962.

226 p. 22 cm.

A series of useful and revealing essays on aspects of Lincoln's life; thirteen writers contributed as many chapters.

Nichols, Edward Jay, 1900–
Toward Gettysburg; a biography of General John F. Reynolds. [University Park] Pennsylvania State University Press, 1958.

x, 276 p. illus., ports., maps. 25 cm.

Based on all available sources, this full study does credit to the general who lost his life at Gettysburg.

Nicolay, John George, 1832–1901.
Abraham Lincoln; a history, by John G. Nicolay and John Hay. New York, The Century co., 1890.

10 v. fronts., illus., plates, ports., maps, facsims. 23½ cm.

The first comprehensive biography of Lincoln by two who knew him intimately; uncritical and eulogistic, yet possessed of much useful data not found elsewhere.

Noll, Arthur Howard, 1855–1930.
General Kirby-Smith, by Arthur Howard Noll ... Sewanee, Tenn., The University press at the University of the South [©1907]

3 p. l., v–vi p., 1 l., 293 p. front. (port.) 21cm.

Inasmuch as Noll included long excerpts from Kirby Smith's letters, he regarded his study as chiefly autobiographical.

Nye, Russel Blaine, 1913–
William Lloyd Garrison and the humanitarian reformers. [1st ed.] Boston, Little, Brown [1955]

215 p. 21 cm.

A brief interpretive study, focusing on Garrison's role in the pre-Civil War reform movements.

Oberholtzer, Ellis Paxson, 1868–1936.
Jay Cooke, financier of the civil war, by Ellis Paxson Oberholtzer ... Philadelphia, G. W. Jacobs & co. [1907]

2 v. fronts., illus., plates, ports., fold. map, facsims. (part fold.) 23 cm.

Comprehensive and reliable as a study of the Civil War banker; includes many documents pertaining to wartime finance.

O'Connor, Richard, 1915–
Hood, cavalier general. [1st ed.] New York, Prentice-Hall [1949]

x, 316 p. port., plans. 24 cm.

A rather general, somewhat uncritical account; based on standard sources, the book lacks documentation.

O'Connor, Richard, 1915–
Sheridan, the inevitable. Maps by Wilson R. Springer. [1st ed.] Indianapolis, Bobbs-Merrill [1953]

400 p. illus., ports., maps. 23 cm.

A careful though partial study of Sheridan; based on a wide collection of sources and written in a fluent and interesting style.

O'Connor, Richard.
Thomas, Rock of Chickamauga. [1st ed.] New York, Prentice-Hall [1948]

viii, 385 p. port., maps. 24 cm.

An uncritical study, vivid in its stylistic presentation but without adequate documentation.

O'Flaherty, Daniel.
General Jo Shelby, undefeated rebel. Chapel Hill, University of North Carolina Press [1954]

xiv, 437 p. port., map. 24 cm.

Popularly written; O'Flaherty regarded his Confederate subject as "the greatest cavalryman of them all."

Orrmont, Arthur.
Mr. Lincoln's master spy: Lafayette Baker. New York, Messner [1966]

191 p. 22 cm.

A shallow study of one whose truthfulness--if not his sanity--has long been questioned; Baker headed Lincoln's secret service.

Osterweis, Rollin, 1907–

Judah P. Benjamin, statesman of the lost cause, by Rollin Osterweis; foreword by Horace D. Taft ... New York, London, G. P. Putnam's sons, 1933.

3 p. l., v–xi, [1] p., 3 l., 19–205 p. front., plates, ports., facsim. 21cm.

Undocumented and brief; adds little to a knowledge of Benjamin's role in the war.

O'Sullivan, Timothy H.

T. H. O'Sullivan: photographer, by Beaumont and Nancy Newhall, with an appreciation by Ansel Adams. [Rochester, N. Y.] G. Eastman House [©1966]

1 v. (chiefly illus.) 21 x 22 cm.

This volume on a wartime photographer many regard as second only to Brady is composed more of O'Sullivan's pictures than of data on his unique career.

Page, Thomas Nelson, 1853–1922.

Robert E. Lee, the southerner, by Thomas Nelson Page ... with portrait. New York, C. Scribner's sons, 1908.

xiii, 312 p. front. (port.) 19½ cm.

A "brief memoir" that emphasizes Lee the man and attempts to restore the high reputation of the South.

[Palmer, Loomis T] *b.* 1844, *ed.*

The life of General U. S. Grant, his early life, military achievements, and history of his civil administration, his sickness and death, together with his tour around the world ... Ed. by L. T. Remlap [*pseud.*] ... Chicago, Fairbanks & Palmer pup. [!] co., 1885.

iv, 5–772 p. incl. illus., plates, ports., map, facsim. front., plates. 22 cm.

Highly laudatory; over half of the book treats of Grant's postwar journey around the world.

Palmer, George Thomas, 1875–

A conscientious turncoat; the story of John M. Palmer, 1817–1900, by George Thomas Palmer, with an introduction by Lloyd Lewis. New Haven, Yale university press; London, H. Milford, Oxford university press, 1941.

xi, 297 p. front. (port.) 24 cm.

A fast-moving, documented study of a Democrat-turned-Republican who followed a gallant Civil War career in the field by becoming governor of Illinois.

Parker, William Belmont, 1871–1934.

The life and public services of Justin Smith Morrill, by William Belmont Parker ... Boston and New York, Houghton Mifflin company, 1924.

viii p., 2 l., 378 p. incl. front. (port.) plates. 22½ cm.

A sympathetic study, told "as far as possible" in Morrill's own words; includes extensive quotations from his speeches, letters, diaries, etc.

Parks, Joseph Howard.

General Edmund Kirby Smith, C. S. A. Baton Rouge, Louisiana State University Press [1954]

viii, 537 p. illus., ports., maps. 22 cm.

Balanced and judicious, this study is based on a rich collection of source material; able in its analysis of Kirby Smith's wartime role.

Parks, Joseph Howard.

General Leonidas Polk, C. S. A., the fighting bishop. [Baton Rouge] Louisiana State University Press [1962]

408 p. illus., ports., maps. 24 cm.

An exhaustive and lucid presentation, emphasizing Polk's military career; carefully researched.

Parks, Joseph Howard.

John Bell of Tennessee. Baton Rouge, Louisiana State University Press [1950]

viii, 435 p. illus., port. 23 cm.

Sound, scholarly, documented, and well-written; the emphasis naturally is on Bell's unsuccessful candidacy for the presidency in 1860.

Parrish, William Earl, 1931–

David Rice Atchison of Missouri, border politician. Columbia, University of Missouri Press [1961]

271 p. illus. 23 cm.

A scholarly, reliable study of a controversial figure; the author attempted to treat Atchison and his career with understanding and impartiality.

Parton, James, 1822–1891.
The life of Horace Greeley, editor of "the New-York tribune," from his birth to the present time. By James Parton ... Boston, J. R. Osgood and co., 1872.
xi, [1], 548 p. front., plates, ports., facsim. 19cm.

An expanded edition of an earlier work; sketchy in content; includes many reprinted documents.

Pemberton, John Clifford, 1893–
Pemberton, defender of Vicksburg, by John C. Pemberton, with a foreword by Douglas Southall Freeman. Chapel Hill, The University of North Carolina press, 1942.
xiv p., 2 l., [3]–350 p. front., illus. (maps) plates, ports. 23½ cm.

As one might expect, this biography by a grandson is not without bias; adds little to the story of the Vicksburg campaign.

Pearce, Haywood Jefferson, 1893–
Benjamin H. Hill, secession and reconstruction [by] Haywood J. Pearce, jr. ... Chicago, Ill., The University of Chicago press [1928]
ix, 330 p. 20 cm.

A general but scholarly study based almost entirely on printed sources; only three of fourteen chapters treat of the war period.

Pendleton, Louis Beauregard, 1861–1939.
... Alexander H. Stephens, by Louis Pendleton. Philadelphia, G. W. Jacobs & company [1908]
406 p. front. (port.) 19½ cm.

A fairly balanced biography, based on a variety of printed sources.

Pearson, Henry Greenleaf, 1870–
James S. Wadsworth of Geneseo, brevet major-general of United States volunteers, by Henry Greenleaf Pearson ... New York, C. Scribner's sons, 1913.
vi p., 4 l., 321 p. front., plates, ports., maps (1 fold.) fold. facsims., fold. geneal. tab. 26½ cm.

Marred by a lack of source material, this is still a creditable biography of a politician-soldier killed in 1864.

Pennypacker, Isaac Rusling, 1852–1935.
... General Meade, by Isaac R. Pennypacker ... New York, D. Appleton and company, 1901.
ix, 402 p. front. (port.) plates, maps (part fold.) facsim. 19½cm.

A general and uncritical account of Meade's Civil War campaigns, with almost no coverage of his prewar or postwar years.

Pearson, Henry Greenleaf, 1870–
The life of John A. Andrew, governor of Massachusetts, 1861–1865, by Henry Greenleaf Pearson ... Boston and New York, Houghton, Mifflin and company, 1904.
2 v. fronts., double pl., ports., facsims. 22½ cm.

Focuses almost exclusively on Andrew's years as Massachusetts' war governor; based on his personal and official correspondence.

Pereyra, Lillian A
James Lusk Alcorn; persistent Whig [by] Lillian A. Pereyra. [Baton Rouge] Louisiana State University Press, 1966.
xv, 237 p. illus., ports. 24 cm.

Based on primary sources and analytical in approach; the author attempts to place the "contradictions and ambiguities" of Alcorn's career in a meaningful context.

Peele, William Joseph, 1855– *comp.*
Lives of distinguished North Carolinians, with illustrations and speeches; collected and compiled by W. J. Peele ... Raleigh [The North Carolina publishing society] 1898.
605 p. front., ports. 23 cm.

Included in this work are short sketches of J. J. Pettigrew, W. D. Pender, S. D. Ramseur, Bryan Grimes, and D. H. Hill.

Perkins, Jacob Randolph, 1878–
Trails, rails and war: the life of General G. M. Dodge, by J. R. Perkins ... Indianapolis, The Bobbs-Merrill company [c1929]
xix p., 1 l., 371 p. front., plates, ports., facsims. 23 cm.

Contains all the weaknesses that one would expect in a sympathetic biography by a nonprofessional.

Peterson, Norma Lois.

Freedom and franchise; the political career of B. Gratz Brown, by Norma L. Peterson. Columbia, University of Missouri Press [1965]

252 p. 24 cm.

Scholarly and competent in its portrayal of a minor political figure who left few papers.

Petigru, James Louis, 1789–1863.

Life, letters and speeches of James Louis Petigru, the Union man of South Carolina, by James Petigru Carson, E. M.; with an introduction by Gaillard Hunt ... Washington, D. C., W. H. Lowdermilk & co., 1920.

xxiii, 497 p. front., plates, ports., facsim. 23 cm.

Essentially a collection of Petigru's letters and speeches, with some connecting and explanatory material by the author, Petigru's grandson.

Phelps, Mary Merwin.

Kate Chase, dominant daughter; the life story of a brilliant woman and her famous father, by Mary Merwin Phelps. New York, Thomas Y. Crowell company [c1935]

2 p., 1 l., 316 p. front., plates, ports. 23 cm.

A fair and full study of the cabinet member's daughter who dominated wartime Washington society.

Phillips, Ulrich Bonnell, 1877–1934.

The life of Robert Toombs, by Ulrich Bonnell Phillips ... New York, The Macmillan company, 1913.

ix p., 2 l., [3]–281 p. front. (port.) 21½cm.

Though somewhat dated, this is still a judicious and scholarly biography by one of the South's great interpreters.

Phillips, Wendell, 1811–1884.

Speeches, lectures, and letters, by Wendell Phillips. Boston, Lee and Shepard, 1892, '91.

2 v. fronts. (ports.) 20½ cm.

A selection, without editorial comment, of Phillips' public statements.

Piatt, Donn, 1819–1891.

General George H. Thomas, a critical biography, by Donn Piatt; with concluding chapters by Henry V. Boynton. Cincinnati, R. Clarke & co., 1893.

viii, 13–658 p. front. (port.) maps. 24cm.

A defensive study of the general whose "great life is a lesson and an example to the living"; prefaced by a discussion of the causes of the war.

Piatt, Donn, 1819–1891.

Memories of the men who saved the union, by Donn Piatt. New York and Chicago, Belford, Clarke & company, 1887.

3 p. l., [v]–xxvi, [27]–302 p. front., plates, ports. 19½ cm.

Another group of shallow, eulogistic essays; the subjects here are Lincoln, Stanton, Chase, Seward and G. H. Thomas.

Pierce, Edward Lillie, 1829–1897.

Memoir and letters of Charles Sumner. By Edward L. Pierce ... Boston, Roberts brothers, 1877–93.

4 v. fronts. (ports.) plan, facsims. 23 cm.

A full and useful collection, documented and with considerable connecting material by Pierce.

Pinchon, Edgcumb, 1883–

Dan Sickles, hero of Gettysburg and "Yankee king of Spain," by Edgcumb Pinchon. Garden City, New York, Doubleday, Doran and company, inc., 1945.

xiii p., 1 l., 276 p., 1 l., 277–280 p. front., illus. (facsims.) plates, ports. 22cm.

A dramatic, but not altogether successful, attempt to relate Sickles' life in novel form.

Pinkerton, Allan, 1819–1884.

The spy of the rebellion; being a true history of the spy system of the United States Army during the late rebellion. Revealing many secrets of the war hitherto not made public. Comp. from official reports prepared for President Lincoln, General McClellan and the provost-marshal-general. By Allan Pinkerton ... New York, G. W. Carleton & co., 1883.

[ix]–xxxii, 33–688 p. illus., 24 pl. (incl. front.) 24 cm.

The personal story of one of the war's top secret agents; however, great caution must be exercised in accepting any part of Pinkerton's account.

Pleasants, Samuel Augustus, 1918–

Fernando Wood of New York. New York, Columbia Univ. Press, 1948.

216 p. 23 cm.

A satisfactory study; limited in its portrayal of Wood's character and activities by the fragmentary nature of his papers.

Polk, William Mecklenburg, 1844–1918.

Leonidas Polk, bishop and general, by William M. Polk ... New York, Longmans, Green, and co., 1893.

2 v. illus., plates (part fold.) ports. (incl. fronts.) maps. 20 cm.

Written by Bishop Polk's son and others; some value lies in the many documents reproduced (although their transcription was not always correct).

Pollard, Edward Alfred, 1831–1872.

Lee and his lieutenants; comprising the early life, public services, and campaigns of General Robert E. Lee and his companions in arms, with a record of their campaigns and heroic deeds ... By Edward A. Pollard ... New York, E. B. Treat & co.; Baltimore, Md., J. S. Morrow; [etc., etc.] 1867.

vi p., 1 l., [9]–851 p. front., pl., ports. 25cm.

A volume showing that the outspoken Richmond newspaper editor at times wrote too much and said too little; this inferior work was republished in 1870 under its subtitle.

Pollard, Edward Alfred, 1831–1872.

Life of Jefferson Davis, with a secret history of the Southern Confederacy, gathered "behind the scenes in Richmond." Containing curious and extraordinary information of the principal southern characters in the late war, in connection with President Davis, and in relation to the various intrigues of his administration. By Edward A. Pollard ... Philadelphia, Chicago [etc.] National pub. co. [1869]

viii, 536 p. front. (port.) 22½ cm.

Pollard regarded his subject with thinly veiled hostility; he charged him with incompetence, self-delusion--and responsibility for the failure of the Confederacy.

Poore, Benjamin Perley, 1820–1887.

The life and public services of Ambrose E. Burnside, soldier, — citizen, — statesman. By Ben: Perley Poore, with an introduction by Henry B. Anthony ... Providence, R. I., J. A. & R. A. Reid, 1882.

448 p. front., illus. (incl. maps) ports. 23½cm.

An old and ineffectual attempt to refurbish the reputation of Burnside; less than half of the book treats of the Civil War.

Poore, Benjamin Perley, 1820–1887.

Perley's reminiscences of sixty years in the national metropolis ... By Ben: Perley Poore ... Philadelphia [etc.] Hubbard brothers; New York, W. A. Houghton; [etc., etc., 1886]

2 v. fronts., illus. (incl. ports., facsims.) 23 cm.

Volume II covers the war period; best for comments on public men.

Pratt, Fletcher, 1897–

Stanton, Lincoln's Secretary of War. [1st ed.] New York, Norton [1953]

xiii, 520 p. port., maps. 22 cm.

A popularly written study, emphasizing Stanton's prewar and wartime careers.

Procter, Ben H

Not without honor; the life of John H. Reagan. Austin, University of Texas Press [1962]

xii, 361 p. illus., ports. 24 cm.

A sympathetic but scholarly study of the long career of the man who served as Confederate Postmaster General.

Quarles, Benjamin.

Frederick Douglass. Washington, Associated Publishers [1948]

xi, 378 p. illus., ports. 21 cm.

A sound, critical and scholarly study based on extensive research; the biography of Douglass.

Quynn, Dorothy Louise (Mackay) 1899–

Barbara Frietschie, by Dorothy Mackay Quynn and William Rogers Quynn ... Baltimore, Maryland historical society, 1942.

2 p. l., 45 p. front. (port.) 1 illus. 23½cm.

The deepest treatment of a still-unresolved controversy.

Ranck, James Byrne.

... Albert Gallatin Brown, radical southern nationalist, by James Byrne Ranck ... New York, London, D. Appleton-Century company, incorporated [c1937]

xiv p., 3 l., 320 p. front. (port.) maps. 23 cm.

A fine study of one of the South's ardent nationalists; based on thorough examination of sources and scholarly in its presentation.

Randall, James Garfield, 1881–

Lincoln and the South [by] J. G. Randall ... Baton Rouge, Louisiana state university press, 1946.

viii p., 2 l., 161 p. ports., facsims. 21 cm.

Four lectures reveal in provocative and interesting style Lincoln's strong sympathies throughout the war for the area of his heritage.

Randall, James Garfield, 1881–1953.

Lincoln, the President. New York, Dodd, Mead, 1945–55.

4 v. illus., ports., maps, facsims. 25 cm.

A definitive, scholarly biography, encompassing more than the title indicates; probably the best and most complete study of Lincoln's life.

Randall, Ruth (Painter)

Colonel Elmer Ellsworth; a biography of Lincoln's friend and first hero of the Civil War. [1st ed.] Boston, Little, Brown [1960]

295 p. illus. 22 cm.

A sensitive, sympathetic account of the youthful leader popularly regarded as the first casualty of the Civil War.

Rawley, James A

Edwin D. Morgan, 1811–1883; merchant in politics. New York, Columbia University Press, 1955.

321 p. port., map. 24 cm.

The definitive study of one of New York's wartime senators and national chairman of the Republican Party from 1856 to 1864.

Raymond, Henry Jarvis, 1820–1869.

The life and public services of Abraham Lincoln ... Together with his state papers, including his speeches, addresses, messages, letters, and proclamations, and the closing scenes connected with his life and death. To which are added anecdotes and personal reminiscences of President Lincoln, by Frank B. Carpenter. New York, Derby and Miller, 1865.

808 p. plates, ports., facsim. 24 cm.

An attempt to bring together every speech and document from Lincoln's pen; connected by a rather sketchy narrative; much of Lincoln's life is omitted.

Rea, Ralph R

Sterling Price; the Lee of the West. Little Rock, Ark., Pioneer Press [1959]

229 p. illus. 24 cm.

A rather inadequate, unbalanced study, overly detailed in some respects.

Reagan, John Henninger, 1818–1905.

Memoirs, with special reference to secession and the civil war, by John H. Reagan ... ed. by Walter Flavius McCaleb ... with introduction by George P. Garrison ... New York and Washington, The Neale publishing company, 1906.

351 p. front., pl., ports. 23 cm.

These recollections by the Confederate Postmaster General were written in part to justify the South's cause.

Reavis, Logan Uriah, 1831–1889.

The life and military services of Gen. William Selby Harney. By L. U. Reavis ... Introduction by Gen. Cassius M. Clay. Saint Louis, Bryan, Brand & co., 1878.

2 p. l., [iii]–xvii, 18–477 p. incl. illus., plates, ports. front., ports. 22cm.

An outdated biography of a professional soldier and Mexican War hero deprived of active Civil War command because of suspected Southern sympathies.

Rice, Harvey Mitchell, 1907–

The life of Jonathan M. Bennett, a study of the Virginias in transition, by Harvey Mitchell Rice. Chapel Hill, The University of North Carolina press, 1943.

xiii p., 1 l., 300 p. front. (port.) facsim. 23½cm.

The definitive biography of a prominent Virginian who served during the war as the state's auditor.

Rice, Jessie Pearl, 1901–
J. L. M. Curry, southerner, statesman and educator. New York, King's Crown Press, 1949.
xii, 242 p. 24 cm.

A sympathetic but not uncritical study based on extensive research.

Richards, Laura Elizabeth (Howe) 1850–1943.
Julia Ward Howe, 1819–1910, by Laura E. Richards and Maud Howe Elliott, assisted by Florence Howe Hall; with portraits and other illustrations ... Boston and New York, Houghton Mifflin company, 1915.
2 v. fronts., plates, ports., fold. facsim. 24cm.

A biography of the author of the "Battle Hymn of the Republic;" by her two daughters; includes extensive excerpts from her letters and diary.

Richardson, Albert Deane, 1833–1869.
A personal history of Ulysses S. Grant, illustrated by twenty-six engravings; eight fac-similes of letters from Grant, Lincoln, Sheridan, Buckner, Lee, etc.; and six maps. With a portrait and sketch of Schuyler Colfax, by Albert D. Richardson ... Hartford, Conn., American publishing company; Chicago, Ill., G. & C. W. Sherwood; [etc., etc.] 1868.
xiv p., 1 l., [17]–560 p. front., illus. (maps, facsims.) plates, ports. 23cm.

An undistinguished campaign biography, episodic and replete with improbable dialogue.

Richardson, Elmo R
John Palmer Usher, Lincoln's Secretary of the Interior, by Elmo R. Richardson and Alan W. Farley. Lawrence, University of Kansas Press, 1960.
152 p. illus. 22 cm.

An unspectacular study of an unspectacular official.

Richardson, Eudora (Ramsay) 1892–
Little Aleck; a life of Alexander H. Stephens, the fighting vice-president of the confederacy, by E. Ramsay Richardson ... Indianapolis, The Bobbs-Merrill company [c1932]
5 p. l., xiii–xiv p., 1 l., 17–359 p. front., pl., ports. 22½ cm.

This smooth-flowing narrative emphasizes Stephens' personal life; yet it lacks satisfactory analysis, adequate background data, and documentation.

Riddle, Albert Gallatin, 1816–1902.
The life of Benjamin F. Wade, by A. G. Riddle ... Cleveland, O., W. W. Williams, 1887.
310 p. front. (port.) 19 cm.

Brief, superficial, and full of praise for the subject; originally a series of articles in the Magazine of Western History.

Riddle, Albert Gallatin, 1816–1902.
Recollections of war times; reminiscences of men and events in Washington, 1860–1865. By Albert Gallatin Riddle ... New York [etc.] G. P. Putnam's sons, 1895.
xii p., 1 l., 380 p. 23½ cm.

Colorful pictures of wartime politics by a congressman who spent most of his time in Washington.

Riddleberger, Patrick W
George Washington Julian, radical Republican; a study in nineteenth-century politics and reform, by Patrick W. Riddleberger. [Indianapolis] Indiana Historical Bureau, 1966.
xiii, 344 p. ports. 24 cm.

A sound, critical and scholarly study; the product of an examination of Julian's papers.

Robertson, Archibald Thomas, 1863–
Life and letters of John Albert Broadus. By Archibald Thomas Robertson ... Philadelphia, American Baptist publication society, 1901.
xiv, 462 p. 3 port. (incl. front.) 2 fold. facsim. 20 cm.

The only worthwhile study of a prominent Baptist clergyman who served in the last months of the war as an aide-de-camp to Gov. Zebulon Vance.

Robins, Edward, 1862–
... William T. Sherman, by Edward Robins ... Philadelphia, G. W. Jacobs & company [c1905]
352 p. front. (port.) double map. 19½cm.

A standard, undistinguished account of "one of the greatest figures in the history of the nineteenth century."

Roland, Charles P

Albert Sidney Johnston, soldier of three republics, by Charles P. Roland. Austin, University of Texas Press [1964]

xi, 384 p. illus., plans, ports. 24 cm.

Complete, well-rounded and scholarly; the author made excellent use of Johnston's papers.

Roman, Alfred, 1824–

The military operations of General Beauregard in the war between the states, 1861 to 1865; including a brief personal sketch and a narrative of his services in the war with Mexico, 1846–8, by Alfred Roman ... New York, Harper & brothers, 1884.

2 v. fronts. (ports.) pl., map. 23 cm.

This work is highly laudatory of its subject and highly critical of Beauregard's enemies; the General himself penned a good part of the text.

Rose, Victor M

The life and services of Gen. Ben McCulloch, by Victor M. Rose. Philadelphia, Pictorial bureau of the press, 1888.

2 p. l., [25]–260 p. illus., port. 23 cm.

The standard study of the ill-fated Texas Ranger; its age becomes increasingly glaring.

Ross, Ishbel, 1897–

Angel of the Battlefield; the life of Clara Barton. [1st ed.] New York, Harper [1956]

xi, 305 p. illus., ports., facsims. 22 cm.

Popularly written and weakly researched, this work is markedly inferior to William E. Barton's older study.

Ross, Ishbel, 1897–

Rebel Rose; life of Rose O'Neal Greenhow, Confederate spy. [1st ed.] New York, Harper [1954]

294 p. illus. 22 cm.

A popular biography of a spirited and controversial woman.

Ross, Sam, 1912–

The empty sleeve, a biography of Lucius Fairchild. Madison, State Historical Society of Wisconsin for the Wisconsin Civil War Centennial Commission, 1964.

291 p. illus., facsim., map, ports. 24 cm.

A well-balanced, documented study of the Wisconsin soldier-politician; yet only a small portion of the book treats of the war.

Rowland, Eron Opha (Moore)

Varina Howell, wife of Jefferson Davis, by Eron Rowland (Mrs. Dunbar Rowland) ... New York, The Macmillan company, 1927–31.

2 v. front., pl., ports. 22½ cm.

Extensively researched, but seriously impaired by the author's extravagant admiration of her subject.

Ruffin, Thomas, 1787–1870.

... The papers of Thomas Ruffin; collected and ed. by J. G. de Roulhac Hamilton ... Raleigh, Edwards & Broughton printing co., state printers, 1918–20.

4 v. front. (port.) geneal. tab. 25 cm.

Ruffin served in the pre-war period as chief justice of the North Carolina Supreme Court; in his last years he was an ardent secessionist and supporter of the Confederate cause.

Russell, Charles Edward, 1860–1941.

The story of Wendell Phillips: soldier of the common good, by Charles Edward Russell ... Chicago, C. H. Kerr & company [c1914]

185 p. 17cm.

A brief, appreciative study, focussing on Phillips' labor reform activity.

Sanborn, Franklin Benjamin, 1831–1917.

Dr. S. G. Howe, the philanthropist, by F. B. Sanborn. New York [etc.] Funk & Wagnalls, 1891.

viii p., 1 l., [11]–370 p. front. (port.) 19 cm.

A eulogistic and superficial study of the great 19th century reformer.

Sanborn, Margaret.
Robert E. Lee. [1st ed.] Philadelphia, Lippincott [1966–

v. illus., ports. 25 cm.

Too much reliance on outdated sources, plus the author's slow but steady emotional involvement with Lee, sap the strength of this two-volume biography.

Sandburg, Carl, 1878–
Abraham Lincoln, the prairie years, by Carl Sandburg; with 105 illustrations from photographs, and many cartoons, sketches, ~~maps, and letters~~ ... New York, Harcourt, Brace & company [1927]

2 v. fronts., illus. (incl. maps) plates, ports., facsims. 24 cm.

Sandburg, Carl, 1878–
Abraham Lincoln; the war years, by Carl Sandburg. With 414 half-tones of photographs and 249 cuts of cartoons, letters, documents ... New York, Harcourt, Brace & company [©1939]

4 v. fronts., illus. (incl. maps) plates, ports., facsims. 24½ cm.

Classics in the Lincoln field, these works qualify as literature as well as history; a sensitive, sympathetic portrayal, in essentially human terms, of Lincoln and his age.

Sanger, Donald Bridgman, 1889–1947.
James Longstreet: I. Soldier, by Donald Bridgman Sanger. II. Politician, officeholder, and writer, by Thomas Robson Hay. Baton Rouge, Louisiana State University Press [1952]

viii, 460 p. ports, maps, facsim. 25 cm.

The first section is a competent and sympathetic re-evaluation of Longstreet's military career; the second sheds considerable light on the obscurity of his postwar career.

Sarmiento, Ferdinand L.
Life of Pauline Cushman. The celebrated Union spy and scout. Comprising her early history; her entry into the secret service of the Army of the Cumberland, and exciting adventures with the rebel chieftains and others while within the enemy's lines: together with her capture and sentence to death by General Bragg and final rescue by the Union army under General Rosecrans. The whole carefully prepared from her notes and memoranda. By F. L. Sarmiento ... Philadelphia, J. E. Potter, 1865.

374 p. incl. front. (port.) plates. 18cm.

This voluminous collection of fact and fantasy must be handled with extreme care; where Miss Cushman's notes end and the author's imagination begins is never made clear.

Schafer, Joseph, 1867–
Carl Schurz, militant liberal, by Joseph Schafer ... [Evansville, Wis., The Antes press, ©1930]

xxi, 270 p. front., plates, ports. 22½cm.

Emphasizes Schurz's early career; only two chapters treat of the Civil War and Reconstruction periods.

Schaff, Morris, 1840–1929.
Jefferson Davis, his life and personality, by Morris Schaff ... Boston, J. W. Luce and company [©1922]

4 p. l., 277 p. 21cm.

An attempt to do justice to Davis; the author, a Northern veteran of the Civil War, was concerned with Davis' "inner life" or personality.

Schuckers, Jacob W
The life and public services of Salmon Portland Chase, United States senator and governor of Ohio; secretary of the treasury, and chief-justice of the United States. By J. W. Schuckers. To which is added, the eulogy on Mr. Chase, delivered by William M. Evarts, before the alumni of Dartmouth college, June 24, 1874. New York, D. Appleton and company, 1874.

xv, 669 p. incl. front. (port.) illus. plates, facsims. 23½ cm.

A comprehensive, but uncritical and laudatory, study; contains extensive quotations from Chase's letters and other statements.

Schwartz, Harold.
Samuel Gridley Howe, social reformer, 1801–1876. Cambridge, Harvard University Press, 1956.

viii, 348 p. 22 cm.

An able, thorough study of Howe's career as a social reformer; based on an exhaustive use of the Howe manuscripts; scholarly and well-documented.

[**Searing,** *Mrs.* **Laura Catherine (Redden)**] 1840–
Notable men in "the House." A series of sketches of prominent men in the House of representatives, members of the Thirty-seventh Congress. Written and ed. by Howard Glyndon [*pseud.*] New York, Baker & Godwin, 1862.

103, [1] p. 23½cm.

Written by a Maryland newspaperwoman who used the pen name, "Howard Glyndon;" her sketches are rather disappointing.

Sears, Lorenzo, 1838–1916.
Wendell Phillips, orator and agitator, by Lorenzo Sears ... New York, Doubleday, Page & company, 1909.

xv, 379 p. front. (port.) 20 cm.

Sympathetic in its treatment; emphasizes Phillips' oratory, with analyses of his addresses and rhetoric.

Seitz, Don Carlos, 1862–1935.

Braxton Bragg, general of the confederacy, by Don C. Seitz. Columbia, S. C., The State company, 1924.

5 p. l., 544 p. front. (port.) 24½cm.

A detailed account of Bragg's wartime service, with copious quotations from letters and documents; the study places the General in a favorable perspective.

Seitz, Don Carlos, 1862–1935.

Horace Greeley, founder of the New York tribune, by Don C. Seitz ... Indianapolis, The Bobbs-Merrill company [©1926]

6 p. l., 433 p. front., plates, ports., facsim. 22½ cm.

A somewhat superficial, journalistic account; undocumented; the author emphasizes Greeley's journalistic career.

Sensing, Thurman, 1900–

Champ Ferguson, Confederate guerilla, by Thurman Sensing. Nashville, Tenn., Vanderbilt university press, 1942.

xi, 256 p. front. (group port.) map. 23½cm.

Ferguson merits only one study; fortunately, this one is more than adequate.

Seward, William Henry, 1801–1872.

The works of William H. Seward, ed. by George E. Baker ... New York, Redfield, 1853–84.

5 v. fronts. (ports.: v. 1, 5) facsim. 22½ cm.

Primarily a collection of speeches and public statements, with a brief biographical memoir.

Seymour, Horatio, 1810–1886.

Public record: including speeches, messages, proclamations, official correspondence, and other public utterances of Horatio Seymour; from the campaign of 1856 to the present time. With an appendix. Comp. from the most authentic sources, and printed exclusively for the use of editors and public speakers. Comp. and ed. by Thomas M. Cook and Thomas W. Knox. New York, I. W. England, 1868.

xi, 413 p. 24cm.

A standard volume of Seymour documentary materials.

Shanks, William Franklin Gore, 1837–1905.

Personal recollections of distinguished generals. By William F. G. Shanks. New York, Harper & brothers, 1866.

xiii, [14]–352 p. incl. front., port. 19½ cm.

More capsule biographies than personal recollections; unreliable and now badly outdated.

Shepherd, Henry Elliot, 1844–

Life of Robert Edward Lee, by Henry E. Shepherd ... New York and Washington, The Neale publishing company, 1906.

280 p. front., plates, ports. 24cm.

Not a biography but a series of laudatory, uncritical essays designed to reveal and exhibit the character of Lee.

Sheppard, Eric William, 1890–

Bedford Forrest, the Confederacy's greatest cavalryman, by Captain Eric William Sheppard ... with plates from engravings and six sketch maps. New York, L. MacVeagh, The Dial press; Toronto, Longmans, Green & co., 1930.

320 p. front., ports., maps (part fold.) facsim. 23 cm.

An adequate military biography, but includes imaginary conversations and weaves fictitious incidents and characters among the real ones.

Sheridan, Philip Henry, 1831–1888.

Personal memoirs of Philip Henry Sheridan, general, United States Army. New and enl. ed., with an account of his life from 1871 to his death, in 1888, by Brig.-Gen. Michael V. Sheridan ... New York, D. Appleton and company, 1902.

2 v. fronts., illus., ports., maps, facsims. 22½ cm.

Emphasizes the military campaigns of the war; entertaining but somewhat superficial.

Sherman, John, 1823–1900.

John Sherman's Recollections of forty years in the House, Senate and cabinet. An autobiography ... Chicago, New York [etc.] The Werner company, 1895.

2 v. fronts., plates, ports., facsims. 24½ cm.

Though self-justifying in tone, these memoirs are still extremely useful; Sherman was a senatorial power throughout the war years.

Sherman, William Tecumseh, 1820–1891.
Home letters of General Sherman; ed. by M. A. De Wolfe Howe. New York, C. Scribner's sons, 1909.

1 p. l., 412 p. front. (port.) $21\frac{1}{2}$cm.

Letters written by Sherman to his wife, and made avaliable to the editor by Sherman's daughter; frank and outspoken in tone but highly informative.

Sherman, William Tecumseh, 1820–1891.
Memoirs of General William T. Sherman. By himself ... New York, D. Appleton and company, 1875.

2 v. fold. map. $22\frac{1}{2}$ cm.

The oft-consulted and much-quoted reminiscences of one of the most famous generals of the war; Sherman wrote as he fought; dynamically and bluntly.

Sherman, William Tecumseh, 1820–1891.
The Sherman letters; correspondence between General and Senator Sherman from 1837 to 1891, ed. by Rachel Sherman Thorndike. With portraits. New York, C. Scribner's sons, 1894.

viii p., 1 l., **398 p. front., ports. 23 cm.**

These letters, invaluable as a source for the ideas of both men, are connected by the editor's brief, explanatory notes.

Sherwin, Oscar, 1902–
Prophet of liberty; the life and times of Wendell Phillips. New York, Bookman Associates [1958]

814 p. illus. 24 cm.

A sympathetic, careful and exhaustive study of Phillips'; thorough in its treatment of the man as well as the events with which he was related.

Shoemaker, Henry Wharton, 1880–
The last of the war governors; a biographical appreciation of Colonel William Sprague, governor of Rhode Island, 1860–1863, with special reference to his participation in the Loyal war governors' conference at Altoona, Pennsylvania, September, 1862, by Henry W. Shoemaker ... Altoona, Pa., Altoona tribune publishing company, 1916.

2 p. l., 3–103 p. ports. 19 x 15cm.

Based on a 1913 interview with Sprague, this rambling narrative treats largely of his role in the 1862 Altoona governors' conference.

Shotwell, Walter Gaston, 1856–
Life of Charles Sumner, by Walter G. Shotwell. New York, T. Y. Crowell & company [©1910]

ix, [1], 733 p. front., port. 21 cm.

A heavy, detailed but undocumented study.

Sievers, Harry Joseph, 1920–
Benjamin Harrison. Introd. by Hilton U. Brown. Chicago, H. Regnery Co., 1952–

v. illus., ports., maps. 24 cm.

The best biography of Harrison in existence; painstakingly researched and written; Vol. I treats of the war period.

Sigaud, Louis Adrien.
Belle Boyd, Confederate spy, by Louis A. Sigaud ... Richmond, Va., The Dietz press, incorporated [1944]

xii p., 1 l., 254 p. pl., ports., facsim. $23\frac{1}{2}$cm.

A biography based on original sources, and demonstrating, in the author's words, "that Belle Boyd was what she said she was, and did what she said she did."

Simms, Henry Harrison, 1896–
Life of Robert M. T. Hunter; a study in sectionalism and secession [by] Henry Harrison Simms ... Richmond, Va., The William Byrd press [©1935]

5 p. l., 3–234 p. **front. (port.) 21 cm.**

A brief and superficial study of the eminent Virginia politician; based almost entirely on printed source material.

Singmaster, Elsie, 1879–
I speak for Thaddeus Stevens, by Elsie Singmaster. Boston, Houghton Mifflin company, 1947.

vi p., 1 l., 446 p. 21 cm.

A fictionalized biography, intended to redress the balance in favor of Stevens.

Skipper, Ottis Clark, 1898–
J. D. B. De Bow, magazinist of the Old South. Athens, University of Georgia Press [1958]
269 p. illus. 25 cm.

A thorough and detailed study that devotes as much space to a history of DeBow's influential magazine as it does to a biography of the noted Southern nationalist.

Smith, Nicholas, 1836–1911.
Grant, the man of mystery, by Colonel Nicholas Smith ... Milwaukee, The Young churchman co., 1909.
xiii, 281 p. 2 pl., 5 port. (incl. front) map. 19½ cm.

A superficial attempt to discover the "mystery" of Grant's character through an illumination of his qualities.

Sloan, Edward William.
Benjamin Franklin Isherwood, naval engineer; the years as engineer in chief, 1861–1869, by Edward William Sloan, III. Annapolis, United States Naval Institute [1966]
xiii, 299 p. illus., ports. 24 cm.

A scholarly study of the head of the Navy's engineering branch during the war; includes much on naval engineering.

Smith, Theodore Clarke, 1870–
The life and letters of James Abram Garfield, by Theodore Clarke Smith ... New Haven, Yale university press; [etc., etc.] 1925.
2 v. fronts. (ports.) illus. (maps) 24 cm.

Only five chapters of this overly detailed study pertain to Garfield's war service as a Union brigadier in the West.

Smith, Arthur Douglas Howden, 1887–1945.
... Old Fuss and Feathers; the life and exploits of Lt.-General Winfield Scott, the only American commander who never lost a battle, the one victorious general to lose a presidential election, patron of Lee, protector of Lincoln, most inept of politicians, strategist, statesman, humanitarian. New York, The Greystone press, 1937.
viii p., 4 l., 3–386 p. front., illus., plates, ports. 22 cm.

Popularly written; markedly inferior to C. W. Elliott's biography of the same subject.

Smith, Willard H 1900–
Schuyler Colfax; the changing fortunes of a political idol. Indianapolis, Indiana Historical Bureau, 1952.
475 p. illus., port. 24 cm.

A scholarly and competent study, based on a thorough examination of primary and secondary sources; judicious in its portrait of Colfax.

Smith, Charles William, 1904–
Roger B. Taney: Jacksonian jurist, by Charles W. Smith, jr. ... Chapel Hill, The University of North Carolina press, 1936.
xi, 242 p. 22 cm.

An analysis of Taney's legal and political ideas; contains a brief biographical essay.

[**Snow, William Parker**] 1817–1895.
Southern generals, who they are, and what they have done. New York, C. B. Richardson, 1865.
[3]–473 p. 18 port. (incl. front.) 23 cm.

One of the first series of biographies published after the war; highly eulogistic in tone; republished in 1867 under the title, Lee and His Generals.

Smith, George Winston.
Henry C. Carey and American sectional conflict. Albuquerque, University of New Mexico Press, 1951.
127 p. 23 cm.

An account of Carey's relation to the Civil War; scholarly but not a deep study of Carey's ideas.

Steiner, Bernard Christian, 1867–1926.
Life of Henry Winter Davis, by Bernard C. Steiner. Baltimore, Md., John Murphy company, 1916.
416 p. front. (port.) 20½ cm.

Superficial; includes extensive summaries of Davis' speeches and numerous long quotations.

Steiner, Bernard Christian, 1867–1926.
Life of Reverdy Johnson, by Bernard C. Steiner ... Baltimore, The Norman, Remington co. [c1914]
v, 284 p. front. (port.) 23cm.

A balanced and careful study; well-researched and still useful.

Steiner, Bernard Christian, 1867–
Life of Roger Brooke Taney, chief justice of the United States Supreme court, by Bernard C. Steiner. Baltimore, Williams & Wilkins company, 1922.
2 p. l., [3]–553 p. front., ports. 23½ cm.

Essentially a study of Taney as a judge; excessively detailed and somewhat lacking in interpretation.

Steiner, Paul Eby, 1902–
Physician-generals in the Civil War; a study in nineteenth mid-century American medicine, by Paul E. Steiner. Springfield, Ill., C. C. Thomas [1966]
xv, 194 p. ports. 24 cm.

From a study--individually and collectively--of thirty-three officers, Steiner concluded that each was more interested in combat than medicine.

Stephens, Alexander Hamilton, 1812–1883.
A constitutional view of the late war between the states; its causes, character, conduct and results. Presented in a series of colloquies at Liberty hall. By Alexander H. Stephens ... Philadelphia, Pa. [etc.] National publishing company; Chicago, Ill. [etc.] Zeigler, McCurdy & co. [c1868–70]
2 v. front., ports., plan, facsims. 23½ cm.

An elaborate, legalistic argument to vindicate the South; considerably more pro-Confederate in tone than the author was as Vice President during the war.

Stephens, Alexander Hamilton, 1812–1883.
A letter for posterity: Alex Stephens to his brother Linton, June 3, 1864. Edited by James Z. Rabun. Atlanta, Library, Emory University, 1954.
24 p. 24 cm.

A nineteen-page letter in which the Confederacy's vice president voiced suspicions that Jefferson Davis was "dishonest and treacherous;" excellent editorial comments.

Stephens, Alexander Hamilton, 1812–1883.
Recollections of Alexander H. Stephens; his diary kept when a prisoner at Fort Warren, Boston harbour, 1865; giving incidents and reflections of his prison life and some letters and reminiscences. Ed., with a biographical study, by Myrta Lockett Avary. New York, Doubleday, Page & company, 1910.
xiii, 572 p. front. (port.) 23 cm.

Concentrates on Stephens' imprisonment, but includes fundamental material on his entire life.

Stephens, Alexander Hamilton, 1812–1883.
The reviewers reviewed; a supplement to the "War between the states," etc., with an appendix in review of "reconstruction," so called. By Alexander H. Stephens. New York, D. Appleton and company, 1872.
273 p. 24 cm.

A collection of attacks on A Constitutional View, accompanied by Stephens' rebuttal.

Stephenson, Wendell Holmes.
... The political career of General James H. Lane, by Wendell Holmes Stephenson ... Topeka, Kansas state printing plant, 1930.
196 p. front. (port.) illus., 2 fold. maps. 23 cm.

As much a history of tumultuous Kansas as a biography of the man who made it so; based on a multitude of source material.

Stickles, Arndt Mathias, 1872–
Simon Bolivar Buckner; borderland knight, by Arndt M. Stickles ... Chapel Hill, The University of North Carolina press, 1940.
xi p., 1 l., 446 p. front., pl., ports., map, facsim. 23½ cm.

A well-documented, analytical study, emphasizing the Civil War years and covering military operations in detail.

Stillwell, Lucille, 1905–
... John Cabell Breckinridge, by Lucille Stillwell. Caldwell, Id., The Caxton printers, ltd., 1936.
3 p. l., [5]–196 p. front., plates, ports. 19½ cm.

Brief and non-critical; little more than an introduction to the subject.

Stoddard, Henry Luther, 1861–

Horace Greeley, printer, editor, crusader, by Henry Luther Stoddard. New York, G. P. Putnam's sons [1946]

xiv, 338 p. front., plates, ports., facsims. 22cm.

A limited interpretation written by "one newspaperman of another"; the study is intended as a "tribute" to Greeley the editor.

Stoddard, William Osborn, 1835–1925.

Inside the White House in war times. By William O. Stoddard ... Illustrated by Dan Beard. New York, C. L. Webster & co., 1890.

244 p. front., pl. 19 cm.

Eulogistic reminiscences by one of Lincoln's secretaries; useful if handled with care.

Storey, Moorfield, 1845–1929.

... Charles Sumner, by Moorfield Storey. Boston and New York, Houghton, Mifflin and company [c1900]

3 p. l., 466 p., 1 l. 18 cm.

A typical eulogistic study, but one of some importance for the flavor of the times.

Stovall, Pleasant A.

Robert Toombs, statesman, speaker, soldier, sage; his career in Congress and on the hustings—his work in the courts—his record with the army—his life at home, by Pleasant A. Stovall ... New York, Cassell publishing company [c1892]

4 p. l., vii–viii, 396 p. 2 pl., 3 port. (incl. front.) 21½cm.

More a memoir than a biography; moderate in tone, though warmly affectionate toward Toombs.

Stowe, Charles Edward, 1850–

Harriet Beecher Stowe: the story of her life, by her son, Charles Edward Stowe, and her grandson Lyman Beecher Stowe ... Boston and New York, Houghton Mifflin company, 1911.

vi p., 2 l., 313, [1] p. front., plates, ports., double facsim. 21 cm.

A sympathetic and uncritical study by two of Mrs. Stowe's descendants.

Stowe, Harriet Elizabeth (Beecher) 1811–1896.

Life of Harriet Beecher Stowe, comp. from her letters and journals, by her son Charles Edward Stowe. Boston and New York, Houghton Mifflin and company, 1889.

xii, 530 p. front., illus., plates, ports., facsims. (1 fold.) 23 cm.

Mrs. Stowe's letters and selections from her journals, with connecting material by her son.

Strode, Hudson, 1893–

Jefferson Davis. [1st ed.] New York, Harcourt, Brace [1955–64]

3 v. ports. 25 cm.

An ambitious and sympathetic biography, meticulously researched and well-written; Davis, the author hopes, will no longer be "either misunderstood or begrudged."

Strong, George Templeton, 1820–1875.

Diary of the Civil War, 1860–1865. Edited by Allan Nevins. New York, Macmillan, 1962.

664 p. illus. 25 cm.

Essentially a reissue of Vol. III of Strong's voluminous diary of a lifetime; contains a poignant and candid observations by a prominent resident of New York City.

Stryker, Lloyd Paul, 1885–

Andrew Johnson; a study in courage, by Lloyd Paul Stryker. New York, The Macmillan company, 1929.

xvi p., 1 l., 881 p. front., illus. (facsim.) plates (1 double) ports. 24 cm.

The author felt that it was time justice was done to Johnson; hence, this biography is as detailed as it is sympathetic.

Sumner, Charles, 1811–1874.

The works of Charles Sumner ... Boston, Lee and Shepard, 1870–73.

15 v. front. (port.) 20½cm.

Volumes VI and VII contain a selection of Sumner's speeches and lectures; only a small portion of his public utterances are included, however.

Swanberg, W A 1907–
Sickles the incredible. New York, Scribner, 1956.
xii, 433 p. illus., ports., map. 24 cm.

A popularly written and carefully documented study of one of the Civil War's fabulous characters.

Swift, Lindsay, 1856–1921.
... William Lloyd Garrison, by Lindsay Swift ... Philadelphia, G. W. Jacobs & company [©1911]
412 p. front. (port.) 19½ cm.

A sympathetic and general account, emphasizing the earlier years of the antislavery crusade.

Swiggett, Howard, 1891–
The rebel raider; a life of John Hunt Morgan, by Howard Swiggett. Garden City, N. Y., The Garden City publishing co., inc. [1937]
7 p. l., 13–341 p. illus. 21½ cm.

The author is critical of Morgan and his reputation; he maintains that the General suffered increasing mental disintegration during his last days.

Swisher, Carl Brent, 1897–
Roger B. Taney, by Carl Brent Swisher. New York, The Macmillan company, 1935.
x p., 2 l., 608 p. front., illus. (facsim.) pl., ports. 24 cm.

Not a biography as much as it is a study of the Chief Justice's environment and an analysis of his judicial and political thoughts.

Swisher, Carl Brent, 1897–
Stephen J. Field, craftsman of the law, by Carl Brent Swisher ... Washington, The Brookings institution, 1930.
viii p., 3 l., 473 p. front., ports., facsim. 23½ cm.

A critical, scholarly study of the California jurist and Civil War Supreme Court justice; based on a wide range of sources.

Sylvis, William H 1828–1869.
The life, speeches, labors and essays of William H. Sylvis, late president of the Iron moulders' international union; and also of the National labor union. By his brother James C. Sylvis ... Philadelphia, Claxton, Remsen & Haffelfinger, 1872.
xi, 13–456 p. front. (port.) 19cm.

The only collection of the famous labor leader's works; marred by weak and eulogistic editing.

Tankersley, Allen P 1906–1957.
John B. Gordon: a study in gallantry. Atlanta, Whitehall Press, 1955.
xii, 400 p. illus., ports. 24 cm.

An admiring study; the author viewed Gordon as a "national pacificator," pledged to a reconciliation of the sections.

Tarbell, Ida Minerva, 1857–
The life of Abraham Lincoln, drawn from original sources and containing many speeches, letters, and telegrams hitherto unpublished, by Ida M. Tarbell ... New York, The Doubleday & McClure co., 1900.
2 v. fronts., illus., plates, ports., facsims. 23 cm.

Based on a thorough search for source material and hence containing much material that was not available to earlier writers; an honest and judicious study.

Tate, Allen, 1899–
Jefferson Davis: his rise and fall, a biographical narrative, by Allen Tate ... New York, Minton, Balch & company, 1929.
6 p. l., 3–311 p. front., ports. 21 cm.

A fine, perceptive character study; the author does not carry his story beyond the fall of the Confederacy.

Tate, Allen, 1899–
Stonewall Jackson, the good soldier; a narrative by Allen Tate ... New York, Minton, Balch & company, 1928.
viii p., 2 l., 3–322 p. front., illus. (maps) plates, ports. 21 cm.

A sensitive and sympathetic narration of the brief career of one of the Confederacy's greatest heroes.

Taylor, Richard, 1826–1879.
Destruction and reconstruction: personal experiences of the late war. By Richard Taylor ... New York, D. Appleton and company, 1879.
274 p. 23 cm.

Regarded as the finest of Confederate memoirs, Taylor's story covers only the war and immediate postwar periods; reprinted in 1955.

Thomas, Benjamin Platt, 1902–
Abraham Lincoln, a biography. [1st ed.] New York, Knopf, 1952.
xiv, 548, xii p. illus., ports., maps. 22 cm.

The best one-volume biography of Lincoln; well-balanced, critical and scholarly, the book is written in a fine, moving style.

Thomas, Benjamin Platt, 1902–
Portrait for posterity: Lincoln and his biographers; illus. by Romaine Proctor. New Brunswick, Rutgers Univ. Press, 1947.
xvii, 329 p. ports. 21 cm.

This series of critical essays on the major Lincoln biographers illuminates the writers themselves and adds much to an understanding of the volumes they produced.

Thomas, Benjamin Platt, 1902–1956.
Stanton; the life and times of Lincoln's Secretary of War [by] Benjamin P. Thomas and Harold M. Hyman. [1st ed.] New York, Knopf, 1962.
xvii, 642, xii p. illus., ports., facsim. 25 cm.

A definitive study of a controversial figure; balanced and judicious, although generally sympathetic to Stanton.

Thomas, John L
The liberator, William Lloyd Garrison, a biography. [1st ed.] Boston, Little, Brown [1963]
502 p. illus. 22 cm.

A sound, critical, and scholarly study; Garrison's reform activities are placed against the social background of the times.

Thomas, Wilbur D
General George H. Thomas, the indomitable warrior, supreme in defense and in counterattack; a biography, by Wilbur Thomas. [1st ed.] New York, Exposition Press [1964]
649 p. illus., map, plans, ports. 24 cm.

Detailed and documented, yet marred by the author's high regard for his subject: "the greatest Union general in the Civil War."

Thomason, John William, 1893–
Jeb Stuart, by John W. Thomason, jr. ... with illustrations and maps by the author. New York, London, C. Scribner's sons, 1930.
xiv p., 1 l., 512 p. incl. front., plates, ports., maps. 23 cm.

Strongly sympathetic in tone, this study is fairly successful at capturing Stuart's personality but includes little on the larger struggle in which Stuart was engaged.

Thompson, William Y
Robert Toombs of Georgia, by William Y. Thompson. Baton Rouge, Louisiana State University Press, 1966.
xiii, 281 p. illus., ports. 24 cm.

By far the most thorough biography in existence of the Georgia politician.

Tiffany, Francis, 1827–1908.
Life of Dorothea Lynde Dix, by Francis Tiffany. Boston, and New York, Houghton, Mifflin and company, 1890.
xiii, 392 p. front. (port.) 20½ cm.

A sympathetic "memoir," published a few years after Miss Dix's death; includes many letters of the reformer not now available.

Tilden, Samuel Jones, 1814–1886.
Letters and literary memorials of Samuel J. Tilden; ed. by John Bigelow, LL. D. New York and London, Harper & brothers, 1908.
2 v. 23cm.

A small section of this work treats of the future presidential candidate's wartime career as a New York attorney.

Tinkcom, Harry Marlin.
John White Geary, soldier-statesman, 1819–1873, by Harry Marlin Tinkcom. Philadelphia, University of Pennsylvania press, 1940.
vi p., 1 l., 155 p. front. (port.) 21cm.

Tinkcom takes an uncritical view of the man who was mayor of San Francisco and governor of territorial Kansas before his service as a Federal general.

Todd, Helen, 1912–
A man named Grant, by Helen Todd; illustrated by John O'Hara Cosgrove. Boston, Houghton, Mifflin company, 1940.
6 p. l., [3]–598 p. illus. 23½ cm.

A semi-fictional account; the characters, incidents, motives and states of mind are fact; beyond these are the probabilities.

Toombs, Robert Augustus, 1810–1885.
The correspondence of Robert Toombs, Alexander H. Stephens, and Howell Cobb, ed. by Ulrich B. Phillips. Washington, 1913.
759 p. 25 cm.

A comprehensive edition with brief introduction by Phillips; an invaluable collection of source material.

Trefousse, Hans Louis.
Ben Butler, the South called him Beast! New York, Twayne Publishers [1957]
365 p. illus. 23 cm.

A competent, thoroughly researched analysis of Butler, whose achievements as a reformer--whatever his motives--accord him a lasting place in history.

Trefousse, Hans Louis.
Benjamin Franklin Wade, radical Republican from Ohio. New York, Twayne Publishers [1963]
404 p. illus. 22 cm.

A sympathetic, thoroughly researched study of Wade's political life; focuses on the Civil War and early Reconstruction years.

Trescot, William Henry, 1822–1898.
The late General Stephen Elliott. Eulogy by the Hon. William Henry Trescot. Delivered in the House of representatives of South Carolina, Friday, September 7, 1866. London, Saunders, Otley and co., 1867.
23 p. 25 x 20cm.

A too-brief eulogy of a North Carolina brigadier mortally wounded in the battle of the Crater.

Trescot, William Henry, 1822–1898.
Memorial of the life of J. Johnston Pettigrew, brig.-gen. of the Confederate States army, by Wm. Henry Trescot. Charleston, J. Russell, 1870.
65 p. 20½cm.

This eulogy to a dependable South Carolina general is too shallow to be of great value.

Trietsch, James H
The printer and the prince; a study of the influence of Horace Greeley upon Abraham Lincoln as candidate and President. [1st ed.] New York, Exposition Press [1955]
332 p. 21 cm.

The last half of this book covers the war years; highly favorable to both subjects; based almost entirely on secondary sources.

Tucker, Glenn.
Hancock the Superb. Maps by Dorothy Thomas Tucker. [1st ed.] Indianapolis, Bobbs-Merrill [1960]
368 p. illus. 22 cm.

A well-written, well-documented study of one of the North's more neglected officers; contains dramatic and vivid battle accounts.

Tucker, Glenn.
Zeb Vance: champion of personal freedom. Indianapolis, Bobbs-Merrill [1966, ©1965]
viii, 564 p. maps, port. 24 cm.

Sympathetic and sometimes defensive, this study is unbalanced in its coverage of Vance's life.

Tyler, Samuel, 1809–1877.
Memoir of Roger Brooke Taney, LL. D., chief justice of the Supreme court of the United States. By Samuel Tyler ... Baltimore, J. Murphy & co., 1872.

1 p. l., vii–xv, 17–659 p. front. (port.) 24½ cm.

A laudatory attempt to vindicate Taney by one who knew him personally; some of Taney's letters and several of his judicial opinions are reprinted.

U. S. *Lincoln Sesquicentennial Commission.*
Lincoln day by day; a chronology, 1809–1865. Earl Schenck Miers, editor-in-chief. Washington, 1960.

3 v. 24 cm.

One of the most unique and highly useful tools in the field of Lincolniana; Lincoln's daily movements have been pinpointed from a multitude of sources.

U. S. *War dept.*
List of field officers, regiments, and battalions in the Confederate States army, 1861–1865. [Washington, Govt. print. off., 189–?]

131, 91 p. 24 cm.

An old but good reference work, in spite of several omissions.

[**U. S.** *War dept.*]
List of staff officers of the Confederate States army. 1861–1865. Washington. Govt. print. off., 1891.

186 p. 24cm.

This roster, while containing thousands of names, is incomplete; yet it is still a helpful guide for identifications.

Vallandigham, Clement Laird, 1820–1871.
The record of Hon. C. L. Vallandigham on abolition, the union, and the civil war ... 6th ed. Columbus, O., J. Walter & co., 1863.

256 p. front. (port.) 22cm.

This defense by a leading Copperhead sags from arguments of legal precedence and includes a variety of legislative proposals made starting in 1855.

Vallandigham, Clement Laird, 1820–1871.
Speeches, arguments, addresses, and letters of Clement L. Vallandigham ... New York, J. Walter & co., 1864.

580 p. front. (port.) 23cm.

A more inclusive collection of Vallandigham's public statements, but marred by extremely poor editing.

Vallandigham, James Laird, 1812–1904.
A life of Clement L. Vallandigham, by his brother, Rev. James L. Vallandigham. Baltimore, Turnbull brothers, 1872.

xii, 573 p. front. (port.) plates. 23½ cm.

A collection of extracts from Vallandigham's speeches and letters, with frequent quotations from newspapers.

Vance, Zebulon Baird, 1830–1894.
Papers. Edited by Frontis W. Johnston. Raleigh, State Dept. of Archives and History, 1963–

v. illus., ports. 24 cm.

Well-edited and extremely useful for Vance's political thoughts and military actions: Vol. II will contain his gubernatorial correspondence.

Vanderbilt, Kermit.
Charles Eliot Norton; apostle of culture in a democracy. Cambridge, Mass., Belknap Press, 1959.

xiii, 286 p. illus., ports., facsim. 22 cm.

The best biography of one of the wartime North's foremost intellectuals.

Van Deusen, Glyndon Garlock, 1897–
Horace Greeley, nineteenth-century crusader. Philadelphia, University of Pennsylvania Press, 1953.

445 p. illus., ports. 23 cm.

A heavily researched and soundly presented study of Greeley the crusader; Van Deusen recreated an old image in very convincing style.

Van Deusen, Glyndon Garlock, 1897–
Thurlow Weed, wizard of the lobby, by Glyndon G. Van Deusen ... Boston, Little, Brown and company, 1947.
xiv, 403 p. plates, ports., facsims. 22 cm.

Scholarly and definitive; based on thorough research in original sources, and includes Weed's letters and papers hitherto closed to investigation.

Van Deusen, Glyndon Garlock, 1897–
William Henry Seward [by] Glyndon G. Van Deusen. New York, Oxford University Press, 1967.
xi, 666 p. illus., ports. 24 cm.

By almost every standard the best biography of Lincoln's secretary of state; the product of exhaustive research.

Van de Water, Frederic Franklyn, 1890–
Glory-hunter; a life of General Custer, by Frederic F. Van de Water ... Indianapolis, New York, The Bobbs-Merrill company [c1934]
394 p. front., plates, ports., maps. 24 cm.

A work of sound research; Custer emerges as an egotist driven by a strong craving for glory.

Vandiver, Frank Everson, 1925–
Mighty Stonewall. New York, McGraw-Hill [1957]
xi, 547 p. illus., ports., maps. 24 cm.

An excellent, definitive study, based on an exhaustive use of primary sources; written in a clear, polished and sometimes picturesque style.

Van Horne, Thomas Budd, *d.* 1895.
The life of Major-General George H. Thomas, by Thomas B. Van Horne ... New York, C. Scribner's sons, 1882.
x p., 1 l., 502 p. front. (port.) 8 fold. maps. 22½cm.

An attempt to vindicate Thomas and to accord him the justice that the author felt had been withheld by previous writers.

Villard, Henry, 1835–1900.
Memoirs of Henry Villard, journalist and financier, 1835–1900 ... Boston and New York, Houghton, Mifflin and company, 1904.
2 v. fronts., ports., maps (part double). 22½ cm.

The highly useful memoirs of a famous war correspondent; the descriptions of such officers as W. T. Sherman are particularly revealing.

Von Abele, Rudolph Radama, 1922–
Alexander H. Stephens, a biography by Rudolph Von Abele ... New York, A. A. Knopf, 1946.
xiii, 337, x p., 1 l. front., pl., ports. 22 cm.

A critical study, fluently written and scholarly in its documentation; devotes some attention to an analysis of Stephens' personality as it affected his career.

Wagenknecht, Edward Charles, 1900–
Harriet Beecher Stowe; the known and the unknown [by] Edward Wagenknecht. New York, Oxford University Press, 1965.
267 p. port. 21 cm.

A "psychograph," or character study, of Mrs. Stowe; not a biography in the traditional sense.

Walker, Charles Manning, 1834–
Sketch of the life, character, and public services of Oliver P. Morton. Prepared for the Indianapolis journal by Charles M. Walker. Indianapolis, Indianapolis journal, 1878.
vi, 191 p. front. (port.) 18 cm.

A brief eulogistic biography written for a local paper shortly after Morton's death; based largely on reminiscences and public records.

Walker, Cornelius Irvine, 1842–
The life of Lieutenant General Richard Heron Anderson, of the Confederate States army, by C. Irvine Walker. Charleston, S. C., Art publishing company [c1917]
269 p. front. (port.) plates. 20½cm.

So few of Anderson's papers survived the war that this inadequate study remains the sole biography.

Walker, Francis Amasa, 1840–1897.
... General Hancock, by General Francis A. Walker. New York, D. Appleton and company, 1894.

vi p., 2 l., 332 p. front. (port.) maps, plans. 19½ cm.

More a reminiscence of service in Hancock's command than a biography of Hancock; undistinguished and inadequately researched.

Walker, Robert James, 1801–1869.
Jefferson Davis. Repudiation, recognition and slavery. Letter[s] of Hon. Robert J. Walker ... [I–II] London, W. Ridgway, 1863.

2 v. in 1. 21 cm.

An Englishman casts a critical eye at some of Davis' policies--notably repudiation; written during wartime, when passions were high.

Wall, Alexander James, 1884–
A sketch of the life of Horatio Seymour, 1810–1886, with a detailed account of his administration as governor of the state of New York during the war of 1861–1865. By Alexander J. Wall ... New York, 1929.

v, 111 p. front., illus. (incl. ports., facsims.) pl. 26½ cm.

A superficial tribute, antiquarian in character; contains a list of Seymour's addresses, speeches and published writings.

Wall, Joseph Frazier.
Henry Watterson, reconstructed rebel. With an introd. by Alben W. Barkley. New York, Oxford University Press, 1956.

362 p. illus. 24 cm.

A sound and readable study, friendly yet judicious in its appraisal.

Wallace, Lewis, 1827–1905.
Lew Wallace; an autobiography ... New York and London, Harper & brothers, 1906.

2 v. fronts., illus., plates, ports., facsims. 21½ cm.

Balanced in its coverage, but somewhat superficial in its treatment of war incidents; reflects Wallace's literary talent.

Wallace, Willard Mosher, 1911–
Soul of the lion; a biography of General Joshua L. Chamberlain. New York, T. Nelson [1960]

357 p. illus. 22 cm.

A balanced biography of the leader of the 20th Maine who later served as governor of Maine and president of Bowdoin College.

Warden, Robert Bruce, 1824–1888.
An account of the private life and public services of Salmon Portland Chase, by Robert B. Warden ... Cincinnati, Wilstach, Baldwin & co., 1874.

xxiii, [11]–838 p. front. (port.) 25 cm.

A voluminous work, uncritical in approach and lacking in historical perspective.

Warner, Ezra J
Generals in blue; lives of the Union commanders, by Ezra J. Warner. [Baton Rouge] Louisiana State University Press [1964]

xxiv, 679, [1] p. ports. 24 cm.

The best biographical dictionary for Federal generals; photographs of each are included; brevity occasionally precludes needed details.

Warner, Ezra J
Generals in gray; lives of the Confederate commanders. [1st ed. Baton Rouge] Louisiana State University Press [1959]

xxvii, 420 p. ports. 25 cm.

The Southern companion to the above, in both format and content.

Washington, Booker Taliaferro, 1859?–1915.
... Frederick Douglass, by Booker T. Washington ... Philadelphia and London, G. W. Jacobs & company [1907]

14 p., 1 l., [15]–365 p. front. (port.) 19½ cm.

A successful and fairly impartial study, focusing principally on Douglass' pre-Civil War and Civil War years.

Watterson, Henry, 1840–1921.
"Marse Henry"; an autobiography, by Henry Watterson ... New York, George H. Doran company [c1919]
2 v. fronts., plates, ports. 22 cm.

These memoirs by an editor-politician throw little light on Watterson's enigmatic army career during the war.

Weed, Thurlow, 1797–1882.
Life of Thurlow Weed including his autobiography and a memoir ... [Boston, New York, Houghton, Mifflin and company; etc., etc., 1884]
2 v. fronts., pl., ports. 24½cm.

Good only for the facts; untrustworthy and outdated in its interpretations; Weed's daughter compiled Vol. I, and his grandson wrote Vol. II.

Weigley, Russell Frank.
Quartermaster general of the Union Army; a biography of M. C. Meigs. New York, Columbia University Press, 1959.
396 p. illus. 23 cm.

A thoroughly researched, highly useful study of the North's ingenious Quartermaster General and the department he headed.

Welles, Gideon, 1802–1878.
Diary. Edited by Howard K. Beale, assisted by Alan W. Brownsword. With an introd. by Howard K. Beale and appendices drawn from Welles's correspondence. New York, W. W. Norton [1960]
3 v. ports. 25 cm.

The first correct text of a diary first published in 1911; an invaluable source for wartime life--official and unofficial--in Washington.

Welles, Gideon, 1802–1878.
Selected essays. Compiled by Albert Mordell. New York, Twayne Publishers [1959–60]
2 v. 22 cm.

These postwar observations by Lincoln's Sec. of the Navy form a valuable addenda to Welles's incomparable diary.

Wellman, Manly Wade, 1905–
Giant in gray; a biography of Wade Hampton of South Carolina. New York, C. Scribner's Sons, 1949.
xv, 387 p. ports. 24 cm.

A popularly written, documented study of the famed South Carolina cavalry commander and political figures.

Wells, Anna Mary.
Dear preceptor; the life and times of Thomas Wentworth Higginson. Boston, Houghton Mifflin, 1963.
363 p. illus. 22 cm.

An effective study of Higginson's life; the author places strong emphasis on Higginson's friendship with Emily Dickinson.

Werstein, Irving.
Abraham Lincoln versus Jefferson Davis. New York, Crowell [1959]
272 p. illus. 24 cm.

A superficial comparison in which both subjects suffer from the treatment.

Werstein, Irving.
Kearny, the magnificent; the story of General Philip Kearny, 1815–1862. New York, John Day Co. [1962]
248 p. illus. 21 cm.

This brief, romanticized narrative is based (according to the author) on Kearney's private papers; lacks documentation.

West, Richard Sedgewick, 1902–
Gideon Welles, Lincoln's navy department, by Richard S. West, jr. Indianapolis, New York, The Bobbs-Merrill company [1943]
379 p. front., plates, ports. 24 cm.

A documented, well-written and thoroughly researched study.

West, Richard Sedgewick, 1902–
Lincoln's scapegoat general; a life of Benjamin F. Butler, 1818–1893, by Richard S. West, Jr. Boston, Houghton Mifflin, 1965.

xvi, 462 p. maps, port. 23 cm.

The author, seeking to disentangle Butler from the "myths" that have grown up about him, sees him as "an intensely puritanical idealist."

Whaley, Elizabeth J
Forgotten hero: General James B. McPherson; the biography of a Civil War general. [1st ed.] New York, Exposition Press [c1955]

203 p. 21 cm.

An incomplete and rather unbalanced study, but containing useful information for later students of McPherson's life and career.

Wheare, Kenneth Clinton, 1907–
Abraham Lincoln and the United States. New York, Macmillan Co., 1949.

xiv, 286 p. port., col. maps (on lining papers) 18 cm.

This small volume was designed to acquaint Englishmen with the essential facts of Lincoln's life and the times in which he lived.

White, Henry Alexander, 1861–1926.
Robert E. Lee and the Southern confederacy, 1807–1870 by Henry Alexander White ... New York [etc.] G. P. Putnam's sons, 1902.

1 p. l., xiii, 467 p. front., plates, ports., maps (part fold.) fold. facsim. 19½cm.

A sympathetic, standard study of Lee's life; the author used a wide range of published sources.

White, Horace, 1834–1916.
The life of Lyman Trumbull, by Horace White. Boston and New York, Houghton Mifflin company, 1913.

xxxv, 458 p., 1 l. pl., 2 port. (incl. front.) 22½ cm.

White, who was closely associated with Trumbull, concentrated sympathetically on the senator's congressional career.

White, Laura Amanda.
... Robert Barnwell Rhett; father of secession, by Laura A. White ... New York, London, The Century co. [c1931]

ix, 264 p. front. (port.) pl., map. 23cm.

A significant contribution to Confederate history, especially in the treatment of causative factors and immediate prewar events.

White, Ruth (Morris)
Yankee from Sweden; the dream and the reality in the days of John Ericsson. [1st ed.] New York, Holt [1960]

299 p. 22 cm.

An undocumented, somewhat sketchy account of the scientist and inventor who developed the ironclad Monitor.

Williams, Ben Ames, 1915–
"Mr. Secretary," by Ben Ames Williams, jr. New York, The Macmillan company, 1940.

viii, 507 p. 22 cm.

Presented in autobiographical form, as if Stanton himself might have written it; a mixture of history and fiction.

Williams, Frances Leigh.
Matthew Fontaine Maury, scientist of the sea. New Brunswick, Rutgers University Press [1963]

xx, 720 p. illus., ports., charts, forms. 25 cm.

A significant and comprehensive study, based on thorough research in original manuscript materials, some not previously used.

Williams, Samuel Cole, 1864–
General John T. Wilder, commander of the Lightning brigade, by Samuel C. Williams ... Bloomington, Indiana university press, 1936.

2 p. l., [vii]–viii, [2], 105 p. illus. 24cm.

A thin biographical sketch of an Indiana brigadier who achieved a high reputation in the Western campaigns.

Williams, Thomas Harry, 1909–
McClellan, Sherman, and Grant. New Brunswick, N. J., Rutgers University Press [1962]

113 p. illus. 20 cm.

These character-studies show as well the development of military thought in the source of the war; an excellent starting point.

Williams, Thomas Harry, 1909–
P. G. T. Beauregard; Napoleon in gray. Baton Rouge, Louisiana State University Press [1955, ©1954]

xiii, 345 p. illus., ports., maps. 23 cm.

The thorough and definitive study of the paradoxical Creole who never quite achieved greatness as a Confederate general.

Wilson, James Grant, 1832–1914.
The life and public services of Ulysses Simpson Grant, general of the United States army, and twice president of the United States. By James Grant Wilson ... Rev. ed. New York, De Witt [©1885]

168 p. front. (port.) facsim. 23½cm.

An enlarged edition of a campaign biography; uncritical and superficial.

Wilson, James Harrison, 1837–1925.
The life of Charles A. Dana, by James Harrison Wilson ... New York and London, Harper & brothers, 1907.

xi, [1] p., 1 l., 544, [1] p. front. (port.) 21½ cm.

A thorough study of Dana's career in journalism and politics; based largely on material made available by Dana's family.

Wilson, James Harrison, 1837–1925.
The life of John A. Rawlins, lawyer, assistant adjutant-general, chief of staff, major general of volunteers, and secretary of war, by James Harrison Wilson ... New York, The Neale publishing company, 1916.

514 p. front. (port.) 22½ cm.

Of some use for insights into Grant's principal staff member; a new appraisal in depth of Rawlins is badly needed.

Wilson, James Harrison, 1837–1925.
The life of Ulysses S. Grant, general of the armies of the United States. By Charles A. Dana ... and J. H. Wilson ... Springfield, Mass., Gurdon Bill & company; Cincinnati, H. C. Johnson; [etc., etc.] 1868.

xvi, [17]–424 p. front. (port.) maps. 22 cm.

A eulogistic biography issued during a presidential year; Dana wrote three of the forty-odd chapters and approved the remainder.

Wilson, Robert Forrest, 1883–1942.
Crusader in crinoline, the life of Harriet Beecher Stowe, by Forrest Wilson. 30 illustrations. Philadelphia, London [etc.] J. B. Lippincott company [©1941]

706 p. incl. illus., geneal. tab. front., plates, ports., fold. facsim. 23½ cm.

An intimate picture of the author of Uncle Tom's Cabin, but Wilson's errors of judgement and fact mar the Civil War chapters.

Wilson, Rufus Rockwell, 1865–1949.
Lincoln in caricature; a historical collection, with descriptive and biographical commentaries by Rufus Rockwell Wilson. Introd. by R. Gerald McMurtry. New York, Horizon Press, 1953.

xix, 327 p. 163 illus. 26 cm.

A collection of political cartoons and caricatures depicting Lincoln; explanatory commentaries.

Wing, Henry Ebeneser, 1839–1925.
When Lincoln kissed me: a story of the Wilderness campaign, by Henry E. Wing ... New York, Eaton & Mains; Cincinnati, Jennings & Graham [©1913]

39 p. plates, ports. (incl. front.) 17½cm.

The highly dramatic reminiscences of a noted New York Tribune reporter; must be handled carefully.

Winston, Robert Watson, 1860–1944.
Andrew Johnson, plebeian and patriot, by Robert W. Winston. New York, H. Holt and company [©1928]

xvi, 549 p. front., plates, ports., map, facsims. 23½ cm.

A thorough, though uncritical attempt to "rehabilitate" Johnson; well-researched and documented.

Winston, Robert Watson, 1860–1944.
High stakes and hair trigger; the life of Jefferson Davis, by Robert W. Winston ... New York, H. Holt and company [c1930]

viii p., 1 l., 306 p. 2 port. (incl. front.) plates, map. 22½ cm.

An undistinguished study; Davis's weakness was his inability "to sink himself in the cause."

Winston, Robert Watson, 1860–1944.
Robert E. Lee; a biography, by Robert W. Winston. New York, W. Morrow & company, 1934.

xi p., 2 l., 3–428 p. front., illus. (maps) 2 pl., ports., 2 double facsim. 22½ cm.

A sympathetic and successful study of Lee; emphasizes his human qualities, character and personality.

Wise, Barton Haxall, 1865–1899.
The life of Henry A. Wise of Virginia, 1806–1876. By his grandson, the late Barton H. Wise. New York, The Macmillan company; London, Macmillan & co., ltd., 1899.

xiii, 434 p. front. (port.) 23½ cm.

A fair, accurate biography by a grandson of a distinguished figure in Virginia and Confederate history.

Wise, John Sergeant, 1846–1913.
The end of an era, edited and annotated by Curtis Carroll Davis. New York, T. Yoseloff [1965]

lxiii, 498 p. ports. 22 cm.

A qualitative reprint of a classic memoir (see I, 181), with valuable introduction and notes appended.

Wister, Owen, 1860–
Ulysses S. Grant, by Owen Wister. [2d ed.] Boston, Small, Maynard & company, 1901.

1 p. l., xvii p., 1 l., 145 p. front. (port.) 14½cm.

A brief, compact and very readable summary of Grant's life; "none of our public men have a story so strange as this."

Woodburn, James Albert, 1856–1943.
The life of Thaddeus Stevens; a study in American political history, especially in the period of the civil war and reconstruction, by James Albert Woodburn ... Indianapolis, The Bobbs-Merrill company [c1913]

6 p. l., 620 p. front., ports. 21 cm.

This sympathetic study makes no pretense at completeness; it concentrates on Stevens' role in the war and Reconstruction periods.

Woodford, Frank Bury, 1903–
Lewis Cass, the last Jeffersonian. New Brunswick, Rutgers University Press, 1950.

ix, 380 p. port. 22 cm.

A competent, sympathetic study; broadly researched but not sufficiently related to the great issues of the period.

Woodley, Thomas Frederick, 1894–
Thaddeus Stevens, by Thomas Frederick Woodley. Harrisburgh, Pa., The Telegraph press, 1934.

1 p. l., [v]–xv, 664 p. front., plates, ports., facsims. 23 cm.

This charitable study emphasizes Stevens' activities and inadequately treats the historical context in which he operated.

Woodward, Ashbel, 1804–1885.
Life of General Nathaniel Lyon. By Ashbel Woodward, M. D. Hartford, Case, Lockwood & co., 1862.

xii, [13]–360 p. front. (port.) 2 pl., plan. 18½cm.

This sentimental eulogy was begun shortly after Lyon's death at Wilson's Creek and adds nothing of value to any understanding of the Union commander.

Woodward, William E 1874–1950.
Meet General Grant, by W. E. Woodward; with twenty illustrations. New York, H. Liveright, 1928.

512 p. front., plates, ports, facsim. 25 cm.

A popularly written, free-flowing study of Grant's career; unburdened by excessive military detail.

Worth, Jonathan, 1802–1869.

... The correspondence of Jonathan Worth, collected and ed. by J. G. de Roulhac Hamilton ... Raleigh, Edwards & Broughton printing company, 1909.

2 v. front. (port.: vol. I) 24cm.

Valuable letters of a prominent member of the North Carolina legislature and, after 1862, public treasurer of the state.

Wright, Marcus Joseph, 1831–1922, *comp.*

General officers of the Confederate army, officers of the executive departments of the Confederate States, members of the Confederate congress by states, comp. and prepared by General Marcus J. Wright. New York, The Neale publishing company, 1911.

188 p. 19cm.

Rosters rather than biographical sketches, yet painstakingly thorough as only Gen. Wright could be.

Wyeth, John Allan, 1845–1922.

Life of General Nathan Bedford Forrest, by John Allan Wyeth, M. D., with illustrations by T. de Thulstrup, Rogers, Klepper, Redwood, Hitchcock, & Carleton. New York and London, Harper & brothers, 1899.

xix, [1] p., 1 l., 655, [1] p. front., plates, ports., 2 maps (1 double) 3 facsim. (1 double) 23½ cm.

Written by a Confederate veteran who served under Forrest, this detailed and uncritical study is concerned almost entirely with military operations.

Yates, Richard, 1860–1936.

Richard Yates, Civil War governor, by Richard Yates and Catharine Yates Pickering. Edited by John H. Krenkel. Danville, Ill., Interstate Printers & Publishers [1966]

300 p. illus., ports. 24 cm.

A collection of some of Yates' letters and speeches, with lengthy quotations from other sources; generally inadequate as a study of Illinois's wartime governor.

Yates, Richard Edwin, 1910–

The Confederacy and Zeb Vance. Tuscaloosa, Ala., Confederate Pub. Co., 1958.

132 p. port. 22 cm.

A brief study of Vance's relations with the Confederate government; not a biography nor even a full study of his governorship.

Young, James Capers, 1892–

Marse Robert, knight of the confederacy, by James C. Young ... New York, Rae D. Henkle co., inc. [c1929]

6 p. l., 362 p. front., plates, ports., double map. 23½ cm.

An uncritical, superficial work that adds little to a knowledge of Lee's life and career.

Young, John Russell, 1841–1899.

Men and memories; personal reminiscences, by John Russell Young; ed. by his wife, May D. Russell Young ... New York, F. T. Neely [c1901]

2 v. front. (port.) 21cm.

Factual, reliable vignettes by a wartime correspondent, founder of the Union League of Philadelphia, and--later--prominent newspaperman.

Zabriskie, Francis Nicoll, 1832–1891.

... Horace Greeley, the editor. By Francis Nicoll Zabriskie. New York [etc.] Funk & Wagnalls, 1890.

vii, [9]–398 p. front. (port.) 19cm.

A sympathetic, superficial study, making no pretense to coverage of the times in which Greeley lived, or the causes to which he attached himself.

Zuber, Richard L

Jonathan Worth; a biography of a Southern Unionist, by Richard L. Zuber. Chapel Hill, University of North Carolina Press [1965]

351 p. port. 24 cm.

The only worthwhile biography of an experienced North Carolina politician who supported the Confederacy with reluctant devotion.

THE UNION

Government and Politics

Rodney C. Loehr

American union commission.

The American union commission: its origin, operations and purposes. Organized to aid in the restoration of the Union upon the basis of freedom, industry, education, and Christian morality ... October 1865. New York, Sanford, Harroun & co., printers, 1865.

cover-title, 24 p. $22\frac{1}{2}^{cm}$.

Organized in 1864, this agency began operations in Tennessee but later increased its activities in scope and area; a precursor of the Freedman's Bureau.

Arnold, Isaac Newton, 1815–1884.

Confiscate the property and free the slaves of rebels. Speech of Hon. I. N. Arnold, of Ill., in the House of representatives, May 23, 1862. [Washington, Scammell & co., printers, 1862]

8 p. $21\frac{1}{2}^{cm}$.

An argument that confiscation of rebel property was legal, expedient, reassuring to the North, and an economic weapon of good use.

Ashley, James Monroe, 1824–1896.

The rebellion—its causes and consequences. A speech delivered by Hon. J. M. Ashley, at College hall in the city of Toledo, Tuesday evening, Nov. 26, 1861. Toledo, Pelton and Waggoner, printers, 1861.

16 p. $23\frac{1}{2}^{cm}$.

A short but rousing oration; slavery was at the root of a criminal, causeless rebellion, and a bold, vigorous policy on the part of the Union was warranted.

Ayer, I Winslow.

The great north-western conspiracy in all its startling details. The plot to plunder and burn Chicago—release of all Rebel prisoners—seizure of arsenals—raids from Canada—plot to burn New York, piracy on the Lakes—parts for the Sons of liberty—trial of Chicago conspirators—inside views of the temples of the Sons of liberty—names of prominent members ... By I. Winslow Ayer ... [3d ed.] Chicago, Rounds & James, book and job printers, 1865.

iv, [5]–112 p. illus. (incl. ports.) 23^{cm}.

Propagandistic, unbalanced and too bent on sensationalism to be used for anything more than contrast.

Babbitt, Elijah, 1796–1887.

Speech of Hon. Elijah Babbitt, of Pennsylvania, on the confiscation of rebel property. Deliverd in the House of representatives, May 22, 1862. [Washington, L. Towers & co., printers, 1862]

8 p. 21cm.

Another proposal that the North confiscate slaves, employ them as soldiers, and use Rebel property to help pay for the cost of the war.

Barnard, Job, 1844–

An address delivered at the thirtieth annual banquet, February 7, 1912, by Justice Job Barnard ... Washington, D. C., 1912.

12 p. front. (port.) 23cm.

Barnard's address, entitled "The Place of the Union Soldier in History," pointed out the many Civil War soldiers who had distinguished public and political careers after the war.

Barrows, William, 1815–1891.

The war and slavery; and their relations to each other. A discourse, delivered in the Old South church, Reading, Mass., December 28, 1862. By Rev. William Barrows ... Boston, J. M. Whittemore & co., 1863.

18 p. 23½cm.

Slavery and the feudal, medieval civilization of the South, Barrows stated, were the major causes of civil war.

Barstow, George, 1812-1883.

War the only means of preserving our nationality. An oration, delivered at San Jose, Santa Clara County, Cal., July 4, 1864, by George Barstow. San Francisco, Printed by Towne & Bacon, 1864.

16 p. 23cm.

In this political reassurances, Barstow reminded Americans that other great nations had suffered reverses but ultimately triumphed; the North would do the same.

Bartley, Thomas Welles, 1812–1885.

The rights of the owners of private property taken in war, to just compensation, without regard to political status, where there has been no adjudication of confiscation. By T. W. Bartley ... Washington, D. C., Chronicle publishing company, 1873.

14 p. 23cm.

A concise, curt argument that the North should reimburse the South for cotton seized during the war.

Bartol, Cyrus Augustus, 1813–1900.

Conditions of peace: a discourse delivered in the West church, in memory of David Kimball Hobart, June 14, 1863. By C. A. Bartol. Boston, Walker, Wise, and company, 1863.

28 p. 23½cm.

A eulogy with strong political overtones; the war must continue, Bartol asserted, until its objects are secured; the South was a danger to free thought, free schools and free pulpits.

[Belmont, August] 1816–1889.

A few letters and speeches of the late civil war. New York [Priv. print.] 1870.

2 p. l., 126 p. 26cm.

Straightforward comments by a prominent New York banker whose friendly connections with the Rothschilds proved to be distinct advantages for the Union.

Benton, Josiah Henry, 1843–1917.

Voting in the field; a forgotten chapter of the civil war, by Josiah Henry Benton ... Boston, Priv. print., 1915.

vi p., 2 l., [3]-332 p. front. (map) ports. 25½ cm

A solitary study; emphasizes the importance of the soldier vote, notably in the 1864 re-election of Lincoln.

Binney, Horace, 1780–1875.

The privilege of the writ of habeas corpus under the Constitution. Philadelphia, T. B. Pugh, 1862.

2 v. 19 cm.

Three well-known treatises that provide strong arguments on the question.

Birkhimer, William Edward, 1848–1914.

Military government and martial law, by William E. Birkhimer ... Washington, D. C., J. J. Chapman, 1892.

xv, 521 p. 23½cm.

A popular discourse on martial law; drawn for the most part from the author's own experiences.

Blair, Montgomery, 1813–1883.

Speech of the Hon. Montgomery Blair, on the causes of the rebellion and in support of the president's plan of pacification, delivered before the legislature of Maryland, at Annapolis, on the 22d of January, 1864. Baltimore, Printed by Sherwood & co., 1864.

22 p. 23cm.

In this slim pamphlet a noted politician defended Lincoln's "10% Plan," attacked Southern chivalry, and concluded with a fervent plea for the Union.

Boutwell, George Sewall, 1818–1905.

Confiscation of rebel property. Speech of Hon. George S. Boutwell, of Massachusetts, delivered in the House of representatives, January 19, 1864. [Washington, McGill & Witherow, printers, 1864]

8 p. 24cm.

Boutwell justified the confiscation of rebel property on legal and constitutional grounds.

Boykin, Edward Carrington, 1889–

Congress and the Civil War. New York, McBride Co. [1955]

352 p. illus. 22 cm.

That only forty-one pages treat of the wartime Congress is but the first disappointment of this shallow study.

Bradley, Erwin Stanley.

The triumph of militant Republicanism; a study of Pennsylvania and presidential politics, 1860–1872. Philadelphia, University of Pennsylvania Press [1964]

467 p. ports. 22 cm.

A full study of the interrelation between state and national politics; weak in spots, and similar in many respects to the approach of A. K. McClure.

Brough, John, 1811–1865.

The defenders of the country and its enemies. The Chicago platform dissected. Speech of Governor Brough, delivered at Circleville, Ohio, Sept. 3 ... Cincinnati, Gazette co. printing house, 1864.

16 p. 23cm.

Good 1864 campaign literature by the staunch Unionist and Republican governor of Ohio.

Burgess, John William, 1844–1931.

... The civil war and the Constitution, 1859–1865, by John W. Burgess ... New York, C. Scribner's sons, 1901.

2 v. maps (part double) 19 cm.

An older, undocumented work heavy on the military and political history of the war; though outdated, it provides good chronology.

Carman, Harry James, 1884–

Lincoln and the patronage, by Harry J. Carman and Reinhard H. Luthin. New York, Columbia university press, 1943.

x, 375 p. front., plates, ports. 23½ cm.

An exhaustively researched treatment of Lincoln's appointments to major and minor government posts.

Carpenter, Stephen D.

Logic of history. Five hundred political texts: being concentrated extracts of abolitionism; also, results of slavery agitation and emancipation; together with sundry chapters on despotism, usurpations and frauds. By S. D. Carpenter ... 2d ed. Madison, Wis., 1864.

2 p. l., 351 p. 23cm.

A wartime example of sensationalism and "waving the bloody shirt;" illustrative of the heated tempers of the day.

Chanler, John Winthrop, 1826–1877.

Down with the black flag of confiscation; up with the union jack. Speech of Hon. John W. Chanler, of New York, in the House of representatives, December 10, 1867. In reply to Mr. Stevens, of Pennsylvania, on his southern confiscation bill. [Washington, 1867]

8 p. 24cm.

In contrast to Boutwell's tract, this one states that confiscation was intolerant, unjust, despotic, unnecessary, unwise and impossible.

Clemens, Jeremiah, 1814–1865.

Letter from Hon. Jere. Clemens. [Philadelphia, 1864]

16 p. 18½cm.

An avowed Unionist from Alabama levied damnation against his state and called for the reelection of Lincoln.

Conkling, Henry, 1814–

An inside view of the rebellion, and American citizens' text-book. By Henry Conkling ... Chicago, Tribune book and job printing establishment, 1864.

24 p. 21cm.

Pro-Republican arguments against the Conservatives and Peace Democrats; Conkling also defended the use of Negro troops.

Conkling, Roscoe, 1829–1888.

Special committee on government contracts—what it has done. Speech of Roscoe Conkling, of New York, in the House of representatives, April 29, 1862. [Washington, Printed at the office of the Congressional globe, 1862]

8 p. 24½cm.

The Republican boss of New York strongly criticized the Congressional Committee on Government Contracts for its handling of alleged corruption, swindles and theft.

Contrabands' relief commission, *Cincinnati.*

Report by the committee of the Contrabands' relief commission of Cincinnati, Ohio, proposing a plan for the occupation and government of vacated territory in the seceded states. Cincinnati, Gazette steam printing house, 1863.

16 p. 22½cm.

A short, early statement of Radical Reconstruction.

Dana, Charles Anderson, 1819–1897.

Lincoln and his cabinet; a lecture delivered on Tuesday, March 10, 1896, before the New Haven Colony historical society, by Charles Anderson Dana ... Cleveland and New York, Printed at the DeVinne press, 1896.

70 p. front., fold. pl., ports. 17½cm.

Provocative and opinionated; unfortunately, too short to be of greater value.

Donovan, Frank Robert, 1906–

Mr. Lincoln's proclamation; the story of the Emancipation proclamation, by Frank Donovan. New York, Dodd, Mead [1964]

vi, 146 p. illus., ports. 22 cm.

Undocumented but moderately well-written; presents a general view of the Proclamation as a military measure.

Doster, William Émile, 1837–

Lincoln and episodes of the civil war, by William E. Doster ... New York and London, G. P. Putnam's sons, 1915.

v, 282 p. 20½ cm.

Includes essays on such topics as Lincoln, Washington in wartime, and the U. S. War Department; rather restricted in value.

Eisenschiml, Otto, 1880–

In the shadow of Lincoln's death, by Otto Eisenschiml. New York, W. Funk, inc., 1940.

xii, 415, [1] p. illus. (maps) plates, ports., facsims. 23½ cm.

A supplement to Why Was Lincoln Murdered?; the author here looks more sternly at Stanton and his possible involvement in the assassination.

Eisenschiml, Otto, 1880–

Why was Lincoln murdered? By Otto Eisenschiml ... Boston, Little, Brown and company, 1937.

x, 503 p. illus. (maps) plates, ports., facsims. 23½ cm.

Appropriately titled, the book asked a multitude of questions and offered few definite answers; the impetus for many succeeding studies on the same enigmatic subject.

Farrar, C C S.

The war, its causes and consequences. By C. C. S. Farrar, of Bolivar County, Miss. Cairo, Ills., Memphis, Tenn. [etc.] Blelock & co., 1864.

260 p. 19cm.

This strange commentary upholds states' rights, criticizes both democracy and secession, and blames the South for the war.

Fisher, Sidney George, 1809–1871.

The trial of the Constitution. By Sidney George Fisher ... Philadelphia, J. B. Lippincott & co.; [etc., etc.] 1862.

xv, [17]–391 p. 24 cm.

An argument that the Federal government must have unlimited power if the Union is to be preserved; Fisher blamed the war on slavery and Democrats.

Franklin, John Hope, 1915–
The Emancipation proclamation. [1st ed.] **Garden City, N. Y., Doubleday, 1963.**

181 p. illus. 22 cm.

A solid though sometimes overstated treatment; still remains the best study on the subject.

Franklin, William Buel, 1823–1903.
A reply of Maj.-Gen. William B. Franklin, to the report of the joint committee of Congress on the conduct of the war, submitted to the public on the 6th of April, 1863 ... New York, D. Van Nostrand, 1863.

31 p. 2 fold. maps (incl. front.) 23½ cm.

One of the more bitter attacks against the meddling Committee; the Democrats made capital of Gen. Franklin's diatribe.

Garfield, James Abram, *pres. U. S.*, 1831–1881.
Speech of Hon. James A. Garfield, of Ohio, on the confiscation of property of rebels. Delivered in the House of representatives, January 28, 1864. [Washington, Printed by L. Towers, 1864]

8 p. 22½ cm.

Professing to speak for the army, Garfield asserted that the law of confiscation rested on the rights of belligerents; hence, the Rebels had no privileges.

Gates, Paul Wallace, 1901–
Free homesteads for all Americans; the Homestead act of 1862. Washington, Civil War Centennial Commission, 1962 [i. e. 1963]

11 p. 23 cm.

A brief history of the developments leading to the Homestead Act; a good introduction to a comparatively neglected subject.

Gooch, Daniel Wheelwright, 1820–1891.
Secession and reconstruction. Speech of Hon. Daniel W. Gooch, of Mass., delivered in the House of representatives, May 3, 1864. [Washington, Printed by L. Towers for the Union congressional committee, 1864]

8 p. 22½ cm.

The urging of a Massachusetts Radical congressman that the North bring to bear against the South "all the power human ingenuity can devise or human agency can execute."

Gray, Wood, 1905–
The hidden civil war; the story of the Copperheads, by Wood Gray ... New York, The Viking press, 1942.

314 p. illus. (maps) plates, ports., facsims. 24 cm.

A study of Northern defeatism during the war; Gray concentrated on Midwestern dissatisfaction, notably Vallandigham and the Northwest Conspiracy.

Gunderson, Robert Gray.
Old gentlemen's convention; the Washington Peace Conference of 1861. Madison, University of Wisconsin Press, 1961.

xiii, 168 p. illus., ports. 23 cm.

In this slim but incisive study, the author relied heavily on memoirs and letters to reveal the motives of the individual delegates.

Gurowski, Adam, *hrabia*, 1805–1866.
Diary ... By Adam Gurowski. Boston [etc.] 1862–66.

3 v. 19 cm.

Gossipy journals by a European radical who gained employment in the State Department; Gurowski was highly critical of just about everything he saw and heard.

Handlin, William Wallace, *b.* 1830.
American politics, a moral and political work, treating of the causes of the civil war, the nature of government, and the necessity for reform. By W. W. Handlin. New Orleans, I. T. Hinton, 1864.

108 p. 20½ cm.

The traditional argument that slavery caused the war, but Handlin added that political and journalistic agitation also played deadly roles.

Hendrick, Burton Jesse, 1870–1949.
Lincoln's war cabinet, by Burton J. Hendrick ... Boston, Little, Brown and company, 1946.

6 p. l., [3]–482 p. front., pl., ports. 22 cm.

Standard interpretations of Lincoln's cabinet members, with emphasis on such troublemakers as Stanton and Chase; popularly written but not thoroughly researched.

Hesseltine, William Best, 1902–
Lincoln and the war governors. [1st ed.] New York, A. A. Knopf, 1948.
x, 405, xxii p. 25 cm.

Detailed analyses of federal-state conflicts, with an excellent picture of how inharmonious states were welded into a cohesive Union.

Hesseltine, William Best, 1902–
Lincoln's plan of reconstruction. Tuscaloosa, Ala., Confederate Pub. Co., 1960.
154 p. 22 cm.

A refutation that Lincoln alive could have or would have prevented "the age of hate."

Howard, Hamilton Gay.
Civil war echoes: character sketches and state secrets, by a United States senator's son and secretary, Hamilton Gay Howard ... illustrated by V. Floyd Campbell ... Washington, D. C., Howard publishing company, 1907.
xvi, 317 p. incl. ports., facsims. 2 port. (incl. front.) 21½ cm.

A highly partisan and untrustworthy account of men and events in Washington during and after the war.

Hyman, Harold Melvin, 1924–
Era of the oath; Northern loyalty tests during the Civil War and reconstruction. Philadelphia, University of Pennsylvania Press, 1954.
229 p. illus. 24 cm.

Hyman concluded that efforts to clean disloyal elements out of the government met with little success and that the loyalty oaths generally failed to achieve desired goals.

Indiana. *Draft commissioner.*
Report of J. P. Siddall, draft commissioner ... Indianapolis, J. J. Bingham, state printer, 1863.
30 p., 1 l. 23cm.

These county statistics placed the number of "conscientious exempts" at 1.5% of the available manpower.

Kelley, William Darrah, 1814–1890.
Speeches of Hon. William D. Kelley. Replies of the Hon. William D. Kelley to George Northrop, esq., in the joint debate in the Fourth congressional district. Philadelphia, Collins, printer, 1864.
89 p. 22½cm.

Campaign utterances by a prominent Pennsylvania congressman, and good sources for Republican policies at the height of the war.

Kendall, Amos, 1789–1869.
Letters exposing the mismanagement of public affairs by Abraham Lincoln, and the political combinations to secure his re-election. By Amos Kendall. Washington, D. C., Printed at the Constitutional union office, 1864.
46 p. 23½cm.

A bitter Democratic document circulated during the 1864 presidential campaign; Kendall's unbridled vehemence centered on Lincoln and the Peninsular Campaign.

Kirkland, Edward Chase.
The peacemakers of 1864, by Edward Chase Kirkland. New York, The Macmillan company, 1927.
5 p. l., 279 p. 20½ cm.

An authoritative work still valuable in spite of its age; Kirkland is at his best in the handling of personalities.

Klement, Frank L
The Copperheads in the Middle West. [Chicago] University of Chicago Press [1960]
xiii, 341 p. ports., facsims. 23 cm.

A re-appraisal of Copperheads that runs counter to Wood Gray's study of the same subject.

Ladies' relief association of the District of Columbia.
Proceedings attending the opening of the Patent office fair, under the auspices of the Ladies' relief association of the District of Columbia. February 22, 1864. Washington, Printed for the benefit of the fair, 1864.
30 p. 25cm.

Contains an address by L. E. Chittenden, Register of the Treasury and later author of a well-known memoir.

[Leland, Charles Godfrey] 1824–1903.
Ye book of copperheads. Philadelphia, F. Leypoldt, 1863.
1 p. l., 24, [6] p. illus. 13 x 23 cm.

A collection of cartoons and rhyming comments on Fernando Wood, Vallandigham, the New York World and others; this study must have delighted school children of the day.

[Lester, Charles Edwards] 1815–1890.
The light and dark of the rebellion ... Philadelphia, G. W. Childs, 1863.
303 p. 19½cm.

A disjointed, unusable narrative in which the author compared Northern politics and politicians with events and men of antiquity.

Locke, David Ross, 1833–1888.
The struggles of Petroleum V. Nasby [pseud.] Original illus. by Thomas Nast. Abridged ed. selected, edited, and with an introd. by Joseph Jones. Notes to the chapters by Gunther Barth. Boston, Beacon Press [1963]
246 p. illus. 21 cm.

Locke's satirical pen continually pricked Northern politicians throughout the war period; this work contains 189 of the most famous and biting letters of the bombastic "Nasby."

The lost "spade"; or, The grave digger's revenge. With appendix. A great political, martial, serio-comic legendary, romantic and farcial drama. Written by the happy Democratic family, expressly for the peace democracy. Performed for over three months in the Canadian provinces (Holcomb & Clay's theatre,) and in the Chicago Wigwam (since demolished.) It is now brought out by Messrs. Rebel &'Sympathizer, and is respectfully dedicated by them to the northern Scum and Mudsills. The managers flatter themselves that no expense has been spared by them, through the kindness of their British friends, to make this the most peaceable drama of the age. New York, 1864.
16 p. 18cm

A satire on Southern news and propaganda, and Northern Democrats, in the 1864 election; Bully Boy (McClellan) is one of the leading actors.

Lowell, James Russell, 1819–1891.
Political essays, by James Russell Lowell. Boston and New York, Houghton Mifflin and company, 1889.
3 p. l., 326 p. 20 cm.

Contains the famed New Englander's views on the Union, the war, McClellan, Lincoln, and the election of 1864.

McCarthy, Charles Hallan, 1860–1941.
Lincoln's plan of reconstruction, by Charles H. McCarthy ... New York, McClure, Phillips & co., 1901
xxiv, 504 p. 24½ cm.

An early but valuable treatment of Lincoln's hopes for a restored Union; largely superseded now by the studies of J. G. Randall and T. H. Williams.

Markens, Isaac.
President Lincoln and the case of John Y. Beall, by Isaac Markens. New York, Printed for the author, 1911.
cover-title, 11 p. port. 25 cm.

Markens sought to spotlight Lincoln's noncompassionate side by showing that the President refused clemency when 91 congressmen urged mercy.

Meneely, Alexander Howard, 1899–
The War department, 1861; a study in mobilization and administration, by A. Howard Meneely ... New York, Columbia university press; London, P. S. King & son, ltd., 1928.
400 p. front. (port.) 23 cm.

Although outdated, still a good treatment; concentrates on Sec. Cameron's mismanagement.

Milton, George Fort, 1894–
Abraham Lincoln and the fifth column, by George Fort Milton. New York, The Vanguard press, 1942.
ix p., 1 l., xi–xiv p., 1 l., 17–364 p. front., plates, ports., facsim. 24 cm.

A classic work on creative conspiracies, espionage and counter-espionage; Milton relied heavily on governmental records.

Nevins, Allan, 1890– *ed.*
Lincoln and the Gettysburg address; commemorative papers [by] John Dos Passos [and others] Urbana, University of Illinois Press, 1964.
133 p. facsim. (on lining papers) 22 cm.

A series of incisive essays by several of the nation's leading intellectuals; excellent for an understanding of the meaning of the address.

Newman, Francis William, 1805–1897?

The good cause of President Lincoln. A lecture by Professor F. W. Newman ... [London] The Emancipation society [1863]

24 p. 17½cm.

An Englishman heaped propagandistic praise on Lincoln in general and the Emancipation Proclamation in particular.

Paine, Levi Leonard, 1837–1902.

Political lessons of the rebellion. A sermon delivered at Farmington, Connecticut, on fast day, April 18, 1862. By Rev. Levi L. Paine. Farmington, S. S. Cowles, 1862.

19 p. 21cm.

A brief discourse alleging that American faults were the conflict between law and liberty and the widespread corruption; war came as a chastisement.

Parker, Joel, 1795–1875.

Constitutional law: with reference to the present condition of the United States. By Joel Parker. Cambridge, Welch, Bigelow, and company, printers to the university, 1862.

35 p. 22 cm.

A pessimistic treatise by a Harvard professor who abhorred the war; useful as a contemporary piece.

Phillips, Wendell, 1811–1884.

... The war of the union; a lecture; by Wendell Phillips, esq., delivered in New York and Boston, December, 1861. New York, E. D. Barker; [etc., etc.] 1862.

cover-title, [7]–30 p. 21cm.

As expected, this noted abolitionist blamed everything on slavery; his style and content are outdated.

Pierrepont, Edwards, 1817–1892.

A review by Judge Pierrepont of Gen. Butler's defense, before the House of representatives, in relation to the New Orleans gold. New York, W. C. Bryant & co., printers, 1865.

cover-title, 27 p. 20½cm.

An interesting commentary on "Beast" Butler's seizure of gold in Louisiana and the General's initial reluctance to relinquish it to the public domain.

Potter, David Morris.

Lincoln and his party in the secession crisis, by David M. Potter .... New Haven, Yale university press; London, H. Milford, Oxford university press, 1942.

x p., 1 l., 408 p. 23 cm.

Treats "intelligently and in critically scholarly fashion" Lincoln's handling--or mishandling--of Southern secession in the period Nov., 1860-Mar., 1861.

Randall, James Garfield, 1881–

... The confiscation of property during the civil war ... by James Garfield Randall. Indianapolis, Mutual printing and lithographing co., 1913.

vi, 7–72 p. 24cm.

Originally the doctoral dissertation of the eminent historian; still used widely and quoted often.

Randall, James Garfield, 1881–

Constitutional problems under Lincoln, by James G. Randall ... New York, London, D. Appleton and company, 1926.

xviii p., 1 l., 580 p. illus. (map) 22cm.

Perhaps the most underrated volume on the Civil War; absolutely indispensable to any study of Northern wartime politics.

Randall, James Garfield, 1881–

Lincoln and the South [by] J. G. Randall ... Baton Rouge, Louisiana state university press, 1946.

viii p., 2 l., 161 p. ports., facsims. 21 cm.

Very incisive essays that emphasize Lincoln's Southern background and his practical thinking about a restored Union.

Republican party. *National convention.*

Proceedings of the first three Republican national conventions of 1856, 1860 and 1864, including proceedings of the antecedent national convention held at Pittsburgh, in February, 1856, as reported by Horace Greeley. Minneapolis, Minn., C. W. Johnson [1893]

264 p. 23 cm.

Its age notwithstanding, this work is still revealing for Republican strategy in the two national elections associated with the war.

Republican party. *New York (State)*

The Union state ticket. Personal character and military services. Gallantry which, under the first Napoleon, would have made French marshals. New York, Baker & Godwin, printers, 1865.

24 p. 22½cm.

A good example of the slanted campaign literature of the period; this one supported the Republican Party.

Review of Hon. J. Collamer's speech, made in the Senate, on the 16th January, 1865, on the bill for the repeal of the eighth section of the Act of July 2d, 1864, respecting trade with the people of the revolted states. Washington, D. C., McGill & Witherow, printers, 1865.

35 p. 22½cm.

An argument that Collamer was wrong in wanting to repeal the law allowing trade with the South, for such trade would benefit the North more.

The **rightful** power of Congress to confiscate and emancipate ... Reprinted from the Law reporter for June, 1862. Boston, C. H. Crosby, printer [1862]

cover-title, 24 p. 22cm.

An interesting monograph, allegedly written by Charles F. Blake, in which the author opposed both emancipation and confiscation.

Rollins, Edward Henry, 1824–1889.

Confiscation and emancipation. Speech of Hon. Edward H. Rollins, of New Hampshire, delivered in the House of representatives, Thursday, May 22, 1862. [Washington, Scammell & co., printers, 1862]

8 p. 25cm.

A radical cry for confiscation of Rebel property, lest treason be given a premium.

Roscoe, Theodore.

The web of conspiracy; the complete story of the men who murdered Abraham Lincoln. Englewood Cliffs, N. J., Prentice-Hall [1959]

xiv, 562 p. illus., ports., maps, facsims. 24 cm.

An intriguing though unconvincing work in which Roscoe joined others in pointing an accusing finger at Stanton as a conspirator in Lincoln's murder.

[**Rush, Benjamin**] 1811–1877.

Letter on the rebellion, to a citizen of Washington, from a citizen of Philadelphia. Philadelphia, C. Sherman & son, printers, 1862.

23 p. 23½cm.

Rush supported Wilkes in the Trent Affair, asserted that the South had long had too much national power, and approved the revolution then in progress.

[**Searing,** *Mrs.* **Laura Catherine (Redden)**] 1840–

Notable men in "the House." A series of sketches of prominent men in the House of representatives, members of the Thirty-seventh Congress. Written and ed. by Howard Glyndon [*pseud.*] New York, Baker & Godwin, 1862.

103, [1] p. 23½cm.

Weak sketches on such individuals as Grow, Stevens, Voorhees, Colfax and Lovejoy.

Shapiro, Henry D

Confiscation of Confederate property in the North. Ithaca, N. Y., Cornell University Press [1962]

58 p. 23 cm.

A study of confiscated acts, with disappointingly little attention on such points as the motivations of those who sought confiscation.

Shepard, S E

The duty of Christians to civil government. By S. E. Shepard ... [Cincinnati, H. S. Bosworth, 186–?]

24 p. 19cm.

Shepard gave religious support to the Union government and argued that it was the duty of all ministers to support the war cause.

Silver, David Mayer, 1915–

Lincoln's Supreme Court. Urbana, University of Illinois Press, 1956.

ix, 272 p. ports. 26 cm.

Includes biographical sketches of wartime justices, as well as a summary of Lincoln's attempt to pack the court; a good introduction to a subject that merits more.

Smith, Donnal Vore, 1901–

Chase and civil war politics, by Donnal V. Smith, PH. D. ... Columbus, O., The F. J. Heer printing co., 1931.

3 p. l., 5–181 p. front. (port.) 23½ cm.

Little more than an introduction to the subject; originally appeared as a journal article.

Smith, William Ernest, 1892–

The Francis Preston Blair family in politics, by William Ernest Smith ... New York, The Macmillan company, 1933.

2 v. fronts., plates, ports., fold. geneal. tab. 24 cm.

A primary source for the political and personal relationships between the Blairs and Lincoln.

Spence, James, *b.* 1816.

L'Union américaine; ses effets sur le caractère national et la politique; causes de la dissolution et étude du droit constitutionnel de séparation; tr. de l'anglais de James Spence. Paris, Michel Lévy frères, 1862.

434 p. 22cm.

Southern propaganda for European audiences, this anti-Northern tract argued that a struggle for political dominance, and not slavery, was the primary cause of the war.

Stevens, Thaddeus, 1792–1868.

Government contracts. Speech of Hon. Thad. Stevens, of Pennsylvania, in the House of representatives, April 28, 1862, on the report of the select committee on government contracts. Washington, D. C., Scammell & co., printers, 1862.

15 p. 24½cm.

A defense against charges of fraud levied on Cameron and Fremont.

Stevens, Thaddeus, 1792–1868.

Speech of Hon. T. Stevens, in reply to the attack on Gen. Hunter's letter. [n. p., 1862]

15 p. 24cm.

Stevens here urged support of Hunter's policy of enlisting emancipated slaves; he felt that such a policy would shorten the war and save lives.

Stevens, Thaddeus, 1792–1868.

Speech of Hon. T. Stevens, of Pennsylvania, delivered in the House of representatives, March 19, 1867, on the bill (H. R. no. 20) relative to damages to loyal men, and for other purposes ... [Washington, 1867]

8 p. 24cm.

An advocation of punishment of traitors by confiscating their property and using it for despoiled loyal men and wounded veterans.

Stevens, Thaddeus, 1792–1868.

Speech of Hon. Thaddeus Stevens, of Pennsylvania, on the bill to raise additional soldiers. Delivered in the House of representatives, Feb. 2, 1863. [Washington, Towers & co., printers, 1863]

8 p. 25 cm.

With the terms of service of 300,000 men soon expiring, Stevens proposed replacing them all with Negro troops.

Stevens, Thaddeus, 1792–1868.

The tax bill. Speech of Hon. Thaddeus Stevens, of Pennsylvania, in the House of representatives, April 8, 1862. [Washington, Scammell & co., printers, 1862]

4 p. 24cm.

In this defense of the bill, the House leader of the Republicans showed that this tax measure could be limited to two years--if Rebel property were sold to pay the war costs.

Stidger, Felix Grundy, 1836– *ed.*

Treason history of the order of Sons of liberty, formerly Circle of honor, succeeded by Knights of the golden circle, afterward Order of American knights. The most gigantic treasonable conspiracy the world has ever known. 1864 ... Ed. by Felix G. Stidger ... [Chicago, The author] 1903.

246, 30 p. front., illus., ports. 20cm.

This voluminous study is too filled with sensationalisms and exaggerations to be of any more than minimal use today.

Sumner, Charles, 1811–1874.

The rebellion:—its origin and main-spring. An oration delivered by Hon. Charles Sumner, under the auspices of the Young men's Republican union of New York, November 27, 1861. New York. Printed for the Young men's Republican union. 1861.

16 p. 24cm.

The senator asserted that slavery--the cause of the war--must be completely abolished; the Democrats must also be weakened.

Sumner, Charles, 1811–1874.

Rights of sovereignty and rights of war: two sources of power against the rebellion. Speech of Hon. Charles Sumner ... on his bill for the confiscation of property and the liberation of slaves belonging to rebels, in the Senate of the United States, May 19, 1862. [n. p., New York young men's Republican union, 1864]

16 p. 23½cm.

In this tirade, Sumner believed that Southern state government had committed political suicide. All rebels should be treated as common criminals.

[Swinton, William] 1833–1892.

The military and naval situation, and the glorious achievements of our soldiers and sailors. Washington, Union congressional committee, 1864.

15 p. 24½cm.

Republican ammunition in the national elections of 1864; Swinton is better known for his many military studies.

Thomas, Benjamin Franklin, 1813–1878.

Remarks of the Hon. B. F. Thomas, of Massachusetts, on the relation of the "seceded states" (so called) to the Union, and the confiscation of property and emancipation of slaves in such states; in the House of representatives, April 10, 1862. Boston, Printed by J. Wilson and son, 1862.

37 p. 23½cm.

The confiscation act, Thomas believed, did not provide for degrees of guilt, would create strong motives for continued resistance, and thus defeat the objectives of the government.

Tilley, John Shipley, 1880–

Lincoln takes command, by John Shipley Tilley. Chapel Hill, The University of North Carolina press, 1941.

xxxvii, 334 p. 22 cm.

This controversial study placed squarely on Lincoln's shoulders the responsibility for war; necessary for any investigation of the Sumter crisis.

Townsend, S P.

A speech by Dr. S. P. Townsend. The nation saved by interposition of Providence—the abolitionists—Wm. Lloyd Garrison—Abraham Lincoln—The financial question, etc., etc. Delivered November 3d, 1864, at Elizabeth city, New Jersey. [New York? 1864]

16 p. 23½cm.

A radical abolitionist blamed for the war; he also accepted the conspiracy theory, legal tender and the protective tariff.

Trimble, Robert.

Popular fallacies relating to the American question. A lecture, delivered in November, 1863. By Robert Trimble. London, Whittaker & co.; [etc., etc.] 1863.

36 p. 20½cm.

In this pro-Union lecture delivered in Great Britain, Trimble stressed slavery as the cause of the war and warned against revolutions begun from evil bases.

Trollope, Anthony, 1815–1882.

... Four lectures: The civil service as a profession (1861); The present condition of the northern states of the American union (1862 or 1863); Higher education of women (1868); On English prose fiction as a rational amusement (1870). Printed verbatim from the original texts. Edited with collations, notes, etc., by Morris L. Parrish and published for him by Constable & co., ltd. London [1938]

vii, 139 p. 20½cm.

An English visitor with strong Union sympathies subtly advocated British support of the North.

Trumbull, Lyman, 1813–1896.

The constitutionality and expediency of confiscation vindicated. Speech of Hon. Lyman Trumbull, of Illinois, on the bill to confiscate the property and free the slaves of rebels; delivered in the Senate of the United States, April 7, 1862. Washington, Printed at the Congressional globe office, 1862.

15 p. 24cm.

Confiscation was both constitutional and expedient, for strenuous measures must be used to preserve the Union.

Ulrich, Bartow Adolphus, 1840–1930.

Abraham Lincoln and constitutional government, by Bartow A. Ulrich ... [Chicago] Chicago legal news [©1916–21]

3 v. in 2. front., plates, ports., facsim. 23½cm.

This largely neglected study contains a provocative appendix of the views of Lincoln and Grant "on the Jew question."

U. S. *Circuit court (4th circuit)*

Reports of cases decided by Chief Justice Chase in the Circuit court of the United States for the Fourth circuit, during the years 1865 to 1869, both inclusive, in the districts of Maryland, Virginia, North Carolina, and South Carolina. Revised and corrected by the Chief Justice. Containing an appendix with the constitution of the Confederate States of America, and the Conscription, Impressment, and Sequestration acts of that government. By Bradley T. Johnson ... New York, Diossy & company, 1876.

xx, 637 p. 23 cm.

Contains the principal court cases of the war, including that of Jefferson Davis; also has a copy of the Confederate Constitution.

U. S. *Civil War Centennial Commission.*
Emancipation centennial, 1962; a brief anthology of the preliminary proclamation. Washington, 1962.
27 p. illus. 24 cm.

A useful guide for the background forces and development of Lincoln's most famous proclamation.

U. S. *Congress.*
... A biographical congressional director with an outline history of the national Congress, 1774–1911. The Continental Congress: September 5, 1774–October 21, 1788. The United States Congress from the First to the Sixty-second Congress, March 4, 1789–March 3, 1911. Washington, Govt. print. off., 1913.
1136 p. 27 cm.

Lists senators and representatives by congress and includes concise sketches of each; essential for any study of the national legislature.

U. S. *Congress.*
The Congressional globe ... [23d Congress to the 42d Congress, Dec. 2, 1833, to March 3, 1873] Washington, Printed at the Globe office for the editors [etc.] 1834–73.
46 v. in 111. plans. 30 cm.

The indispensable record of congressional debates and legislation; as useful for politics as the War of the Rebellion is for military campaigns.

U. S. *Congress. House. Committee on claims.*
... T. T. Garrard and others. <To accompany bill H. R. no. 568> ... Report ... [Washington, Govt. print. off., 1864]
31 p. illus. (map) 25cm.

Typical of claims cases, this one involved the destruction of Garrard's salt works at Manchester, Ky.; Garrard's petition was denied.

U. S. *Congress. Joint Committee on the Conduct of the War.*
Report. Washington, Govt. Print. Off., 1863.
3 v. 23 cm.

A detailed report on the first battles in the East, and indicative of the actions of the most meddlesome of congressional committees.

U. S. *Congress. House. Committee on military affairs.*
... Study and investigation of battle fields in the United States for commemorative purposes ... Report. <To accompany H. R. 11613> ... [Washington, Govt. print. off., 1926]
10 p. 23cm. (69th Cong., 1st sess. House. Rept. 1071)

U. S. *Congress. Senate. Committee on military affairs.*
... Study and investigation of battle fields in the United States for commemorative purposes ... Report. <To accompany H. R. 11613> ... [Washington, Govt. print. off., 1926]
10 p. 23cm. (69th Cong., 1st sess. Senate. Rept. 917)

These two study-reports treat of battles from the Revolution through the Civil War and the possibility of converting several of the fields into national military parks.

U. S. *Congress House. Committee on war claims.*
... Claim of the city of New York ... Report. <To accompany S. 1694> ... [Washington, U. S. Govt. print. off., 1934]
14 p. incl. tables. 23½cm.

One of several thousand claims cases; this one is of interest because Congress agreed to reimburse New York $650,000 for that city's support of troops.

U. S. *Congress. House. Committee on war claims.*
... War-claims and claims of aliens. March 26, 1874.—Recommitted to the Committee on war-claims and ordered to be printed ... Report: <to accompany H. R. 2659.> [Washington, Govt. print. off., 1874]
104 p. 22½cm.

An outline of the legal principles involved in weighing damages to Rebel property by Union forces.

U. S. *Congress. House. Select committee on the war debts of the loyal states.*
... War debts of the loyal states. [Washington, 1866]
8 p. 23cm.

These debts amounted to $467,954,364; the committee recommended paying $118,487,105 in 20-year, five-percent U. S. Bonds.

U. S. *Congress. House. Select committee to inquire into the contracts of the government.*
... Government contracts. [Washington, Govt. print. off., 1861]
147, ii, 1109 p. 24 cm.

The examination testimony of 165 witnesses relative to army supplies, steamer charters, fortifications, etc.

U. S. *Congress. House. Special Committee on the Treatment of Prisoners of War and Union Citizens.*

Report on the treatment of prisoners of war by the rebel authorities during the War of the Rebellion: to which are appended the testimony taken by the committee, and official documents and statistics, etc. Washington, Govt. Print. Off., 1869.

1205 p. 23 cm.

One of the early examples of "waving the bloody shirt;" other, similar works may be found in the bibliographical section on prisons and prisoners of war.

U. S. *District court. New York (Southern district)*

... The United States *vs.* The steamer Peterhoff and her cargo. In prize. Opinion of the court, by Judge Betts. With an appendix, containing the opinions of Judge Marvin, in the District court of the United States for the Southern district of Florida, in the cases of the Dolphin and the Pearl. New-York, J. W. Amerman, printer, 1864.

116 p. 22½cm.

Lower courts had condemned the vessel and cargo, but the Supreme Court reversed the decision except for a portion of the cargo.

U. S. *President.*

A compilation of the messages and papers of the presidents, 1789–1902, by James D. Richardson ... [New York] Bureau of national literature and art, 1903.

10 v. fronts., illus., plates, ports. 23½ cm.

Volume VI spans the Civil War period but provides little material not available in other more useful sources.

U. S. *President, 1861–1865 (Lincoln)*

General order respecting the observance of the Sabbath Day in the Army and Navy. Washington, 1862.

sheet. 18 x 11 cm.

A decree roughly parallel to Washington's First General Order; also printed in the Official Records, Ser. III, Vol. II.

U. S. *President, 1861–1865 (Lincoln)*

A proclamation respecting soldiers absent without leave. [Washington] 1863.

4 p. 19 cm.

Lincoln's famous decree granting amnesty to all AWOL soldiers who voluntarily returned to their commands.

U. S. *Treasury dept.*

Commercial intercourse with, and in, states declared in insurrection, and the collection of abandoned and captured property. Embracing the Treasury department circulars and regulations; the executive proclamations and license; and the War and Navy department orders relating to those subjects. September 11, 1863. Washington, Gov't print. off., 1863.

2 p. l., [3]–56 p. 21½cm.

Contains definitions of captured and abandoned property, rules and regulations pertaining to trade and special agents, plus a series of presidential proclamations.

U. S. *Treasury dept.*

... Letter from the secretary of the Treasury, transmitting, in response to Senate resolution of March 8, 1880, a statement showing the expenditures of the government on account of the war of the rebellion from July 1, 1861, to June 30, 1879, inclusive, &c. [Washington, Govt. print. off., 1880]

7 p. 22cm.

This report by John Sherman showed that expenditures growing out of the war amounted to $6,189,929,000, and that, in Aug., 1865, the public debt was in excess of $2,756,431,000.

U. S. *War dept.*

Report of the secretary of war. [Washington, 1865]

cover-title, 47 p. 22½cm.

In addition to Stanton's report, this pamphlet also contains reports by various provost marshals.

Upton, Emory, 1839–1881.

... The military policy of the United States. By Bvt. Maj. Gen. Emory Upton, United States Army. 3d impression. Washington, Govt. print. off., 1912.

1 p. l., xxiii, 495 p. fold. map. 23 cm.

A highly respected general pointedly criticized the weaknesses of civilians attempting to formulate military policies.

Wade, Benjamin Franklin, 1800–1878.

Facts for the people. Ben Wade on McClellan. And Gens. Hooker & Heintzelman's testimony. A crushing review of little Napoleon's military career. [Cincinnati, C. Clark, 1864]

8 p. 24½cm.

A radical Republican strongly criticized McClellan for his caution; Wade pointedly hinted that treason might have been involved.

Wade, Benjamin Franklin, 1800–1878.

Traitors and their sympathizers. Speech of Hon. B. F. Wade, of Ohio, in the Senate of the United States, April 21, 1862. [Washington, Scammell & co., printers, 1862]

8 p. 24½cm.

In another tirade Wade justified the meddling of his Committee on the Conduct of the War.

Warren, Charles, 1868–

The supreme court in United States history, by Charles Warren ... Boston, Little, Brown, and company, 1922.

3 v. fronts., plates, ports. 23½ cm.

An adequate portrayal of a tribunal whose wartime activities were largely passive.

Weeden, William Babcock, 1834–1912.

War government, federal and state, in Massachusetts, New York, Pennsylvania and Indiana, 1861–1865, by William B. Weeden ... Boston and New York, Houghton, Mifflin and company, 1906.

xxv, 389, [1] p. 21½ cm.

A still-valuable study; emphasizes that not only was war government on all levels in chaos but also that public business was badly handled.

Whiting, William, 1813–1873.

Military arrests in time of war. By William Whiting. Washington, Govt. print. off., 1863.

59 p. 22 cm.

A short but pointed essay on the subject by a leading Northern political philosopher.

Williams, Thomas Harry, 1909–

Lincoln and the radicals [by] T. Harry Williams. [Madison] The University of Wisconsin press [°1941]

6 p. l., 3–413 p. illus., ports. 22½ cm.

This traditional interpretation is now under challenge by the revisionists; Williams emphasized the sordid factionalism within Lincoln's party.

Wilson, Henry, 1812–1875.

Military measures of the United States Congress. 1861–1865. By Henry Wilson ... Printed from advance sheets of the Rebellion record. New York, D. Van Nostrand, 1866.

v, 88 p. front. (port.) 25½cm.

Wilson's radical views weakened this summary of congressional wartime actions.

Zornow, William Frank.

Lincoln & the party divided. [1st ed.] Norman, University of Oklahoma Press [1954]

xi, 264 p. ports. 23 cm.

A thoroughly researched study of the 1864 election, though lacking in interpretations and conclusions.

THE UNION

Economic and Social Studies

John T. Hubbell

Adams, Randolph Greenfield, 1892–
Hudibrastic aspects of some editions of the Emancipation proclamation [by] Randolph G. Adams ... Philadelphia, 1946.
1 p. l., 11–17 p. 23cm.

This too-slim essay on various editions of Lincoln's document has now been superseded by a number of studies.

Alcott, Louisa May, 1832–1888.
Hospital sketches and Camp and fireside stories. By Louisa M. Alcott ... Boston, Roberts brothers, 1892.
1 p. l., ii p., 1 l., 3–379 p. front., plates. 18 cm.

This interesting account by a remarkable woman forms a long introduction to the subject of Civil War hospitals.

American anti-slavery society.
Proceedings of the American anti-slavery society, at its third decade, held in the city of Philadelphia, Dec. 3d and 4th, 1864 [*i. e.* 1863] Phonographic report by Henry M. Parkhurst. New York, American anti-slavery society, 1864.
175 p. 22cm.

Contains a masterful speech by W. L. Garrison on how superbly the Negro had adjusted to new freedom.

Ames, Blanche (Butler) 1847–1939.
Chronicles from the nineteenth century; family letters of Blanche Butler and Adelbert Ames, married July 21st, 1870, compiled by Blanche Butler Ames, 1935. [Clinton? Mass.] 1957.
2 v. plans. 25 cm.

Only the first 100 pages treat of the war--and the letters reprinted are too personal to be revealing of anything but the prominent Ames family.

Ames, Mary (Clemmer) 1839–1884.
Ten years in Washington. Life and scenes in the national capital, as a woman sees them. By Mary Clemmer Ames ... Hartford, Conn., A. D. Worthington & co.; [etc., etc.] 1873.
xx, [21]–587 p. plates, ports. (incl. front.) 21½ cm.

Superficial description of Washington and its people during the Civil War era.

Andreano, Ralph, *ed.*
The economic impact of the American Civil War. Cambridge [Mass.] Schenkman Pub. Co., 1962.
203 p. illus. 22 cm.

An excellent study of the subject.

Andrews, J. Cutler, 1908–
The North reports the Civil War. [Pittsburgh] University of Pittsburgh Press [1955]

x, 813 p. illus., ports., maps (1 fold.) 24 cm.

The war as newspaper correspondents saw it; a thorough treatment of such subjects as censorship, conflicts between press and officers, and exploits of individual reporters.

Archibald, William Charles, 1842–
Home-making and its philosophy, illustrated by a nesting branch of the Archibalds, by William Charles Archibald. Boston, Mass., The author, 1910.

xii, 506 p. front., plates, ports., facsim. 26cm.

Some sixty pages cover the family's homelife in New England during the war.

Armitage, Thomas, 1819–1896.
The past, present, and future of the United States. A discourse, delivered by Rev. Thomas Armitage, pastor of the Fifth avenue Baptist church, on Thanksgiving day, Nov. 27, and repeated by request, December 18, 1862. New York, T. Holman, 1862.

31 p. 23cm.

A typical Northern sermon of the period: heavy on patriotism, rich in religion, and as stirring as the minister could make it.

Armory square hospital gazette.
Armory square, Washington, D. C., J. E. Walker [etc.] 186

v. 23–34cm. weekly.

A weekly newspaper that provided a running commentary on events inside one of the North's larger army hospitals.

[**Bacon,** *Mrs.* **Georgeanna Muirson (Woolsey)**] 1833– *ed.*
Letters of a family during the war for the Union. 1861–1865. [New Haven, Conn., Tuttle, Morehouse & Taylor] 1899.

2 v. 20cm.

Penetrating commentaries, by members of the Woolsey family, on Northern hospitals, charities, and the general progress of the war.

[**Bacon,** *Mrs.* **Georgeanna Muirson (Woolsey)**] 1833–
Three weeks at Gettysburg ... New York, A. D. F. Randolph, 1863.

24 p. 14 x 12cm.

A short discourse, privately printed, of a battlefield visit; a later, unchanged edition appeared under the title: <u>What We Did at Gettysburg</u>.

Bagley, William Chandler, 1909–
Soil exhaustion and the civil war, by William Chandler Bagley, jr. Washington, D. C., American council on public affairs [1942]

xi, 101 p. 23½ cm.

A heavily documented, short study; Bagley emphasized soil exhaustion as an impetus for both slavery expansion and civil war.

Baker, Nina (Brown) 1888–
Cyclone in calico; the story of Mary Ann Bickerdyke. [1st ed.] Boston, Little, Brown, 1952.

278 p. port. 22 cm.

A popular sketch of a woman who devoted herself to the improvement of the care of the wounded and sick in the Union army.

Barnes, David M.
The draft riots in New York. July, 1863. The metropolitan police: their services during riot week. Their honorable record. By David M. Barnes. New York, Baker & Godwin, 1863.

117 p., 1 l. 23½ cm.

One of the first studies to appear on the riots; as critical of the rioters as it is laudatory of the city's officials.

Barrett, Don Carlos.
The greenbacks and resumption of specie payments, 1862–1879, by Don C. Barrett. Gloucester, Mass., P. Smith, 1965 [c1931]

x, 259 p. 21 cm.

Only one-fourth of this work treats of the war; the author showed a lack of understanding of its economic problems.

[Bartlett, John Russell] 1805–1886, *comp.*

The barbarities of the Rebels, as shown in their cruelty to the federal wounded and prisoners; in their outrages upon Union men; in the murder of Negroes, and in their unmanly conduct throughout the rebellion. By Colonel Percy Howard, late of the Royal horse guards [*pseud.*] Providence, R. I., Printed for the author, 1863.

40 p. 24½ cm.

One of many highly sensational--and completely unfounded--tract alleging atrocities by the other side; both North and South had a host of such propagandists.

Batcheler, Horatio Pettus.

Jonathan at home: or, A stray shot at the Yankees. By Capt. Horace P. Batcheler ... London, Printed by W. H. Collingridge, 1864.

viii, 287 p. 19½cm.

Highly quotable recollections of society in the wartime North, especially that of New York City.

Belcher, Wyatt Winton, 1907–

The economic rivalry between St. Louis and Chicago, 1850–1880. New York, 1947.

223 p. 23 cm.

The first nine chapters of this neglected work reveal much on two principal Northern cities during wartime.

Bellows, Henry Whitney, 1814–1882.

The state and the nation—sacred to Christian citizens. A sermon preached in All Souls' church, New York, April 21, 1861. By Henry W. Bellows. New York, J. Miller, 1861.

16 p. 22½cm.

An early, rousing sermon by a Unitarian minister who later became president of the U. S. Sanitary Commission.

Beman, Nathan Sidney Smith, 1785–1871.

Our civil war: the principles involved, its causes and cure, being a discourse delivered on Thanksgiving day, Nov. 27, 1862. [By] N. S. S. Beman. Troy, N. Y., A. W. Scribner & co., printers, 1863.

52 p. 22½cm.

Rev. Beman was then president of Rensselaer Polytechnic Institute; caught up by the "hate mood" of the day, he accused Southerners of every known cruelty.

Bernard, Kenneth A 1906–

Lincoln and the music of the Civil War, by Kenneth A. Bernard. Caldwell, Idaho, Caxton Printers, 1966.

xix, 333 p. 49 plates (incl. facsims., music, ports.) 24 cm.

An outgrowth of articles published in the Lincoln Herald; emphasizes the music most familiar to Lincoln, not the wartime favorites.

Billingsley, Amos Stevens, 1818–1897.

From the flag to the cross; or, Scenes and incidents of Christianity in the war. The conversions ... sufferings and deaths of our soldiers, on the battle-field, in hospital, camp and prison; and a description of distinguished Christian men and their labors. By A. S. Billingsley ... Philadelphia, Pa., Boston, Mass. [etc.] New-world publishing company; Burlington, Ia., R. T. Root, 1872.

3 p. l., v–xvi, 15–429 p. 12 pl., 9 port. (incl. front.) 22cm.

Valuable for the attitudes of many Northern clergy; republished under the title, Christianity in the War.

Bingham, Joel Foote, 1827–1914.

Great providences toward the loyal part of this nation. A discourse delivered at a united service of the seven Presbyterian congregations of Buffalo, November 24, 1864, on occasion of the annual thanksgiving, both of the state and of the nation. By Joel F. Bingham ... Buffalo, Breed, Butler and company, 1864.

59 p. 22½cm.

Illustrative of Presbyterian sentiment and sermons in the embattled North.

Blied, Benjamin Joseph, 1908–

Catholics and the Civil War, essays. Foreword by Peter Leo Johnson. Milwaukee, 1945.

162 p. 24 cm.

A good collection of essays on Catholics in the prewar period, as well as the wartime political questions in which they were involved.

Boardman, George Dana, 1828–1903.

Addresses delivered in the meeting-house of the First Baptist church of Philadelphia, April 14th, 16th, and 19th, 1865, by the Reverend George Dana Boardman, pastor. [Philadelphia, Sherman & co., printers, 1865]

cover-title, 64 p. 23cm.

The most climactic in content of scores of printed sermons by a popular Presbyterian minister.

Bogart, Ernest Ludlow, 1870–

... War costs and their financing; a study of the financing of the war and the after-war problems of debt and taxation, by Ernest Ludlow Bogart ... with an introduction by Russell C. Leffingwell ... New York, London, D. Appleton and company, 1921.

xxiii, [1] p., 1 l., 509, [1] p. 20½ cm.

A standard source on the Federal government's attempts to finance the war; still highly useful.

Bolles, Albert Sidney, 1846–1939.

The financial history of the United States, from 1861 to 1885. By Albert S. Bolles ... New York, D. Appleton and company, 1886.

xi, 585 p. 22½cm.

A recognized study for many years; now superseded by a number of more scholarly works.

Borrett, George Tuthill.

Letters from Canada and the United States. By George Tuthill Borrett ... London, Printed for private circulation, by J. E. Adlard, 1865.

2 p. l., 294 p. 20cm.

An English visitor was favorably impressed by the normalcy and solidarity of life in wartime New England.

Brainerd, Cephas, 1831–1910.

The work of the Army committee of the New York Young men's Christian association, which led to the organization of the United States Christian commission: a paper read before the Association at the monthly meeting, 18th December, 1865, at the request of the Board of directors, by Cephas Brainerd. New York, J. Medole, printer, 1866.

40 p. 23cm.

States in interesting fashion the precedent for the U. S. Christian Commission.

Brockett, Linus Pierpont, 1820–1893.

Woman's work in the civil war: a record of heroism, patriotism and patience. By L. P. Brockett ... and Mrs. Mary C. Vaughan. With an introduction, by Henry W. Bellows ... Illustrated with sixteen steel engravings. Philadelphia, Pa. [etc.] Zeigler, McCurdy & co.; Boston, Mass., R. H. Curran, 1867.

3 p. l., 5–799 p. 15 port. (incl. front.) 22½ cm.

A recommended study by a leading figure in social reform during the war period; rapidly becoming outdated.

Brookmire economic service, *New York.*

Economic trends of war and reconstruction, 1860–1870. New York, Brookmire economic service [©1918]

1 p. l., 30 p. diagrs. 23½cm.

This statistical study also compares the economic growth of the Civil War period with that of World War I.

Bucklin, Sophronia E.

In hospital and camp: a woman's record of thrilling incidents among the wounded in the late war. By Sophronia E. Bucklin. With an introduction by S. L. C. Philadelphia, J. E. Potter and company, 1869.

380 p. incl. front. (port.) plates. 22cm.

Of limited value, though it includes descriptions of some army hospitals.

[Burn, James Dawson]

Three years among the working-classes in the United States during the war. By the author of "The autobiography of a beggar-boy." London, Smith, Elder and co., 1865.

xvi, 309, [1] p. 19 cm.

An Englishman employed in the North during the war as a hat finisher continually expressed pessimism about the war's effect on American business.

Burton, Margaret Davis.

The woman who battled for the boys in blue. Mother Bickerdyke; her life and labors for the relief of our soldiers. Sketches of battle scenes and incidents of the sanitary service. Written by Margaret B. Davis [*i. e.* Margaret Davis Burton] Published for the benefit of M. A. Bickerdyke. San Francisco, Calif., Printed and sold by A. T. Dewey, 1886.

xii, [13]–166 p. incl. front. (port.) 19½ cm.

A laudatory essay on one of the most famous and beloved nurses in the Western theater.

[Butterfield, Horatio Quincy] 1822–1894.

U. S. Christian commission. A delegate's story. [Philadelphia? 1863]

cover-title, 8 p. 17½cm.

A eulogy, heavy with religious overtones, to this important commission.

[Campbell, John Francis] 1822–1885.
A short American tramp in the fall of 1864, by the editor of "Life in Normandy." Edinburgh, Edmonston and Douglas, 1865.

2 p. l., vii, 427 p. incl. front., illus., map. 21½ cm.

While Campbell's travels were mainly in Canada, he did journey through and comment on the northern part of the Union.

Carpenter, Hugh Smith, 1824–1899.
The relations of religion to the war: a sermon delivered on fast-day, Sept. 26, 1861. By Rev. Hugh Smith Carpenter ... Published by request. New York, W. A. Townsend, 1861.

23 p. 24cm.

An illuminating justification of the war on religious grounds; by a Presbyterian minister.

Chambrun, Charles Adolphe de Pineton, *marquis* **de,** 1831–1891.
Impressions of Lincoln and the Civil War, a foreigner's account; translated from the French by Aldebert de Chambrun. New York, Random House [1952]

x, 174 p. group port., facsim. 21 cm.

Letters written in the last years of the war by an official French envoy to Washington; the author's pen-pictures of Union leaders are especially useful.

Chase, *Mrs.* **Julia A (Houghton)** 1842–
Mary A. Bickerdyke, "mother". The life story of one who, as wife, mother, army nurse, pension agent and city missionary, has touched the heights and depths of human life. Written by Julia A. Chase. Pub. under the auspices of the Woman's relief corps, (Department of Kansas.) Lawrence, Kans., Journal publishing house, 1896.

viii, 145 p. 2 port. (incl. front.) 23cm.

Another deserved testimonial to a nurse affectionately known to Union soldiers in the West as "mother" Bickerdyke.

Chessman, G Wallace.
Ohio colleges and the Civil War [by] G. Wallace Chessman. [Columbus] Ohio State University Press for the Ohio Historical Society [c1963]

32 p. 24 cm.

A well-researched little survey of the wartime problems faced by Ohio's many colleges.

Christ in the army; a selection of sketches of the work of the U. S. Christian commission, by various writers. Printed for the Ladies Christian commission. [Philadelphia, J. B. Rodgers, pr.] 1865.

144 p. 1 illus. (port.) 14½cm.

This commentary on the activities of the Commission is of mixed value and limited usefulness.

Collis, Septima Maria (Levy) 1842–1917.
A woman's war record, 1861–1865, by Septima M. Collis (Mrs. Genl. Charles H. T. Collis) New York and London, G. P. Putnam's sons, 1889.

3 p. l., 78 p. front., plates, ports. 18 cm.

The bulk of this little memoir recounts how Mrs. Collis accompanied her husband, a Pennsylvania soldier, to the front.

Colyer, Vincent, 1825–1888.
Report of the Christian mission to the United States army, of Vincent Colyer, presented to the N. Y. and Brooklyn Young men's Christian associations, St. George's church, N. Y., Artists' patriotic fund, and other societies, from April 1861 to August 1862, including the battles of Bull Run, Roanoke island and Newbern, New York, G. A. Whitehorne, printer [1862?]

24 p. 22½cm.

This report, by a perceptive New Yorker, gives a clear insight into army social conditions during the first months of the war.

Commons, John Rogers, 1862–1945.
History of labour in the United States, by John R. Commons, David J. Saposs, Helen L. Sumner, E. B. Mittelman, H. E. Hoagland, John B. Andrews [and] Selig Perlman; with an introductory note by Henry W. Farnam ... New York, The Macmillan company, 1935–36.

4 v. diagrs. 22½ cm.

Volume II contains a long section on labor nationalism, 1860-1877; otherwise, this set is of little value to a study of the war period.

Conference on American Economic Institutional Change, 1850–1873, and the Impact of the Civil War, *Greenville, Del., 1964.*
Economic change in the Civil War era; proceedings. Edited by David T. Gilchrist & W. David Lewis. Greenville, Del., Eleutherian Mills-Hagley Foundation, 1965.

ix, 180 p. fold. map. 24 cm.

An excellent collection of essays on the impact of the Civil War on American economic institutions.

Congdon, Charles Taber, 1821–1891.

Tribune essays; leading articles contributed to the New York tribune from 1857 to 1863, by Charles T. Congdon; with an introduction by Horace Greeley ... New York, J. S. Redfield, 1869.

2 p. l., vii–xxiv, 406 p. 19½cm.

The best-known editorials by the journalist regarded as "Greeley's right hand man."

Corliss, Carlton Jonathan, 1888–

Main line of Mid-America; the story of the Illinois Central. New York, Creative Age Press, 1950.

xviii, 490 p. illus., ports., maps (part col.) 22 cm.

This solid study concentrates on economic matters, but it also adds much social data on one of the Union's most important rail lines.

Cross, Andrew Boyd.

The war. Battle of Gettysburg and the Christian commission. By Andrew B. Cross. [Baltimore] 1865.

60, 32 p. 3 fold maps. 22½cm.

A pat on the back to the Christian Commission.

Crozier, Emmet.

Yankee reporters, 1861–65. New York, Oxford University Press, 1956.

441 p. illus. 22 cm.

A reasonably researched account of leading reporters who, Crozier asserts, played a major role in preserving the Union.

The **cruelties** of war. By a churchman. Philadelphia, Printed for the author, 1864.

53 p. 24cm.

Interesting and unique in that a Northern clergyman castigated the Federal government for misconduct and upheld the Confederates as more virtuous belligerents.

Daly, Maria (Lydig) 1824–1894.

Diary of a Union lady, 1861–1865. Edited by Harold Earl Hammond. New York, Funk & Wagnalls [1962]

xlvii, 396 p. 22 cm.

Comparable in length to Mrs. Chesnut's diary, yet Mrs. Daly's observations of New York scenes lack the incisiveness found in the Chesnut journal.

Danforth, Mildred E

A Quaker pioneer: Laura Haviland, superintendent of the Underground. [1st ed. New York, Exposition Press [1961]

259 p. 21 cm.

Especially useful for the pre-war and wartime humanitarian efforts made in Michigan.

Dannett, Sylvia G L 1909– *ed.*

Noble women of the North. New York, T. Yoseloff [1959]

419 p. illus. 22 cm.

A collection of laudatory essays on well-known Northern women; based entirely on printed sources, with fact and legend blended indiscriminately.

Dannett, Sylvia G L 1909–

Our women of the sixties, by Sylvia G. L. Dannett and Katharine M. Jones. Washington, U. S. Civil War Centennial Commission, 1963.

44 p. illus., ports. 23 cm.

A cursory introduction to the subject; discusses in generalities the most outstanding women on both sides.

Darling, *Mrs.* **Flora (Adams)** 1840–1910.

Mrs. Darling's letters, or Memories of the civil war. By Mrs. Flora Adams Darling. New York, J. W. Lovell company [c1883]

2 p. l., 7–223 p. 18½cm.

Sentimental ramblings, restricted in scope and limited in value.

Davis, Andrew McFarland, 1833–1920.
The origin of the national banking system. Washington, Govt. Print. Off., 1910–11.
2 pts. (246 p.) 24 cm.

An uncritical narrative-history of the subject; contains much factual data on the national banking legislation of 1863-1864.

Dean, Henry Clay, 1822–1887.
Crimes of the civil war, and curse of the funding system. By Henry Clay Dean. Baltimore, Printed for the publisher, by J. W. Smith & bro., 1869.
vii, 539 p. 23 cm.

This highly partisan commentary on Civil War finance should be used with extreme care.

Dewey, Davis Rich, 1858–1942.
... Financial history of the United States, by Davis Rich Dewey ... New York [etc.] Longmans, Green, and co., 1903.
xxxv p., 1 l., 530 p. charts. 20½ cm.

Another once-important work now stricken by age.

Deyrup, Felicia Johnson, 1917–
Arms makers of the Connecticut Valley; a regional study of the economic development of the small arms industry, 1798–1870. Northampton, Mass., 1948.
vii, 290 p. illus. 24 cm.

Of value because comparatively little has been done in the area of Northern firearms industries.

Dicey, Edward, 1832–1911.
Six months in the federal states. By Edward Dicey ... London and Cambridge, Macmillan and co., 1863.
2 v. 18½cm.

Observations by a widely traveled Englishman of Northern life and manners; Dicey was an abolitionist in sympathies.

Dunham, Chester Forrester, 1891–
... The attitude of the northern clergy toward the South, 1860–1865 ... by Chester Forrester Dunham. Toledo, O., The Gray company, 1942.
xi, 258 p. 24cm.

A highly confusing treatment of a very important subject.

Edmundson, Sarah Emma, 1841–1898.
Nurse and spy in the Union Army: comprising the adventures and experiences of a woman in hospitals, camps, and battle-fields, by S. Emma E. Edmonds [pseud.] Hartford, W. S. Williams, 1865.
384 p. illus., port. 22 cm.

A sensational account of a woman in the front lines; one of several subsequent editions bore the provocative title, Unsexed.

Epler, Percy Harold, 1872–
The life of Clara Barton, by Percy H. Epler. New York, The Macmillan company, 1915.
xvii, 438 p. front., plates, ports. 20½ cm.

A satisfactory study of the famous Union nurse, though the work has weaknesses of sentimentality.

Erickson, Charlotte.
American industry and the European immigrant, 1860–1885. Cambridge, Harvard University Press, 1957.
x, 269 p. 25 cm.

A scholarly account of contract-labor laws, their repeal, and the general effect of immigration on the labor movement at the time of the war.

Erne, John Henry Crichton, *4th earl of,* **1839–1914.**
A tour in British North America and the United States, 1863; a lecture delivered to the Young men's Christian association at Lisnaskea, by Viscount Crichton. Dublin, Hodges, Smith and co., 1864.
63 p. 18½cm.

This English traveler took a highly critical look at the North, particularly its soldiers.

Erving, *Mrs.* **Annie Priscilla (Zerbe)**

Reminiscences of the life of a nurse in field, hospital and camp during the civil war. By Mrs. Annie Priscilla Erving ... Newburgh, N. Y., Daily news [c1904]

4 p. l., 62 p. incl. illus., 2 port. 19cm.

Short and of limited value; treats almost entirely of hospital life.

Farley, Joseph Pearson, 1839–1912.

West Point in the early sixties, with incidents of the war, by Joseph Pearson Farley ... Troy, N. Y., Pafraets book company, 1902.

vii, 201 p. front., plates. 23cm.

Farley's excellent and personal study becomes even more valuable when used with Morris Schaff's work on the same subject.

Faust, Albert Bernhardt, 1870–

The German element in the United States with special reference to its political, moral, social, and educational influence, by Albert Bernhardt Faust ... New York, The Steuben society of America, 1927.

2 v. in 1. fronts., plates, ports., maps (1 double) facsims. (1 double) 23 cm.

Voluminous and unreliable; Faust accepted all figures that would support his highly prejudiced approach.

Ferguson, Robert, 1817–1898.

America during and after the war. By Robert Ferguson ... London, Longmans, Green, Reader and Dyer, 1866.

4 p. l., ii p., 1 l., 280 p. 19½cm.

In this wordy memoir, an English clergyman-historian was awed by the diligence and hard work of wartime New Englanders.

Ferri-Pisani, Camille.

Prince Napoleon in America, 1861; letters from his aide-de-camp. Translated with a pref. by George J. Joyaux. Foreword by Bruce Catton. Illustrated by Gil Walker. Bloomington, Indiana University Press, 1959.

317 p. illus. 21 cm.

Seven long and extremely descriptive letters by an aide to the cousin of the French monarch; especially good for comments on the larger Northern cities; yet suffers from a lack of an index.

Fisch, Georges, 1814–

Nine months in the United States during the crisis. By the Rev. Georges Fisch ... With an introduction by the Hon. Arthur Kinnaird, M. P., and a preface by the Rev. W. Arthur. London, J. Nisbet & co., 1863.

1 p. l., [v]-xvi, 166 p. 17½cm.

A French minister's commentaries on American religion, education, character, conscience and slavery; much wearing argument is also included.

Fite, Emerson David, 1874–

Social and industrial conditions in the North during the civil war, by Emerson David Fite ... New York, P. Smith, 1930.

vii, 318 p. 21 cm.

Now dated, but still the best general survey of the subject.

Fogel, Robert William.

The Union Pacific Railroad; a case in premature enterprise. Baltimore, Johns Hopkins Press, 1960.

129 p. 24 cm.

A provocative short study that disputes the theme of rapacity among the promoters of the Union Pacific.

Foner, Philip Sheldon, 1910–

Business & slavery; the New York merchants & the irrepressible conflict [by] Philip S. Foner ... Chapel Hill, The University of North Carolina press, 1941.

ix, 356 p., 1 l. 23 cm.

Useful for the economic reactions of New York City to the coming of war.

Fredrickson, George M 1934–

The inner Civil War; northern intellectuals and the crisis of the Union [by] George M. Fredrickson. [1st ed.] New York, Harper & Row [1965]

viii, 277 p. 22 cm.

A detailed and heavily documented study of how the war acted as a catalyst for Northern intellectual change; the best available source on the subject.

Furness, William Henry, 1802–1896.

A voice of the hour: a discourse delivered by W. H. Furness ... Philadelphia, Sunday, January 10, 1864 Philadelphia, Crissy & Markley, printers [1864]

15 p. 22cm.

In a propagandistic sermon typical of that day, a Philadelphia minister termed slavery "a foaming fountain of insecurity and alarm, of violence and crime and blood."

Gobright, Lawrence Augustus, 1816–1879.

Recollection of men and things at Washington, during the third of a century. By L. A. Gobright. Philadelphia, Claxton, Remsen & Haffelfinger; Washington, W. H. & O. H. Morrison, 1869.

xi, 13–420 p. 19cm.

Gobright's reminiscences concentrate more on the prewar period, though the work contains some glimpses of the capital in wartime.

Goodrich, Frank Boott, 1826–1894.

The tribute book, a record of the munificence, self-sacrifice and patriotism of the American people during the war for the union ... By Frank B. Goodrich ... New York, Derby & Miller, 1865.

3 p. l., [3]–512 p. illus., plates. 27½cm.

A voluminous laudation of the Northern people, with emphasis on charities and hospital workers.

[**Green, Benjamin Edwards**] 1822–1907.

The irrepressible conflict between labor and capital: a brief summary of some of the chief causes and results of the late civil war in the United States, as presented in the translator's preface to Adolphe Granier de Cassagnac's History of the working and burgher classes, in which the origin, nature, and objects of the much calumniated French Commune are historically explained. Philadelphia, Claxton, Remsen & Haffelfinger, 1872.

2 p. l., vii–lxv, 329–349, 7–13, 351–352 p. 21½cm.

An early Marxist interpretation of the Civil War.

Grossman, Jonathan Philip, 1915–

William Sylvis, pioneer of American labor; a study of the labor movement during the era of the civil war, by Jonathan Grossman, PH. D. New York, Columbia university press; London, P. S. King & Staples, ltd., 1945.

302 p. front. (port.) 23 cm.

This study--as much a history of the molders' union as a biography of Sylvis--is valuable for insights into labor movements at the time of the war.

Hackett, Horatio Balch, 1808–1875.

Christian memorials of the war; or, Scenes and incidents illustrative of religious faith and principle, patriotism and bravery of our Army. With historical notes. By Horatio B. Hackett ... Boston, Gould and Lincoln; New York, Sheldon and co.; [etc., etc.] 1864.

xiv, 256 p. 20cm.

A collection of 130 episodes, anecdotes and incidents of Christianity's trials by war; some stories are of doubtful authenticity.

Haight, Theron Wilber.

... Three Wisconsin Cushings; a sketch of the lives of Howard B., Alonzo H. and William B. Cushing, children of a pioneer family of Waukesha County, by Theron Wilber Haight ... [Madison] Wisconsin history commission, 1910.

xiv, 109 p. front., ports., facsims. 23½ cm.

Two Cushings served in Midwestern army units; the third was in the U. S. Navy; contains some data on prewar Chicago and Wisconsin.

Hammond, William Alexander, 1828–1900, *ed.*

Military medical and surgical essays, prepared for the United States sanitary commission. Ed. by William A. Hammond ... Philadelphia, J. B. Lippincott & co., 1864.

viii, 9–552 p. illus. 23 cm.

An extremely valuable collection of individually published monographs written by experts in the field; revealing for the state of medicine in the war era.

[**Hammond, William Alexander**] 1828–1900.

... Two reports on the condition of military hospitals at Grafton, Va., and Cumberland, Md. ... New York, W. C. Bryant & co., printers, 1862.

40 p. 23cm.

Early statements by a leading member of the Sanitary Commission.

Hancock, Cornelia, 1840–1926.

South after Gettysburg; letters of Cornelia Hancock from the Army of the Potomac, 1863–1865; edited by Henrietta Stratton Jaquette. Philadelphia, University of Pennsylvania press, 1937.

xiii, 173 p. 2 illus. (plans) plates. 21 cm.

An excellent commentary by a Quaker nurse who concluded, "War is humbug."

Harper, Robert S

Lincoln and the press. New York, McGraw-Hill ⌈1951⌉

xii, 418 p. ports., facsims. 24 cm.

Good study of newspaper reactions to Lincoln; pertinent to the present day.

Haviland, Laura (Smith) 1808–1898.

A woman's life-work: labors and experiences of Laura S. Haviland. Cincinnati, Printed by Walden & Stowe, for the author, 1881.

3 p. l., ⌈3⌉–515 p. front. (port.) plates. 20 cm.

A too-often-overlooked memoir by a Michigan lady who toiled untiringly in local hospitals and for local war causes.

Hawthorne, Frank W

The Episcopal Church in Michigan during the Civil War ⌈by Frank W. Hawthorne. Lansing⌉ Michigan Civil War Centennial Observance Commission ⌈1966⌉

v, 29 p. 23 cm.

One of the better monographs in the Michigan CWCC series.

Hazard, Blanche Evans.

The organization of the boot and shoe industry in Massachusetts before 1875, by Blanche Evans Hazard ... Cambridge, Harvard university press; ⌈etc., etc.⌉ 1921.

3 p. l., v–x, 293, ⌈1⌉ p. maps, 2 facsim. (incl. front.) 23cm.

Relatively little of this work pertains to the war period, yet the study contributes to a better understanding of the shoemaking industry.

Headley, Joel Tyler, 1813–1897.

The great riots of New York, 1712 to 1873. Including a full and complete account of the four days' draft riot of 1863. By Hon. J. T. Headley ... New York, E. B. Treat, 1873.

2 p. l., ⌈7⌉–306, ⌈331⌉–359 p. front., plates. 21cm.

The first study of any depth on the July, 1863, outburst in New York City; now outdated and somewhat superseded.

Heathcote, Charles William, 1882–

The Lutheran church and the civil war, by Charles William Heathcote ... New York, Chicago ⌈etc.⌉ Fleming H. Revell company ⌈c1919⌉

160 p. 19½cm.

Of uneven content and quality; treats somewhat of both Northern and Southern synods.

Henshaw, *Mrs.* **Sarah Edwards (Tyler)** *b.* 1822.

Our branch and its tributaries; being a history of the work of the Northwestern sanitary commission and its auxiliaries, during the war of the rebellion. By Mrs. Sarah Edwards Henshaw. Including a full report of receipts and disbursements, by E. W. Blatchford, treasurer; and an introductory chapter, by Hon. Mark Skinner. Chicago, A. L. Sewell, 1868.

xvi, 17–432 p. pl., double maps. 22½cm.

A somewhat disorganized but still useful study of women's labors in the Midwest on behalf of the Union and its soldiers.

Hepburn, Alonzo Barton, 1846–1922.

History of coinage and currency in the United States and the perennial contest for sound money, by A. Barton Hepburn ... New York, The Macmillan company; London, Macmillan & co., ltd., 1903.

xiv, 666 p. 21½ cm.

A very conservative treatment of Civil War money by a former Comptroller of the Currency.

⌈Holstein, Anna Morris (Ellis) "*Mrs.* W. H. Holstein"⌉

Three years in field hospitals of the Army of the Potomac. By Mrs. H. Philadelphia, J. B. Lippincott & co., 1867.

vii, 9–131 p. 19½ cm.

Perceptive reminiscences of a woman who saw the decidedly unglamorous side of war with the Army of the Potomac.

Howe, Julia (Ward) 1819–1910.

Reminiscences, 1819–1899, by Julia Ward Howe ... Boston and New York, Houghton, Mifflin and company, 1899.

2 p. l., 465, ⌈1⌉ p. front., plates, ports., 2 fold. facsim. 21cm.

Self-confident ramblings of life in Maine; by the author of "The Battle Hymn of the Republic."

Howe, Samuel Gridley, 1801–1876.

A letter to Mrs. --------, and other loyal women, touching the matter of contributions for the army, and other matters connected with the war. By S. G. Howe. Boston, Ticknor & Fields, 1862.

27, 26 p. 23½cm.

A prominent Northern humanitarian says in essence, "Rally 'round the flag, girls!"

Hungerford, Edward, 1875–1948.

The story of the Baltimore & Ohio railroad, 1827–1927, by Edward Hungerford; profusely illustrated with maps, prints, photographs, etc., etc. New York, London, G. P. Putnam's sons, 1928.

2 v. fronts., plates, ports., facsims. (2 fold.) 24½ cm.

A full history of the famous railroad, but inferior to more recent studies by Festus P. Summers.

Hurn, Ethel Alice.

... Wisconsin women in the war between the states, by Ethel Alice Hurn, B. A. [Madison] Wisconsin history commission, 1911.

xix, 190 p. front. (port.) 6 pl. (1 fold.) 23½ cm.

A recounting of the activities of women on the home front in sending supplies, supporting morale, tending farms, etc., while the men were away.

[Jarvis, Mary Caroline] 1840– *comp.*

The services of the Protestant Episcopal church in the United States of America, as ordered by the bishops, during the civil war ... New York, Hatch & co., 1864.

[136] p. 22 x 18½cm.

Of limited value, even though it gives the "official" account; issued "for the benefit" of the Sanaitary Commission.

Jewell, Jacob, 1836–

Heroic deeds of noble master masons during the civil war, from 1861 to 1865, in the U. S. A., by Jacob Jewell ... [Pueblo, Col., The Franklin press, ©1916]

127 p. incl. port. 20cm.

Tributes, some doubtlessly exaggerated, of super patriots among Northern Masons.

Jolly, Ellen Ryan.

Nuns of the battlefield, by Ellen Ryan Jolly, LL. D. [Providence, The Providence visitor press, ©1927]

lx, [1], 336 p. incl. front. 23½ cm.

Surveys Catholic orders and nuns' activities as nurses; contains a useful bibliography.

Jones, Edgar De Witt, 1876–

Lincoln and the preachers; with an introd. by William H. Townsend. [1st ed.] New York, Harper [1948]

xviii, 203 p. ports. 21 cm.

A little-known but revealing work on the varying relations between Lincoln and prominent Northern clergymen.

Jones, Robert Leslie, 1907–

Ohio agriculture during the Civil War. [Columbus] Ohio State University Press for the Ohio Historical Society [1962]

25 p. 24 cm.

This small monograph on regional farming is thoroughly researched and useful to any large study of agriculture.

Kelley, William Darrah, 1814–1890.

Speeches, addresses and letters on industrial and financial questions. To which is added an introduction, together with copious notes and an index. By William D. Kelley, M. C. Philadelphia, H. C. Baird, 1872.

xxx, 5–514 p. 23½ cm.

A heavy collection of soft-money testimonies by one of the most noted protectionists of the period.

Kellogg, Florence Shaw.

Mother Bickerdyke as I knew her, by Florence Shaw Kellogg; with an introduction by Jenkin Lloyd Jones ... Chicago, Unity publishing company, 1907.

176 p. front. (port.) illus., pl. 19cm.

A useful memoir that is also a warm tribute to the famous Union nurse in the Tennessee theater.

Killough, Edward M.

History of the Western Maryland railway company, including biographies of the presidents. Rev. ed. By Edward M. Killough ... Baltimore, Md., 1940.

4 p. l., 128 p. illus., pl., maps (1 fold.) 23cm.

Only the highlights of the history of the railroad appear in this summary; a full and scholarly treatment of the subject remains to be done.

Knapp, Frederick Newman, 1821–1889.

... Two reports concerning the aid and comfort given by the Sanitary commission to sick soldiers passing through Washington. By Frederick N. Knapp, special relief agent. [Washington, 1861]

23, [1] p. 22cm.

Valuable reports of the Commission's first activities.

Knapp, Frederick Newman, 1821–1889.

... Report concerning the aid and comfort given by the Sanitary commission to sick and invalid soldiers, for the quarter ending June 30, 1865. By Frederick N. Knapp ... [Washington, 1865]

47, [1] p. 22½cm.

This report is useful when compared with the 1861 statements (see previous entry). The Sanitary Commission published an entire series of such reports in the course of the war.

Laugel, Auguste, 1830–1914.

The United States during the war. By Auguste Laugel. London, H. Baillière; New York, Baillière brothers [etc.] 1866.

xiii p., 1 l., 313 p. 23cm.

An excellent travel account of an 1864-1865 trip, mainly through the Midwest.

Lawrence, Catherine S.

Autobiography. Sketch of life and labors of Miss Catherine S. Lawrence, who in early life distinguished herself as a bitter opponent of slavery and intemperance ... Rev. ed. Albany, N. Y., J. B. Lyon, printer, 1896.

238 p. front., ports. 20cm.

Amid this stream of abolitionist tirades are a few references to wartime hospitals at the front and behind the lines.

Lecomte, Ferdinand, 1826–1899.

The war in the United States. Report to the Swiss military department; preceded by a discuorse to the Federal military society assembled at Berne, Aug. 18, 1862. By Ferdinand Lecomte ... Tr. from the French. New York, D. Van Nostrand, 1863.

148 p. 19cm.

Typical observations of the wartime North by a foreigner; unique only because of Lecomte's Swiss nationality.

Livermore, Mary Ashton (Rice) 1820–1905.

My story of the war: a woman's narrative of four years personal experience as nurse in the Union army, and in relief work at home, in hospitals, camps, and at the front during the war of the rebellion. With anecdotes, pathetic incidents, and thrilling reminiscences portraying the lights and shadows of hospital life and the sanitary service of the war. By Mary A. Livermore ... Hartford, A. D. Worthington and company, 1888.

700 p. front., plates (part col.) port. 23 cm.

Well-known, valuable reminiscences; especially good for accounts of military hospitals and relief work.

Lockwood, *Mrs.* **Mary (Smith)** 1831–

Yesterdays in Washington, by Mary Smith Lockwood ... Rosslyn, Va., The Commonwealth company [c1915]

2 v. fronts. (v. 1, port.) plates. 20½cm.

Contains only passing references to wartime Washington; of some value for personal and social insights into the nation's capital.

Logan, Mary Simmerson (Cunningham) 1838–1923.

Reminiscences of a soldier's wife; an autobiography, by Mrs. John A. Logan ... New York, C. Scribner's sons, 1913.

xvi, 470 p. front., plates, ports., facsims. 21½ cm.

Perceptive memoirs by the wife of an Illinois general; revealing for scenes of Washington society.

Lomax, Elizabeth (Lindsay) *b.* 1796.

Leaves from an old Washington diary, 1854–1863, written by Elizabeth Lindsay Lomax, edited by Lindsay Lomax Wood. [New York] Books, inc., distributed by E. P. Dutton and company, inc., 1943.

256 p. 21½cm.

Disappointing to the point of uselessness; at most, the journal contains but passing references to life in Washington during wartime.

McNeill, George Edwin, 1837–1906, *ed.*
The labor movement: the problem of to-day. The history, purpose and possibilities of labor organizations in Europe and America ... Ed. by George E. McNeill ... Associate authors: Terence V. Powderly ... Dr. Edmund J. James ... [and others] Boston, A. M. Bridgman & co.; New York, The M. W. Hazen co.; [etc., etc.] 1887.

xiv, [5], 615, [9] p. incl. tables. plates, ports. 24 cm.

Because McNeill was a leading New England labor leader during the war, his first-hand accounts are useful to any study of the subject.

Mackintire, Eliab Parker, 1797–1864.
Letters of Eliab Parker Mackintire, of Boston, written between 1845 & 1863, to Reverend William Salter, of Burlington, Iowa; edited by Philip Dillon Jordan. New York, The New York public library, 1936.

168 p. front. (port.) 25½cm.

A Boston businessman's letters to his son-in-law, a minister in Iowa; in the few wartime epistles, Mackintire believed the war was being fought to uphold the Constitution.

Macmillan, Margaret (Burnham) 1898–
The Methodist Episcopal Church in Michigan during the Civil War [by Margaret B. Macmillan. Lewis Beeson, editor. Lansing] Michigan Civil War Centennial Observance Commission [1965?]

75 p. 23 cm.

A compact and revealing monograph of the problems and activities of one sect in one Northern state.

Mayo, Amory Dwight, 1823–1907.
East and West. By Rev. A. D. Mayo. [Cincinnati? 1865?]

33 p. 23½ cm.

When Western talk began of uniting with the South and leaving New England on its own, a Unitarian minister urged his Western flock to stand fast to the cause.

Merk, Frederick, 1887–
... Economic history of Wisconsin during the civil war decade, by Frederick Merk. Madison, The Society, 1916.

414 p. front. (fold. map) plates, ports., facsim., diagr. 25 cm.

Traces in excellent fashion the effects of war upon the economic life of a "typical" northwestern state; thorough and well-written.

Metcalf, Kenneth Nolan, 1923–1965.
Effects of the Civil War on manufacturing in Michigan [by Kenneth N. Metcalf and Lewis Beeson. Lansing] Michigan Civil War Centennial Observance Commission [1966]

31 p. group port. 23 cm.

This slim monograph is a good introduction to the subject; the text contains some documentation.

Meyer, John F.
The German element in two great crises of American history, 1776–1861, by Rev. J. F. Meyer ... [Columbus, O., ©1915]

cover-title, 29 p. 23cm.

Too short to qualify as more than an introduction to a sadly neglected topic.

Michigan. *Civil War Centennial Observance Commission.*
Michigan institutions of higher education in the Civil War. [Willis F. Dunbar, editor. Lansing, 1964]

123 p. illus. 23 cm.

A fuller summary, with more use of wider sources, than a comparable survey on Ohio colleges by G. W. Chessman.

Michigan. *Civil War Centennial Observance Commission.*
Michigan labor and the Civil War. [Lansing, 1964]

31 p. port. 23 cm.

A monograph that but whets the appetite.

Michigan. *Civil War Centennial Observance Commission.*
Michigan women in the Civil War. [Lansing, 1963?]

144 p. illus., ports. 23 cm.

Another pamphlet more designed to alert than to inform.

Mitchell, Wesley Clair, 1874–1948.
A history of the greenbacks, with special reference to the economic consequences of their issue, 1862–65. ⌊Chicago⌋ University of Chicago Press ⌊1960, ©1903⌋
577 p. illus., tables. 23 cm.

Covers the period 1862-1865; in spite of its age, it remains "a model of dispassionate scholarship."

Mug, Mary Theodosia, *sister*, 1860–
Lest we forget; the Sisters of Providence of St. Mary-of-the-Woods in civil war service, by Sister Mary Theodosia Mug. St. Mary-of-the-Woods, Ind., Providence press ⌊©1931⌋
79 p. plates, ports. 19cm.

The brief and laudatory account of the activities of an Indiana religious order in military hospitals.

New England soldiers' relief association.
Minutes of the organization and proceedings of the New England soldiers' relief association ... New York, J. F. Trow, printer, 1862.
31 p. 23cm.

A self-satisfying summary of benevolent undertakings.

New York Bible society.
The Bible in the army; a statement of the distribution of the Scriptures among the military and naval forces of the Union, by the New York Bible society, 1861. ⌊New York⌋ The New York Bible society, 1862.
31 p. 23cm.

Extracts from an annual report recounting the pleasures of donors and the gratitude of recipients to Bible distribution in Federal armies.

North, *Mrs.* **Mary M** *comp.*
Civil war army nurses' scrap book, compiled by Mary M. North, by whom many of the sketches were written. ⌊n. p.⌋ 1925.
49 p. illus. (incl. ports.) 28½ x 26cm.

Too disorganized and lacking in material to be of any significance.

Norton, Charles Eliot, 1827–1908.
Letters of Charles Eliot Norton, with biographical comment by his daughter Sara Norton and M. A. De Wolfe Howe ... Boston and New York, Houghton Mifflin company, 1913.
2 v. fronts., plates, ports., facsims. 22½ cm.

Contains a few letters on the war by one of the early editors of the North American Review.

Notes of hospital life from November, 1861, to August, 1863 ... Philadelphia, J. B. Lippincott & co., 1864.
xiv, 16-210 p. 19cm.

Anonymously written, but very illustrative of the social horrors of war.

⌊**Olmsted, Frederic Law**⌋ 1822–1903, *comp.*
Hospital transports. A memoir of the embarkation of the sick and wounded from the peninsula of Virginia in the summer of 1862. Compiled and published at the request of the Sanitary commission. Boston, Ticknor and Fields, 1863.
xiv p., 1 l., ⌊17⌋–167 p. 18½cm.

An excellent description of transports, by a master writer of that day; reveals forcefully the Union tragedy of the Peninsular Campaign.

Olnhausen, Mary (Phinney) von, 1818–1902.
Adventures of an army nurse in two wars; ed. from the diary and correspondence of Mary Phinney, baroness von Olnhausen, by James Phinney Munroe ... Boston, Little, Brown, and company, 1903.
2 p. l., 355 p. front. (port.) 21cm.

A comparative commentary by a baroness of hospital life in the Civil and Franco-Prussian wars.

Otis, George Alexander, 1830–1881.
A report on a plan for transporting wounded soldiers by railway in time of war; with descriptions of various methods employed for this purpose on different occasions. By George A. Otis ... Washington, War department, Surgeon general's office, 1875.
56 p. illus. 24cm.

Of some use for data on Northern railroads as transports for Union wounded; an excellent bibliography is appended.

Parsons, Emily Elizabeth, 1824–1880.

Memoir of Emily Elizabeth Parsons. Pub. for the benefit of the Cambridge hospital. Boston, Little, Brown, and co., 1880.

2 p. l., 159 p. 18½cm.

An interesting collection of letters commenting for the most part on military hospitals during the 1862-1864 period.

Pendel, Thomas Franses.

Thirty-six years in the White House, by Thomas F. Pendel, door-keeper; Lincoln-Roosevelt. Washington, The Neale publishing company, 1902.

176 p. front., ports. 20cm.

Shallow and probably exaggerated reminiscences by a White House servant who placed more emphasis on the postwar period.

Perkins, Howard Cecil, *ed.*

... Northern editorials on secession, edited by Howard Cecil Perkins ... New York, London, D. Appleton-Century company, incorporated [©1942]

2 v. 23 cm.

The best collection of editorials on the coming and outbreak of war; D. L. Dumond produced a similar work for the Southern side.

Pivány, Eugene.

Hungarians in the American civil war, by Eugene Pivány. Illustrated by John Kemény. Cleveland, O., 1913.

61 p. illus. (incl. ports.) 19cm.

Biographical sketches of some of the 800 Hungarians who served the Union in various capacities.

Poor, Henry Varnum, 1812–1905.

History of the railroads and canals of the United States ... By Henry V. Poor ... v. 1. New York, J. H. Schultz & co., 1860.

viii, [9]–612 p. maps. 24cm.

Completely outdated, but of some use in showing the overall state of American railroads on the eve of war.

Porter, Mary Harriet, 1846–

Eliza Chappell Porter, a memoir by Mary H. Porter. Published for the benefit of the Oberlin missionary home association, Oberlin, Ohio. Chicago, New York, Fleming H. Revell company [1893]

4 p. l., v–ix, [1], 9–366 p. front., ports. 20cm.

The wife of a Presbyterian minister, Mrs. Porter labored valiantly in several army hospitals in the West; this "memoir" is more a voluminous eulogy.

Pratt, Edwin A 1854–1922.

The rise of rail-power in war and conquest, 1833–1914, with a bibliography, by Edwin A. Pratt ... Philadelphia, J. B. Lippincott company; London, P. S. King & son, ltd., 1916.

xii, 405 p. 22½ cm.

An adequate study only; the first part of the book explains railroad precedents established by the war.

Pringle, Cyrus Guernsey.

The record of a Quaker conscience; Cyrus Pringle's diary, with an introduction by Rufus M. Jones. New York, The Macmillan company, 1918.

93 p. 17½ cm.

An excellent short account of a botanist who refused to serve when drafted in 1863.

Protestant Episcopal Church in the U. S. A. *Liturgy and ritual.*

Pastoral letter and special service for the day of National Thanksgiving, appointed by the President of the United States, Aug. 6th, A. D., 1863. [Burlington, N. J., 1863]

8 p. 21 cm.

Of value only as an example of the feelings of the day; Bishop William H. Odenheimer penned the letter.

Ratner, Sidney, 1908–

American taxation, its history as a social force in democracy [by] Sidney Ratner. New York, W. W. Norton & company, inc. [1942]

561 p. incl. tables. 24 cm.

Written to explain the relation of tax policy to social justice programs; recommended for any study of Civil War finance.

Reinfeld, Fred, 1910–
The story of Civil War money. New York, Sterling Pub. Co. [1959]
93 p. illus. 26 cm.

Concise explanations of the economic factors behind Confederate and Union paper money values.

... **Render** unto Caesar, a collection of sermon classics on all phases of religion in wartime. New York, Lewis publishing company [1943]
223 p. 21cm.

The important sermons included here were all published separately; of some use for the emotions of the era.

Rizk, Estelle (Smith)
No more muffled hoofbeats. Philadelphia, Dorrance [1960]
80 p. illus. 20 cm.

Admittedly a collection of legends about Civil War events and people in Carter County, Ky.; useless as history.

Rothschild, Salomon de, *baron*, 1835–1864.
A casual view of America; the home letters of Salomon de Rothschild, 1859–1861. Translated and edited by Sigmund Diamond. Stanford, Calif., Stanford University Press, 1961.
136 p. 23 cm.

Above-average comments by a Frenchman on the social and political events just prior to the outbreak of war.

Rubinger, Naphtali J
Abraham Lincoln and the Jews. New York, J. David [1962]
75 p. 23 cm.

An interesting monograph that poses more questions than it answers.

Salm-Salm, Agnes (Joy) *prinzessin* **zu,** 1844?–1912.
Ten years of my life, by the Princess Felix Salm-Salm. London, R. Bentley & son, 1876.
2 v. front. (port.) 20½cm.

Although only a portion of Vol. I covers the Civil War, the journal throws some light on behind-the-front-scenes; Gen. Hooker was but one officer thoroughly charmed by the foreign visitor.

Schaff, Morris, 1840–1929.
The spirit of old West Point, 1858–1862, by Morris Schaff, with illustrations. Boston and New York, Houghton Mifflin company, 1909.
x p., 1 l., 289 p. front., 22 pl. (1 double) 23cm.

The still-popular and fairly reliable story of how war clouds and the war itself affected the cadets and administration of the U. S. Military Academy.

Sharkey, Robert P
Money, class, and party; an economic study of Civil War and reconstruction. Baltimore, Johns Hopkins Press, 1959.
346 p. 24 cm.

The best treatment of Northern economics in wartime; based on exhaustive research and handled with scholarly excellence.

Shryock, Richard Harrison, 1893–
The development of modern medicine: an interpretation of the social and scientific factors involved, by Richard Harrison Shryock ... Philadelphia, University of Pennsylvania press; London, H. Milford, Oxford university press, 1936.
xiv p., 1 l., 442 p. front., plates, diagrs. 23½ cm.

A superb study that merits far more attention by historians of all periods.

Sigerist, Henry Ernest, 1891–1957.
American medicine, by Dr. Henry E. Sigerist ... translated by Hildegard Nagel. New York, W. W. Norton & company, inc. [c1934]
xix, 316 p. front., plates (1 double) ports., plans. 22 cm.

Written by one of the foremost medical historians of our day, this study shows the broad and slow development of medicine in America.

Smith, Edward Parmelee, 1827–1876.

Incidents among shot and shell. The only authentic work extant giving the many tragic and touching incidents that came under the notice of the United States Christian commission during the long years of the civil war. By Rev. Edward P. Smith ... [Philadelphia?] Edgewood publishing co. [c1868]

494 p. front., illus., plates. 23cm.

This unbalanced compilation consists of anecdotal accounts of the Christian Commission's work; reissued a year later under a more peaceful title.

Smith, Gerrit, 1797–1874.

Speeches and letters of Gerrit Smith ... on the rebellion ... New York, J. A. Gray & Green, printers [etc.] 1864–65.

2 v. in 1. 22½cm.

This partial collection of the utterances and writings of a noted abolitionist covers only the Jan., 1863-Jan., 1865, period.

Smith, Harry Edwin.

The United States federal internal tax history from 1861 to 1871, by Harry Edwin Smith ... Boston and New York, Houghton Mifflin company, 1914.

xix, 357, [1] p. tables (part fold.) 21cm.

A thorough study; scholarly in content, but now showing age.

Smith, William Prescott, 1822?–1872.

B & O in the Civil War; from the papers of Wm. Prescott Smith. Edited by William E. Bain. [Illus. by Lloyd C. Foltz] Denver, Sage Books [1966]

156 p. illus., facsims., map. 23 cm.

A small but exceedingly revealing collection of material on the B & O and the problems that it faced; Smith was the line's Master of Transportation.

Spaulding, Elbridge Gerry, 1809–1897.

A resource of war—The credit of the government made immediately available. History of the legal tender paper money issued during the great rebellion. Being a loan without interest and a national currency. Prepared by Hon. E. G. Spaulding ... Buffalo, Express printing company, 1869.

vi, [5]-213, 40 p. 23cm.

Written by the "father of the greenbacks," this study contains much original material on the legal Tender Acts and other wartime financial measures.

Stanton, Elizabeth (Cady) 1815–1902.

Eighty years and more (1815–1897). Reminiscences of Elizabeth Cady Stanton ... New York, European publishing company, 1898.

ix, 474 p. 11 port. (incl. front.) 20½cm.

Sprightly recollections by a noted woman reformer who campaigned unceasingly during the war as an abolitionist and defender of the Union.

Stanton, Robert Livingston, 1810–1885.

The church and the rebellion: a consideration of the rebellion against the government of the United States; and the agency of the church, north and south, in relation thereto. By R. L. Stanton ... New York, Derby & Miller, 1864.

xiv, 562 p. 19½ cm.

A rambling account to be used with care; most valuable for the author's attitudes.

Starr, John William, 1888–

Lincoln & the railroads; a biographical study, by John W. Starr, jr. ... New York, Dodd, Mead & company, 1927.

xiii p., 1 l., 325 p. front., plates, ports., map, facsims. 21 cm.

A popularized account more concerned with Lincoln than with railroads; must be handled with caution.

Starr, Louis Morris, 1917–

Bohemian Brigade; Civil War newsmen in action. [1st ed.] New York, Knopf, 1954.

xvii, 367, xix p. illus., ports., map. 22 cm.

An interesting but somewhat romanticized account; non-analytical in content.

Stearns, *Mrs.* **Amanda (Akin)**

The lady nurse of Ward E, by Amanda Akin Stearns. New York, The Baker & Taylor company, 1909.

312 p. front., ports. 18cm.

One of the most informative accounts of Washington's Armory Square Hospital; reliable and void of over-sentimentality.

Stebbins, Henry George, 1811–1881.
... Finances & resources of the United States. Speech of the Hon. Henry G. Stebbins, in the House of representatives, March 3, 1864 ... New York, Loyal publication society, 1864.
22 p., 1 l. 22cm.

An assertion that the dollar was as sound as the Union.

Steiner, Paul Eby, 1902–
Physician-generals in the Civil War; a study in nineteenth mid-century American medicine, by Paul E. Steiner. Springfield, Ill., C. C. Thomas [1966]
xv, 194 p. ports. 24 cm.

A superior study of medicine and physicians of the war period; contains an almost exhaustive bibliography on the two subjects.

Stewart, William Rhinelander, 1852–1929.
The philanthropic work of Josephine Lowell; containing a biographical sketch of her life, together with a selection of her public papers and private letters, collected and arranged for publication, by William Rhinelander Stewart ... New York, The Macmillan company, 1911.
xv, 584 p. 4 pl., 5 port. (incl. front.) 22½ cm.

Interesting commentaries by an intellectual idealist who often viewed the war as a glorious means to more glorious ends.

Stowe, *Mrs.* **Harriet Elizabeth (Beecher) 1811–1896.**
A reply to "The affectionate and Christian address of many thousands of women of Great Britain and Ireland, to their sisters, the women of the United States of America." By Mrs. Harriet Beecher Stowe, in behalf of many thousands of American women. London, S. Low, son, and co., 1863.
3 p. l., [3]–63 p. 17cm.

The author of Uncle Tom's Cabin snarls at British women who sympathize with the Confederacy.

Studenski, Paul, 1887–
Financial history of the United States: fiscal, monetary, banking, and tariff, including financial administration and state and local finance [by] Paul Studenski and Herman E. Krooss. 1st ed. New York, McGraw-Hill, 1952.
528 p. 24 cm.

In this general account is one good section on the Civil War.

Sweet, William Warren, 1881–
The Methodist Episcopal church and the civil war, by William Warren Sweet ... Cincinnati, Methodist book concern press [1912]
228 p. 21cm.

A survey only; based largely on published sources and shallow in content.

Swisshelm, Jane Grey (Cannon) 1815–1884.
Crusader and feminist; letters of Jane Grey Swisshelm, 1858–1865; edited with an introduction and notes by Arthur J. Larsen ... Saint Paul, The Minnesota historical society, 1934.
ix p., 1 l., 327 p. front., plates, ports., fold. facsims. 20½ cm.

The letters of a unique lady whose varied career included newspaper editor, lecturer, government clerk and army nurse; particularly good for views on wartime Washington.

Taylor, George Rogers, 1895–
The American railroad network, 1861-1890 [by] George Rogers Taylor [and] Irene D. Neu. Cambridge, Harvard University Press, 1956.
viii, 113 p. maps (3 fold. col.) 24 cm.

An excellent, concise study of the impact of civil war on the development of a national railroad system.

Tharp, Louise (Hall) 1898–
Three saints and a sinner: Julia Ward Howe, Louisa, Annie, and Sam Ward. [1st ed.] Boston, Little, Brown [1956]
406 p. illus. 23 cm.

Popularly written essays, with novelist Howe holding center stage.

[**Tourgee, Albion Winegar**] 1838–1905.
The veteran and his pipe. Chicago and New York, Belford, Clarke & co., 1886.
269 p. 18cm.

A series of anecdotes, addresses and essays on a variety of Union topics, by a noted Reconstruction governor; the material should be handled with care.

Townsend, George Alfred, 1841–1914.
Campaigns of a non-combatant, and his romaunt abroad during the war. By Geo. Alfred Townsend. New York, Blelock & company, 1866.
368 p. 19 cm.

Written while reporter Townsend was in London; excessively padded with overly dramatic war scenes; reissued in 1960 under the title Rustics in Rebellion.

Tripler, *Mrs.* Eunice (Hunt) 1822–1910.
Eunice Tripler: some notes of her personal recollections. New York, The Grafton press, 1910.
184 p. front., ports. 17cm.

Highly useful for the observations included by Dr. Charles Tripler, an army surgeon who saw much duty in Washington and Detroit, and who met several of the Union's top leaders.

Trollope, Anthony, 1815–1882.
North America. By Anthony Trollope ... New York, Harper & brothers, 1863.
vii, 623 p. 19 cm.

The piercing observations of the North by a famous English writer who visited America in 1861-1862.

Trollope, Anthony, 1815–1882.
North America; edited, with an introd., notes, and new materials, by Donald Smalley and Bradford Allen Booth. New York, Knopf, 1951.
xxxvii, 555, viii p. illus., port. 25 cm.

A qualitative republication of the previous entry, enhanced by a useful introduction, some annotation, and a full index.

U. S. *Military railroad dept.*
... Reports of Bvt. Brig. Gen. D. C. McCallum, director and general manager of the military railroads of the United States, and [of James B. Fry] the provost marshall general. In two parts ... Washington, Govt. print. off. 1866.
2 v. fold. map, tables, diagrs. 23½cm.

One of the fundamental sources for Civil War transportation, even though heavily slanted to military matters.

U. S. *Treasury dept.*
... Cotton sold to the Confederate States. Letter from the secretary of the Treasury transmitting, in accordance with a resolution of the Senate of April 22, 1912, a report of sales of cotton to the Confederate States ... Washington, Govt. print. off., 1913.
314 p. 23cm.

Tables listing such items as the number of bales involved in each sale, its value, where shipped, etc.; incomplete because the Confederate archives are fragmentary.

United States sanitary commission.
The soldier's friend ... By the U. S. sanitary commission. Philadelphia, Perkinpine & Higgins, 1865.
128 p. 11cm.

Largely a handbook of inspirations, hymns, and psalms for Civil War GI's.

Vander Velde, Lewis George, 1890–
The Presbyterian churches and the federal Union, 1861–1869, by Lewis G. Vander Velde ... Cambridge, Harvard university press; London, H. Milford, Oxford university press, 1932.
xv, 575 p. 23 cm.

A thorough study of the relation of church and national politics; no other treatment of wartime Presbyterians exists.

Vasvary, Edmund, 1888–
Lincoln's Hungarian heroes; the participation of Hungarians in the civil war, 1861–1865, by Edmund Vasvary. Washington, D. C., The Hungarian reformed federation of America, 1939.
2 p. l., [11]–171 p. front., illus. (incl. plan) ports., facsims. 27cm.

The only detailed study of this nationality in the Civil War; because the work concentrates on outstanding individuals, it has gaps,

Walker, Robert James, 1801–1869.
... Review of our finances, and of the report of Hon. S. P. Chase, secretary of the Treasury. By Hon. Robert J. Walker ... [New York, J. F. Trow, 1862]
p. [129]–144. 22½cm.

A long treatise in support of the issuance of paper money by national banks as preferable to fiat currency.

Wallace, Mary (Austin) 1837 *or* 8–1921.
Mary Austin Wallace: her diary, 1862; a Michigan soldier's wife runs their farm. Edited by Julia McCune. Lansing, Michigan Civil War Centennial Observance Commission, 1963.

18 p. group port. 23 cm.

Slim but unique recollections by a Michigan soldier's wife left alone to manage a small farm.

Ware, Norman Joseph, 1886–
The labor movement in the United States, 1860–1895; a study in democracy, by Norman J. Ware ... New York, London, D. Appleton and company, 1929.

xviii p., 1 l., 409 p. 21 cm.

A still-useful, though somewhat outdated general history; the first sections show how the war acted as an impetus to late 19th century labor organizations.

Weisberger, Bernard A 1922–
Reporters for the Union. [1st ed.] Boston, Little, Brown [1953]

xi, 316 p. illus. 22 cm.

A superior study, especially of the professionalizing influence of the war.

Wells, David Ames, 1828–1898.
... The recent financial, industrial and commercial experiences of the United States: a curious chapter in politico-economic history. By David A. Wells ... New York, J. H. and C. M. Goodsell, 1872.

61 p. 23cm.

This first-hand account remains useful for the relationship between gold, Union exports, and the war.

[**Weston, David**]
Among the wounded; U. S. Christian commission; experiences of a delegate. Philadelphia, J. B. Rodgers, printer, 1864.

14, [2] p. 16cm.

This too-short memoir throws faint light on a few aspects of religion in the army.

Wilson, William Bender.
A few acts and actors in the tragedy of the civil war in the United States. By William Bender Wilson ... Philadelphia, By the author, 1892.

114 p. 19½cm.

Included in this potpourri of material are chapters on war preparations, ammunition trains, and wartime railroads.

Wittenmyer, *Mrs.* **Annie (Turner)** 1827–
Under the guns; a woman's reminiscences of the civil war, by Mrs. Annie Wittenmyer ... With an introduction by Mrs. General U. S. Grant. Boston, E. B. Stillings & co., 1895.

7 p. l., 272 p. front. (port.) 20cm.

One of the best memoirs by a Northern lady; Mrs. Wittenmyer won fame for her diet kitchens in Western army hospitals.

Wittke, Carl Frederick, 1892–
The Irish in America. Baton Rouge, Louisiana State University Press [©1956]

xi, 319 p. 24 cm.

A full treatment of the subject, with emphasis on the mid-19th century; soundly researched.

Women's loyal national league, *New York.*
Proceedings of the meeting of the loyal women of the Republic, held in New York, May 14, 1863. New York, Phair & co., printers, 1863.

86 p. 23cm.

Of importance chiefly because it contains a patriotic address by the well-known Elizabeth Cady Stanton.

[**Woolsey, Jane Stuart**]
Hospital days. Printed for private use. New York, D. Van Nostrand, 1870.

182, [6] p. 24cm.

One knowledgeable writer has termed this scarce work "perhaps the best book about the Civil War by a woman writer."

Wormeley, Katharine Prescott, 1830–1908.
The other side of war; with the Army of the Potomac. Letters from the headquarters of the United States sanitary commission during the peninsular campaign in Virginia in 1862. By Katharine Prescott Wormeley. Boston, Ticknor and company, 1889 [1888]

ix p., 1 l., 210 p. front., port. 23 cm.

Interesting and perceptive letters by a nurse in the Sanitary Commission.

Young, Agnes (Brooks) 1898–
The women and the crisis; women of the North in the Civil War, by Agatha Young [pseud.] New York, McDowell, Obolensky [1959]

389 p. illus. 24 cm.

Popularly written and anecdotal; should be used with caution.

THE UNION

State and Local Studies

William E. Parrish

Abbott, Richard H
Ohio's war Governors. With an introd. by William B. Hesseltine. [Columbus] Ohio State University Press for the Ohio Historical Society [°1962]
51 p. 24 cm.

A concise introduction to the administrations of Govs. William Denison, David Tod and John Brough.

Adamson, Hans Christian.
Rebellion in Missouri, 1861: Nathaniel Lyon and his Army of the West; the rise of Brigadier General Nathaniel Lyon, USA, who saved Missouri from secession in the Civil War. [1st ed.] Philadelphia, Chilton Co., Book Division [1961]
305 p. illus. 21 cm.

This fast-paced, highly readable account of war's outbreak in Missouri is markedly pro-Lyon.

Ambler, Charles Henry, 1876–
... A history of West Virginia, by Charles Henry Ambler ... New York, Prentice-Hall, inc., 1933.
xvi, 622 p. col. front., illus. 21½ cm.

Still the most reliable volume for West Virginia politics and problems during wartime.

Amherst college.
Roll of the graduates and undergraduates of Amherst college who served in the army or navy of the United States, during the war of the rebellion. Prepared under the direction of the faculty of the college. Amherst, H. M. McCloud, book and job printer, 1871.
48 p. 22cm.

A brief record of Amherst men and their service; revised and enlarged in 1905.

Anderson, Galusha, 1832–1918.
The story of a border city during the civil war, by Galusha Anderson ... with twelve portraits and views ... Boston, Little, Brown, and company, 1908.
viii p., 2 l., 385 p. front., plates, ports., facsim. 21½cm.

An intimate sketch of local conditions and feeling in St. Louis; by a prominent Baptist clergyman; particularly good in revealing political factionalisms.

Appler, Augustus C
The guerrillas of the West; or, The life, character and daring exploits of the Younger brothers; with a sketch of the life of Henry W. Younger, father of the Younger brothers ... The war record of Quantrell ... also a sketch of the life of the James boys ... By Augustus C. Appler ... St. Louis, Eureka publishing company, 1876.
iv, 5–208 p. 4 pl. (incl. front.) 21½ cm.

Biographical sketches of questionable accuracy, not a history of Trans-Mississippi campaigns.

Atkins, Thomas Astley, 1839–1916.

Yonkers in the rebellion of 1861–1865. Including a history of the erection of the monument to honor the men of Yonkers who fought to save the Union. By Thomas Astley Atkins and John Wise Oliver. [Yonkers] The Yonkers Soldiers' and sailors' monument association, 1892.

262 p., 1 l. incl. plates, port. front. 25cm.

The first of many city tributes cited in this section; this one concentrates more on the monument than the reasons for its erection.

Baker, Mary Ellen.

Bibliography of lists of New England soldiers, by Mary Ellen Baker, A. B. Boston, New England historic genealogical society, 1911.

56 p. 25cm.

An incomplete listing; prepared by one more learned in librarianship than in history.

Barnet, James, *ed.*

The martyrs and heroes of Illinois in the great rebellion. Biographical sketches. Ed. by James Barnet ... Chicago, Press of J. Barnet, 1865.

1 p. l., 8, xvi, [9]–263 p. front., ports. 23½cm.

Tributes to a few of the many who upheld the honor of Illinois.

Barnhart, John Donald, 1895–

The impact of the Civil War on Indiana, by John D. Barnhart. Indianapolis, Indiana Civil War Centennial Commission, 1962.

48 p. 23 cm.

A useful introduction to a subject badly in need of fuller treatment; particularly good on Hoosier politics.

Bates, Samuel Penniman, 1827–1902.

History of Pennsylvania volunteers, 1861–5; prepared in compliance with acts of the legislature, by Samuel P. Bates ... Harrisburg, B. Singerly, state printer, 1869–71.

5 v. plates (part col.) maps (part fold.) 27½ cm.

A standard state roster that could have been fuller and more comprehensive.

Bates, Samuel Penniman, 1827–1902.

Martial deeds of Pennsylvania. By Samuel P. Bates ... Author's ed. Philadelphia, T. H. Davis & co., 1875.

1116 p. incl. front. pl., ports., maps (1 fold.) 25½ cm.

Divided into historical and biographical sections; thorough in its coverage but largely uncritical.

Belknap, Charles Eugene, 1846–

The yesterdays of Grand Rapids, by Charles E. Belknap. Grand Rapids, The Dean-Hicks company, 1922.

5 p. l., 15–194 p. front. (port.) 20½cm.

These reminiscences include several references to the Michigan city, as well as Belknap's experiences as a soldier.

Benjamin, Marcus, 1857–1932, *ed.*

Washington during war time, a series of papers showing the military, political, and social phases during 1861 to 1865; official souvenir of the thirty-sixth annual encampment of the Grand army of the republic, collected and edited by Marcus Benjamin under the direction of the Committee on literature for the encampment. Washington city [Press of B. S. Adams] 1902.

xv, 215, [1] p. incl. front. (port.) illus., plates. fold. maps, fold. facsim. 23½ cm.

A series of unrelated essays on various aspects of Washington's wartime history; of variable value.

Berthrong, Donald J

The Civil War collection of the Illinois State Historical Library. Springfield, The Library, 1949.

23 p. 25 cm.

A very useful outline of one of the major sources for original Civil War manuscripts.

Bishop, Albert Webb, 1832–1901.

Loyalty on the frontier, or Sketches of Union men of the South-west; with incidents and adventures in rebellion on the border. By A. W. Bishop ... St. Louis, R. P. Studley and co., printers, 1863.

228 p. 20 cm.

Contains sketches (many of them superficial) of seven men, plus chapters on northwestern Arkansas; of little value today.

Blake, Harold F.

Re-told tales; or, Little stories of war times—French and Indian wars—the revolutionary war—the war of 1812—the Mexican war—the civil war—and the part Kensington played in them, by Harold F. Blake ... Farmington, Me., The Knowlton & McLeary co., 1917.

93 p. pl., port. 18cm.

An historical tribute, heavy on the Civil War period, to Kensington, N. H.

Book, Janet Mae.

Northern rendezvous; Harrisburg during the Civil War. Harrisburg, Pa., Telegraph Press, 1951.

138 p. illus., map. 20 cm.

An effective picture of a wartime state capital and the currents of politics and military strife that swept about it.

Bowdoin college.

Bowdoin in the war. [Brunswick? 1870?]

cover-title, 36 p. 22½ cm.

An inadequate tribute still consulted because it remains the only work on the subject.

Bowen, James Lorenzo.

Massachusetts in the war, 1861–1865. By James L. Bowen. With an introduction by Hon. Henry L. Dawes ... Springfield, C. W. Bryan & co., 1889.

xv, 1029 p. incl. port. front. 24cm.

Largely a regimental history with little on the home front.

Bradley, Isaac Samuel, 1853–1912.

... A bibliography of Wisconsin's participation in the war between the states, based upon material contained in the Wisconsin historical library, comp. by Isaac Samuel Bradley ... [Madison] Wisconsin history commission, 1911.

ix, 42 p. 23½ cm.

Lists published materials--chiefly state documents, regimental histories and rosters--treating of military aspects of the war.

Brand, William A 1837–1879, *comp.*

Roll of honor. The soldiers of Champaign County, who died for the Union. Comp. by W. A. Brand. Urbana, O., Saxton & Brand, printers, 1876.

68 p. 15½cm.

A muster-roll-type listing of those from Champaign County, O., who died in service.

Brooklyn. Brooklyn and Long Island fair in aid of the U. S. sanitary commission.

History of the Brooklyn and Long Island fair, February 22, 1864 ... Prepared and published by authority of the Executive committee. Brooklyn, "The Union" steam presses, 1864.

1 p. l., [5]–189 p. fold. col. plates, plans. 28½cm.

A thorough account of preparations, exhibits, and results of one of the major fairs for the benefit of the Sanitary Commission; illustrated.

Brooks, Noah, 1830–1903.

Washington in Lincoln's time, by Noah Brooks ... New York, The Century co., 1895.

2 p. l., vii–ix p., 1 l., 328 p. 19½ cm.

The wartime reminiscences of the Washington correspondent for the Sacramento Union; based in large part on his daily newsletters.

Brown, Francis Henry, 1835–1917.

Harvard university in the war of 1861–1865. A record of services rendered in the army and navy of the United States, by the graduates and students of Harvard college and the professional schools. By Francis H. Brown ... Boston, Cupples, Upham, and company, 1886.

vi p., 1 l., 407 p. 23½cm.

A simple list of Harvard men and their Civil War records.

Brown, George William, 1812–1891.

Baltimore and the nineteenth of April 1861; a study of the war, by George William Brown ... Baltimore, N. Murray, 1887.

176 p. front (map) 24½ cm.

Attempts by the mayor of Baltimore to describe the political atmosphere of the time and to defend his actions; considerable documentation.

Brown, Ida C
Michigan men in the Civil War. [Ann Arbor] University of Michigan [1959]
31 p. illus. 23 cm.

A summary, with bibliography, of a subject covered fully in several noted works.

Brummer, Sidney David, 1880–
... Political history of New York state during the period of the civil war, by Sidney David Brummer, PH. D. New York, Columbia university, Longmans, Green & co., agents; [etc., etc.] 1911.
451 p. 25 cm.

Based largely on newspaper articles and reports, this fine study treats mainly of political conventions, platforms, leaders and speeches.

Burgess, Milton V
Minute Men of Pennsylvania, with a brief biography of their leader in Blair, Bedford, and Cambria Counties, Col. Jacob C. Higgins. Including a copy of Col. Higgins' diary of the Mexican War. Martinsburg, Pa., Morrisons Cove herald, 1962.
89 p. illus., ports., map, facsim. 24 cm.

A valuable account of the preparations made by citizens of southern Pennsylvania to protect themselves from an expected Confederate invasion in 1863.

Burnap, Willard A.
What happened during one man's lifetime, 1840–1920. A review of some great, near great and little events, by Willard A. Burnap ... Fergus Falls, Minn., W. L. Burnap, 1923.
4 p. l., [11]-461 p. illus., maps. 20½cm.

Helpful for some references to the effect of the war on the Far West.

Burr, Fearing.
The town of Hingham in the late civil war, with sketches of its soldiers and sailors. Also the address and other exercises at the dedication of the soldiers' and sailors' monument. Prepared by Fearing Burr and George Lincoln. Pub. by order of the town. [Boston, Rand, Avery & co., printers] 1876.
455 p. front., ports. 24cm.

Another city history that contains rosters, reminiscences of varying authenticity, and the inevitable tributes.

[Burrage, Henry Sweetser] 1837–1926, *comp.*
Brown university in the civil war. A memorial. Providence [Providence press company, printers] 1868.
xii p., 1 l., 380 p. 23 x 18cm.

A sketch of the war's effect on the university, with a roll of students and graduates who served; includes biographies of those who died in service.

Burt, Silas Wright, 1830–1912.
My memoirs of the military history of the state of New York during the war for the union, 1861–65. By Colonel Silas W. Burt ... Ed. by the state historian and issued as War of the rebellion series—Bulletin, no. 1. Albany, J. B. Lyon company, state printers, 1902.
192 p. 23cm.

A singular work on military preparations in New York State; spans only the first two years of the war.

Byers, Samuel Hawkins Marshall, 1838–1933.
Iowa in war times, by S. H. M. Byers ... Des Moines, W. D. Condit & co., 1888.
615 p. front., illus., pl., port., maps. 24cm.

Primarily the story of Iowa's regiments, but a good account too of the state's reaction to conflict and its problems of organization.

Carley, Kenneth.
Minnesota in the Civil War. [1st ed.] Minneapolis, Ross & Haines, 1961.
168 p. illus. 23 cm.

This series of unconnected essays portrays the high points of the state's participation; richly informative; the chapters appeared originally as newspaper articles.

[Carpenter, Jesse H] 1838–
The war for the Union, 1861–1865. A record of its defenders, living and dead, from Steuben county, Indiana; and history of veteran organizations and kindred associations ... [Angola, Ind., R. H. Carpenter] 1888–89.
95 p. illus., pl., ports. 18 x 14cm.

One of relatively few local complications for the Midwest; the slim work treats too much of postwar happenings.

Carrington, Henry Beebee, 1824–

Military movements in Indiana in 1864, designed to supplement the military history of Indiana and correct several errors in relation to the raids of Forrest, Morgan and Johnson in 1864, by reference to omitted official documents, orders, telegrams, etc., of that period. By Henry B. Carrington, U. S. A., then commanding the district of Indiana and the Indiana legion. [Boston? 18—]

12 p. front. (double map) 19½cm.

A corrective discourse that only compounds the factual errors.

Castel, Albert E

A frontier state at war: Kansas, 1861–1865. Ithaca, N. Y., Published for the American Historical Association [by] Cornell University Press [1958]

251 p. illus. 24 cm.

Gives a clear reflection of issues and leaders with a good picture of the power struggle between moderates and radicals within the dominant Republican party.

[**Cheever, Noah Wood**] 1839–1905.

Stories and amusing incidents in the early history of the University of Michigan. U. of M. stories of ye olden time. Wit and wisdom in the early history of the U. of M. Fun and frolic of the old boys during the war times. Ann Arbor, Mich., Register publishing co., printers, 1895.

68 p. front. (4 port.) 4 pl. (1 fold.; incl. ports.) 17 cm.

Two sections of this slim pamphlet contain wartime reminiscences of life both at the university and in Ann Arbor.

Chelsea, *Mass.*

Roll of honor of the city of Chelsea. A list of the soldiers and sailors who served on the quota of Chelsea, in the great civil war for the preservation of the Union from 1861 to 1865, with a partial record of each man ... Also an appendix including the names of Chelsea men who served to the credit of other states, cities and towns. Chelsea, H. Mason & son, printers, 1880.

213 p. 13cm.

A list of Chelsea men with their service records.

Chenault, John Cabell, 1855–1924.

Old Cane Springs; a story of the war between the states in Madison county, Kentucky; revised and supplemented by Jonathan Truman Dorris ... from the original by John Cabell Chenault ... introduction by Ivan E. McDougle ... Louisville, Ky., The Standard printing co., incorporated, 1936.

xvi, 257 p. front., illus. (map) plates, ports. 23½ cm.

Memoirs recorded years after the events described; Chenault concentrated on slavery in the Bluegrass country.

Chetlain, Augustus Louis, 1824–1914.

Recollections of seventy years, by Augustus L. Chetlain, brigadier, and brevet major general U. S. vols., civil war, 1861–65. Galena, The Gazette publishing company, 1899.

304 p. front. (port.) 22cm.

Although the great bulk of these memoirs recounts Chetlain's experiences as a soldier, the book also contains many insights of wartime Galena, Ill.

Church, Charles A., 1857–

History of the Republican party in Illinois 1854–1912; with a review of the aggressions of the slave-power, by Charles A. Church ... Rockford, Ill., Press of Wilson brothers company, printers [©1912]

xiii, 248 p. incl. port. front., ports. 21 cm.

Informative, but narrow in treatment and now outdated.

Clark, Charles Branch, 1913–

Politics in Maryland during the Civil War. Chestertown, 1952.

201 p. 24 cm.

A detailed and well-documented study of the intricate political framework of this border state; originally published as a series of journal articles.

Clark, Lewis H.

Military history of Wayne County, N. Y. The county in the civil war. By Lewis H. Clark. Sodus, N. Y., L. H. Clark, Hulett & Gaylord [1883]

[933] p. 23cm.

Brief histories of fifteen Empire State regiments comprise the bulk of this older study.

Clark, Olynthus Burroughs, 1864–1936.

The politics of Iowa during the civil war and reconstruction ... Iowa City, Ia., The Clio press, 1911.

vi, 204 p., 1 l. 25cm.

The standard study of political forces on the move in a state that became a key Republican stronghold.

Clark, Rufus Wheelwright, 1813–1886.

The heroes of Albany. A memorial of the patriot-martyrs of the city and county of Albany, who sacrificed their lives during the late war in defence of our nation, 1861–1865, with a view of what was done in the county to sustain the United States government; and also brief histories of the Albany regiments. By Rufus W. Clark, D. D. Albany, S. R. Gray, 1867.

viii p., 1 l., [11]–870 p. col. front., illus., plates, ports. 25 cm.

A voluminous collection of eulogies, heavily padded and weakeningly sentimental.

Coatsworth, Stella S (Flood)

The loyal people of the North-west, a record of prominent persons, places and events, during eight years of unparalleled American history. By Stella S. Coatsworth, with an introductory note by Rev. T. M. Eddy ... Illustrated with fine steel engravings. Chicago, Church, Goodman & Donnelley, printers, 1869.

402 p. front., plates, ports. 23cm.

A general survey of civil participation in the war by the people of this area.

Cole, Arthur Charles, 1886–

... The era of the civil war, 1848–1870, by Arthur Charles Cole ... Springfield, Illinois centennial commission, 1919.

7 p. l., 499 p. front., ports., maps. 24 cm.

In spite of its age, Cole's study remains the most authoritative on non-military aspects of wartime Illinois; has an excellent bibliography.

Coleman, John Winston, 1898–

Lexington during the civil war, by J. Winston Coleman, jr. ... Lexington, Ky., Commercial printing co., 1938.

51 p. front., plates, facsim. 18cm.

A valuable introduction to the subject; the major emphasis is on Bragg's 1862 campaign in Kentucky.

Coles, Harry Lewis, 1918–

Ohio forms an Army. [Columbus] Ohio State University Press for the Ohio Historical Society [1962]

26 p. 24 cm.

This brief work gives a good description of the processes and problems in recruiting and equipping Ohio regiments.

Colton, Ray Charles, 1907–

The Civil War in the western territories: Arizona, Colorado, New Mexico, and Utah. [1st ed.] Norman, University of Oklahoma Press [1959]

ix, 230 p. illus., ports., maps. 24 cm.

The chapters in this broad picture of war in the Southwest lack correlation, but the work as a whole is based on sound research and thought.

Connecticut. *Adjutant-general's office.*

Record of service of Connecticut men in the army and navy of the United States during the war of the rebellion. Comp. by authority of the General assembly under direction of the adjutants-general Brig.-Gen. Stephen R. Smith ... Brig.-Gen. Frederick E. Camp ... Brig.-Gen. Lucius A. Barbour ... Col. George M. White ... Hartford, Conn., Press of the Case, Lockwood & Brainard company, 1889.

xiii, 1071 p. 30½cm.

Practically every Northern state issued such a roster of its Civil War soldiers; this one, like most others, suffers from lack of an index.

Connelley, William Elsey, 1855–1930.

Quantrill and the border wars, by William Elsey Connelley ... Cedar Rapids, Ia., The Torch press, 1910.

542 p. front., illus. (incl. ports., facsim.) fold. map, fold. plan. 24½ cm.

A general account of border warfare in which Quantrill was so prominent; probably the best study on the subject; reprinted in 1965.

Cook, Frederick Francis.

Bygone days in Chicago; recollections of the "Garden city" of the sixties, by Frederick Francis Cook ... with nearly one hundred illustrations from rare prints and photographs. Chicago, A. C. McClurg & co., 1910.

xvi, [5], 400 p. incl. front. plates, ports., facsims. 21½ cm.

An old but very revealing memoir of life in one of the North's most important wartime cities; heavily slanted toward social matters.

Cook, Roy Bird.

Lewis county in the civil war, 1861–1865 [by] Roy Bird Cook ... Charleston, W. Va., Jarrett printing co., 1924.

155 p. front., pl., ports., map. 23½cm.

The story of a West Virginia county that found itself frequently at the crossroads of war; based on fragmented and scattered records, official and otherwise.

Coolidge, John Phillips, 1913–
... Mill and mansion, a study of architecture and society in Lowell, Massachusetts, 1820–1865. New York, Columbia university press, 1942.

xi p., 2 l., [3]–261 p. front., plates, maps (1 double) plans, diagrs. 24 cm.

Rich in local material on one of New England's most important wartime cities.

Coulter, Ellis Merton, 1890–
The civil war and readjustment in Kentucky, by Merton Coulter ... Chapel Hill, The University of North Carolina press; [etc., etc.] 1926.

viii p., 2 l., 468 p. illus. (maps) 24 cm.

A good account of the history and character of this key border state; embraces all facets of life there.

Crawford, Samuel Johnson, 1835–1913.
Kansas in the sixties, by Samuel J. Crawford ... Chicago, A. C. McClurg & co., 1911.

xvii, 441 p. front., ports. 21½ cm.

Memoirs of a "war governor" (1865-1868) who also served in the 2d Kansas Infantry and participated in many local campaigns.

Creasey, George W[illiam] 1840–
The city of Newburyport in the civil war from 1861 to 1865 with the individual records of the soldiers and sailors who served to its credit, also the war records of many natives and residents of the city, credited to other places, by George W. Creasey ... Boston, Griffith-Stillings press, 1903.

539, [1] p. front. (port.) 24cm.

A typical city history for the war period, with much data for genealogists and some facts for the historian.

Crittenden, Henry Huston, 1859– *comp.*
The Crittenden memoirs, compiled by H. H. Crittenden ... New York, G. P. Putnam's sons, 1936.

xv, 17–542 p. front., plates, ports., fold. geneal. tab., facsim., coat of arms. 24 cm.

Useful for a few insights into lawlessness in Civil War Missouri.

Croffut, William Augustus, 1835–1915.
The military and civil history of Connecticut during the war of 1861–65. Comprising a detailed account of the various regiments and batteries, through march, encampment, bivouac, and battle; also instances of distinguished personal gallantry, and biographical sketches of many heroic soldiers: together with a record of the patriotic action of citizens at home, and of the liberal support furnished by the state in its executive and legislative departments. By W. A. Croffut and John M. Morris ... New York, L. Bill, 1868.

2 p. l., iii, 5–892 p. front., port. 23½ cm.

Largely regimental histories, with a sketchy outline of political events within the state.

Cullom, Shelby Moore, 1829–1914.
Fifty years of public service; personal recollections of Shelby M. Cullom, senior United States senator from Illinois. Chicago, A. C. McClurg & co., 1911.

xi, 467 p. front., ports. 21½ cm.

A very revealing insight into Illinois politics during the secession and war crises; balanced and reliable.

Curry, Richard Orr.
A house divided; a study of statehood politics and the Copperhead movement in West Virginia. [Pittsburgh] University of Pittsburgh Press [1964]

203 p. maps. 24 cm.

Curry shows that half the counties and 40% of the population favored the Confederacy, yet the majority wanted home rule. Copperheadism is equated with conservatism.

Davis, Stanton Ling.
Pennsylvania politics, 1860–1863, by Stanton Ling Davis ... Cleveland, O., The Bookstore, Western Reserve university, 1935.

ix, 334 numb. l. 27cm.

Treats of a period when Pennsylvania was being transformed into a Republican state; a skillful discussion of political intricacies and intra-party struggles.

Decker, Eugene Donald.
A selected, annotated bibliography of sources in the Kansas State Historical Society pertaining to Kansas in the Civil War. Emporia, Kansas State Teachers College, 1961.

95 p. illus., map. 23 cm.

A good reference guide to Civil War materials.

Delano, Jesse Lemuel, 1835–

A record of Sunderland in the civil war of 1861 to 1865. Comp. by Jesse L. Delano, in 1881. According to vote of the town. Amherst, Mass., J. E. Williams, printer, 1882.

43, [3] p. 23½cm.

One of the weaker community chronicles, owing to brevity.

Delaware. *Civil War Centennial Commission.*

Delaware in the Civil War. Edited by W. Emerson Wilson. Dover, 1962.

48 p. illus. 23 cm.

A taste of a subject that desperately needs full and scholarly treatment.

DeWitt, John Doyle, 1902–

Lincoln in Hartford. [n. p., n. d.]

15 p. illus., ports. 25 cm.

A brief account of a brief visit made in March, 1860.

District of Columbia. *Civil War Centennial Commission.*

The symbol and the sword; Washington, D. C., 1860–1865. [Washington] ©1962.

71 p. illus. 22 cm.

This survey of wartime Washington emphasizes its psychological importance to the Union and its status as a center of operations.

Doremus, Philip, 1825–

Reminiscences of Montclair, with some account of Montclair's part in the civil war, by Philip Doremus. Montclair, N. J., 1908.

2 p. l., 111 p. plates, ports. 21½cm.

Only 27 pages of this slim memoir treat of the war, and the treatment is rather superficial.

Eddy, Thomas Mears, 1823–1874.

The patriotism of Illinois. A record of the civil and military history of the state in the war for the Union, with a history of the campaigns in which Illinois soldiers have been conspicuous, sketches of distinguished officers, the roll of the illustrious dead, movements of the sanitary and Christian commissions. By T. M. Eddy ... Chicago, Clarke & co., 1865–66.

2 v. front., pl., port. 22½cm.

Volume I affords a clear picture of the inner workings of the Yates administration; Vol. II is military in content.

Edom, Clifton Cedric.

Missouri sketch book; a collection of words and pictures of the Civil War. [n. p.] Lucas Bros. [1963]

163 p. illus. 29 cm.

A pictorial history of the Civil War in Missouri, with heavy emphasis on the Union side and a somewhat inadequate running commentary.

Edwards, John Newman, 1839–1889.

Noted guerrillas, or The warfare of the border. Being a history of the lives and adventures of Quantrell, Bill Anderson, George Todd, Dave Poole, Fletcher Taylor, Peyton Long, Oll Shepherd, Arch Clements, John Maupin, Tuck and Woot Hill, Wm. Gregg, Thomas Maupin, the James brothers, the Younger brothers, Arthur McCoy, and numerous other well known guerrillas of the West. By John N. Edwards ... St. Louis, Bryan, Brand & company; Chicago, Thompson & Wakefield; [etc., etc.] 1877.

2 p. l., ix–xi, [13]–488 p. front., plates, ports. 22cm.

Romanticized glorification of the James boys, Quantrill, and others; by one who knew many of them personally.

Eliot, Ellsworth, 1864–

Yale in the civil war, by Ellsworth Eliot, jr. New Haven, Yale university press; London, H. Milford, Oxford university press, 1932.

xiv, 222 p. front., plates, ports., facsim. 30½ cm.

Most of this study is a service roll of Yale men; also included is a brief account of college life at the outbreak of war.

Evans, Samuel Minis, 1843–

Allegheny County, Pennsylvania, in the war for the suppression of the rebellion, 1861–1865. Roll of honor, defenders of the flag, attack on Fort Sumter, S. C., April 12, 1861, surrender at Appomattox, Va., April 9, 1865. Published by authority of the Board of managers, Soldiers and sailors memorial hall; compiled and arranged by and under the direction of Samuel M. Evans ... Pittsburgh, Pa., 1924.

1 p. l., 7–610 p., 1 l. front. 24½cm.

This cursory summary of the county's role also contains a complete roster of its servicemen.

The Evening star, *Washington, D. C.*
Mirror of war; the Washington star reports the Civil War. Compiled and edited by John W. Stepp and I. William Hill. Englewood Cliffs, N. J., Prentice-Hall [1961]

vi, 378 p. illus., ports. 28 cm.

Highlights of the Evening Star's coverage of the Civil War; well-edited, enlightening and entertaining.

Everett, Lloyd Tilghman, 1875–
For Maryland's honor; a story of the war for southern independence, by Lloyd T. Everett ... Boston, The Christopher publishing house [°1922]

229 p. col. front., pl. 21cm.

This work of fiction is included because it too often has been erroneously regarded as a volume of facts.

Fisher, *Mrs.* **Margaret May (Merrill)** 1872– *comp.*
Utah and the civil war, being the story of the part played by the people of Utah in that great conflict, with special reference to the Lot Smith expedition and the Robert T. Burton expedition; compiled and edited by Margaret M. Fisher, assisted by C. N. Lund and Judge Nephi Jensen, under direction of the J. Q. Knowlton post of the G. A. R. ... [Salt Lake City, The Deseret book company, °1929]

173 p. incl. illus., pl., ports. 22½cm.

This little-known and shallow study throws a minimum of light on a comparison that hardly merits more.

Fiske, John, 1842–1901.
The Mississippi valley in the civil war, by John Fiske ... Boston and New York, Houghton, Mifflin and company, 1900.

xxv, 368 p. front., maps, plans. 20 cm.

An overrated, outdated study that concentrates on the major military campaigns from Belmont to Nashville.

Foster, John Young.
New Jersey and the rebellion: a history of the services of the troops and people of New Jersey in aid of the Union cause. By John Y. Foster. Published by authority of the state. Newark, M. R. Dennis & co., 1868.

viii, 872 p. incl. maps. front. (port.) fold. map. 23½cm.

Largely regimental summaries; three chapters cover the home front and touch on state politics and society.

Freitag, Alfred John, 1916–
Detroit in the Civil War; illustrated by Betty Huffman, edited by Joe L. Norris. Detroit, Wayne University Press [1951]

19 p. illus. 22 cm.

A slim survey of the wartime activities, military and civilian, in this Northern city.

Fry, James Barnet, 1827–1894.
New York and the conscription of 1863; a chapter in the history of the civil war, by James B. Fry ... New York & London, G. P. Putnam's sons, 1885.

1 p. l., 85 p. 20cm.

Interestingly relates the draft riots and their manifestations within a latently hostile population; based on contemporary records and interviews.

[**Fullbrook, Earl Stanfield**] 1892–
... Sanitary fairs, a method of raising funds for relief work in Iowa during the civil war. Iowa City, Ia., The State historical society of Iowa [1917]

cover-title, 23 p. 18cm.

A brief sketch of the efforts of Iowans to aid the war effort through the fair method, with particular emphasis on the 1864 fair at Dubuque.

Gibson, Florence Elizabeth.
The attitudes of the New York Irish toward state and national affairs, 1848–1892. New York, 1951.

480 p. 22 cm.

Only a small part of this excellent study relates the actions of New York's Irishmen in the war; the bibliography contains many leads to additional material.

Gilmore, George Clinton, *d.* 1912.
Manchester men. Soldiers and sailors in the civil war, 1861–'66. By George C. Gilmore. Concord, N. H., The Rumford press, 1898.

167 p. incl. pl. front. (port.) 25cm.

Too short and superficial to be of use to anyone but genealogists.

Goulding, Joseph Hiram, 1842–1916, *comp.*

Official military and naval records of Rutland, Vermont, in the war of the rebellion, 1861–1866. Men credited to town; residents since the war or buried in cemeteries within the limits of the original town. Compiled by vote of the towns of Rutland, West Rutland and Proctor, by J. H. Goulding. 1889–90–91. Rutland, The Tuttle company, printers, 1891.

100 p. 23cm.

More eulogistic than informative.

Graham, Robert Henry, 1865–

Yates County's "boys in blue", 1861–1865; who they were—what they did; compiled by Robert H. Graham. Penn Yan, N. Y. [1926]

204 p. 22cm.

One of the larger county registers for the men in blue; as with all such compilations, of value primarily to genealogists.

Green, Constance (McLaughlin) 1897–

Washington. Princeton, N. J., Princeton University Press, 1962–63.

2 v. illus. 25 cm.

Two gossipy chapters on the Civil War tell little not already known.

Greene, Nancy Lewis.

Ye olde Shaker bells, by Nancy Lewis Greene ... Lexington, Ky. [Transylvania printing co.] ©1930.

83 p. front., plates. 23cm.

Records and pictures of the Shaker colony at Pleasanthill, Ky.; a unique diary is included and underscores the effect of the war on the group.

Grinnell, Josiah Bushnell, 1821–1891.

Men and events of forty years. Autobiographical reminiscences of an active career from 1850 to 1890, by the late Josiah Busnell [!] Grinnell. With introduction by Prof. Henry W. Parker, D. D. Boston, D. Lothrop company [©1891]

1 p. l., [vii]–xvi, 426 p. front., plates, ports. 22½cm.

The reliable and highly useful memoirs of a prominent Iowa statesman of the war period.

Gue, Benjamin F 1828–1904.

History of Iowa from the earliest times to the beginning of the twentieth century ... by Benjamin F. Gue; illustrated with photographic views of the natural scenery of the state, public buildings, pioneer life, etc., with portraits and biographies of notable men and women of Iowa ... New York, The Century history company [1903]

4 v. fronts., illus., plates, ports., maps, facsims. 24 cm.

A generally creditable reference work; eight chapters treat of the home front and politics; the remaining twenty-two are regimental histories.

Hall, Clifton Rumery, 1884–

Andrew Johnson, military governor of Tennessee, by Clifton R. Hall ... Princeton, Princeton university press; [etc., etc.] 1916.

iv p., 1 l., 234 p. 23cm.

A solid work, based in large part on Johnson's then-unpublished papers.

Hamand, Lavern Marshall, 1918– *ed.*

Coles County in the Civil War, 1861–1865. Charleston [Ill.] Division of Regional Services [Eastern Illinois University] 1961.

112 p. illus., ports. 22 cm.

Brief but interesting, this monography summarizes one Illinois county's response to war.

Hamilton, James Alexander, 1788–1878.

Reminiscences of James A. Hamilton; or, Men and events, at home and abroad, during three quarters of a century. New York, C. Scribner & co., 1869.

ix, 647 p. 24 cm.

Hamilton played a somewhat influential role in New York politics during the war; his memoirs therefore can have value.

Hancock, Harold Bell, 1913–

Delaware during the Civil War, a political history. Wilmington, Historical Society of Delaware [1961]

197 p. illus., ports., facsims. 25 cm.

A good survey of Delaware politics in wartime and of the effect of the war generally upon the state and its people; originally published as a series of articles in Delaware History.

Harper, Robert S
Ohio handbook of the Civil War. [Columbus] Published by the Ohio Historical Society for the Ohio Civil War Centennial Commission, 1961.
78 p. illus. 24 cm.

An interesting, well-written summary prepared for the Centennial by the late director of the Ohio Commission.

Harris, Norman Dwight, 1870–
The history of negro servitude in Illinois, and of the slavery agitation in that state, 1719–1864, by N. Dwight Harris ... Chicago, A. C. McClurg & co., 1904.
x p., 1 l., 276 p. front., ports., facsim. 20½cm.

A long-consulted social study, but annually weakened by age.

Headley, Phineas Camp, 1819–1903.
Massachusetts in the rebellion. A record of the historical position of the commonwealth, and the services of the leading statesmen, the military, the colleges, and the people, in the civil war of 1861–65. By P. C. Headley ... Boston, Walker, Fuller and co., 1866.
xii, 688 p. front., port. 23cm.

Heavy on military topics, this remains a good contemporary account of the Bay State's reaction to war.

Hicken, Victor, 1921–
Illinois in the Civil War. Urbana, University of Illinois Press, 1966.
xiv, 391 p. 24 cm.

A somewhat limited study that concentrates almost exclusively on Illinois individuals and units in battle. Yet Hicken makes good use of the sources at hand.

[**Higginson, Thomas Wentworth**] 1823–1911, *ed.*
Harvard memorial biographies ... Cambridge, Sever and Francis, 1866.
2 v. 24cm.

Memoirs of Harvard men who died in service.

Higginson, Thomas Wentworth, 1823–1911.
Massachusetts in the Army and Navy during the war of 1861–65. Prepared under the authority of the state by Thomas Wentworth Higginson ... Boston, Wright & Potter printing co., state printers, 1895–96.
2 v. 26½ cm.

The standard authority for Massachusetts's role in the war, at the front, and at home.

Hildebrand, Samuel S 1836–1872.
Autobiography of Samuel S. Hildebrand, the renowned Missouri "bushwacker" ... being his complete confession, recently made to the writers, and carefully compiled by James W. Evans and A. Wendell Keith ... Together with all the facts connected with his early history. Jefferson City, Mo., State times printing house, 1870.
312 p. incl. front., plates. 19cm.

Unique--but sometimes untrustworthy--reminiscences of a "backshooter;" throws some light on wartime chaos in Missouri.

Hoke, Jacob.
... Reminiscences of the war; or, Incidents which transpired in and about Chambersburg, during the war of the rebellion. By J. Hoke ... Chambersburg, Pa., M. A. Foltz, 1884.
211, [1] p. 24 cm.

A detailed account, padded with reprinted official correspondence, of life in Chambersburg, Pa.; the chapters on the burning of the city were published separately in book form.

Holliday, John Hampden, *b.* 1846.
... Indianapolis and the civil war, by John H. Holliday. Indianapolis, E. J. Hecker, printer, 1911.
1 p. l., p. [525]–595. 24 cm.

Provides an adequate and general account of the city's responses to war.

Hooper, Osman Castle, 1858–1941.
The Crisis and the man, an episode in civil war journalism, by Osman Castle Hooper ... Columbus, The Ohio state university press, 1929.
35 p. port. 21½cm.

A monograph on the Columbus (O.) Crisis and its active editor, Samuel Medary; a worthwhile introduction to subjects that merit more.

Hornbeck, Betty (Dutton)

Upshur brothers of the Blue and the Gray, by Betty Hornbeck. Parsons, W. Va., McClain Print. Co., 1967.

259 p. illus., maps, ports. 23 cm.

Above-average monographs on life in wartime Upshur County, W. Va.; three rosters are included; the short chapters originally appeared as newspaper articles.

Howe, Henry, 1816–1893.

The times of the rebellion in the West: a collection of miscellanies, showing the part taken in the war by each western state—notices of eminent officers—descriptions of prominent battles—conspiracies in the West to aid the rebellion—incidents of guerrilla and border warfare—individual adventures—anecdotes illustrating the heroism of western soldiers, etc. ... By Henry Howe. Cincinnati, Howe's subscription book concern, 1867.

252 p. incl. col. front., illus., plates. plates. 22cm.

Brief summaries of a wide variety of incidents and events; presented on a state-by-state basis.

Hubbart, Henry Clyde, 1882–

... The older Middle West, 1840–1880, its social, economic and political life and sectional tendencies before, during and after the civil war, by Henry Clyde Hubbart ... New York, London, D. Appleton-Century company, incorporated [©1936]

ix, 305 p. illus. (maps) 23 cm.

The only general treatment of the subject; weak in some areas and void in others; still a good starting point.

Hunt, Gaillard, 1862–1924, *comp.*

Israel, Elihu and Cadwallader Washburn; a chapter in American biography, compiled by Gaillard Hunt. New York, The Macmillan company, 1925.

vi p., 1 l., 397 p. front., ports. 22½cm.

Mainly valuable as a source book on Maine's war governor (Israel Washburn); more a compilation of letters and speeches than a biography.

Hutchinson, Vernal.

A Maine town in the Civil War; a chronicle of the vanished town of Old Deer Isle, Maine, during the crucial years 1861–65, as found in town, State, and national records, and as retained in the memories of the last survivors of that generation. Freeport, Me., Bond Wheelwright Co. [1967]

114 p. illus., map (on lining papers), ports. 21 cm.

A rather weak compilation that concentrates more on individual soldiers from Deer Isle than on the social and economic aspects of the community itself.

Illinois. *Military and naval dept.*

Report of the adjutant general of the state of Illinois ... Containing reports for the years 1861–66. Revised by Brigadier General J. W. Vance, adjutant general. Springfield, Ill., H. W. Rokker, state printer and binder, 1886.

8 v. 22½cm.

One of the better adjutant general's compilations; descriptive rosters are given for most units; yet suffers from extremely small type.

Illinois. *State sanitary commission.*

Report of transactions of the Illinois State sanitary bureau from its organization December 18th, 1862, to September 12th, 1863. And also of the Illinois State sanitary commission from September 12th, 1863, to January 1st, 1864. Springfield, Steam press of Baker & Phillips, 1864.

98 p. 21cm.

A report of operations to the General Assembly; largely statistical.

Indiana. *Adjutant general's office.*

Report of the adjutant general of the state of Indiana ... Indianapolis, A. H. Conner [etc.] state printer, 1865–69 [v. 1, '69]

8 v. 23½ cm.

Volume I (reprinted in 1960) contains much of value on the state's civil participation; the remaining volumes house rosters and regimental histories.

Indiana. *Battle flag commission.*

Indiana battle flags and Indiana war organizations. Pub. by Indiana Battle flag commission. [Indianapolis] 1928.

8 p. 22½cm.

Too short to be of significance.

Indiana sanitary commission.

Report of the Indiana sanitary commission, made to the governor. January 2, 1865. Indianapolis, W. R. Holloway, state printer, 1865.

132 p. 22cm.

This summary of operations and accomplishments was made at the conclusions of the war.

Iowa. *Adjutant-general's office.*
Roster and record of Iowa soldiers in the war of the rebellion, together with historical sketches of volunteer organizations, 1861–1866 ... Published by authority of the General assembly, under the direction of Brig. Gen. Wm. H. Thrift, adjutant general. Des Moines, E. H. English, state printer, 1908–11.
6 v. 23cm.

One of the better and more readable state rosters.

Iowa. *Governor.*
The messages and proclamations of the governors of Iowa; comp. and ed. by Benjamin F. Shambaugh ... v. I–
Iowa City, Ia., The State historical society of Iowa, 1903–
v. 25½ cm.

Volume II contains the papers of Gov. Kirkwood; Vol. III the papers of Gov. William M. Stone; biographical sketches of each are included.

Johns, *Mrs.* **Jane Martin.**
Personal recollections of early Decatur, Abraham Lincoln, Richard J. Oglesby and the civil war, by Jane Martin Johns, ed. by Howard C. Schaub. [Decatur, Ill.] Decatur chapter Daughters of the American revolution, 1912.
268 p. front. (port.) 22½cm.

Feminine viewpoints of Illinois in general and the city of Decatur in particular; overly chauvinistic and sentimental.

Jones, Robert Huhn, 1927–
The Civil War in the Northwest: Nebraska, Wisconsin, Iowa, Minnesota, and the Dakotas. [1st ed.] Norman, University of Oklahoma Press [1960]
216 p. illus. 24 cm.

Indian uprisings and military administrations are the main topics in this study of the Wisconsin-Minnesota-Iowa region.

Jordan, Ewing, 1847– *comp.*
University of Pennsylvania men who served in the civil war, 1861–1865; Department of arts (the college) compiled by Ewing Jordan ... [Philadelphia, 19—]
cover-title, [63] p. 24½cm.

A simple roster; of value solely to descendants of the soldiers.

Kennedy, Elijah Robinson, 1844–1926.
The contest for California in 1861; how Colonel E. D. Baker saved the Pacific States to the Union. Boston, Houghton Mifflin Co., 1912.
xiv, 361 p. front., ports. 22 cm.

Although weakened by age, this study remains the best for divided sentiment in California during the war's first days; much attention is also given to the battle of Ball's Bluff.

Kimmel, Stanley Preston.
Mr. Lincoln's Washington. New York, Coward-McCann [1957]
224 p. illus., ports., maps, facsims. 29 cm.

So weak a picture-book as to be worthless to all but the beginning reader.

King, John W.
The silent dead, or Roll of honor; comprising the names of all soldiers from Muskingum County, who lost their lives in battle or by disease, during the war of rebellion. Reported to date Jan. 1, 1866, by John W. King ... Zanesville, O., Logan & Dodd, 1866.
42 p. 21cm.

A list of Ohio soldiers who died in service along with the circumstances of their deaths.

Klein, Frederic Shriver, 1904– *ed.*
Just south of Gettysburg: Carroll County, Maryland, in the Civil War. Personal accounts and descriptions of a Maryland border county, 1861–1865, edited by Frederic Shriver Klein, with the collaboration of W. Harold Redcay [and] G. Thomas LeGore, for the Civil War Centennial Committee of the Historical Society of Carroll County, Md. Westminster, Newman Press, 1963.
247 p. illus. 23 cm.

An excellent compilation of letters, diaries, clippings and documents; the bulk of the study centers on the Gettysburg campaign.

Knapp, Charles Merriam, 1892–
New Jersey politics during the period of the civil war and reconstruction, by Charles Merriam Knapp ... Geneva, N. Y., W. F. Humphrey, 1924.
v, 212 p., 1 l. front. (map) 23cm.

An adequate treatment of a limited subject; based largely on newspaper sources; insufficient use of manuscript materials.

Laciar, Jacob D.

Patriotism of Carbon County, Pa., and what her people contributed during the war for the preservation of the Union. By J. D. Laciar. Mauch Chunk, Pa., 1867.

2 p. l., v–viii, [9]–120 p. front., ports. 21½cm.

This typical local production extolls the county's citizens and their contributions to war.

Ladies' hospital relief association, *Rochester, N. Y.*

Report of the Christmas bazaar, held under the auspices of the Ladies' hospital relief association, from December 14 to December 22, inclusive, at Corinthian hall, Rochester, N. Y. Rochester, Printed by Benton & Andrews, 1863.

48 p. illus. (plan) 23cm.

Another self-praising statement of local work done in the fields of hospitals and charities.

Lane, Jarlath Robert, *brother*, 1910–

... A political history of Connecticut during the civil war ... by Brother J. Robert Lane, F. S. C. Washington, D. C., The Catholic university of America press, 1941.

x, 321 p. 23 cm.

Includes four chapters on the pre-war and five on the war period; thoroughly researched and well-written; good bibliographical essay.

Lang, Theodore F.

Loyal West Virginia from 1861 to 1865. With an introductory chapter on the status of Virginia for thirty years prior to the war. By Theodore F. Lang ... Baltimore, Deutsch publishing co., 1895.

xix, 382 p. front., port., maps. 27½ cm.

Mostly a military history with regimental rosters; contains good sections on the attitudes that existed between Virginians and West Virginians.

Lanman, Charles, 1819–1895.

The red book of Michigan; a civil, military and biographical history. By Charles Lanman ... Detroit, E. B. Smith & company; Washington, Philp & Solomons, 1871.

1 p. l., xiv p., 1 l., [9]–549 p. 24 cm.

Primarily military in content; the Civil War material was the work of John Robertson, who later expanded the section for his Michigan and the War.

Laughlin, Sceva Bright, 1881–

Missouri politics during the civil war, by Sceva Bright Laughlin ... [Salem, Or., 1930]

vi, 116 p. illus. (maps) 23cm.

Shallow and brief, this study is primarily a summation of conventions and elections.

Leech, Margaret, 1893–

Reveille in Washington, 1860–1865, by Margaret Leech. New York and London, Harper & brothers [c1941]

x p., 1 l., 423, [1] p. illus. (maps, facsim.) plates. 24½ cm.

This Pulitzer Prize-winning volume is colorful and dramatic in presentation, but possessed of several small errors in fact.

Leftwich, William M.

Martyrdom in Missouri; a history of religious proscription, the seizure of churches, and the persecution of ministers of the gospel, in the state of Missouri during the late civil war, and under the "test oath" of the new constitution. By Rev. W. M. Leftwich ... Saint Louis, S. W. book & pub. co., 1870.

2 v. 19 cm.

The story of the persecution of ministers suspected of disloyalty; by a leading Methodist preacher; possesses a strong emotional undercurrent.

Love, William De Loss, 1819–1898.

Wisconsin in the war of the rebellion; a history of all regiments and batteries the state has sent to the field, and deeds of her citizens, governors and other military officers, and state and national legislators to suppress the rebellion. By Wm. De Loss Love. Chicago [etc.] Church and Goodman; New York, Sheldon & co., 1866.

vi p., 1 l., [vii]–xxi, [17]–1140 p. front., illus., port., diagr. 23½cm.

Essentially short regimental summaries; contains disappointingly little on the homefront.

Lusk, David W

Politics and politicians: a succinct history of the politics of Illinois from 1856 to 1884, with anecdotes and incidents, and appendix from 1809 to 1856 ... By D. W. Lusk. Springfield, Ill. [H. W. Rokker, printer] 1884.

xiii, 526 p. front., ports. 23 cm.

An old, standard study, still of value--especially when used in conjunction with the Raum volume on Illinois Republicanism.

McClure, Alexander Kelly, 1828–1909.
Old time notes of Pennsylvania: a connected and chronological record of the commercial, industrial and educational advancement of Pennsylvania, and the inner history of all political movements since the adoption of the constitution of 1838, by A. K. McClure, LL. D. Illustrated with portraits of over one hundred distinguished men of Pennsylvania, including all the governors, senators, judges of the courts of today, leading statesmen, railroad presidents, business men and others of note. Autograph ed. Philadelphia, The J. C. Winston company, 1905.
2 v. fronts., plates, ports. 23 cm.

A standard, widely used work on the Keystone State; Vol. I contains much data on wartime happenings.

McDowell, Robert Emmett.
City of conflict: Louisville in the Civil War, 1861–1865. With an introd. by Barry Bingham. [1st ed.] Louisville, Ky., Louisville Civil War Round Table [1962]
259 p. illus. 23 cm.

Largely local color; based on secondary accounts, it is lacking in penetrating analyses of the city's deeper sympathies, feelings, etc.

McElroy, John, 1846–1929.
The struggle for Missouri, by John McElroy ... Washington, D. C., The National tribune co., 1909.
3 p. l., ix, 3–342 p. col. front., illus., col. pl., ports., maps. 21½ cm.

Highly readable, though based largely on secondary sources; surveys the conflict through the battle of Pea Ridge.

McKelvey, Blake, *ed.*
... Rochester in the civil war. Blake McKelvey, editor. Edited under the supervision of Dexter Perkins, city historian under the authority of the Board of trustees of the Rochester public library ... Rochester, N. Y., The Society, 1944.
9 p. l., 5–266 p. front., plates, ports., map, facsim. 24cm.

A lively account, based largely on newspaper sources, of one city's reactions to war; includes letters, diaries and reminiscences of several of the city's recruits.

Maine. *Adjutant-general's office.*
Annual report. 1861–1866. Augusta, Stevens & Sayward, printers to the state, 1862–67.
7 v. 23 cm.

This standard compilation initially appeared as supplements to the Adjutant-General's annual reports for the war years.

Manakee, Harold Randall, 1908–
Maryland in the Civil War. Baltimore, Maryland Historical Society [1961]
173 p. illus., ports., maps. 24 cm.

This skillfully presented summary strikes a fair balance between military and civil topics; thumbnail sketches of prominent Marylanders are included.

Marietta college, *Marietta, O.*
Marietta college in the war of secession, 1861–1865. Cincinnati, P. G. Thomson, 1878.
96 p. 23cm.

A brief sketch of the effect of the war on this small school, along with a record of the students and faculty who served.

Marvin, Abijah Perkins.
History of Worcester in the war of the rebellion. By Abijah P. Marvin ... Worcester [Mass.] The author, 1870.
582 p. front., ports., plan. 23½ cm.

Probably the best city-history published in the immediate postwar years, though the book is heavily padded with useless statistics and varying trivia.

Maryland. *Board of trustees of the Antietam national cemetery.*
A descriptive list of the burial places of the remains of Confederate soldiers, who fell in the battles of Antietam, South Mountain, Monocacy, and other points in Washington and Frederick counties, in the state of Maryland. Pub. by direction of His Excellency, Oden Bowie, governor of Maryland. Hagerstown, Md., "Free press" print [1868]
84 p. 22cm.

Of value primarily to descendants of the soldiers listed; the list was prepared by Moses Poffinberger and Aaron Good.

Maryland. *Board of trustees of the Antietam national cemetery.*
History of Antietam national cemetery, including a descriptive list of all the loyal soldiers buried therein: together with the ceremonies and address on the occasion of the dedication of the grounds, September, 17th, 1867. Baltimore, J. W. Woods, printer, 1869.
202 p. 2 phot. 23cm.

Still the best history of the Civil War's second most famous cemetery; a folded map is included.

Maryland. *Commission on the publication of the histories of the Maryland volunteers during the civil war.*
History and roster of Maryland volunteers, war of 1861-5. Prepared under authority of the General assembly of Maryland, by L. Allison Wilmer, J. H. Jarrett, Geo. W. F. Vernon ... Baltimore, Md., Press of Guggenheimer, Weil & co., 1898-99.

2 v. front. (port.) 19 cm.

Another, typical state roster of troops; this one is more scarce to locate than most of the others.

Maryland union commission.
Services held by the Maryland union commission, in Charles street M. E. church, on the evening of June 1st, 1865, being the day of humiliation and prayer appointed by the President of the United States of America. Baltimore, Sherwood & co., printers [1865]

22 p. 18cm.

Includes a short sketch of the wartime activities of the Maryland Branch, U. S. Christian Commission.

Mason, Philip Parker, 1927-
From Bull Run to Appomattox: Michigan's role in the Civil War, by Philip P. Mason and Paul J. Pentecost. Detroit, Wayne State University, 1961.

vii, 63 p. illus., ports., map. 23 cm.

Brief sketches covering a wide variety of topics of the Wolverine State at war; succinct and well-researched; appeared originally as a series of newspaper articles.

Massachusetts. *Adjutant-general's office.*
Massachusetts soldiers, sailors, and marines in the civil war. Compiled and published by the adjutant-general in accordance with chapter 475, Acts of 1899 and chapter 64, Resolves of 1930 ... Norwood, Mass., Printed at the Norwood press, 1931-

v. 26½cm.

This most recently published adjutant general's report, nine volumes in all, provides valuable background and service data on each Bay State soldier.

Massachusetts. *Governor, 1861-1866 (John A. Andrew)*
Correspondence between Gov. Andrew and Maj.-Gen. Butler. Boston, J. J. Dyer, 1862.

86 p. 23½cm.

Letters relative to the raising of troops in the first year of the war.

Massachusetts in the Civil War. Boston, Massachusetts Civil War Centennial Commission, 1960-

v. 22 cm.

A series of well-researched and highly readable monographs; heavy on military affairs.

May, George Smith, 1924-
Michigan and the Civil War years, 1860-1866; a wartime chronicle, by George S. May. [Lansing] Michigan Civil War Centennial Observance Commission [1964]

vii, 124 p. 23 cm.

Journal-like entries give a concise and helpful picture of both military and political events.

May, George Smith, 1924- *ed.*
Michigan Civil War history; an annotated bibliography. Compiled by James M. Babcock [and others] Detroit, Wayne State University Press, 1961.

xii, 128 p. 23 cm.

A thorough, useful and annotated bibliography of Michigan's participation in the war.

Michigan. *Adjutant general's dept.*
Annual report. 1862-66. Lansing, J. A. Kerr & co., 1863-66.

6 v. 22cm.

As in the case of all such state reports, this one treats almost exclusively of military units, actions and casualties.

Michigan. *Adjutant general's dept.*
Michigan in the war. Comp. by Jno. Robertson, adjutant general. Rev. ed. ... Lansing, W. S. George & co., state printers, 1882.

1039 p. front., pl., ports. 24 cm.

Revised edition of an 1880 work; primarily military history, regiment by regiment, with only incidental reference to non-military events.

Michigan. *Adjutant general's dept.*
Record of service of Michigan volunteers in the civil war, 1861–1865. Pub. by authority of the Senate and House of representatives of the Michigan Legislature under the direction of Brig. Gen. Geo. H. Brown, adjutant general. ⌈Kalamazoo, Mich., Ihling bros. & Everhard, printers, 190–⌉
46 v. fronts., ports. 23½ cm.

Another descriptive state roster; inferior to those published by such states as Iowa and Massachusetts.

Michigan. *Governor.*
Messages of the governors of Michigan ... Ed. by George N. Fuller. Lansing, The Michigan Historical commission, 1925–
v. ports., tables. 23½ cm.

Includes the public messages of Govs. Austin Blair and Henry H. Crapo, with brief biographical sketches of each.

Miers, Earl Schenck, 1910– *ed.*
New Jersey and the Civil War: an album of contemporary accounts. Princeton, N. J., Van Nostrand, 1964.
xii, 135 p. illus., ports., col. maps (on lining papers) 22 cm.

Written for popular consumption; lacks documentation, bibliography and index; concentrates on New Jersey in the field.

Millbrook, Minnie (Dubbs) *ed.*
Twice told tales of Michigan and her soldiers in the Civil War. ⌈Lansing⌉ Michigan Civil War Centennial Observance Commission ⌈1966⌉
84 p. illus., port. 23 cm.

This slim collection of anecdotes is useful for color and relaxation; many of the stories are obviously suspect.

Milwaukee sentinel. (*Indexes*)
The Civil War, from the Milwaukee sentinel index. Reproductions of card entries filed under the subject "Civil War" in the Milwaukee Public Library's catalog of the Milwaukee sentinel index (1837–1880) A bibliography of "Wisconsin in the Civil War," compiled by the staff of the Milwaukee Public Library. Prepared for publication by the Milwaukee Public Library. Milwaukee, 1962.
vi, 62 p. port. (on cover) 33 cm.

A natural starting-point for any study of an important Midwestern city in wartime.

Minnesota. *Board of commissioners on publication of history of Minnesota in civil and Indian wars.*
Minnesota in the civil and Indian wars 1861–1865. Prepared and published under the supervision of the Board of commissioners appointed by the act of the Legislature of Minnesota of April 16, 1889. St. Paul, Minn., Printed for the state by the Pioneer press company, 1890–93.
2 v. 26½ cm.

These two large volumes, now badly dated, nevertheless contain much data on a state removed from the scene of war; the best sections treat of the Sioux uprisings.

Minnesota historical society.
Minnesotans in the civil and Indian wars, an index to the rosters in Minnesota in the civil and Indian wars, 1861–1865; compiled as a W. P. A. project for the Minnesota historical society under the direction of Irene B. Warming, reference assistant. Saint Paul, The Minnesota historical society, 1936.
2 p. l., 2, 488 numb. l. 28½ x 22½cm.

A WPA project that makes Minnesota in the Civil and Indian Wars useful and usable; regrettably, few copies exist.

Missouri. *Adjutant-general's office.*
Annual report ... 1862/1865. Jefferson City ⌈1862⌉–66.
4 v. 23cm.

Similar in most respects to the reports of the Michigan Adjutant General (see previous entry).

Missouri. *Governor.*
The messages and proclamations of the Governors of the State of Missouri. v. 1–
⌈1820–44—
Columbia, State Historical Society of Missouri.
v. ports. 24 cm.

Contains the official papers of Govs. Jackson and Fletcher, plus a brief biographical sketch of each.

Monks, William.
A history of southern Missouri and northern Arkansas; being an account of the early settlements, the Civil war, the Ku-klux, and times of peace. By William Monks ... West Plains, Mo., West Plains journal co., 1907.
247 p. incl. front., illus., ports. 20cm.

Personal reminiscences of a militia officer; rambling but good in showing divided loyalties and suffering at the hands of guerrillas.

Moore, George Ellis.
A banner in the hills; West Virginia's statehood. New York, Appleton-Century-Crofts [1963]
256 p. illus. 24 cm.

Published by the state centennial commission, this work contains a satisfactory narrative of military and political affairs relative to the new commonwealth.

Mudd, Joseph Aloysius, 1842–1916.
With Porter in north Missouri; a chapter in the history of the war between the states, by Joseph A. Mudd. Washington, D. C., The National publishing company, 1909.
452 p. front., ports. 23½cm.

Largely military in content, with a few allusions to the Missouri countryside and populace.

Murdock, Eugene Converse.
Ohio's bounty system in the Civil War [by] Eugene C. Murdock. [Columbus] Ohio State University Press for the Ohio Historical Society [1963]
58 p. map. 24 cm.

Small in size but heavy with little-known facts and startling revelations about the evils of the bounty system.

Musgrove, Richard Watson, 1840–1914.
Autobiography. [n. p.] M. D. Musgrove, 1921.
230 p. illus. 23 cm.

Of limited usefulness for references to the 1862-1865 Indian wars in the then-Northwest.

Nason, Elias, 1811–1887.
A brief record of events in Exeter, N. H. during the year 1862; together with the names of the soldiers of this town in the war. By Rev. Elias Nason ... Exeter, Fogg & Fellowes, 1863.
20 p. 18½cm.

Even briefer than the title implies; a similar work was issued for the year 1861.

Naylor, Colin T
Civil War days in a country village. Peekskill, N. Y., Highland Press, 1961.
122 p. illus. 29 cm.

An interesting examination of wartime Peekskill, N. Y.; largely a collection of community miscellany.

Nebraska. *Governor.*
Messages and proclamations of the governors of Nebraska, 1854–1941. A special publication of the Nebraska state historical society ... Published as a report of Work projects administration ... Sponsored by the Nebraska state historical society and the University of Nebraska. [Lincoln?] 1941–42.
4 v. ports., tables. 28½cm.

Contains the public papers of Govs. Alvin Saunders and Algernon S. Paddock, with brief biographical sketches of each.

New Hampshire. *Adjutant-general's office.*
Revised register of the soldiers and sailors of New Hampshire in the war of the rebellion. 1861–1866. Prepared and published by authority of the legislature, by Augustus D. Ayling, adjutant general. Concord, I. C. Evans, public printer, 1895.
xli p., 1 l., 1347 p. 32½cm.

Somewhat more skimpy on information than the average state roster, but still the best source for individual soldier's records.

New Hampshire and the Civil War. no. 1–[4]. [Concord] New Hampshire Civil War Centennial Commission [1962–65?]
4 no. illus., ports. 21 cm.

Similar in format and content to periodicals issued by the centennial commissions of Massachusetts and New York.

New Jersey. *Adjutant-general's office.*
Annual report of the adjutant-general of the state of New Jersey, for ... 1861[–1865] Trenton, 1862–66.
4 v. in 1. 22cm.

Each volume summarizes recruiting problems and contains a roster of officers recruited.

New Jersey. *Adjutant-general's office.*

Record of officers and men of New Jersey in the civil war, 1861 1865. Compiled in the office of the adjutant general. Published by authority of the Legislature. William S. Stryker, adjutant general. Trenton, J. L. Murphy, printer, 1876.

2 v. 31cm.

Two huge volumes that are more difficult to use than similar state rosters for Iowa, Ohio, et al.

New York (*State*) *Adjutant-general's office.*

A record of the commissioned officers, non-commissioned officers, and privates, of the regiments which were organized in the state of New York and called into the service of the United States to assist in suppressing the rebellion, caused by the secession of some of the southern states from the Union, A. D. 1861, as taken from the muster-in rolls on file in the adjutant-general's office, S. N. Y. Albany, Comstock & Cassidy, printers, 1864–68.

8 v. 30½cm.

Supplementary volumes to the Adjutant-General's annual reports for 1893-1905; comparable to other state compilations.

New York (*State*) *Board of managers of the soldiers' depot.*

Report of the Board of managers of the New York state soldiers' depot, and of the fund for the relief of sick, wounded, furloughed and discharged soldiers. Transmitting the report of the general agent of the state. Albany, Van Benthuysen's steam printing house, 1864.

160 p. 5 fold. pl. (part col.) 2 maps (1 fold.) 2 fold. plans. 25cm.

Largely a statistical accounting of work done by the board.

New York (*State*) *General agent for the relief of sick and wounded soldiers.*

Annual report.

Albany, 186

v. plates, plans. 23½cm.

Summarizes with statistics work done through official state channels.

New York (*State*) *Governor.*

State of New York. Messages from the governors, comprising executive communications to the Legislature and other papers relating to legislation from the organization of the first colonial Assembly in 1683 to and including the year 1906, with notes. Ed. by Charles Z. Lincoln; pub. by authority of the state ... Albany, J. B. Lyon company, state printers, 1909.

11 v. ports. 24cm.

Contains the public papers of Govs. Edwin D. Morgan and Horatio Seymour.

New York. Union defence committee.

The Union defence committee of the city of New York. Minutes, reports, and correspondence; with an historical introduction by John Austin Stevens. [New York] The Union defence committee, 1885.

3 p. l., 286 p. 26½cm.

A useful volume for behind-the-lines examples of devotion to the Union.

New York State and the Civil War. v. 1– July 1961–

[Albany, New York State Civil War Centennial Commission]

v. illus., ports. 20 cm.

This valuable series of monthly publications covered all aspects of the war in New York but regrettably ceased with the Commission's disbandment in 1963.

Niven, John.

Connecticut for the Union; the role of the State in the Civil War. New Haven, Yale University Press, 1965.

xviii, 493 p. illus., facsim., maps, ports. 25 cm.

A superb study, utilizing all of the tools of modern scholarship; unfortunately heavy on things military.

[Norton, John Foote] 1809–1892.

The record of Athol, Massachusetts, in suppressing the great rebellion. Prepared for publication by a committee of the town. Boston, G. C. Rand & Avery, 1866.

264 p. 19½cm.

While containing much local history, this study suffers from weaknesses of scholarship and an excess of eulogium.

Ohio. *Roster commission.*

Official roster of the soldiers of the state of Ohio in the war of the rebellion, 1861–1866 ... Compiled under direction of the Roster commission ... Published by authority of the General assembly. Akron, Werner co., 1886–95.

12 v. 25½ cm.

Another full, descriptive roster, yet one--like many--that could have benefitted from larger type.

Owens, Kenneth N

Galena, Grant, and the fortunes of war; a history of Galena, Illinois, during the Civil War. DeKalb, Ill., Northern Illinois University, in cooperation with the Galena Historical Society, Galena, Ill., 1963.

v, 67 p. illus., ports. 23 cm.

A monograph, without footnotes or index, of the wartime social life in the town that gave Grant to the Union.

[Painter, Henry M]

Brief narrative of incidents in the war in Missouri, and of the personal experience of one who has suffered. Boston, Press of the Daily courier, 1863.

28 p. 24cm.

An untrustworthy and exaggerated narrative, yet illustrative of the vehemence of war in a divided state.

Parrish, William Earl, 1931–

Turbulent partnership: Missouri and the Union, 1861–1865. With an introd. by Robert L. D. Davidson. Columbia, University of Missouri Press [1963]

242 p. illus. 23 cm.

A penetrating study of internal political problems and the inter-relationships between a key border state and the federal government.

Patton, John, 1850–

An address by John Patton, delivered at Lansing, Mich., October 12, 1898, at the unveiling of the statue, erected by the state of Michigan, in the Capitol grounds, to the memory of Austin Blair, war governor. [Lansing? 1898?]

20 p. illus. 26cm.

A eulogistic sketch of Michigan's war governor.

Paul, William G

Wisconsin's Civil War archives, compiled by William G. Paul, with the assistance of David J. Delgado and Jack K. Jallings. Madison, State Historical Society of Wisconsin, 1965.

v, 66 p. 23 cm.

A descriptive listing of 173 manuscript collections pertaining to Wisconsin's responses to war.

Pennsylvania. *Governor.*

... Papers of the governors. 1681–1902. Harrisburg, The State of Pennsylvania, 1900–02.

12 v. fronts., illus., pl., ports., facsims. (part double, 1 fold.) 21½cm.

Contains the official messages and proclamations of Gov. Andrew G. Curtin, with a brief sketch of his administration.

Philadelphia. Great Central Fair for the U. S. Sanitary Commission, *1864.*

The haversack. Philadelphia, Published by the Committee on Hospitals for the Great Central Fair for the U. S. Sanitary Commission, 1864.

60 p. 23 cm.

This fund-raising publication, issued by one of the more active homefront organizations, contains sketches of both civilian and military life.

Philadelphia. *Home guard.*

Report of Brigadier Gen'l A. J. Pleasonton, commanding the Home guard of the city of Philadelphia, to the Hon. Alexander Henry, mayor ... for ... 1861, 1862, 1863. Philadelphia, 1862–64.

3 v. in 1. 1 illus. 21½–23cm.

Essentially statistical in content; its major value is its pinpointing of defense efforts in the Philadelphia area.

Phisterer, Frederick, 1836–1909, *comp.*

New York in the war of the rebellion, 1861 to 1865. Comp. by Frederick Phisterer. 3d ed. ... Albany, J. B. Lyon company, state printers, 1912.

6 v. col. fronts. (incl. col. port.) col. plates, col. maps. 28½ cm.

Primarily regimental histories with very little on civil affairs; Vol. I contains a list of Assembly members and congressmen.

Pittsburgh sanitary committee.

First report, address and proceedings of the Pittsburgh sanitary committee, February, 1863. Pittsburgh, Printed by W. S. Haven, 1863.

16 p. 22½cm.

An official summation of its work at the time of its consolidation with the U. S. Sanitation Commission.

Plank, Will.
Banners and bugles; a record of Ulster County, New York and the mid Hudson region in the Civil War. Marlborough, N. Y., Centennial Press [1963]

164 [4] p. illus., maps, ports. 27 cm.

A superior compilation of one county in the war; based on a wide variety of primary sources, this study also pays more-than-usual attention to civilian affairs.

Pompey, Sherman Lee.
New Mexico honor roll. Independence, Calif., Historical and Genealogical Pub. Co., ©1965.

[10] l. 28 cm.

A simple register of names; of use for selected genealogists only.

Porter, George Henry, 1878–
Ohio politics during the civil war period ... New York, 1911.

1 p. l., 257 p. maps. 24½cm.

Somewhat colorless and overly objective, yet a comprehensive view of the internal history of state administrations.

Quiner, Edwin Bentlee, *d.* 1868.
The military history of Wisconsin: a record of the civil and military patriotism of the state, in the war for the union, with a history of the campaigns in which Wisconsin soldiers have been conspicuous — regimental histories — sketches of distinguished officers—the roll of the illustrious dead—movements of the Legislature and state officers, etc. By E. B. Quiner ... Chicago, Clarke & co., 1866.

1022 p. front., illus., port. 23½cm.

Histories of several Wisconsin units, plus a summary of legislative and executive steps taken in support of the war.

Radcliffe, George Lovic Pierce, 1877–
... Governor Thomas H. Hicks of Maryland and the civil war, by George L. P. Radcliffe. Baltimore, the Johns Hopkins press, 1901.

141 p. 24½ cm.

A generally favorable account based largely on personal papers and newspapers; especially good for Hicks's stand in the secession crisis.

Raum, Green Berry, 1829–1909.
History of Illinois Republicanism, embracing a history of the Republican party in the state to the present time ... with biographies of its founders and supporters ... also a chronological statement of important political events since 1774. By Green B. Raum. Chicago, Rollins publishing company, 1900.

815 p. front., illus., ports. 28cm.

Like the companion study by Lusk, this work shows age; yet it remains revealing for the political infighting in one key state.

Raymond, Samuel, *b.* 1814, *comp.*
... The record of Andover during the rebellion. Comp. by Samuel Raymond. Andover [Mass.] W. F. Draper, printer, 1875.

viii, 232 p. 24cm

An above-average city history--though, like its many associates, it suffers from sentimentalism.

Redington, Edward Dana, 1839– *comp.*
Military record of the sons of Dartmouth in the Union army and navy, 1861–1865, comp. by Major E. D. Redington, '61; rev. and ed. by Major W. H. Hodgkins, hon. '97; pub. by the trustees of the college. Boston, Mass., 1907.

vi, 137 p. 23½cm.

Brief sketches of the military service of Dartmouth graduates and students.

Refugee relief commission of Ohio, *Cincinnati.*
... Semi-annual report of the Refugee relief commission of Ohio ... [1st]– [March, 1864]–
Cincinnati, Times steam book and job printing establishment, 1864–

21½cm.

A largely statistical account of work done within the state.

Reid, Whitelaw, 1837–1912.
Ohio in the war: her statesmen, her generals, and soldiers. By Whitelaw Reid ... Cincinnati, New York, Moore, Wilstach & Baldwin, 1868.

2 v. front., pl., port., map. 25cm.

Volume I covers the home front and concentrates on politics; Vol. II treats of things military; still a valuable source for the Buckeye State.

Rhode Island. *Adjutant-general's office.*
Annual report of the adjutant general of Rhode Island and Providence Plantations, for the year 1865. Cor., rev., and republished ... by Brigadier-General Elisha Dyer, adjutant general. Providence, E. L. Freeman & son, printers to the state, 1893–95.
2 v. 25½cm.

A very comprehensive state listing that would have been more usable had it been printed in four average volumes rather than in two weighty tomes.

Rittenhouse, Jack DeVere, 1912–
New Mexico Civil War bibliography, 1861–1865; an annotated checklist of books & pamphlets. [Enl. ed.] Houston, Stagecoach Press, 1961.
36 p. 24 cm.

Well annotated; valuable for research in this area.

Robinson, H L.
History of Pittsfield, N. H. in the great rebellion, by H. L. Robinson ... Pittsfield, N. H. [Concord, N. H., Printed by the Republican press association] 1893.
217 p. front., pl., ports. 19cm.

Concentrates almost totally on men from Pittsfield in the Federal armies; many of the biographical sketches are useful.

Rombauer, Robert Julius, 1830–
The Union cause in St. Louis in 1861; an historical sketch, by Robert J. Rombauer ... [St. Louis, Press of Nixon-Jones prtg. co.] 1909.
xiv p., 1 l., 475 p. front., illus. (maps, plans) pl., ports. 23½cm.

A thorough, favorable account, with much background material, of Union operations in St. Louis; an appendix contains rosters of Missouri soldiers.

Rose Hill Seminar. *1st, Waynesboro, Pa., 1963.*
The Cumberland Valley of Pennsylvania in the 1860's; proceedings. Edited with an introd. by Francis Coleman Rosenberger. [Gettysburg? Pa., ©1963]
vii, 72 p. 23 cm.

A collection of six essays, by as many scholars, on an area of Pennsylvania that witnessed several scenes of war; the longest essay treats of the burning of Chambersburg.

Ryan, Daniel Joseph, 1855–1923.
The civil war literature of Ohio; a bibliography with explanatory and historical notes, by Daniel J. Ryan ... Cleveland, O., The Burrows brothers company, 1911.
ix, 518 p. 27½cm.

Still useful but badly in need of updating; contains most of the works that appeared immediately after the war.

Ryle, Walter Harrington.
Missouri: union or secession, by Walter Harrington Ryle, PH. D. Nashville, Tenn., George Peabody college for teachers, 1931.
4 p. l., 247 p. 22½cm.

An able discussion of the Missouri election campaign of 1860 and the events leading through the secession convention of March, 1861.

Scharf, John Thomas, 1843–1898.
History of Baltimore city and county, from the earliest period to the present day: including biographical sketches of their representative men. By J. Thomas Scharf ... Philadelphia, L. H. Everts, 1881.
x, 13–947 p. front., illus., plates, ports., fold. maps. 28cm.

Sadly lacking in many details, but the best source for this Southern city in a Northern state.

Schmidt, Royal Jae, 1915–
Bugles in a dream; Du Page County in the Civil War. Elmhurst, Ill., Historical Society of Du Page County, 1962.
31 p. 23 cm.

This brief sketch recounts one Illinois county's role in the national holocaust.

Schouler, William, 1814–1872.
A history of Massachusetts in the civil war. By William Schouler ... Boston, E. P. Dutton & co., 1868–71.
2 v. front. (port.) fold. map. 23½ cm.

Volume I is a political history strongly pro-Andrew in sentiment; Vol. II recounts the contributions of cities and counties.

Schrantz, Ward L.

Jasper County, Missouri, in the civil war, compiled by Ward L. Schrantz. Carthage, Mo., The Carthage press, ©1923.

xxi, [23]–269 p. front. (map) plates 20cm.

The story of a border county in southwest Missouri caught in the turmoil of guerrilla warfare; based on county histories, official records and newspaper accounts.

Seabrook, William Luther Wesley, 1833–

Maryland's great part in saving the Union; the loyalty of her governor, Thomas Holliday Hicks, and a majority of her people; from personal participation in and knowledge of events at Annapolis, and observation of the attitude of the people throughout the state, by William L. W. Seabrook, commissioner of the Land office from January 1858, till March, 1868. [Westminster, Md., Printed by the American sentinel company, ©1913]

2 p. l., 58 p. plates, ports. 21cm.

Personal reminiscences of a minor political figure intimately acquainted with Gov. Hicks and others; Seabrook viewed Maryland as a pivotal border state.

Secret correspondence illustrating the condition of affairs in Maryland. Baltimore, 1863.

42 p. 23 cm.

Letters from Maryland Unionists in regards to Confederate sympathizers in the state; unique and useful.

Shetler, Charles.

West Virginia Civil War literature; an annotated bibliography. Morgantown, West Virginia University Library, 1963.

xii, 184 p. illus., facsims. 23 cm.

A reference guide as useful to the scholar as it is informative to the layman.

Shippensburg Historical Society. *Publication Committee.*

Shippensburg in the Civil War. Authors: William H. Burkhart [and others] Shippensburg, Pa., Shippensburg Historical Society, 1964.

313 p. illus., ports. 24 cm.

An indexed potpourri of local items; muster rolls, newspaper accounts, soldiers' recollections, postwar memorials and modern narratives.

Simms, Henry Harrison, 1896–

Ohio politics on the eve of conflict. [Columbus?] Ohio State University Press for Ohio Historical Society [1961]

34 p. 24 cm.

Ohioans favored compromise, but felt that neither the Mississippi River nor tariffs should be divided among two nations.

Smith, Edward Conrad, 1891–

The borderland in the civil war, by Edward Conrad Smith ... New York, The Macmillan company, 1927.

5 p. l., 412 p. illus. (maps) 22½ cm.

An important study for a better understanding of the intricacies of border state feelings; shows the problems confronting these states during the war.

Smith, George Washington, 1855–1945.

A history of southern Illinois: a narrative account of its historical progress, its people, and its principal interests, by George Washington Smith ... Chicago and New York, The Lewis publishing company, 1912–

v. front. (port.) illus. 27½ cm.

The most detailed study to date of the area known as "Little Egypt;" the age of the three-volume work is now beginning to show.

Soldiers aid society of Hartsville, Pa.

History of the Hartsville ladies' aid society. Organized November 15, 1861. Pub. by the society. [Hartsville? W. W. H. Davis, printer, 1867.

26 p. 22½cm.

Contains an account of the society's activities, names of members, and a list of material supplied to soldiers.

Soldiers' and citizens' album of biographical record [of Wisconsin] containing personal sketches of army men and citizens prominent in loyalty to the Union. Also a chronological and statistical history of the civil war, and a history of the Grand army of the republic; with portraits of soldiers and prominent citizens. Chicago, Grand army publishing company, 1890.

880, [8] p. incl. front., col. plates, ports. ports. 26½cm.

The usual "mug" book in which veterans emphasized individual war records; also contains some biographical material.

Speed, Thomas, 1841–1906.

The Union cause in Kentucky, 1860–1865, by Captain Thomas Speed, adjutant 12th Kentucky infantry and veteran infantry vols. 1861–65 ... New York and London, G. P. Putnam's sons, 1907.

xxiii, 355 p. front. (port.) 23½ cm.

A strongly favorable account of Kentucky Unionists' efforts to hold their state and of the contribution of Kentuckians in the Union forces.

Spruance, John S

Delaware stays in the Union; the Civil War period, 1860–1865. With drawings by Frank E. Schoonover. Newark, University of Delaware Press, 1955.

34 p. illus. 22 cm.

Another small sampling of a subject still in need of full and scholarly treatment.

Stampp, Kenneth Milton.

Indiana politics during the Civil War. Indianapolis, Indiana Historical Bureau, 1949.

xiii, 300 p. 24 cm.

This basic study emphasizes economic motivations behind political differences within the state; Stampp is overly critical of Republicans.

Stanley, Ruel H.

Eastern Maine and the rebellion: being an account of the principal local events in eastern Maine during the war. And brief histories of eastern Maine regiments. Contains accounts of mobs, riots, destruction of newspapers, war meetings, drafts, Confederate raids, peace meetings, celebrations, soldiers' letters, and scenes and incidents at the front, never before in print. By R. H. Stanley and Geo. O. Hall. Bangor, Me., R. H. Stanley & company, 1887.

392 p. 3 pl., 17 port. (incl. front.) 23cm.

A good picture of local response in rock-ribbed New England to the conflict, with regimental histories of those groups from the area.

[Stevens, A Parsons]

... The military history of Ohio. Its border annals, its part in the Indian wars, in the war of 1812, in the Mexican war, and in the war of the rebellion, with a prefix, giving a compendium of the history of the United States ... Special local department in editions by counties, giving a roster of Ohio's rank and file from the county in the war of the rebellion ... New York, Toledo [etc.] The Transcontinental publishing co., 1885.

308 p. front., illus. (incl. maps) ports. 38cm.

Recounts Ohio's role in all wars to that time; skimpy on non-military aspects; special county editions listed local soldiers.

Stevenson, David.

Indiana's roll of honor. By David Stevenson, A. M. Indianapolis, A. D. Streight, 1864–66.

2 v. front., port. 23cm.

Largely regimental histories, with biographical sketches of the leading civil and military figures.

Stutler, Boyd Blynn, 1889–

West Virginia in the Civil War. Charleston, W. Va., Education Foundation, 1963.

vii, 304 p. 24 cm.

Gives a brief account of the state's formation, but devotes much space to the military encounters that took place in the area.

Tallmadge Historical Society.

The Civil War and Tallmadge, Ohio, 1861–1865; excerpts from reports made at the annual meetings, and other data. Tallmadge, °1961.

30 p. map. 23 cm.

Excerpts from reports concerning various aspects of the county's participation in the war.

Thornbrough, Emma Lou.

Indiana in the Civil War era, 1850–1880. Indianapolis, Indiana Historical Bureau, 1965.

xii, 758 p. illus., facsims., ports. 24 cm.

Volume III treats of the war and contains a wealth of information on politics and society inside the Hoosier State.

Townsend, Thomas Seaman, 1829–1908.

The honors of the Empire state in the war of the rebellion, by Thomas S. Townsend ... New York, A. Lovell & co., 1889.

vi, 7–416 p. 20½cm.

Largely a regimental history; approximately one-fifth is devoted to civilian aspects with interesting chapters on the professions, women in war, colleges, etc.

United States sanitary commission. *Cincinnati branch.*

... Report of the operations of the Cincinnati branch of the United States sanitary commission, to March 1, 1862. [New York? 1862]

12 p., 2 l. 22½cm.

A summary of work accomplished at the Cincinnati post.

United States sanitary commission. *General aid society for the army, Buffalo.*

Report of delegates from the General aid society for the army, at Buffalo, N. Y., to visit the government hospitals, and the agencies of the United States sanitary commission. By Rev. George W. Hosmer, D. D. Buffalo, Franklin steam printing house, 1862.

16 p. 22½cm.

A brief account of Buffalo hospital conditions and the need for improvements early in the war.

United States sanitary commission. *Philadelphia branch.*

Report of the general superintendent of the Philadelphia branch of the U. S. sanitary commission, to the Executive committee, February 1st, 1864; Jan. 1st, 1865; Jan. 1st, 1866. Philadelphia, King & Baird, printers, 1864–66.

3 v. 23cm.

Volume I contains a history of operations; statistical tables were issued as supplements.

United States sanitary commission. *Soldiers' aid society of northern Ohio, Cleveland.*

Our acre and its harvest. Historical sketch of the Soldiers' aid society of northern Ohio. Cleveland branch of the United States sanitary commission ... Cleveland, Fairbanks, Benedict & co., printers, 1869.

xiii p., 1 l., 17–511 p. illus. (plan) plates, map. 23½cm.

This historical study is good for showing the general setup and operations of a major branch of the Sanitary Commission.

United States sanitary commission. *Chicago branch.*

... Report on the condition of camps and hospitals at Cairo and vicinity, Paducah and St. Louis, by Rev. W. W. Patton and R. N. Isham, M. D., of the Chicago branch of the U. S. sanitary commission, October, 1861. Chicago, Dunlop, Sewell & Spalding, printers, 1861.

11, [1] p. 21cm.

An early report on the need for more adequate facilities in Chicago.

United States sanitary commission. *New-England women's auxiliary association, Boston.*

... Annual report of the New-England women's auxiliary association ... Boston, Prentiss & Deland, printers, 1863–65.

3 v. 23cm.

Largely a statistical survey of work done by this group.

United States sanitary commission. *Western dept.*

... Report on the operations of the U. S. sanitary commission in the valley of the Mississippi, for the quarter ending Oct. 1st, 1864. By Dr. J. S. Newberry, secretary Western department. [Washington, 1864]

30 p. 22½cm.

A typical report from an untypical department.

Vermont. *Adjutant and inspector-general's office.*

Revised roster of Vermont volunteers and lists of Vermonters who served in the army and navy of the United States during the war of the rebellion, 1861–66. Compiled by authority of the General assembly under direction of Theodore S. Peck, adjutant-general. Montpelier, Press of the Watchman publishing co., 1892.

vii, 863 p. 31 x 23cm.

Comparable in strengths and weaknesses to similar compilations for other Northern states.

Waite, Otis Frederick Reed, 1818–1895.

Claremont war history; April, 1861, to April, 1865: with sketches of New-Hampshire regiments, and a biographical notice of each Claremont soldier, etc. By Otis F. R. Waite. Concord [N. H.] McFarland & Jenks, printers, 1868.

xi, [13]–300 p. 19 cm.

This overrated work contains little more than summaries of regiments containing men from the Claremont area.

Waite, Otis Frederick Reed, 1818–1895.

New Hampshire in the great rebellion. Containing histories of the several New Hampshire regiments, and biographical notices of many of the prominent actors in the civil war of 1861–65. By Major Otis F. R. Waite ... Claremont, N. H., Tracy, Chase & co., 1870.

vi p., 1 l., [9]–608 p. front., pl., port. 23cm.

Primarily devoted to battle accounts and regimental summaries; some of the biographical sketches are of civilian leaders.

Waite, Otis Frederick Reed, 1818–1895.

Vermont in the great rebellion. Containing historical and biographical sketches, etc. By Maj. Otis F. R. Waite. Claremont, N. H., Tracy, Chase and company, 1869.

288 p. front., plates, ports. 19½cm.

Similar in format and organization to the same author's compilation for New Hampshire.

Ware, Edith Ellen.

Political opinion in Massachusetts during civil war and reconstruction, by Edith Ellen Ware ... New York, 1916.

1 p. l., 5–219 p., 1 l. diagrs. (1 fold.) 25cm.

Changes in public opinion, and evaluations of the press, are this work's most valuable contents; the weakest points are the shallow characterizations of individuals.

Wayland, ***Mass***

The town of Wayland in the civil war of 1861–1865, as represented in the army and navy of the American union ... Prepared and published by order of the town of Wayland. Wayland [Mass.] 1871.

452 p. 22½cm.

One of the largest histories of a Northern city in wartime; suffers the usual weaknesses of home-grown historians.

Webb, William Larkin, 1856–

Battles and biographies **of Missourians**; or, The civil war period of our state. By W. L. Webb. Kansas City, Mo., Hudson-Kimberly pub. co., 1900.

369, [1] p. front., plates, ports. 20cm.

Brief, superficial accounts of leading actions in Missouri, plus biographies of a variety of Missourians, civil and military, on both sides.

Weeden, William Babcock, 1834–1912.

War government, federal and state, in Massachusetts, New York, Pennsylvania and Indiana, 1861–1865, by William B. Weeden ... Boston and New York, Houghton, Mifflin and company, 1906.

xxv, 389, [1] p. 21½ cm.

Uses states mentioned to show the far-reaching readjustment accomplished in federal-state relations by wartime government at both levels; a useful reference.

Weisenburger, Francis Phelps, 1900–

Columbus during the Civil War. [Columbus] Ohio State University Press for the Ohio Historical Society [1963]

33, [1] p. 24 cm.

A fully annotated monograph that concentrates on the city's social and economic sides during war.

Wells, Robert W

Wisconsin in the Civil War. [Milwaukee, Milwaukee journal, 1962]

102 p. illus. 31 cm.

Thirty-nine popularly written vignettes; originally appeared serially in the Milwaukee Journal.

Western sanitary commission.

Report to the Western sanitary commission on the general military hospitals of St. Louis, Mo. St. Louis, R. P. Studley and co., printers, 1862.

75, [1] p. 22½cm.

A detailed survey of the hospital situation in St. Louis; the emphasis is on administrative problems.

Western sanitary commission.

Report of the Western sanitary commission for the year ending June 1st, 1863. St. Louis, Mo., Western sanitary commission rooms, 1863.

cover-title, 32 p. 23cm.

Nothing more than a general and laudatory survey of the Commission's work.

Wiel, Samuel Charles, 1878–

Lincoln's crisis in the far West. San Francisco, Priv. print., 1949.

v, 130 p. facsim. 24 cm.

A weak study that centers too much on California gold mining and the disposition of public lands.

Willis, Henry Augustus, 1830–1918.

Fitchburg in the war of the rebellion. By Henry A. Willis ... Fitchburg [Mass.] S. Shepley, 1866.

202 p. incl. tables. 24cm.

Superior to the other community histories published immediately after the war; contains prison accounts as well as biographical sketches and the usual rosters.

Wilson, James Grant, 1832–1914.

Biographical sketches of Illinois officers engaged in the war against the rebellion of 1861. By James Grant Wilson ... Chicago, J. Barnet, 1862.

vi, [7]–106 p. front., ports. 24cm.

Incomplete and unreliable sketches; designed largely as an enlistment inducement.

Wilson, Rufus Rockwell, 1865–1949.

Washington, the capital city, and its part in the history of the nation, by Rufus Rockwell Wilson ... Philadelphia & London, J. B. Lippincott co., 1901.

2 v. front., pl. 21 cm.

Another inadequate history, especially weak on social happenings inside the national capital.

Wisconsin. *Adjutant-general's office.*

Roster of Wisconsin volunteers, war of the rebellion, 1861–1865 ... Compiled by authority of the Legislature, under the direction of Jeremiah M. Rusk, governor, and Chandler P. Chapman, adjutant general. Madison, Democrat printing co., state printers, 1886.

2 v. 23cm.

One of the poorer of such compilations; difficult to find and even more difficult to use.

Wisconsin. *Commission on civil war records.*

Records and sketches of military organizations, population, legislation, election and other statistics relating to Wisconsin in the period of the civil war. Charles E. Estabrook, editor; Duncan McGregor, Orlando Holway, associate commissioners. Pub. by the state. [Madison?] Democrat printing company, 1914.

3 p. l., 220 p. 23cm.

Contains a chronological list of battles and engagements in which Wisconsin units participated, plus regimental sketches.

Wisconsin. *Commission on civil war records.*

Wisconsin losses in the civil war; a list of the names of Wisconsin soldiers killed in action, mortally wounded or dying from other causes in the civil war; arranged according to organization, and also in a separate alphabetical list ... Charles E. Estabrook, editor; Duncan McGregor, Orlando Holway, associate commissioners. Pub. by the state. [Madison?] Democrat printing company, state printer, 1915.

vi p., 1 l., 343 p. 23cm.

The official list of Wisconsin soldiers who died in service.

Wisconsin. *Governor.*

... Civil war messages and proclamations of Wisconsin war governors; ed. by Reuben Gold Thwaites in collaboration with Asa Currier Tilton and Frederick Merk. [Madison] Wisconsin history commission, 1912.

xvi, 319 p. 5 port. (incl. front.) 23 cm.

The official papers of Govs. Randall, Harvey, Salomon and Lewis; largely unannotated.

Wisconsin state historical society. *Library.*

... Catalogue of books on the war of the rebellion, and slavery, in the library of the State historical society of Wisconsin. Madison, Democrat printing company, 1887.

1 p. l., 61 p. 22½cm.

A general bibliography on the Civil War, based on holdings at that time of the Society library; the emphasis is on military affairs.

Wisconsin. State historical society. *Library.*

The Keyes and the civil war manuscript collections in the Wisconsin historical library. [Madison] 1916.

20 p. 2 port. (incl. front.) 24cm.

A two-part pamphlet; the last half describes the Civil War manuscripts collection: some 30,000 loose papers and 28 bound volumes.

Wittke, Carl Frederick, 1892– *ed.*

The history of the state of Ohio, edited by Carl Wittke ... Published under the auspices of the Ohio state archaeological and historical society ... Publication committee: Harlow Lindley, chairman, Carl Wittke, William T. Utter. [Columbus, O., 1941–44]

6 v. illus. (incl. ports., facsims.) maps (1 fold.) diagrs. (1 double) 23½ cm.

Volume IV, written by Eugene H. Roseboom, remains the best study of the Buckeye State in wartime.

Wolcott, Walter, 1859–

The military history of Yates county, N. Y. ... By Walter Wolcott ... Penn Yan, N. Y., Express book and job printing house, 1895.

viii, 157, [1] p. 24cm.

This slim compilation concentrates on military units rather than the communities that contributed them.

Woodford, Frank Bury, 1903–

Father Abraham's children; Michigan episodes in the Civil War. Detroit, Wayne State University Press, 1961.

305 p. illus. 24 cm.

A collection of twenty-one popularly written, unrelated essays; lacks documentation, bibliography and index.

Woodruff, George H *b.* 1814.

Fifteen years ago: or, The patriotism of Will County, designed to preserve the names and memory of Will County soldiers, both officers and privates—both living and dead: to tell something of what they did, and of what they suffered, in the great struggle to preserve our nationality. By George H. Woodruff ... Joliet, Pub. for the author by J. Goodspeed, 1876.

xiv, [15]-515, 82 p. front. (port.) 24cm.

Tributes to and laudations of Ohio soldiers; several of the many deeds recounted are of doubtful authenticity.

Woodward, Walter Carleton, 1878–1942.

The rise and early history of political parties in Oregon 1843–1868, by Walter Carleton Woodward ... Portland, Ore., The J. K. Gill company, 1913.

xiii, 276, [1] p. front., ports. 22½cm.

Notwithstanding its age, this work is still useful for an insight into wartime politics in the Far West.

THE CONFEDERACY

Government and Politics

Martin Abbott

Akin, Warren, 1811–1877.

Letters of Warren Akin, Confederate Congressman, edited by Bell Irvin Wiley. Athens, University of Georgia Press [1959]

v, 151 p. ports. 24 cm.

Carefully edited letters between a Confederate congressman and his wife; informative on life in Richmond and Georgia.

Beals, Carleton, 1893–

War within a war; the Confederacy against itself. [1st ed.] Philadelphia, Chilton Books [1965]

xi, 177 p. maps. 21 cm.

The story of the "fifth column" within the Confederacy; overstated and overdone, with inadequate documentation.

Bell, Hiram Parks, 1827–1907.

Men and things, by Hiram P. Bell, being reminiscent, biographical and historical. Atlanta, Press of the Foote & Davies company, 1907.

vii, 449 p. front. (port.) 20cm.

Rambling reminiscences of a Confederate congressman from Georgia; virtually worthless as history.

Bledsoe, Albert Taylor, 1809–1877.

Is Davis a traitor; or, Was secession a constitutional right previous to the war of 1861? By Albert Taylor Bledsoe ... Baltimore, Printed for the author by Innes & company, 1866. ○

vi, 263, [1] p. 20 cm.

Perhaps the classic statement of the South's "right" of secession; also adds interesting information on Confederate personalities and politics.

Booth, Edwin Gilliam, 1810–1886.

In war time. Two years in the confederacy and two years north. With many reminiscences of the days long before the war. By Edwin G. Booth. Philadelphia, J. D. Avil & co., 1885.

3 p. l., [3]–141, xii, 142–221 p. pl., ports. 22½cm.

Of limited use for Confederate politics in general and Virginia wartime politics in particular.

Brooks, Robert Preston, 1881–

... Conscription in the Confederate States of America, 1862–1865, by R. P. Brooks ... [Athens, Ga.] The University [1917]

1 p. l., p. [419]–442. 23cm.

A succinct introduction to a subject far better covered by A. B. Moore's classic study.

Brownlow, William Gannaway, 1805–1877.

Sketches of the rise, progress, and decline of secession; with a narrative of personal adventures among the rebels. By W. G. Brownlow ... Philadelphia, G. W. Childs; Cincinnati, Applegate & co., 1862.

458 p. front. (port.) plates, facsim. 17½ cm.

Fascinating experiences of an avowed biased Tennessee Unionist; revealing on conditions in East Tennessee during the first two years of the war.

Campbell, John Archibald.

Reminiscences and documents relating to the civil war during the year 1865. By John Campbell. Baltimore, J. Murphy & co., 1887.

68 p. 23½cm.

Mainly an account of the 1865 meeting between Lincoln and Confederate commissioners, of whom Campbell was one.

Cardozo, Jacob Newton.

A plan of financial relief, addressed to the legislature of Georgia, and Confederate States Congress, as originally published in the Atlanta southern confederacy, by J. N. Cardozo. Atlanta, Ga., J. H. Seals & co.'s power press, 1863.

37 p. 21cm.

The plan was based more on hope than on reality; yet the monograph is an interesting commentary on the sad state of Confederate finance.

Carpenter, Jesse Thomas.

The South as a conscious minority, 1789–1861; a study in political thought, by Jesse T. Carpenter ... New York city, The New York university press, 1930.

x, 315 p. 23½ cm.

A highly regarded treatise on Southern politics in the mid-nineteenth century; the title notwithstanding, the study contains some discussion on the Confederate government.

Confederate States of America. *1st Cong., 1st sess.,* Feb. 18–Apr. 22, 1862.

... Proceedings of First Confederate Congress—First session.

(*In* Southern historical society. Papers. Richmond, Va. [1923– 24½cm. v. 44, p. 1–206

A fuller, more informative account of congressional activity than that given in the official Journal.

Confederate States of America. *Congress.*

Address of Congress to the people of the Confederate States. [Richmond, 1864]

8 p. 23 cm.

A wordy reminder by both houses of the Congress that the Southern people were in "a struggle for the preservation of liberty and civilization . . . "

Confederate States of America. *Congress.*

... Journal of the Congress of the Confederate States of America, 1861–1865. Washington, Govt. print. off., 1904–05.

7 v. 23 cm.

A sparse and rather unenlightening chronicle of what transpired within the Congress.

Confederate States of America. *Conscript dept.*

... Communication from secretary of war ... transmit[ting] a report from Colonel J. S. Preston, chief of the Conscript bureau, of "the number of exempts in the Confederate States, the states in which they reside, and the reasons for the exemption from military service ... [Richmond, 1863]

4 p. 24cm.

Indicative of why many Southerners considered the conflict "a rich man's war but a poor man's fight."

Confederate States of America. *Dept. of Justice.*

The opinions of the Confederate attorneys general, 1861–1865, edited by Rembert W. Patrick, with a foreword by Harold L. Sebring. Buffalo, Dennis [1950]

xxiv, 608 p. 26 cm.

A convenient collection for the student of Confederate legal affairs.

Confederate States of America. *Laws, statutes, etc.*

Acts and resolutions of the first session of the Provisional congress of the Confederate States, held at Montgomery, Ala. Richmond, Enquirer book and job press, by Tyler, Wise, Allegre & Smith, 1861.

(*In* Provisional and permanent constitutions, of the Confederate States. Richmond, Tyler, Wise, Allegre and Smith, printers, 1861. 159 p. 22cm. p. [33]–159)

The major source for the official acts of the provisional government.

Confederate States of America. *Laws, statutes, etc.*
Laws and joint resolutions of the last session of the Confederate Congress (November 7, 1864–March 18, 1865) together with the Secret acts of previous congresses, with an introduction and a bibliographical note, by Charles W. Ramsdell, editor. Durham, N. C., Duke university press [c1941]
xxvii, 183 p. front., illus. (facsims.) 23½cm

A scholarly compilation, with full annotations, of the acts and resolutions of the last Confederate Congress.

Confederate States of America. *Laws, statutes, etc.*
... The statutes at large of the provisional government of the Confederate States of America, from the institution of the government, February 8, 1861, to its termination, February 18, 1862, inclusive. Arranged in chronological order. Together with the constitution for the provisional government, and the permanent constitution of the Confederate States, and the treaties concluded by the Confederate States with Indian tribes. Ed. by James M. Matthews ... Richmond, R. M. Smith, printer to Congress, 1864.
xv, [1], 411, xlviii p. 24cm.

Contains all non-secret acts and resolutions of the Confederacy's provisional government; by a law clerk experienced in compiling such legal digests.

Confederate States of America. *Laws, statutes, etc.*
Tariff (of 1857) made of force by act of Congress of the Confederate States of America, 9th February, 1861. With additional free list under act 18th February, 1861. Charleston, Steam-power presses of Evans & Cogswell, 1861.
40 p. 23cm.

A documentary history of the Confederacy's early trade regulations.

Confederate States of America. *Patent office.*
Rules and directions for proceedings in the Confederate States Patent office. Richmond, Tyler, Wise, Allegre & Smith, 1861.
47, ix p. 15cm.

Self-explanatory; Rufus R. Rhodes was commissioner of patents.

Confederate States of America. *Post-Office Dept.*
Report of the Postmaster General. Nov. 27th, 1861. [Richmond, 1861]
66 p. 22 cm.

This and reports for 1862, 1863, and 1864 contain accountings of the department's receipts and expenditures, plus other important information.

Confederate States of America. *President.*
A compilation of the messages and papers of the confederacy, including the diplomatic correspondence, 1861–1865; pub. by permission of Congress by James D. Richardson ... Nashville, United States publishing company, 1905.
2 v. front., ports. 24 cm.

An indispensable collection: Vol. I relates to Davis and his cabinet; Vol. II treats of diplomacy; reprinted without change in 1966.

Confederate States of America. *President.*
Correspondence between the President and General Joseph E. Johnston, together with that of the secretary of war and the adjutant and inspector general, during the months of May, June and July, 1863. Published by order of Congress. Richmond, R. M. Smith, public printer, 1864.
64 p. 23½cm.

Concerned mainly with military affairs; the growing rift between Davis and Johnston is easily visible here.

Confederate States of America. *President.*
The messages and papers of Jefferson Davis and the Confederacy, including diplomatic correspondence, 1861–1865. Edited and compiled by James D. Richardson. A new ed. with a comprehensive introd. by Allan Nevins. New York, Chelsea House-R. Hector, 1966.
2 v. illus., ports. 25 cm.

A new edition of the classic study, this set has increased value because of Nevin's twenty-two-page introductory essay, "The Embattled Confederacy: Its Tasks and Leadership."

Confederate States of America. *Treasury dept.*
Information from the various state governments in regard to the value of the property, the revenue system, and the amount collected during the last fiscal year in each of the Confederate States. [Richmond, 1861]
7 p. 21 cm.

A source for the comparative wealth of Southern states at the beginning of the war.

Confederate States of America. *Treasury dept.*
Message of the President ... Feb. 25, 1863 [transmitting communications from the secretary of the Treasury and the attorney general, in regard to the sequestration of real estate belonging to alien enemies] [Richmond, 1863]
7 p. 24½ cm.

Statistics on sequestration of enemy property by the Confederate government in Feb., 1863.

Confederate States of America. *Treasury dept.*

... Response of the secretary of the Treasury to the resolution of the Senate of the 5th December 1864, respecting operations under the act to impose regulations upon the foreign commerce of the Confederate States. [Richmond, 1864]

7 p. incl. tables. 24½ cm.

An explanation for the need of the act and charts showing cargoes received on government account at Wilmington and Charleston in the Oct.-Dec., 1864, period.

Confederate States of America. *War dept.*

[Letter of secretary of war relative to contracts made by the War department, in the Trans-Mississippi department, for supplies of any sort to be paid for in cotton. Richmond, 1864]

[2] p. 25cm.

Report of a contract with Marmaduke & Thornton for 10,000 Enfield rifles--to be paid for in cotton at San Antonio, Tex.

Coulter, Ellis Merton, 1890–

The Confederate States of America, 1861–1865. [Baton Rouge] Louisiana State University Press, 1950.

x, 644 p. illus., ports., fold. map. 25 cm.

This title is repeated here because Coulter's general history remains the best account of the Confederate Congress.

Curry, Jabez Lamar Monroe, 1825–1903.

Civil history of the government of the Confederate States, with some personal reminiscences. By J. L. M. Curry ... Richmond, Va., B. F. Johnson publishing company, 1901.

318 p. incl. front. (port.) 20cm.

Essentially a defense of secession and an outline of the political history of the Confederacy; moderate tone, pleasant style, but superficial substance.

Davis, Jefferson, 1808–1889.

A short history of the Confederate States of America, by Jefferson Davis ... New York, Belford co., 1890.

xii, 505 p. front. (port.) 24½ cm.

Mainly concerned with the deep commitment of Confederates to their cause and also Confederate treatment of prisoners and neutrals.

Derry, Joseph Tyrone, 1841–

Story of the Confederate States; or, History of the war for southern independence, embracing a brief but comprehensive sketch of the early settlement of the country, trouble with the Indians, the French, revolutionary and Mexican wars ... By Joseph T. Derry ... with an introduction by Gen. Clement A. Evans ... designed especially for the boys and girls of the South ... Over 130 fine engravings. Richmond, Va., B. F. Johnson publishing company, 1895.

4, [v]–xvi p., 1 l., 19–448 p. front., illus. (incl. ports., maps) 24½cm.

Neo-Confederate propaganda that is virtually worthless as history.

Dietz, August, 1869–

The Confederate States Post-Office Department, its stamps & stationery; a record of achievement. Richmond, Dietz Press [1948]

48 p. illus. (part col.) ports. 23 cm.

A summary of the longer work published in 1929, with emphasis on the achievements of the department, and biographical sketches of its personnel.

Dietz, August.

The postal service of the Confederate States of America, by August Dietz. Richmond, Va., Press of the Dietz printing company, 1929.

4 p. l., v–xi, 439 p. incl. map. col. front., illus. (incl. facsims.) col. pl. diagr. 26cm.

A detailed study of one Confederate department; buttressed with official documents, letters and illustrations.

[**Donnell, Richard Spaight**] 1820–1867. *supposed author.*

A voice from North-Carolina. The secessionists: their promises and performances; the conditions into which they have brought the country; the remedy, etc. Reprinted from the Raleigh (N. C.) standard, of July 31, 1863. New-York, A. D. F. Randolph, 1863.

21 p. 18cm.

A frank and open plea for peace negotiations; highly critical of secessionists.

Dumond, Dwight Lowell, 1895–

The secession movement, 1860–1861, by Dwight Lowell Dumond ... New York, The Macmillan company, 1931.

vi p., 2 l., 294 p. 20½ cm.

Long recognized as a classic study of the subject; now coming under some fire from the revisionists.

Eggleston, George Cary, 1839–1911.

The history of the Confederate war; its causes and its conduct; a narrative and critical history, by George Cary Eggleston ... New York, Sturgis & Walton company, 1910.

2 v. 21½cm.

An account of high literary merit; remarkably objective, though inaccurate in some details.

Evans, Clement Anselm, 1833–1911.

The civil history of the Confederate States. By Brig.-Gen. Clement A. Evans.

(*In* Evans, Clement A., ed. Confederate military history. Atlanta, Ga., 1899. 24cm. v. 1, p. ⌊247⌋–570. port.)

This first volume of Confederate Military History is included here because of Evan's lengthy and provocative discussion on the wartime Southern government.

Hall, *Rev.* **William A.**

The historic significance of the southern revolution. A lecture delivered by invitation in Petersburg, Va., March 14th and April 29th, 1864. And in Richmond, Va., April 7th and April 21st, 1864. By Rev. William A. Hall of New Orleans ... Petersburg, Printed by A. F. Crutchfield & co., 1864.

45 p. 23cm.

The Confederacy is viewed as an heroic effort to preserve republican government against the onslaughts of democracy.

Hanna, Alfred Jackson, 1893–

Flight into oblivion, by A. J. Hanna. ⌊Richmond⌋ Johnson publishing company ⌊c1938⌋

xiii, 306 p. incl. front., illus. 21½ cm.

The major, detailed study of the exodus of the Confederate government from Richmond; thoroughly researched and well-written.

Hendrick, Burton Jesse, 1870–1949.

Statesmen of the lost cause; Jefferson Davis and his cabinet, by Burton J. Hendrick ... Boston, Little, Brown and company, 1939.

xvii, 452 p. front., pl., ports. 24 cm.

A fascinating presentation, based on sound scholarship; an enduring contribution to Confederate history.

Hill, Louise Biles, 1891–

... State socialism in the Confederate States of America, by Louise B. Hill ... Charlottesville, Va., The Historical publishing co., inc., 1936.

31 p. 24½cm.

An interesting study of the Confederate government's attempts to nationalize foreign trade.

Hoole, William Stanley, 1903–

Alias Simon Suggs; the life and times of Johnson Jones Hooper. University, Ala., University of Alabama Press, 1952.

xxiii, 283 p. port. 23 cm.

The only useful study of an Alabama newspaperman who assisted in the formation of the Confederacy and who remained on intimate terms with its leaders until his untimely death in 1862.

... **Humanistic** studies in honor of John Calvin Metcalf. Charlottesville, Va. ⌊New York, N. Y., Columbia university press⌋ 1941.

x, 338 p. 1 illus., pl. 23½ cm.

Highly useful for Lester J. Cappon's monograph, "Government and Private Industry in the Southern Confederacy."

Jones, Charles Colcock, 1831–1893.

A roster of general officers, heads of departments, senators, representatives, military organizations, &c., &c., in Confederate service during the war between the states. By Charles C. Jones, jr. ... Richmond, Southern historical society, 1876.

135 p. 23½ cm.

This handy guide appeared originally as a supplement to Vols. I-III of the Southern Historical Society Papers; still useful, in spite of several factual gaps.

Jones, John Beauchamp, 1810–1866.

A Rebel war clerk's diary at the Confederate States capital. By J. B. Jones ... Philadelphia, J. B. Lippincott & co., 1866.

2 v. 20cm.

An interesting commentary on life and people in the Confederacy, but marred by the author's strong prejudices and his editing of the narrative after the events described.

Jones, John Beauchamp, 1810–1866.
A rebel war clerk's diary. Condensed, edited, and annotated by Earl Schenck Miers. New York, Sagamore Press [1958]
xiv, 545 p. 24 cm.

An overly condensed version of original, with a short introduction by the editor.

Kean, Robert Garlic Hill, 1828–1898.
Inside the Confederate Government; the diary of Robert Garlick Hill Kean, head of the Bureau of War. Edited by Edward Younger. New York, Oxford University Press, 1957.
241 p. illus. 23 cm.

The well-edited diary of one close to the seat of war; observations are sharp, keen, perceptive; especially revealing of the character and inner workings of government.

Klingberg, Frank Wysor.
The Southern Claims Commission. Berkeley, University of California Press, 1955.
ix, 261 p. map, tables. 24 cm.

A penetrating study that emphasizes the great amount of Unionism present in the Confederacy.

Lee, Charles Robert.
The Confederate Constitutions. Chapel Hill, University of North Carolina Press [1963]
viii, 225 p. tables. 24 cm.

A valuable study of the provisional and permanent Confederate constitutions, along with biographical profiles of the men who framed them.

Lester, William Wharton, 1827–1899.
A digest of the military and naval laws of the Confederate States, from the commencement of the Provisional congress to the end of the First Congress under the permanent constitution. Analytically arranged by Capt. W. W. Lester ... and Wm. J. Bromwell ... Columbia [S. C.] Evans and Cogswell, 1864.
vii p., 1 l., [11]–329, [1] p. 21cm.

Incomplete and extremely scarce; still, a starting point for a study of Confederate military law.

Moore, Albert Burton, 1887–
Conscription and conflict in the Confederacy, by Albert Burton Moore ... New York, The Macmillan company, 1924.
ix p., 2 l., 367 p. 22½ cm.

Details the nature and operation of the Confederate draft system, and adds an exhaustive description of resentment to conscription.

Norwood, Thomas Manson, 1830–1913.
A true vindication of the South, in a review of American political history, by Thomas Manson Norwood ... [Savannah, Ga., Braid & Hutton, inc., printers, ©1917]
5 p. l., xvi, 450 [1] p. 23½ cm.

This wordy, voluminous work fails to achieve what its title states.

... An **official** guide of the Confederate government from 1861 to 1865 at Richmond; showing the location of the public buildings and offices of the Confederate, state and city governments, residences of the principal officers, etc. [Richmond, 190–?]
cover-title, 32 p. 20 x 16cm.

Still useful for capsule summaries of the organization and administration of the Confederate government.

Owsley, Frank Lawrence, 1890–1956.
State rights in the Confederacy. Gloucester, Mass., Peter Smith, 1961 [©1925]
289 p. 21 cm.

Still regarded as a major contribution toward understanding the internal disension and particularism that hastened Confederate defeat--even though the thesis is overstated.

Patrick, Rembert Wallace, 1909–
Jefferson Davis and his cabinet [by] Rembert W. Patrick. Baton Rouge, Louisiana state university press, 1944.
x, 401 p. 23½ cm.

This well-done study stresses more the six individual Confederate departments than the workings of the Davis government; Davis himself receives favorable treatment.

[Pollard, Edward Alfred] 1831-1872.

Echoes from the South. Comprising the most important speeches, proclamations, and public acts emanating from the South during the late war. New York, E. B. Treat & co.; Baltimore, Md., L. T. Palmer & co.; [etc., etc., 1866]

vi, [7]-211 p. 19½ cm.

A miscellany of documents undistinguished by any critical judgment concerning the value of the documents selected.

Pollard, Edward Alfred, 1831-1872.

The first year of the war. By Edward A. Pollard ... Corr. and improved ed. Richmond, West & Johnston, 1862.

xvi, [17]-406 p. 22½ cm.

Pollard, Edward Alfred, 1831-1872.

The second year of the war. By Edward A. Pol .rd ... Richmond, West & Johnston, 1863.

x, 17-326 p. 23 cm.

Pollard, Edward Alfred, 1831-1872.

Southern history of the war. The third year of the war. By Edward A. Pollard ... New York, C. B. Richardson, 1865.

391 p. front., port. 22½ cm.

Pollard, Edward Alfred, 1831-1872.

Southern history of the war. The last year of the war. By Edward A. Pollard ... New York, C. B. Richardson, 1866.

363 p. front., port. 22½cm.

The first popular history of the war from the Confederate point of view, Pollard's works are seriously marred by venomous anti-Davis feeling and bitter anti-Northern prejudice.

Pollard, Edward Alfred, 1831-1872.

The lost cause; a new southern history of the war of the Confederates. Comprising a full and authentic account of the rise and progress of the late southern Confederacy—the campaigns, battles, incidents, and adventures of the most gigantic struggle of the world's history. Drawn from official sources, and approved by the most distinguished Confederate leaders. By Edward A. Pollard ... With numerous splendid steel portraits ... New York, E. B. Treat & co., Baltimore, Md., L. T. Palmer & co.; [etc., etc.] 1866.

xxx p., 1 l., [33]-752 (*i. e.* 740) p. front., ports. 24½ cm.

A condensation of the author's four-volume history--and reproduced with all the faults of the larger work.

Ringold, May Spencer.

The role of the State legislatures in the Confederacy. Athens, University of Georgia Press [©1966]

viii, 141 p. 23 cm.

This scholarly, mature work sheds much light on a little-known chapter in Confederate history.

Robinson, William Morrison, 1891-

Justice in grey; a history of the judicial system of the Confederate States of America, by William M. Robinson, jr. Cambridge, Mass., Harvard university press, 1941.

xxi, 713 p. double map. 23½ cm.

The definitive study of the administration of justice in the Confederacy; scholarly, comprehensive, detailed.

Scott, John, 1820-1907.

Letters to an officer in the army; proposing constitutional reform in the Confederate government after the close of the present war. A supplement to "The lost principle." By John Scott, of Fauquier ... Richmond, A. Morris, 1864.

iv, [5]-82 p. 21½cm.

Unfounded opinions on how the Confederate government could best carry out its functions; Scott's basic weakness was his assumption that the South was going to win the war.

Stephens, Alexander Hamilton, 1812-1883.

Speech of Hon. Alex. H. Stephens, delivered before the Georgia legislature, on Wednesday night, March 16th, 1864. Reported for the Atlanta intelligencer by A. E. Marshall, and revised by himself. Atlanta, Intelligencer steam power presses, 1864.

28 p. 21½cm.

A bitter attack on government policies; calculated to destroy morale.

Stewart, William Henry, 1838-1912.

The spirit of the South; orations, essays, and lectures, by Colonel William H. Stewart. New York and Washington, The Neale publishing company, 1908.

238 p. 21cm.

A miscellaneous collection of essays that are virtually worthless as history.

Stonebraker, J Clarence.

The unwritten South. 3d ed. Cause, progress and result of the civil war. Relics of hidden truth after forty years. By J. Clarence Stonebraker. [n. p., ©1908]

224 p., 1 l. col. front., illus. 18cm.

A brief work whose fervent ardor in defending the South renders it useless as history.

Studies in southern history and politics; inscribed to William Archibald Dunning, PH. D., LL. D., Lieber professor of history and political philosophy in Columbia university, by his former pupils, the authors. New York, Columbia university press, 1914.

viii, 394 p. 24 cm.

Contains a highly useful essay by S. D. Brummer on "The Judicial Interpretation of the Confederate Constitution."

Tansill, Robert.

A free and impartial exposition of the causes which led to the failure of the Confederate States to establish their independence. By Colonel Robert Tansill, of the late Confederate States army. Washington, 1865.

24 p. 21½cm.

Written by a former Confederate officer soon after the war, this rationale is both short and unconvincing.

Tatum, Georgia Lee.

Disloyalty in the confederacy, by Georgia Lee Tatum, PH. D. Chapel Hill, The University of North Carolina press, 1934.

xi, 176 p. 23½ cm.

A scholarly, well-written account of internal opposition to the Confederate government; the analysis of factors involved is penetrating.

The **times!** or The flag of truce, dedicated to the cabinets at Washington and Richmond, by a white Republican. Richmond, Ritchie & Dunnavant, printers, 1863.

18 p. 21cm.

An amazing condemnation of the Confederacy's aims; published under the nose of the Confederate administration.

Vandiver, Frank Everson, 1925–

Rebel brass; the Confederate command system. Introd. by T. Harry Williams. Baton Rouge, Louisiana State University Press [c1956]

142 p. illus. 21 cm.

A sharp, provocative look at the Confederate high command; contains much food for digestion.

Vanfelson, Charles A.

The little red book, or department directory. For the use of the public in the Confederate States of America. Pub. by C. A. Vanfelson. Richmond, Tyler, Wise and Allegre, printers, 1861.

24 p. 22½cm.

A little-known but valuable work on the physical layout and organization in Richmond of the Confederate Navy Department.

Virginia. *Governor, 1864–1865 (Smith)*

Letter from the Governor of Virginia, communicating a series of resolutions passed at a meeting of the Governors of the States of Virginia, North Carolina, South Carolina, Georgia, Alabama, and Mississippi, held in Augusta, Ga., on Monday, the 17th day of October, 1864. [Richmond, 1864]

3 p. 23 cm.

Useful as an expression of gubernatorial discontent with Confederate affairs late in the war.

Warren, Edward, 1828–1893.

A doctor's experiences in three continents. By Edward Warren. In a series of letters addressed to John Norris, M. D., of Baltimore, Md. Baltimore, Md., Cushings & Bailey, 1885.

xiv, [15]–613 p., 1 l. front., ports. 19½cm.

Warren served as Surgeon General of North Carolina during the war; his articulate memoir provides good material on the administration of Gov. Vance.

Wesley, Charles Harris, 1891–

The collapse of the confederacy, by Charles H. Wesley ... Washington, D. C., The Associated publishers, inc., 1937.

xiii, 225 p. 18½ cm.

A not-too-successful attempt to compress economic and social problems of the South into a small synthesis.

Wiley, Bell Irvin, 1906–

The road to Appomattox. Memphis, Memphis State College Press [1956]

121 p. 23 cm.

Three incisive essays that evaluate Jefferson Davis, trace the rise and fall of Confederate morale, and describe internal factors hastening Confederate collapse.

Williams, James, *d.* 1869.

The South vindicated; being a series of letters written for the American press during the canvass for the presidency in 1860, with a letter to Lord Brougham on the John Brown raid, and a survey of the result of the presidential contest, and its consequences, by the Hon. James Williams ... with an introduction by John Baker Hopkins ... London, Longman, Green, Longman, Roberts, & Green, 1862.

lx, 444 p. 22cm.

An overly strong, unconvincing defense of Confederate constitutional questions.

Wooster, Ralph A

The secession conventions of the South. Princeton, N. J., Princeton University Press, 1962.

viii, 294 p. maps. 23 cm.

The best study on the subject; well-researched and ably presented; much statistical data.

Wright, Marcus Joseph, 1831–1922, *comp.*

General officers of the Confederate army, officers of the executive departments of the Confederate States, members of the Confederate congress by states, comp. and prepared by General Marcus J. Wright. New York, The Neale publishing company, 1911.

188 p. 19cm.

An old but still valuable compilation; by one of the most painstaking of Confederate historians.

Yearns, Wilfred Buck, 1918–

The Confederate Congress. Athens, University of Georgia Press [1960]

293 p. 25 cm.

The first and only systematic study of the Congress; mainly a history of legislation, though it provides some insights into personalities and problems.

THE CONFEDERACY

Economic and Social Studies

May S. Ringold

Abel, Annie Heloise, 1873–

The American Indian as slaveholder and secessionist; an omitted chapter in the diplomatic history of the Southern Confederacy, by Annie Heloise Abel, PH. D. Cleveland, The Arthur H. Clark company, 1915.

394 p. incl. front., ports., maps, plan. 24½ cm.

Abel concentrates on the background and general situation in the Indian Territory, then covers its relationship to Texas and Arkansas.

Abrams, Alexander St. Clair.

A full and detailed history of the siege of Vicksburg, by A. S. Abrams ... Atlanta, Ga., Intelligencer steam power presses, 1863.

80 p. 21½cm.

Useful for its one chapter on the condition and conduct of the inhabitants of the city; the rest of the text is military.

Alexander, John Brevard, 1834–

Reminiscences of the past sixty years, by Dr. John Brevard Alexander ... Charlotte, N. C., 1908. Charlotte, N. C., Presses of Ray printing co. [1908]

513 p. port. 24cm.

A series of completely unrelated and disorganized recollections, touching but lightly on the war period.

[**Alexander, William**] 1808–1875.

... Elements of discord in Secessia, &c., &c. New York, May, 1863. New York, W. C. Bryant & co., printers, 1863.

cover-title, 16 p. 22½cm.

Alexander asserted that disenchantment prevailed because of distrust of leaders, flight of capital abroad, and second thoughts on secession.

Allan, Elizabeth Randolph (Preston) 1848–
The life and letters of Margaret Junkin Preston, by Elizabeth Preston Allan. Boston and New York, Houghton, Mifflin and company, 1903.

4 p. l., 878 p., 1 l. front. (port.) 20cm.

By a Southern writer, wife and mother; gives an all-too-brief account of wartime life in Lexington, Va.

Anderson, *Mrs.* **Lucy Worth (London)**
North Carolina women of the Confederacy, written and published by Mrs. John Huske (Lucy London) Anderson ... [Fayetteville, N. C., Cumberland printing co.] 1926.

141 p. 2 pl. 24cm.

Drawn from North Carolinians' reminiscences and, occasionally, from community war associations' minutes.

Andrews, Eliza Frances, 1840–
The war-time journal of a Georgia girl, 1864–1865, by Eliza Frances Andrews; illustrated from contemporary photographs. New York, D. Appleton and company, 1908.

4 p. l., 387 p. front., plates, ports. 21½cm.

An account of social life in Georgia after Sherman's march; told by an intelligent, observing, quite partisan Southern girl.

Andrews, Eliza Frances, *b.* 1840.
The war-time journal of a Georgia girl, 1864–1865. Edited by Spencer Bidwell King, Jr. Macon [Ga.] Ardivan Press, 1960.

396 p. illus. 21 cm.

A reprinting rather than an editing of the previous title; contributes nothing to the original except a sketch of the author's life.

Andrews, Marietta (Minnigerode) 1869–1931.
Scraps of paper, by Marietta Minnigerode Andrews ... New York, E. P. Dutton & co., inc. [©1929]

xv, 381 p. incl. front., illus., plates, ports. 21½cm.

Contains Mrs. Henry Dulany's 1862-1863 diary of life in Virginia, the Civil War letters of Charles Minnigerode, and a chapter on Confederate flags and seals.

Andrews, Matthew Page, 1879–
The women of the South in war times, comp. by Matthew Page Andrews ... Baltimore, The Norman, Remington co., 1920.

xvii p., 2 l., 3–466 p. front., pl., ports. 19½ cm.

Selected excerpts from wartime reminiscences and stories of Southern women, with one good Civil War diary--that of Judith B. McGuire.

Armstrong, George Dodd, *b.* 1813.
"The good hand of our God upon us." A thanksgiving sermon preached on occasion of the victory of Manassas, July 21st, 1861, in the Presbyterian church, Norfolk, Va., by Rev. Geo. D. Armstrong ... Norfolk, Va., J. D. Ghiselin, jr., 1861.

15 p. 23cm.

A sermon correlating Confederate victory with God's will.

Atkinson, Joseph Mayo, 1820–1891.
God, the giver of victory and peace. A thanksgiving sermon, delivered in the Presbyterian church, September 18, 1862, Raleigh, N. C. By Rev. Joseph M. Atkinson. [n. p., 1862]

15 p. 20½cm.

This minister explained the reverses of the winter in the light of a need for more trust in God and things spiritual.

Atlanta daily register, *Atlanta, Ga.*
Address of the Atlanta register to the people of the Confederate States. One dollar per copy. Atlanta, Ga., J. A. Sperry & co.; Augusta, Ga., G. B. Mitchell [1864]

1 p. l., 16 p. 23½cm.

An appeal to the people for an all-out war effort; linked their efforts with God's providence.

Aughey, John Hill, *b.* 1828.
The iron furnace: or, Slavery and secession. By Rev. John H. Aughey, a refugee from Mississippi ... Philadelphia, W. S. & A. Martien, 1863.

206 p. front. (port.) 2 pl. 18 cm.

A somewhat restrained attack on Southern institutions in general and slavery in particular, written by a Unionist parson.

Aughey, John Hill, 1828–

Tupelo. By Rev. John H. Aughey ... Lincoln, Neb., State journal company, printers, 1888.

595 p. plates, ports. $20\frac{1}{2}^{cm}$.

An enlarged, greatly embellished sequel to the previous--and far less trustworthy.

Augusta and Savannah Railroad.

Report.
Savannah, Ga.

v. 24 cm.

The eleventh annual report (1861) is a veritable encyclopedia of statistics vital to any study of Confederate railroads.

Avary, Myrta (Lockett)

Dixie after the war; an exposition of social conditions existing in the South, during the twelve years succeeding the fall of Richmond. By Myrta Lockett Avary ... With an introduction by General Clement A. Evans; illustrated from old paintings, daguerreotypes and rare photographs. New York, Doubleday, Page & company, 1906.

5 p. l., [ix]–x, 435 p. front., plates, ports. $23\frac{1}{2}$ cm.

A revealing companion to Mrs. Avary's wartime reminiscences; most of this work tells of Virginia in the days immediately after Appomattox.

Avary, *Mrs.* **Myrta (Lockett)** *ed.*

A Virginia girl in the civil war, 1861–1865; being a record of the actual experiences of the wife of a Confederate officer; collected and ed. by Myrta Lockett Avary. New York, D. Appleton and company, 1903.

x, 384 p. $19\frac{1}{2}^{cm}$.

Not history, but charming and revealing in its delineation of Confederate figures as seen through the eyes of an impressionable maiden.

Baird, Washington.

The Confederate spelling book: interspersed with choice reading lessons in poetry and in prose ... By Washington Baird ... Macon, Ga., Burke, Boykin & company, 1864.

190 p. 18^{cm}.

An adaptation of an old text to the views and sentiments of the people of the Confederate States.

Bank convention of the Confederate States, *Richmond, Va.,* 1861.

Proceedings of the Bank convention of the Confederate States, held at Richmond, Va., July 24th, 25th, and 26th, 1861. Charleston, Steam-power press of Evans & Cogswell, 1861.

14 p. 24^{cm}.

Contains bank officials' pledges of support for the Confederacy and suggestions for maintaining fiscal stability.

Banks, John, 1797–1870.

A short biographical sketch of the undersigned by himself. [Austell? Ga., 1936?]

38 p. 22 cm.

Diary entries for the war years contain a good (though brief) description of Banks's business activities and family affairs.

Battle, Kemp Plummer, 1831–1919.

History of the University of North Carolina ... by Kemp P. Battle ... Raleigh, N. C., Printed for the author by Edwards & Broughton printing company, 1907–12.

2 v. front., plates, ports., facsims. $24\frac{1}{2}^{cm}$.

A slightly biased account of the college in war and of Sherman's "influence" on the campus.

Battle, Kemp Plummer, 1831–1919.

Memories of an old-time tar heel, by Kemp Plummer Battle ... edited by his son William James Battle ... Chapel Hill, The University of North Carolina press, 1945.

xii, 296 p. plates, ports. 23 cm.

Weak on the war years, this is still a sometimes charming memoir by a man whose varied career included that of a Confederate soldier, public official and history professor.

Beaumont, *Mrs.* **Betty (Bentley)** *b.* 1828.

Twelve years of my life. An autobiography. By Mrs. B. Beaumont, of Woodville, Miss. Philadelphia, T. B. Peterson & brothers [c1887]

1 p. l., 19–366 p. 19^{cm}.

Vivid observations by an Englishwoman who operated a store during the war in Woodville, Miss.

Beers, Fannie A

Memories. A record of personal experience and adventure during four years of war. By Mrs. Fannie A. Beers. Philadelphia, Press of J. B. Lippincott co., 1888.

336 p. front. 20 cm.

Vivid recollections by a nurse and administrator in Confederate hospitals, plus some stories of less value "told" to the writer.

Bennett, William Wallace, 1821–1887.

A narrative of the great revival which prevailed in the southern armies during the late civil war between the states of the federal union. By William W. Bennett ... Philadelphia, Claxton, Remsen & Haffelfinger, 1877.

vi, [7]–427 p. front., plates, ports. 19½ cm.

A pioneer study of the two major waves of religious fever that swept through the Confederate armies; too emotional in spots.

Bishop, Albert Webb, 1832–1901.

Loyalty on the frontier, or Sketches of Union men of the South-west; with incidents and adventures in rebellion on the border. By A. W. Bishop ... St. Louis, R. P. Studley and co., printers, 1863.

228 p. 20 cm.

Written by and about Unionists in Arkansas, with some description of life around Elk Horn Tavern and Fayetteville in 1862.

Bivins, Viola (Cobb)

Echoes of the Confederacy. Longview, Tex., Mrs. J. K. Bivins [1950]

197 p. illus. 24 cm.

Of little value except for one eulogistic chapter on Southern women.

Blackford, Launcelot Minor, 1894–

Mine eyes have seen the glory; the story of a Virginia lady, Mary Berkeley Minor Blackford, 1802–1896, who taught her sons to hate slavery and to love the Union. Cambridge, Harvard University Press, 1954.

293 p. illus. 22 cm.

The revealing war experiences of a mother of five Confederate soldiers; the narrative is composed primarily of excerpts from Mrs. Blackford's writings.

Blanton, Wyndham Bolling, 1890–

Medicine in Virginia in the nineteenth century, by Wyndham B. Blanton, M. D. Richmond, Garrett & Massie, incorporated, 1933.

xii p., 1 l., 466 p. front., plates, ports., facsims. 27 cm.

Chapter 13 describes medicine, medical treatment, hospitals, and famous cases in the Confederacy.

Bonham, Milledge Louis, 1880–

The British consuls in the Confederacy ... New York, 1911.

269 p. 25cm.

A study of the consular defense of English aliens in the Confederacy and of wartime commercial functions of the consulates.

Boykin, Richard Manning.

Captain Alexander Hamilton Boykin, one of South Carolina's distinguished citizens, by Richard Manning Boykin ... New York, 1942.

2 p. l., ii numb. l., 1 l., 263 p., 1 l. incl. illus., plates, ports., facsim. fronts. 22½cm.

Though spotty in value and undocumented, this biography gives glimpses of a proud South Carolina family caught in the turmoil of war.

Bradbeer, William West.

Confederate and southern state currency; historical and financial data, biographical sketches, descriptions ... by William West Bradbeer. Mt. Vernon, N. Y., 1915.

162 p. illus. (facsims.) 25½cm.

This descriptive catalogue lists the currency of all Confederate states except Tennessee.

Brantley, Rabun Lee.

Georgia journalism of the civil war period, by Rabun Lee Brantley, PH. D. Nashville, Tenn., George Peabody college for teachers, 1929.

4 p. l., xi–xvi p., 1 l., 134 p. illus. (map) fold. facsims. 24cm.

Useful "exhibits" of 111 Georgia newspapers, with histories of each and a chapter on publication difficulties.

Brice, Marshall Moore.
The Stonewall Brigade Band. Verona, Va.. McClure Print. Co. [1967]
viii, 213 p. illus., ports. 24 cm.

The fullest history possible of a still-active military band whose roots stretch back to 1845; only 31 pages cover the Civil War years.

Brown, Albert Gallatin, 1813–1880.
State of the country. Speech in the Confederate Senate, December 24, 1863. [n. p., 1863?]
16 p. 24 cm.

A summary of economic conditions, with taxation suggested to pay the indebtedness of the Confederacy.

Brown, William Garrott, 1868–1913.
The lower South in American history, by William Garrott Brown ... New York, The Macmillan company; London, Macmillan & co., ltd., 1902.
xi, 271 p. 20 cm.

An old book with an unusually perceptive section on the resources of the Confederacy.

Bruce, Kathleen.
... Virginia iron manufacture in the slave era, by Kathleen Bruce ... with illustrations and map. New York, London, The Century co. [c1930]
xiii, 482 p. front. (port.) plates, fold. map. 22½ cm.

Especially valuable for data on the Tredegar Iron Works and other Confederate foundries.

Buck, Lucy Rebecca, 1842–1918.
Diary of Lucy Rebecca Buck, 1861–1865. [n. p.] 1940.
cover-title, 2 p. l., 2–240 numb. l. mounted plates, mounted port., map. 27½cm.

Descriptive of life in Front Royal, Va., during the 1860's.

Burckmyer, Cornelius L 1822–1877.
The Burckmyer letters, March, 1863–June, 1865. Columbia, S. C., The State company, 1926.
476 p. 21cm.

Informative on Confederate social and business affairs in France and in Charleston and other South Carolina communities.

Burge, Dolly Sumner (Lunt) 1817–1891.
A woman's wartime journal; an account of the passage over a Georgia plantation of Sherman's army on the march to the sea, as recorded in the diary of Dolly Sumner Lunt (Mrs. Thomas Burge) with an introduction and notes by Julian Street. Macon, The J. W. Burke co., 1927.
xii p., 1 l., 15–65 p. 19 cm.

A second edition of an abridgement poorly edited and first published in 1918; less than half of the original diary is included.

Burge, Dolly Sumner (Lunt) 1817–1891.
Diary. Edited by James I. Robertson, Jr. Athens, University of Georgia Press [1962]
141 p. 24 cm.

Well-edited, indexed, and published in its entirety, this diary is a valuable source on plantation life in Confederate Georgia.

Burns, Amanda (McDowell)
Fiddles in the Cumberlands, by Amanda McDowell, 1861–1865 [and] Lela McDowell Blankenship, 1943. New York, R. R. Smith, 1943.
ix, 310 p. 24½cm.

A sprightly diary of events in Northern Tennessee; weakened by imaginary conversation at the start of each chapter; some entries were later rewritten from memory.

Campbell, John Archibald, 1811–1889.
Recollections of the evacuation of Richmond, April 2d, 1865. By John A. Campbell. Baltimore, J. Murphy & co., 1880.
27 p. 24 cm.

A distinguished jurist captured the social and political chaos as a national capital collapsed.

Cartland, Fernando Gale.

Southern heroes; or, The Friends in war time, by Fernando G. Cartland, with an introduction by Benjamin F. Trueblood ... Cambridge, Riverside press, 1895.

xxviii, 480 p. front., pl., ports. 22½ cm.

The unhappy story of wartime mistreatment of North Carolina Quakers.

Castlen, Harriet (Gift)

Hope bids me onward, by Harriet Gift Castlen ... Biography of George Gift arranged by his daughter, from letters George Gift wrote to her mother before they were married. ⌊Savannah, Chatham printing company, 1945⌋

2 p. l., 7–198 p. 23½cm.

Emphasizes social life in Georgia and Alabama, and contains revealing data on the blockade.

Cato, *pseud.*

"Cato" on constitutional "money" and legal tender. In 12 no. from the Charleston mercury. Charleston, Evans & Cogswell, 1862.

38 p. 23 cm.

A pamphlet condemning the government's monetary policy and the Confederacy's trend toward "consolidation."

Champomier, P A

Statement of the sugar crop made in Louisiana ... By P. A. Champomier.

New Orleans, Printed by Magne & Weisse, 18

v. in 15½–19½ cm.

The 1862 volume is a list, by parish, of sugar planters and the number of hogsheads produced by each.

Chase, Philip Hartley, 1886–

Basic classification and listing Confederate States of America paper money, 1861–1865, by P. H. Chase. Bala-Cynwyd, Pa. ⌊c1936⌋

31 p. illus. 21½ cm.

This is but an introduction to Chase's more thorough 1947 volume.

Chase, Philip Hartley, 1886–

Confederate Treasury notes; the paper money of the Confederate States of America, 1861–1865. Philadelphia, 1947.

148 p. illus. 24 cm.

This illustrated and descriptive volume is a valuable guide to Confederate notes.

Cheshire, Joseph Blount, *bp.*, 1850–1932.

The church in the Confederate States; a history of the Protestant Episcopal church in the Confederate States, by Joseph Blount Cheshire ... New York, London ⌊etc.⌋ Longmans, Green, and co., 1912.

ix, 291 p. 19½ cm.

An old study of the Episcopal Church and its adjustment to war, with emphasis on its work among soldiers and Negroes; inadequate by modern scholarship.

Chesnut, Mary Boykin (Miller) 1823–1886.

A diary from Dixie, as written by Mary Boykin Chesnut, wife of James Chesnut, jr., United States senator from South Carolina, 1859–1861, and afterward an aide to Jefferson Davis and a brigadier-general in the Confederate army; ed. by Isabella D. Martin and Myrta Lockett Avary. New York, D. Appleton and company, 1905.

xxii, 424 p. front., plates, ports., facsim. 21½ cm.

A Civil War classic; covers social and economic conditions, morale, and major events stretching from Alabama to Virginia.

Chesnut, Mary Boykin (Miller) 1823–1886.

A diary from Dixie; edited by Ben Ames Williams. Boston, Houghton Mifflin Co., 1949.

xii, 572 p. port. 21 cm.

The best edition of the famous diary.

The **city** intelligencer; or, Stranger's guide. By V. & C. Richmond, Macfarlane & Fergusson, printers, 1862.

24 p. 19½cm.

A directory giving the location of various government offices, banks, hotels, churches, hospitals, etc.

Clay-Clopton, Virginia, 1825–1915.

A belle of the fifties; memoirs of Mrs. Clay, of Alabama, covering social and political life in Washington and the South, 1853–66, put into narrative form by Ada Sterling. Illustrated from contemporary portraits. New York, Doubleday, Page & company, 1905.

xxii, 386 p. 24 port. (part col. incl. front.) 23½cm.

Descriptive largely of wartime life in Richmond and Macon, with good accounts of shortages and substitutes.

Clayton, Victoria Virginia (Hunter)

White and black under the old régime; by Victoria V. Clayton ... with introduction by Frederic Cook Morehouse ... Milwaukee, The Young churchman co.; [etc., etc., ©1899]

195 p. front., illus., plates, ports. 17½ cm.

Contains chapters on the problems in Alabama of maintaining normal home life and controlling servants.

Collins, Elizabeth.

Memories of the southern states. By Elizabeth Collins ... Taunton [Eng.] Barnicott, 1865.

3 p. l., 116 p. 18cm.

A highly sympathetic view of Confederate South Carolina; by an Englishwoman who successfully ran the blockade on her return home in 1863.

Confederate receipt book. A compilation of over one hundred receipts, adapted to the times. Richmond, Va., West & Johnston, 1863.

28, [1] p. 21½cm.

Social and economic history revealed in the adaptation of old Southern recipes to Confederate shortages.

Confederate receipt book; a compilation of over one hundred receipts adapted to the times. Introd. by E. Merton Coulter. Athens, University of Georgia Press [1960]

38 p. illus. 23 cm.

A reprint of the original, with an interesting introduction and useful index added.

The **Confederate States** almanac, and repository of useful knowledge. v. [1]–4; 1862–65. Compiled and published by H. C. Clarke. Vicksburg, Miss. [etc., ©1861–64]

4 v. 18cm.

Convenient, miscellaneous statistical data on agricultural production, Confederate soldiers' pay, postal rates, etc.

Confederate States medical & surgical journal. v. 1, v. 2, no. 1–2; Jan. 1864–Feb. 1865. Richmond [Ayres & Wade, etc.] 1864–65.

2 v. in 1. illus. 29½cm.

A compendium of medical knowledge in the Confederacy.

Confederate States of America. *Congress. House of Representatives. Committee on Quartermaster and Commissary Departments.*

Report on the subject of tobacco rations for the Army. [Richmond, 1865]

2 p. 25 cm.

A recommendation that the government manufacture of tobacco be expanded to accomodate the needs of the army.

Confederate States of America. *Congress. House of representatives. Committee on salt supply.*

Report of the Committee on salt supply. [Richmond, 1864]

11 p. 23cm.

An evaluation of the salt wells of Smyth and Washington Counties, Va., as supplementary sources to the mines of Saltville, Va.

Confederate States of America. *Dept. of state.*

Correspondence of the Department of state, in relation to the British consuls resident in the Confederate States. Richmond, Printed at the Sentinel office, 1863.

55 p. 21cm.

Generally informative documents on the work of British consuls; emphasizes the work of Consul Magee relative to Alabama loans and bonds.

Confederate States of America. *Post-office dept.*

Advertisement of January 31, 1862, inviting proposals for carrying the mails of the Confederate States in the states of Alabama, Mississippi and Tennessee, from July 1, 1862, to June 30, 1866. John H. Reagan, postmaster general ... [Richmond, 1862]

96 p. 24 cm.

Inadvertently stresses some of the major problems Sec. Reagan had to face; a unique publication.

Confederate States of America. *Produce loan office.*

[Report of chief of Produce loan office. Richmond, 1864]

5 p. 23½cm.

Government cotton in N. C., S. C., Ga. and Ala. was reported in good shape, while Miss. cotton was classified as unsatisfactory.

Confederate States of America. *Treasury dept.*

... Communication of secretary of Treasury [relative to unpaid requisitions upon the Treasury, drawn by the quartermaster general and the commissary general] [Richmond, 1865]

5 p. 23½cm.

All extant printed reports of the Treasury Department serve as sources for the economic history of the Confederacy.

Confederate States of America. *Treasury dept.*

Tabular statement ... showing the rates of duty upon merchandise under the Tariff act of 1857, of the United States, as amended by the Provisional congress of the Confederate States of America; the rates under the proposed tariff bill now pending before the said Provisional congress; and the rates under the act of Congress of the United States of 1861. [Montgomery? 1861]

47 p. 25 cm.

This statement proposed new rates to adjust the existing tariff schedule.

Confederate States of America. *War Dept.*

Uniform and dress of the Army and Navy of the Confederate States of America. Introd. by Richard Harwell. [Rev. ed.] Philadelphia, R. Riling, 1960.

[12] p., reprint: 5, [4] p. plates (part col.) 29 cm.

The most revealing study of Confederate uniforms, insignia, etc; this reprint contains three descriptive works published during the war.

Cook, Anna Maria (Green) 1844–1936.

The journal of a Milledgeville girl, 1861–1867. Edited by James C. Bonner. Athens, University of Georgia Press, 1964.

vii, 131 p. plan. 22 cm.

Useful in its details of Georgia life during the war; a model for careful, exhaustive editing.

Criswell, Grover C

Confederate and Southern State bonds; a descriptive listing, including rarity ... **Including "the Territory of Florida" and "the Republic" and "Government of Texas," by Grover C. Criswell, Jr. [and] Clarence L. Criswell. St. Petersburg Beach, Fla., 1961.**

310 p. illus. 27 cm.

Of value for the highly specialized researcher.

Criswell, Grover C

Confederate and southern state currency; a descriptive listing, including rarity. By Grover C. Criswell, Jr. [and] Clarence L. Criswell. [Pass-A-Grille Beach, Fla., Criswell's] 1957.

277 p. illus. 26 cm.

A useful catalogue for those saving their Confederate money.

Cumming, Kate, 1835–

Gleanings from Southland; sketches of life and manners of the people of the South before, during and after the war of secession, with extracts from the author's journal and epitome of the new South. By Kate Cumming ... Birmingham [Ala.] Roberts & son, 1895.

277 p. front. (port.) 20cm.

Less valuable than the author's journal, with some excerpts from the journal and summaries of journal entries; written a generation after the war.

Cumming, Kate, 1835–

A journal of hospital life in the Confederate army of Tennessee, from the battle of Shiloh to the end of the war: with sketches of life and character, and brief notices of current events during that period. By Kate Cumming. Louisville, J. P. Morgan & co.; New Orleans, W. Evelyn [c1866]

199, [1] p. 23½ cm.

A fine personal narrative, realistic in its depiction of Confederate hospital conditions.

Cumming, Kate, 1835–1909.
Kate: the journal of a Confederate nurse. Edited by Richard Barksdale Harwell. Baton Rouge, Louisiana State University Press [1959]

xx, 321 p. plates, port., facsim. 24 cm.

Skillful editing made a valuable journal even more valuable and usable.

Curtis, Walter Gilman.
... Reminiscences, by Dr. W. G. Curtis. 1848–1900. For thirty years state quarantine surgeon for the port of Wilmington ... Southport, N. C., Herald job office [c1905]

1 p. l., 64 p. front. (port.) 22 cm.

Unique recollections of wartime Wilmington, N. C.; by the quarantine officer of that important post.

Daniel, John Moncure, 1825–1865.
The Richmond examiner during the war; or, The writings of John M. Daniel. With a memoir of his life, by his brother, Frederick S. Daniel. New York, Printed for the author, 1868.

232 p. front. (port.) 23½ cm.

The bulk of the wartime editorials was critical of the Southern effort, the Confederate president, the cabinet, ad infinitum.

[**Daniel, Lizzie (Cary)**] *comp.*
Confederate scrap-book. Copied from a scrap-book kept by a young girl during and immediately after the war, with additions from war copies of the "Southern literary messenger" and "Illustrated news" loaned by friends, and other selections as accredited. Pub. for the benefit of the Memorial bazaar, held in Richmond, April 11, 1893. Richmond, Va., J. H. Hill printing company, 1893.

2 p. l., iv, 254 p. 2 col. pl. (incl. front.) 22 cm.

Some information on wartime prices, along with songs, poems, addresses, and miscellany.

Davidson, Nora Fontaine M *comp.*
Cullings from the confederacy. A collection of southern poems, original and others, popular during the war between the states, and incidents and facts worth recalling. 1862–1866. Including the doggerel of the camp, as well as a tender tribute to the dead ... Comp. by Nora Fontaine M. Davidson ... Washington, D. C., The Rufus H. Darby printing co., 1903.

5 p. l., 15–163 p. incl. pl., port. pl., 4 port. on 2 pl. 23½cm.

Lists some wholesale and retail prices for needed commodities; also discusses women's work and loyalties.

Dawson, Sarah (Morgan) 1842–1909.
A Confederate girl's diary. Introd. by Warrington Dawson. Edited with a foreword and notes by James I. Robertson, Jr. Bloomington, Indiana University Press [1960]

473 p. illus. 21 cm.

An annotated reissue of a splendid diary first published in 1913; contains unique descriptions of conditions in wartime Louisiana.

Day, Samuel Phillips.
Down South; or, An Englishman's experience at the seat of the American war. By Samuel Phillips Day, special correspondent of the Morning herald ... London, Hurst and Blackett, 1862.

2 v. front. (port.) 19½cm.

Valuable for a foreigner's viewpoint on Southern customs, amusements, dress and women in Richmond and western Virginia.

Dayton, *Mrs.* **Ruth (Woods)** 1894–
Samuel Woods and his family, by Ruth Woods Dayton [Charleston, W. Va., Hood-Hiserman-Brodhag company] 1939.

vii, 170 p. front., plates, ports. 24cm.

Revealing in details of home life in wartime Virginia.

De Leon, Thomas Cooper, 1839–1914.
Belles, beaux and brains of the 60's, by T. C. De Leon ... Illustrated with one hundred and sixty-six portraits. New York, G. W. Dillingham company [c1909]

xi, [9], 9–464 p. front. (port.) illus. 22 cm.

Uncritical recollections of people and society, with interesting chapters on creative art in the South and the origin of Dixie's songs.

De Saussure, *Mrs.* **Nancy (Bostick)** 1837–1915.
Old plantation days; being recollections of southern life before the civil war, by Mrs. N. B. De Saussure. New York, Duffield & company, 1909.

123 p. col. front. 20½cm.

Novel in its account of abundance in wartime South Carolina, exciting in its depiction of the Fort Sumter bombardment, and graphic in its descriptions of a part of Sherman's march.

Devol, George H 1829–

Forty years a gambler on the Mississippi, by George H. Devol ... 1st ed. Cincinnati, Devol & Haines, 1887.

viii, 9–300 p. front. (port.) 4 pl. 22cm.

A gambler's life in New Orleans before and after Federal occupation; includes a description of the author's experiences in a New Orleans jail.

Dew, Charles B

Ironmaker to the Confederacy: Joseph R. Anderson and the Tredegar Iron Works, by Charles B. Dew. New Haven, Yale University Press, 1966.

ix, 345 p. illus., maps, port. 27 cm.

An exhaustive study and a model business history; treats of the Confederacy's largest foundry and of the problems it and its owner constantly faced.

Doggett, David Seth, 1810–1880.

A nation's Ebenezer. A discourse delivered in the Broad st. Methodist church, Richmond, Virginia, Thursday, September 18, 1862: the day of public thanksgiving, appointed by the President of the Confederate States. By Rev. D. S. Doggett ... Richmond, Va., Enquirer book and job press, 1862.

18 p. 21½cm.

Prayers of thanksgiving for the victories of the summer, with an exhortation for further effort.

Doggett, David Seth, 1810–1880.

The war and its close. A discourse, delivered in Centenary church, Richmond, Va., Friday, April 8th, 1864, by Rev. D. S. Doggett ... on the occasion of the national fast. Pub. by the Soldiers' tract association, M. E. church, South. Richmond, Macfarlane & Fergusson, 1864.

20 p. 19cm.

A sermon of the sins attendant upon war, and a summary of the minister's opinions on the issues involved in the crisis.

Dumond, Dwight Lowell, 1895– *ed.*

... Southern editorials on secession, edited by Dwight Lowell Dumond ... New York, London, The Century co. [c1931]

xxxiii, 529 p. 23 cm.

An excellent sampling, enhanced by Dumond's own insertions; H. L. Perkins prepared a similar work for the Northern side.

Dunbar, Mary Conway (Shields) 1845–

My mother used to say; a Natchez belle of the sixties, by Elizabeth Dunbar Murray. Boston, Christopher Pub. House [1959]

224 p. illus. 21 cm.

Natchez before, during and after the war, described in stories told to a daughter.

Dunn, Ballard S 1829–1897.

Brazil, the home for southerners: or, A practical account of what the author, and others, who visited that country, for the same objects, saw and did while in that empire. By Rev. Ballard S. Dunn ... New York, G. B. Richardson [etc.] 1866.

1 p. l., iv, [3]–272, [23] p. incl. tab. front. (port.) 19½cm.

The first insight into Confederate exiles in South America; updated and expanded by the studies of Hanna and Hill.

Edmondston, Catherine (Devereux)

Journal, 1860–1866. Edited by Margaret Mackay Jones (Mrs. George Lyle Jones) [n. p., 1954]

111 p. illus., map. 24 cm.

Day-by-day life on a North Carolina plantation, with detailed remarks on weather, crops, women's work, and farm Negroes.

Elliott, Stephen, *bp.*, 1806–1866.

Ezra's dilemma. A sermon preached in Christ church, Savannah, on Friday, August 21st, 1863, being the day of humiliation, fasting and prayer, appointed by the President of the Confederate States, by the Rt. Rev. Stephen Elliott ... Savannah, Ga., Power press of G. N. Nichols, 1863.

26 p. 21½cm.

Elliott pled for the homefolk to make every effort to bolster the soldiers' will to fight.

Elliott, Stephen, *bp.*, 1806–1866.

God's presence with our army at Manassas! A sermon, preached in Christ church, Savannah, on Sunday, July 28th, being the day recommended by the Congress of the Confederate States, to be observed as a day of thanksgiving, in commemoration of the victory at Manassas Junction, on Sunday the 21st of July, 1861. By the Rt. Rev. Stephen Elliott ... Savannah, W. T. Williams, 1861.

iv, 22 p., 1 l. 22cm.

A caution against over-confidence.

Elliott, Stephen, *bp.*, 1806–1866.

God's presence with the Confederate States. A sermon preached in Christ church, Savannah, on Thursday, the 13th June, being the day appointed at the request of Congress, by the President of the Confederate States, as a day of solemn humiliation, fasting and prayer. By the Rt. Rev. Stephen Elliott ... Pub. by request of the vestry. Savannah, W. T. Williams, 1861.

21 p. 21½cm.

After a statement of principles, Elliott called for further endeavor by all.

Elliott, Stephen, *bp.*, 1806–1866.

"New wine not to be put into old bottles." A sermon preached in Christ church, Savannah, on Friday, February 28th, 1862, being the day of humiliation, fasting, and prayer, appointed by the President of the Confederate States. By the Rt. Rev. Stephen Elliott ... Savannah, Press of J. M. Cooper & co., 1862.

18 p. 23cm.

An interesting equation of the Southern cause with the need to frustrate rampant democracy.

Elliott, Stephen, *bp.*, 1806–1866.

"Samson's riddle." A sermon preached in Christ church, Savannah, on Friday, March 27th, 1863. Being the day of humiliation, fasting and prayer, appointed by the president of the Confederate States. By the Rt. Rev. Stephen Elliott ... Macon, Ga., Burke, Boykin & co., printers, 1863.

24 p. 20½cm.

Shame to those who would too soon seek peace!

Elliott, Stephen, *bp.*, 1806–1866.

"Vain is the help of man." A sermon preached in Christ church, Savannah, on Thursday, September 15, 1864, being the day of fasting, humiliation, and prayer, appointed by the governor of the state of Georgia. By the Rt. Rev. Stephen Elliott ... Macon, Ga., Burke, Boykin & company, 1864.

13 p. 20½cm.

A darkness-before-the-dawn sort of morale-builder.

Ellis, Emily Caroline (Searson) 1838–

The flight of the clan; a diary of 1865; being an account of how the Ellis family of South Carolina, together with their kinsmen, the De Loaches, Hays, and Framptons fled before Sherman's raiders, by Emily Caroline Ellis. Together with an introd. and historical notes by Frampton Erroll Ellis. Atlanta, 1954.

14 p. illus. 24 cm.

A slim, privately printed journal that concentrates on refugees' reactions rather than Sherman's actions.

Eppes, Susan (Bradford) 1845 *or* 6–1942.

Through some eventful years, by Susan Bradford Eppes (Mrs. Nicholas Ware Eppes) ... Macon, Ga., Press of the J. W. Burke company, 1926.

vi p., 2 l., 11–378 p. col. ports., 2 col. coats of arms (incl. front.) 23 cm.

Life on a Florida plantation, as described in memoirs and a diary; the latter paints a vivid picture of social and economic conditions.

Ezekiel, Herbert T.

The Jews of Richmond during the civil war, by Herbert T. Ezekiel. [Richmond, Press of H. T. Ezekiel, 1915]

8 l. 31 x 25½cm.

Hearsay evidence on the contributions of Jews to the war effort; useful in its revelation of outstanding individuals among the Jewish community of Richmond.

Famous adventures and prison escapes of the civil war. New York, The Century co., 1893.

x p., 1 l., 338 p. incl. front., illus. 21 cm.

In this famous compilation is the war diary of a female Unionist who spent part of the war in Arkansas, Mississippi and--especially--Vicksburg.

Fearn, Frances (Hewitt) *ed.*

Diary of a refugee, ed. by Frances Fearn; illustrated by Rosalie Urquhart. New York, Moffat, Yard and company, 1910.

ix, 149 p. front., plates. 19½ cm.

This slim journal recounts the hardships endured by refugees fleeing before the advancing Federal armies.

Field, Henry Martyn, 1822–1907.

Blood is thicker than water: a few days among our southern brethren. By Henry M. Field ... New York, G. Munro, 1886.

viii, [11]–151 p. incl. front. 19 cm.

This postwar travelogue of the South, by a Presbyterian clergyman-author, is inferior to the same writer's better known Bright Skies and Dark Shadows.

Fleet, Benjamin Robert, 1846–1864.
Green Mount; a Virginia plantation family during the Civil War: being the journal of Benjamin Robert Fleet and letters of his family. Edited by Betsy Fleet and John D. P. Fuller. Drawings by Sidney E. King. W. Clement Eaton, editorial consultant. Lexington, University of Kentucky Press [1962]
xxiv, 374 p. illus., ports., map (on lining papers) 24 cm.

Valuable for a young boy's depiction of deteriorating fortunes on a Virginia plantation, and for family letters that supplement the journal.

Flournoy, Mary H
Side lights on southern history, by Mary H. Flournoy ... Richmond, Va., The Dietz press, 1939.
7 p. l., 259 p. front., plates, ports. 20½ cm.

Contains chapters on Confederate newspapers, sources, and relations with Indiana, but lacks documentation, bibliography and index.

Fontaine, Lamar, 1829–
My life and my lectures, by Lamar Fontaine, C. E., PH. D. New York and Washington, The Neale publishing company, 1908.
2 p. l., 3-361 p. front. (port.) 23cm.

The best source on the Confederate soldier who reputedly wrote "All Quiet Along the Potomac Tonight."

Freemasons. *Virginia. Grand lodge.*
Free masonry and the war. Report of the Committee under the resolutions of 1862, Grand lodge of Virginia, in reference to our relations as masonic bodies and as masons, in the North and South, growing out of the manner in which the present war has been prosecuted ... Richmond, C. H. Wynne, printer, 1865.
31 p. 23cm.

A declaration of independence for the Southern lodges.

Fulkerson, Horace Smith, 1818–1891.
A civilian's recollections of the war between the states, by H. S. Fulkerson ... 1886; edited by P. L. Rainwater ... Baton Rouge, La., O. Claitor, 1939.
5 p. l., 253 p. 23½ cm.

Informative on behind-the-lines morale and life, and on the author's purchasing activities for his native state of Mississippi.

Fuller, Claud E 1877–
Confederate currency and stamps, 1861–1865; official acts of Congress authorizing their issue; historical data and official correspondence on the Confederate financial system including sketches on the coins, stamps, medals, seal, and flags. [Nashville, Published by the Parthenon Press under the auspices of the Tennessee Division, United Daughters of the Confederacy, ©1949]
236 p. illus. (part col.) ports., facsims. 32 cm.

A compilation of information on the subjects listed in the title; several are more adequately treated in other studies.

Furman university, *Greenville, S. C.*
A catalogue of the officers and students ... spring term.

Greenville, S. C.
v. front. 22½cm.

The 1861 catalogue provided data on admission requirements, curriculum, etc. for a typical Southern religious school.

Gannon, Michael V
Rebel bishop: the life and era of Augustin Verot, by Michael V. Gannon. With a foreword by John Tracy Ellis. Milwaukee, Bruce Pub. Co. [1964]
xvii, 267 p. illus., map, ports. 22 cm.

The exposition of a Catholic bishop's rationale for slavery and state rights; describes also the work of priests among soldiers and prisoners.

Gay, Mary Ann Harris, *b.* 1827.
Life in Dixie during the war. 1863–1864–1865. [By] Mary A. H. Gay. Atlanta, Ga., Constitution job office, 1892.
255 p. 19½cm.

Recollections penned many years after the war; relives days in Atlanta during the Sherman era.

Georgia. *Comptroller General's Office.*
Report.
[Atlanta, etc.]
v. in tables. 22-26 cm.

Annual reports provide a wealth of material on county economy: slaves, receipts, disbursements, etc.

Goodloe, Albert Theodore.
Confederate echoes: a voice from the South in the days of secession and of the southern confederacy. By Rev. Albert Theodore Goodloe ... Nashville, Tenn., Printed for the author, Publishing house of the M. E. church, South, Smith & Lamar, 1907.

452 p. front., plates, ports. 19 cm.

These wartime experiences, based on memory and a diary, tell of life in Mississippi and northern Alabama.

Gray, Cordelia Lewis (Scales) 1844–1915.
"Dear darling Loulie": letters of Cordelia Lewis Scales to Loulie W. Irby during and after the War Between the States. Edited by Martha Neville Lumpkin. [Boulder? Colo.] ©1955.

viii, 151 p. ports. 28 cm.

A mimeographed publication of chatty letters from a teenage Mississippi girl to her friend in Memphis; a good example of the adolescent excitement of the period.

Green, Beulah Gayle.
Confederate reporter, 1861–64. Austin, Tex., Printed by Burrell Print. Co., 1962.

123 p. illus. 29 cm.

Reproduced clippings from two Virginia newspapers describe events and conditions in the South; arranged in chronological order.

Greenville and Columbia railroad company.
Proceedings.
[Columbia? S. C.,

v. 21cm.

The 1863 minutes give statistical information on the war-ravaged line.

Greenville ladies' association in aid of the volunteers of the Confederate army.
Minutes of the proceedings of the Greenville ladies' association in aid of the volunteers of the Confederate army. Edited by James Welch Patton ... Durham, N. C., Duke university press, 1937.
118 p. 23 cm.

A commentary on the activities of women throughout the war period; gives insight into the social and economic history of the Confederacy.

Habersham, Anna Wylly.
Journal. [New ed.] Darien, Ga., Ashantilly Press, 1961.

23 p. illus., port. 20 cm.

This too-short diary reveals little except the thoughts and interests of one Southern woman.

Habersham, Josephine Clay (Habersham) 1821–1893.
Ebb tide; as seen through the diary of Josephine Clay Habersham, 1863. By Spencer Bidwell King, Jr. Illus. by William Etsel Snowden, Jr. Athens, University of Georgia Press, 1958.

129 p. illus. 22 cm.

A well-edited diary, with supporting chapters drawn from letters, books and another family diary; the whole reveals wartime life among the gentle folk of Savannah.

Hague, Parthenia Antoinette (Vardaman) 1838–
A blockaded family: life in southern Alabama during the civil war, by Parthenia Antoinette Hague. Boston and New York, Houghton, Mifflin and co., 1888.

v, 176 p. 18cm.

Good on war-imposed innovations in farming and experiments in "ersatz" on a plantation near Eufaula, Ala.

Hale, Jonathan D *comp.*
... Continued lifting of masks ... A war courts decree, and one sequal [!] A slight result of Gen. Grant's order no. 4. Copyright secured by Dr. J. D. Hale. [Washington, D. C., 1887?]
cover-title, 31, [1] p. 2 fold. facsim. (incl. port.) 16½cm.

Another protest of the unfortunate consequences of the breakdown of law and order in the South.

Hall, *Mrs.* Frances.
Major Hall's wife. A thrilling story of the life of a southern wife and mother, while a refugee in the confederacy, during the late struggle. Written by herself. Syracuse, N. Y., Weed & company, 1884.

49 p. 22cm.

The experiences of a woman refugee in Louisiana; the ring of truth is somewhat offset by a ghost story seriously related.

Hall, John Lesslie, 1856–

Half-hours in southern history, by Jno: Lesslie Hall ... Richmond, Atlanta [etc.] B. F. Johnson publishing co. [c1907]

320 p. 16 port. (incl. front.) 21cm.

Of doubtful merit despite the chapters on women's role in the war.

Hall, Wade H

Reflections of the Civil War in southern humor. Gainesville, University of Florida Press, 1962.

82 p. 23 cm.

Rewarding interpretation of Southern humor and humorists among soldiers, Negroes, the poor whites, and the folks at home.

Hanna, Alfred Jackson, 1893–

Confederate exiles in Venezuela, by Alfred Jackson Hanna and Kathryn Abbey Hanna. Limited ed. Tuscaloosa, Ala., Confederate Pub. Co., 1960.

149 p. 22 cm.

The only study of a little-known episode attendant to Confederate defeat; well-researched and interestingly written.

Hardin, Elizabeth Pendleton, 1839–1895.

The private war of Lizzie Hardin: a Kentucky Confederate girl's diary of the Civil War in Kentucky, Virginia, Tennessee, Alabama, and Georgia. Edited by G. Glenn Clift. Frankfort, Kentucky Historical Society, 1963.

306 p. illus. 23 cm.

A fascinating journal that details the author's experiences after she was expelled from Kentucky for Confederate sympathies.

Harrison, Constance (Cary) "*Mrs.* Burton Harrison," 1843–1920.

Recollections grave and gay, by Mrs. Burton Harrison. New York, C. Scribner's sons, 1911.

4 p. l., 3–386 p. 21½ cm.

An intelligent woman's memories of social life and economic conditions in Richmond, with good commentaries on Confederate military and political leaders.

Harrison, Mary Douglass (Waring) *b.* 1845.

Miss Waring's journal: 1863 and 1865, being the diary of Miss Mary Waring of Mobile, during the final days of the War Between the States. Edited by Thad Holt, Jr. Chicago, Wyvern Press of S. F. E. [c1964]

17 p. illus. 25 cm.

Filled with too many personal thoughts and events, this skimpy diary provides but hints to wartime Mobile.

Harwell, Richard Barksdale.

Confederate belles-lettres, a bibliography and a finding list of the fiction, poetry, drama, songsters, and miscellaneous literature published in the Confederate States of America, by Richard Barksdale Harwell; foreword by Robert H. Woody. Hattiesburg, Miss., The Book farm, 1941.

79 p. 23 cm.

A useful bibliography of an important aspect of Confederate social history.

Harwell, Richard Barksdale.

Confederate music. Chapel Hill, University of North Carolina Press [1950]

viii, 184 p. illus. 24 cm.

An excellent study of one aspect of Confederate cultural life.

Herr, Kincaid A

The Louisville & Nashville railroad, 1850–1942, by Kincaid A. Herr ... Louisville, Ky., L. & N. magazine, 1943.

ix, 221 p. illus. (incl. ports., facsims.) maps (1 double) diagr. 29 x 22½cm.

This still-reliable work concentrates on the wartime activities of one of the more important lines in the West; originally published serially in a magazine.

Hickerson, Thomas Felix, 1882–

Echoes of Happy Valley; letters and diaries, family life in the South, Civil War history. Chapel Hill, N. C., Distributed by Bull's Head Bookshop [1962]

245 p. illus. 27 cm.

A miscellany of letters, diaries and memoirs, some commenting on everyday life in Virginia.

Hill, Lawrence Francis, 1890–
The Confederate exodus to Latin America, by Lawrence F. Hill ... [Austin? Tex.] 1936.

94 p. 24 cm.

An enlargement of a magazine article, this monograph is inferior to similar studies by Hanna and Rolle.

Hill, Lawrence Francis.
Confederate exiles to Brazil, by Lawrence F. Hill. [Durham? N. C., 1927?]

cover-title, p. 192–210. 26½cm.

More comprehensive than the Dunn volume, but still somewhat shallow and disorganized.

Hoge, Peyton Harrison, 1858–
Moses Drury Hoge: life and letters. By his nephew, Peyton Harrison Hoge. Richmond, Va., Presbyterian committee of publication [1899]

ix, [1] p., 1 l., 518 p. front., plates, ports., facsims. 24½cm.

The best study of a stalwart in Virginia Presbyterian circles; gives some insights into wartime Richmond, as well as religion in the Confederacy.

Holmes, Sarah Katherine (Stone) 1841–1907.
Brokenburn; the journal of Kate Stone, 1861–1868. Edited by John Q. Anderson. Baton Rouge, Louisiana State University Press [1955]

400 p. illus. 22 cm.

A well-edited journal treating of everyday life in Louisiana and Texas during the war.

[**Hopley, Catherine Cooper**]
Life in the South, from the commencement of the war. By a blockaded British subject. Being a social history of those who took part in the battles, from a personal acquaintance with them in their own homes. From the spring of 1860 to August 1862 ... London, Chapman & Hall, 1863.

(American culture series, 196 : 3)

Microfilm copy (positive) made in 1962 by University Microfilms, Ann Arbor, Mich.

Valuable observations on plantation life in Virginia and Florida during the first two years of war.

Horst, Samuel, 1919–
Mennonites in the Confederacy; a study in Civil War pacifism. Scottdale, Pa., Herald Press [1967]

148 p. illus., maps, port. 20 cm.

An excellent summary of the habits and problems of some 400 families residing mostly in the Shenandoah Valley.

Hubbell, Jay Broadus, 1885– *ed.*
The last years of Henry Timrod, 1864–1867, including letters of Timrod to Paul Hamilton Hayne and letters about Timrod by William Gilmore Simms, John R. Thompson, John Greenleaf Whittier, and others. With four uncollected poems and seven uncollected prose pieces. Drawn chiefly from the Paul Hamilton Hayne collection in the Duke university library. Edited by Jay B. Hubbell. Durham, N. C., Duke university press, 1941.

xi, 184 p. 21 cm.

The sometimes revealing letters of wartime Columbia, S. C.; by a leading writer whose poetry ceased with the opening guns of combat.

Hunter, Alexander, 1843–
The women of the Debatable land, by Alexander Hunter ... Illustrated by Miss Elizabeth C. Harmon. Washington, D. C., Cobden publishing company, 1912.

viii p., 2 l., 261 p. front., illus., plates, ports., fold. map. 20cm.

Folklore rather than history; written from stories told to, or experiences remembered by, the author.

Jackson, H[enry] W R.
Historical register and Confederates assistant to national independence. Containing a discovery for the preservation of butter, together with other valuable recipes, and important information for the soldier, and the people in general throughout the Confederate States of America ... By H. W. R. Jackson. Augusta, Ga., Printed at the office of the Constitutionalist, 1862.

47, [1] p. 18cm.

A conglomeration of information on food recipes, substitutes, etc.

Jackson, Henry W R
The southern women of the second American revolution. Their trials, &c. Yankee barbarity illustrated. Our naval victories and exploits of Confederate war steamers. Capture of Yankee gunboats, &c. By H. W. R. Jackson. Atlanta, Ga., Intelligencer steam-power press, 1863.

120, [2] p. 21 cm.

Another miscellany; this one includes atrocity stories, sketches of women, and some military material thrown in for good measure.

Jervey, Susan Ravenel, 1840–

Two diaries from middle St. John's, Berkeley, South Carolina, February–May, 1865; journals kept by Miss Susan R. Jervey and Miss Charlotte St. J. Ravenel, at Northampton and Pooshee plantations, and reminiscences of Mrs. (Waring) Henagan; with two contemporary reports from federal officials. ⌊Pinopolis, S. C.⌋ St. John's hunting club, 1921.

56 p. 23½cm.

Points out the fears of women in areas overrun by soldiers, yet shows remarkably little physical violence done to women.

Johnston, James Houstoun, 1866– *comp.*

Western and Atlantic railroad of the state of Georgia ... compiled by James Houstoun Johnston ... in pursuance of legislative action 1925. Atlanta ⌊Stein printing co., state printers⌋ 1931 ⌊*i. e.* 1932⌋

1 p. l., iii, 364 p. front., plates, ports., mounted fold. map, facsim., diagrs. 23½ cm.

This solitary study of the W & A covers much more ground than the famous foray made on the line by the Andrews Raiders.

Jones, Joseph, 1833–1896.

Medical and surgical memoirs: containing investigations on the geographical distribution, causes, nature, relations and treatment of various diseases ... By Joseph Jones ... New Orleans, Printed for the author, by Clark & Hofeline, 1876–90.

3 v. in 4. front. (v. 3, pt. 2) illus., plates (part col.) fold. maps, fold. plans, fold. charts, fold. tables. 24½cm.

Stimulating reflections by the most active of medical scientists in the Confederacy.

Jones, Katharine M 1900– *ed.*

Heroines of Dixie; Confederate women tell their story of the War. ⌊1st ed.⌋ Indianapolis, Bobbs-Merrill ⌊1955⌋

xiv, 430 p. ports. 23 cm.

Adequately edited excerpts from both published and manuscript sources; chronologically organized to reflect changing conditions.

Jones, Katharine M 1900–

Ladies of Richmond, Confederate capital. With an introd. by Clifford Dowdey. Indianapolis, Bobbs-Merrill ⌊1962⌋

365 p. illus. 24 cm.

Chosen from significant sources on Southern society, economics and morale in the Confederate capital.

Jones, Katharine M 1900– *ed.*

When Sherman came: Southern women and the "great march," by Katharine M. Jones. Indianapolis, Bobbs-Merrill ⌊1964⌋

xiv, 353 p. 24 cm.

Good commentaries on women's reactions to conditions in the wake of Sherman's march; taken largely from manuscript letters, diaries and memoirs.

Jones, Mary Sharpe (Jones) 1808–1869.

Yankees a'coming; one month's experience during the invasion of Liberty County, Georgia, 1864–1865, by Mary Sharpe Jones and Mary Jones Mallard. Edited with a prologue by Haskell Monroe. Tuscaloosa, Ala., Confederate Pub. Co., 1959.

102 p. illus., ports., map, facsim. 22 cm.

Descriptions of the invasion of a Southern home by Northern marauders; rich in detail, interesting in content.

Jordan, Charles Edward, 1851–

A letter from Charles Edward Jordan to his family and friends by whom this little work was inspired ... ⌊n. p.⌋ 1932.

47 p. front. (port.) illus. (plan) plates, facsim. 23½cm.

Memories of wartime life in Haymarket and Greenwich, Va.; brief and interesting.

Kelsey, Albert Warren, 1840–

Autobiographical notes and memoranda, by Albert Warren Kelsey, 1840–1910. <For private circulation only>. ⌊Baltimore, Munder-Thomsen press, 1911⌋

129, ⌊1⌋ p. front. (port.) 24½cm.

The 1864 experiences of a Northern man operating an abandoned plantation ninety miles above Vicksburg.

Kent, *Mrs.* **E C.**

"Four years in Secessia." A narrative of a residence at the South previous to and during the southern rebellion, up to November, 1863, when the writer escaped from Richmond. By Mrs. E. C. Kent. 2d ed.—with additions. Buffalo, Franklin printing house, 1865.

35, ⌊1⌋ p. 22½cm.

Critical views of Southern life by a New Yorker; includes references to economic conditions in Richmond.

Lamb, Sarah Anne (Chaffee) *b.* 1837.
Letters from the colonel's lady: correspondence of Mrs. (Col.) William Lamb written from Fort Fisher, N. C., C. S. A., to her parents in Providence, R. I., U. S. A., December 1861 to January 1865. From the Lamb collection of the Library of the College of William and Mary. Edited by Cornelius M. Dickinson Thomas. [Winnabow, N. C., Charles Towne Preservation Trust, 1965]

xxii, 97 p. illus., facsims., map, ports. 22 cm.

The highly unique letters of the wife of a Confederate commander to her mother in the North; useful in a number of ways.

Lander, S.
Our own school arithmetic. By S. Lander, A. M. Greensboro, N. C., Sterling, Campbell & Albright; Richmond, Va., W. H. White, 1863.

vi, [7]–223, [1] p. 17cm.

Illustrations and problems obviously adjusted to secession and war.

Law, *Mrs.* **Sallie Chapman (Gordon)**
Reminiscences of the war of the sixties beween the North and South, by Mrs. S. C. Law ... Memphis, Tenn., Memphis printing co., 1892.

cover-title, 16 p. 16cm.

An interesting little book on conditions in Confederate Memphis and the hospital work of women there.

LeConte, Emma.
When the world ended; diary. Edited by Earl Schenck Miers. New York, Oxford University Press, 1957.

124 p. illus. 23 cm.

An exciting diary, written in Columbia, S. C., and covering the period Jan.-Aug., 1865.

Le Conte, Joseph, 1823–1901.
The autobiography of Joseph Le Conte; edited by William Dallam Armes. New York, D. Appleton and company, 1903.

xvii, 337 p. front., plates, ports. 19cm.

Revealing memoirs by a famed scientist who served during the war as superintendent of niter works near Columbia, S. C.

Lee, Floride (Clemson) 1842–1871.
A rebel came home; the diary of Floride Clemson tells of her wartime adventures in Yankeeland, 1863–64, her trip home to South Carolina, and life in the South during the last few months of the Civil War and the year following. Editors: Charles M. McGee, Jr. [and] Ernest M. Lander, Jr. Illustrator: Olivia Jackson McGee. Columbia, University of South Carolina Press, 1961.

153 p. illus. 24 cm.

An interesting and well-edited diary; unfortunately, only eleven pages treat of life in wartime South Carolina.

Logan, Kate Virginia (Cox) 1840–1915.
My Confederate girlhood; the memoirs of Kate Virginia Cox Logan, edited by her daughter, Lily Logan Morrill. Richmond, Garrett & Massie, incorporated, 1932.

xv p., 1 l., 150 p. plates, ports. 24 cm.

Life at Clover Hill Plantation, the site of Richmond's source of coal during the war.

Lonn, Ella, 1879–
Salt as a factor in the confederacy, by Ella Lonn ... New York, W. Neale, 1933.

viii p., 2 l., 13–324 p. front., fold. map. 20½ cm.

A definitive study of the complicated efforts to relieve a shortage in this prime necessity.

[**Loughborough, Mary Ann (Webster)**] 1836–1887.
My cave life in Vicksburg. With letters of trial and travel. By a lady. New York [etc.] D. Appleton and company, 1864.

196 p. map. 18½ cm.

A valuable story of a gentlewoman's experiences under siege at Vicksburg.

Loy, *Mrs.* **Linda (Wiley)**
Memories of the sunny South (1860–61–62–63) by Linda Wiley Loy. Effingham, Ill. [Effingham county printing co.] 1933.

2 p. l., 3–66 p. 22½cm.

Wartime experiences of the daughter of an active Unionist in Tennessee.

Lubbock, Francis Richard, 1815–1905.

Six decades in Texas; or, Memoirs of Francis Richard Lubbock, governor of Texas in war time, 1861–63. A personal experience in business, war, and politics. Ed. by C. W. Raines ... Austin, B. C. Jones & co., printers, 1900.

xvi, 685 p. illus., plates, ports., facsims. 23½cm.

Some informative chapters on Texas wartime economy.

McDonald, Cornelia (Peake) 1822–1909.

A diary with reminiscences of the war and refugee life in the Shenandoah valley, 1860–1865 [by] Mrs. Cornelia McDonald ... annotated and supplemented by Hunter McDonald ... Nashville, Cullom & Ghertner co. [c1935]

xvi, 540 p. col. front., plates (part col.) ports. (1 col.) facsims. 24 cm.

A portrayal of wartime life in central and western Virginia.

McGuire, Judith White (Brockenbrough) "*Mrs.* John P. McGuire."

Diary of a southern refugee, during the war. By a lady of Virginia ... New York, E. J. Hale & son, 1867.

360 p. 19cm.

Detailed on conditions in Richmond, where the writer served for a time as a clerk in the commissary department.

McHenry, George.

... A paper containing a statement of facts relating to the approaching cotton crisis. By George McHenry. Richmond, Dec. 31, 1864. [Richmond, 1865]

87 p. 22½cm.

An essay on the importance of closing off the supply of cotton to Europe as a means of obtaining British recognition.

McMaster, *Mrs.* Elizabeth (Waring)

The Girls of the sixties; this memorial volume is lovingly dedicated to Malvina Sarah Waring (Mrs. Clark Waring) by her daughter, Elizabeth Waring McMaster. Columbia, S. C. [The State co.] 1937.

175 p. ports. 23½cm.

Biographical sketches, mostly of little-known figures, and of use only to genealogists.

Macon, Emma Cassandra (Riely) 1847–

Reminiscences of the civil war, by Emma Cassandra Riely Macon and Reuben Conway Macon, adjutant, Thirteenth Virginia infantry, Ewell's division, Stonewall Jackson's corps, C. S. A., 1861–5; written 1896. [Cedar Rapids, Ia.] Priv. print. [The Torch press] 1911.

158, [2] p. pl., 2 port. (incl. front.) 24½ cm.

Revealing for glimpses of civilian life in the Shenandoah Valley, especially around the Winchester area.

Malet, William Wyndham, 1804–1885.

An errand to the South in the summer of 1862. By the Rev. William Wyndham Malet ... London, R. Bentley, 1863.

viii, 312 p. front. 17 cm.

Detailed reminiscences and descriptions by an English vicar who spent six months on a visit to wartime South Carolina.

Massey, Mary Elizabeth.

Ersatz in the Confederacy. Columbia, University of South Carolina Press, 1952.

xii, 233 p. illus. 24 cm.

An interesting presentation of shortages in the Confederacy and imaginative improvisations to remedy the scarcity of needed commodities.

Massey, Mary Elizabeth.

Refugee life in the Confederacy. Baton Rouge, Louisiana State University Press, 1964.

xii, 327 p. illus. 24 cm.

A beautifully researched and useful study of a difficult subject.

Maury, *Mrs.* Betty Herndon (Maury)

The Confederate diary of Betty Herndon Maury, daughter of Lieut. Commander M. F. Maury ... 1861–1863. Edited by Alice Maury Parmelee. Washington, Priv. print., 1938.

2 p. l., 102 p. front. (port.) 24½cm.

Day-to-day events, first in Fredericksburg, then Richmond; chronicled by an intelligent and observant Southern woman.

Mays, Samuel Elias, 1834–1906.

Genealogical notes on the family of Mays, and reminiscences of the war between the states, from notes written around the campfires by Samuel Elias Mays, born in South Carolina, Nov. 12th, 1834; died at Plant City, Florida, Nov. 27th, 1906; and some references to the Earle family. ₍Plant City, Printed by Plant City enterprise, 1927₎

324 p. 2 port. (incl. front.) 23½ cm.

Good commentaries on social and economic problems, as well as military experiences; written from notes taken during the war.

Meade, William, *bp.*, 1789–1862.

Address on the day of fasting and prayer, appointed by the president of the Confederate States, June 13, 1861. Delivered at Christ church, Millwood, Va., by Bishop Meade ... Richmond, Enquirer book and job press, 1861.

19 p. 20½cm.

This morale-builder called attention to the needs of soldiers' families.

Means, Alexander, 1801–1883.

Diary for 1861; edited by Ross H. McLean. Atlanta, The Library, Emory University, 1949.

46 p. 24 cm.

The detailed daily jottings of a prominent minister-physician-teacher; useful for insights into Georgia during the early months of the war.

Merrick, *Mrs.* **Caroline Elizabeth (Thomas)** 1825–

Old times in Dixie land; a southern matron's memories, by Caroline E. Merrick. New York, The Grafton press, 1901.

241 p. front., port. 19½cm.

Covers the war years in Louisiana and includes excerpts from a family diary; an excess of quoted conversations weakens credibility.

Mikell, Isaac Jenkins, 1851–

Rumbling of the chariot wheels, by I. Jenkins Mikell. Columbia, S. C., The State company, 1923.

273 p. front. 19½cm.

Recollections of a young boy during the war, with descriptions of Charleston and Aiken, S. C.

Moore, *Mrs.* **M B.**

Dixie primer. For the little folks. By Mrs. M. B. Moore. 2d ed. Raleigh, N. C., Branson, Farrar & co., 1863.

3 p. l., 5–26, ₍2₎ p. 14½cm.

Propaganda for juveniles; many stories encouraged the belief that the Negroes were better off as slaves.

Moore, *Mrs.* **M B.**

The geographical reader, for the Dixie children. By Mrs. M. B. Moore. Raleigh, Branson, Farrar & co., 1863.

48 p. double maps. 20 x 17cm.

Brainwashing, 1863-style, intended to sustain the righteousness of secession and the Confederate cause.

Mordecai, John Brooke, 1878–

A brief history of the Richmond, Fredericksburg and Potomac railroad, by John B. Mordecai ... February, 1940. ₍Richmond, Old Dominion press, inc., 1941₎

86 p. plates, map, facsims. 27 cm.

An outdated introduction to a subject still awaiting full treatment.

Morgan, Julia.

How it was; four years among the Rebels. By Mrs. Irby Morgan ... Nashville, Tenn., Printed for the author, Publishing house, Methodist Episcopal church, South, 1892.

204 p. front., ports. 19 cm.

The well-told experiences of a refugee in Tennessee and Georgia.

Morrow, Decatur Franklin, 1856–

Then and now; reminiscences and historical romance, 1856–1865, by D. F. Morrow ... Macon, Ga., Press of the J. W. Burke company, 1926.

346 p. incl. front., illus., ports. 19½cm.

Recollections of life in the North Carolina Piedmont; fictionalized to conceal the identities of persons mentioned.

Muir, Dorothy Troth, 1905–

Presence of a lady; Mount Vernon, 1861–1868, by Dorothy Troth Muir ... [Washington, Printed by Mount Vernon publishing company, 1946]

90 p. incl. front. plates (1 double) 24cm.

The secretary to the first regent of the Mount Vernon Ladies' Association relates wartime problems in maintaining the historic site.

News and courier, *Charleston, S. C.*

"Our women in the war." The lives they lived; the deaths they died. From the weekly News and courier, Charleston, S. C. ... Charleston, S. C., The News and courier book presses, 1885.

xii, [3]–482 p. 23½cm.

Accounts--some romantic and idealized, some graphic and realistic--recounted many years after the conflict.

Nightingale, Florence, 1820–1910.

Directions for cooking by troops, in camp and hospital. Prepared for the Army of Virginia, and published by order of the Surgeon General. With essays on Taking food, and What food. Richmond, J. W. Randolph, 1861.

35 p. 15 cm.

Self-explanatory, and still possessed of some interest.

North Carolina. *State dept. of archives and history.*

Addresses at the unveiling of the memorial to the North Carolina women of the confederacy presented to the state by the late Ashley Horne. Compiled by R. D. W. Connor. Raleigh, Edwards & Broughton printing co., state printers, 1914.

26, [1] p. front., plates, port. 23cm.

Connor's moving tribute highlights this collection of eulogies to embattled women.

Ozanne, T D.

The South as it is, or Twenty-one years' experience in the southern states of America. By the Rev. T. D. Ozanne, M. A. London, Saunders, Otley, and co., 1863.

v, [1], 306 p. 20cm.

Overly sanguine in generalizations on Southern life and Negro-white relations; trustworthy in descriptions of economic conditions.

Palmer, Benjamin Morgan, 1818–1902.

A discourse before the General assembly of South Carolina, on December 10, 1863, appointed by the legislature as a day of fasting, humiliation and prayer. By B. M. Palmer ... Columbia, S. C., C. P. Pelham, state printer, 1864.

24 p. 22cm.

An equating of the Confederate cause with the struggle for republican government.

Palmer, Sarah L.

Six months among the secessionists. A reliable and thrilling narrative of the sufferings and trials of Miss Sarah L. Palmer, a native of Pennsylvania, who, at the opening of the great southern rebellion, was teaching school in Knoxville, the home of Parson Brownlow ... Philadelphia, Barclay & co., 1862.

[9]–40 p. incl. front., pl. 25cm.

So exaggerated and confusing that in a subsequent edition Miss Palmer listed herself as a native of Massachusetts.

Partridge, J Arthur.

The false nation and its "bases"; or, Why the south can't stand. By J. Arthur Partridge ... London, E. Stanford, 1864.

xiii, [3]–60 p. 21½cm.

A view of the South's social, economic and political structure; represents the region as lacking in the qualities of a nation.

Pember, Phœbe Yates, 1823–1913.

A southern woman's story. By Phœbe Yates Pember. New York, G. W. Carleton & co.; London, S. Low, son & co., 1879.

192 p. 17 cm.

Memoirs of experiences in a Richmond hospital; especially good for accounts of hospital adjustments to wartime privations.

Pember, Phoebe Yates, 1823–1913.

A Southern woman's story; life in Confederate Richmond. Including unpublished letters written from the Chimborazo Hospital. Edited by Bell Irvin Wiley. Jackson, Tenn., McCowat-Mercer Press, 1959.

199 p. illus. 25 cm.

A completely new edition of the previous entry, enhanced by Wiley's elaborate introduction and some useful notes.

Petersburg, Va. Merchants and millers.

To the Senate and House of representatives of the Confederate States. [Petersburg, 1863]

3 p. 22cm.

Vigorous reactions to a Confederate commissary officer's threat to confiscate half of the available flour.

Peyton, John Lewis, 1824–1896.

The American crisis; or, Pages from the note-book of a state agent during the civil war. By John Lewis Peyton ... London, Saunders, Otley and co., 1867.

2 v. front. (port.) 21 cm.

The experiences of a North Carolina state agent in England, with too little on his trading operations.

Philpott, William Bledsoe, *ed.*

The sponsor souvenir album and history of the United Confederate veterans' reunion, 1895. Patriotic poems, war songs, romantic incidents, biographical and historical sketches. Ed. by William Bledsoe Philpott ... Houston, Tex., Sponsor souvenir co., 1895.

241, [124] p. incl. illus., ports. col. front. 26cm.

Contains some stories of the work of Southern women during the war.

Pickett, La Salle (Corbell) "*Mrs.* G. E. Pickett," 1848–1931.

What happened to me, by La Salle Corbell Pickett ... New York, Brentano's, 1917.

vi p., 1 l., 366 p. front., plates, ports. 19½cm.

Describes wartime improvisations in trousseau, gifts and entertainment for a young bride in Virginia.

Porcher, Francis Peyre, 1825–1895.

Resources of the southern fields and forests, medical, economical, and agricultural. Being also a medical botany of the Confederate States: with practical information on the useful properties of the trees, plants, and shrubs. By Francis Peyre Porcher ... Prepared and published by order of the surgeon-general, Richmond, Va. Charleston, Steampower press of Evans & Cogswell, 1863.

xxv, 601 p. 22½cm.

A contemporary survey of scientific and popular knowledge of the medicinal, economic and useful properties of trees, plants, and shrubs in the South.

Pringle, Elizabeth Watris (Allston) 1845–1921.

Chronicles of Chicora Wood, by Elizabeth W. Allston Pringle ... New York, C. Scribner's sons, 1922.

ix, 366 p. front., pl., ports. 21½ cm.

Household problems and experiences during wartime comprise one-third of this memoir by a member of one of South Carolina's distinguished families.

Protestant Episcopal Church in the Confederate States of America.

Journals. Centenary ed. in facsimile. Edited by William A. Clebsch. Austin, Tex., Church Historical Society, 1962.

1 v. (various pagings) facsims. 24 cm.

These journals of annual conventions are valuable contributions to church history. The short introduction is a tribute to the church.

Protestant Episcopal church in the U. S. A. *South Carolina (Diocese)*

Report of the Committee on the destruction of churches in the diocese of South Carolina during the late war. Presented to the Protestant Episcopal convention, May, 1868. Charleston, J. Walker, printer, 1868.

16 p. 23 cm.

Describes in detail the extent of destruction to church properties in the diocese that, by 1865, had been forced to suspend virtually all services.

Pruitt, Olga Reed, 1896–

It happened here; true stories of Holly Springs. Photos by the author. [Holly Springs? Miss., 1950]

115 p. illus. 23 cm.

Pictures of Civil War homes, stores and public buildings, with some stories taken from letters, interviews and newspapers.

Pryor, Sara Agnes (Rice) 1830–1912.

Reminiscences of peace and war, by Mrs. Roger A. Pryor ... New York, The Macmillan company; London, Macmillan & co., ltd., 1904.

xiv p., 2 l., 3–402 p. 1 illus., 6 port. (incl. front.) 21 cm.

Written years after hostilities, this is nevertheless an interesting account of a woman's reaction to war.

Pryor, Sara Agnes (Rice) "*Mrs.* R. A. Pryor," 1830–1912.
My day; reminiscences of a long life, by Mrs. Roger A. Pryor ... New York, The Macmillan company, 1909.

ix, 454 p. front., plates, ports. 21 cm.

A condensation of Mrs. Pryor's Reminiscences, with little new material added.

[**Putnam, Sallie A (Brock) "*Mrs.* Richard Putnam"**] 1845?–
Richmond during the war; four years of personal observation. By a Richmond lady. New York, G. W. Carleton & co.; [etc., etc.] 1867.

2 p. l., [ix]–xiv, [15]–389 p. 19 cm.

Soberer, and frequently more perceptive, than Mrs. Chesnut's celebrated diary; in many ways, this is a source just as valuable for events, observations, and impressions of wartime Richmond.

Putnam, Sallie A (Brock) *b.* 1845?
In Richmond during the Confederacy, by a lady of Richmond (Sallie A. Putnam) New York, R. M. McBride Co. [1961]

[4] p., reprint: 389 p. 21 cm.

An offset reproduction, badly done, of the previous entry; the short introduction adds nothing worthwhile, and no index is provided.

Raleigh and Gaston railroad company.
Proceedings of the stockholders ... at their ... annual meeting.
Raleigh, 18

v. tables (part fold.) 19–23cm.

The 1861 report gives revealing statistical information on railroad operations.

Ramsdell, Charles William, 1877–1942.
Behind the lines in the Southern Confederacy [by] Charles W. Ramsdell, edited with a foreword by Wendell H. Stephenson. Baton Rouge, La., Louisiana state university press, 1944.

xxi p., 1 l., 136 p. front. (port.) 21 cm.

Suggestive, rather than definitive, in its study of homefront problems.

Ravenel, Henry William, 1814–1887.
The private journal of Henry William Ravenel, 1859–1887; ed. by Arney Robinson Childs. Columbia, University of South Carolina Press, 1947.

xxi, 428 p. port., facsim. (on lining-papers) 24 cm.

Remembered as one of America's greatest botanists, as well as a friend of freedmen, Ravenel kept an emotional and highly revealing diary of life in war-torn South Carolina.

The **Record** of news, history and literature. v. 1; June 18–Dec. 10, 1863. Richmond, Va. [West & Johnston] 1863.

248 p. 31 x 24cm.

A miscellany of information on the Confederacy.

Remarks on the manufacture of bank notes, and other promises to pay. Addressed to the bankers of the Southern confederacy. Columbia, S. C., Steam power-press of F. G. De Fontaine & co., 1864.

31 p. front. (facsim.) 23cm.

Discusses the dangers of counterfeiting and the proper safeguards against the crime.

Richard, Jacob Fraise, 1844–
The Florence Nightingale of the Southern army; experiences of Mrs. Ella K. Newsom, Confederate nurse in the great war of 1861–65. By J. Fraise Richard. New York and Baltimore, Broadway publishing co. [c1914]

1 p. l., 5–101 p. 19½cm.

A source of some usefulness on the work of Southern women in soldiers' hospitals.

Ripley, Eliza Moore (Chinn) McHatton, 1832–1912.
From flag to flag; a woman's adventures and experiences in the South during the war, in Mexico, and in Cuba, by Eliza McHatton-Ripley ... New York, D. Appleton and company, 1889.

296 p. 18½ cm.

These reminiscences cover the Federal occupation of New Orleans and a flight to Mexico; contains a standard account of Confederate life.

Ripley, Eliza Moore (Chinn) McHatton, 1832–1912.
Social life in old New Orleans, being recollections of my girlhood, by Eliza Ripley ... New York and London, D. Appleton and company, 1912.

6 p. l., 331, ⌊1⌋ p. front., illus., plates, ports. 21½ cm.

Two interesting chapters on ersatz in the Confederacy and on a wartime wedding.

Roland, Charles P
Louisiana sugar plantations during the American Civil War. Leiden, E. J. Brill, 1957.

150 p. 25 cm.

A good monograph on one aspect of Louisiana agriculture; other, similar studies are badly needed.

Rolle, Andrew F
The lost cause; the Confederate exodus to Mexico, by Andrew F. Rolle. With a foreword by A. L. Rowse. ⌊1st ed.⌋ Norman, University of Oklahoma Press ⌊1965⌋

xv, 248 p. illus., map, ports. 23 cm.

The moving odyssey of Confederate exiles who went south of the border; well-documented.

Russell, John Henderson, 1884–
... The free Negro in Virginia, 1619–1865, by John H. Russell ... Baltimore, The Johns Hopkins press, 1913.

viii, 9–194 p. 24½ cm.

Touches but lightly on the plight of freedmen in Confederate Virginia.

Russell, *Sir* **William Howard,** 1820–1907.
Pictures of southern life, social, political, and military. Written for the London times, by William Howard Russell ... New York, J. G. Gregory, 1861.

143 p. 20½cm.

The observations of a skillful reporter during an 1861 journey from Charleston to Cairo, Ill., via New Orleans and Natchez.

Rutherford, Mildred Lewis, 1852–1928, *ed.*
Miss Rutherford's scrap book; valuable information about the South ... v. 1– Jan. 1923–
Athens, Ga., Mildred L. Rutherford ⌊1923–

v. illus. (incl. ports., music) 23 cm. 10 nos. a year.

—— Index, vol. I ... 1923–⌊vol. V ... 1927⌋ ⌊Athens? Ga., 1927⌋

7, ⌊1⌋ p. 25½ cm.

In these scraps of miscellany are articles on women's war work, army religion, Southern agriculture and medicine.

Rutherford, Mildred Lewis, 1852–1928.
Wrongs of history righted; address delivered by Miss Mildred Lewis Rutherford, historian general, United Daughters of the Confederacy ⌊at⌋ Savannah, Georgia, Friday, Nov. 13, 1914. ⌊Athens? Ga., 1914⌋

34 p. 23 cm.

Restatements in 1914 of views typical of the 1860's regarding the righteousness of the Southern cause.

Saint-Amand, Mary Scott.
A balcony in Charleston, by Mary Scott Saint-Amand, with a foreword by Archibald Rutledge. Richmond, Va., Garrett and Massie, incorporated ⌊©1941⌋

xii p., 1 l., 157 p. front. (port.) plates, facsim. 23½cm.

Contains eighteen vividly written, wartime letters from Charleston by Caroline Howard Gilman, a well-known Old South author; an excellent source for Confederate social history.

Salley, Katherine Batts, *ed.*
Life at Saint Mary's, by Katherine Batts Salley, editor, Katharine Drane Perry ⌊and others⌋ ... Chapel Hill, The University of North Carolina press, 1942.

xii, 288 p. front., plates, ports., facsims. 22cm.

An excellent firsthand account of wartime life at a fashionable N. C. girl's school.

Saxon, Elizabeth (Lyle)
A southern woman's war time reminiscences, by Mrs. Elizabeth Lyle Saxon, for the benefit of the Shiloh monument fund. ⌊Memphis, Tenn., Press of the Pilcher printing co., 1905⌋

3 p. l., ⌊9⌋–72 p. 18 cm.

Describes life in Alabama and Georgia, notably a trip from Mobile to Memphis.

Schwab, John Christopher, 1865–1916.
The Confederate States of America, 1861–1865; a financial and industrial history of the South during the civil war, by John Christopher Schwab ... New York, C. Scribner's sons, 1901.
xi, 332 p. fold. tab. 23 cm.

Still the best treatment of financial and industrial developments in wartime South.

Seat, W H.
The Confederate States of America in prophecy. By the Rev. W. H. Seat ... Nashville, Tenn., Printed for the author, at the Southern Methodist publishing house, 1861.
vi, 7–144 p. 15½cm.

An amazing interpretation of Old Testament prophecies applied to the Civil War; justified the South's cause against the forces of evil.

Silver, James Wesley, 1907–
Confederate morale and church propaganda. Tuscaloosa, Ala., Confederate Pub. Co., 1957.
120 p. 22 cm.

A first-rate book on a limited aspect of Confederate church history.

Simkins, Francis Butler, 1898–
The women of the Confederacy, by Francis Butler Simkins and James Welch Patton. Richmond and New York, Garrett and Massie, incorporated [©1936]
xiii p., 1 l., 306 p. front., port., plates, facsim. 23½ cm.

This pioneer study concentrated on social and economic aspects; contains a highly useful bibliography.

Siviter, Anna (Pierpont) 1858–1932.
Recollections of war and peace, 1861–1868, by Anna Pierpont Siviter; edited by Charles Henry Ambler ... New York, G. P. Putnam's sons, 1938.
xxxviii p., 2 l., 43–393 p. front., illus. (facsim.) plates, ports. 19½ cm.

An exhaltation of West Virginia and its first governor--who was Mrs. Siviter's father; inferior to Ambler's biography of Gov. Pierpont.

Smedes, Susan (Dabney) 1840–
A southern planter. By Susan Dabney Smedes ... 7th ed. New York, J. Pott & co., 1899.
342 p. facsim. 19½ cm.

Treats of slaves in wartime, life within Federal lines, and refugees in Macon, Ga.; first published in 1887 under the title, Memorials of a Southern Planter.

Smith, Daniel Elliott Huger.
A Charlestonian's recollections, 1846–1913. Introd. by Harold A. Mouzon, pref. by Alice R. Huger Smith. Charleston, S. C., Carolina Art Association [1950]
162 p. 23 cm.

Of value here only for the author's brief recollections of wartime life at the University of Virginia.

Smith, Ernest Ashton, 1868–
The history of the Confederate Treasury ... by Ernest Ashton Smith ... Harrisburg, Pa., Press of Harrisburg publishing co., 1901.
1 p. l., 126 p., 1 l. 25cm.

An old study that gives a survey of the experimental devices employed by the department to supply war needs.

Smith, Mary Shannon.
... Union sentiment in North Carolina during the civil war [by] Mary Shannon Smith ... [Raleigh, N. C., Meredith college, 1915]
21 p. 22½cm.

North Carolina factionalism, political and otherwise, is briefly treated.

[**Smith, Richard McAllister**] 1819–1870.
The Confederate first reader: containing selections in prose and poetry, as reading exercises for the younger children in the schools and families of the Confederate states. Richmond, Va., G. L. Bidgood, 1864.
viii, [9]–120 p. 18cm.

Prepared for Southern children "to elevate their ideas, form correct tastes, and instill proper sentiments;" must be seen to be believed!

Smith, *Mrs.* **S E D** *b.* 1817.

The soldier's friend; being a thrilling narrative of Grandma Smith's four years' experience and observation, as matron, in the hospitals of the South, during the late disastrous conflict in America. By Mrs. S. E. D. Smith. Rev. by Rev. John Little, and dedicated to the rebel soldiers. Memphis, Tenn., Printed by the Bulletin publishing company, 1867.

300 p. incl. front. (port.) 19½cm.

Mrs. Smith served in Tenn., Ga. and Miss.; almost 100 pages of this work consists of wartime letters from former patients.

The **Southern** illustrated news. v. 1– Sept. 13, 1862– [Richmond, Va., Ayres & Wade] 1862–

v. illus. (incl. ports.) 42cm.

The Confederacy's answer to Harper's Weekly, this Richmond publication contained--among other things--woodcuts and sketches of Confederate generals.

Southwood, Marion.

"Beauty and booty", the watchword of New Orleans. By Marion Southwood, a lady of New Orleans ... New York, Pub. for the author by M. Doolady, 1867.

303 p. front. 19½cm.

These personal observations describe New Orleans both before and during Federal occupation; especially good for social history.

Spencer, Carrie Esther (Samuels) *ed.*

A Civil War marriage in Virginia; reminiscences and letters, collected by Carrie Esther Spencer, Bernard Samuels [and] Walter Berry Samuels. [Boyce? Va., °1956]

vi, 267 p. illus., ports., facsims. 24 cm.

These heart-warming letters also contain information on prices and home conditions.

Steel, Samuel Augustus, 1849–

The sunny road; home life in Dixie during the war, by S. A. Steel. [Memphis, Latsch & Arnold, °1925]

160 p. front. (port.) 19½cm.

Life on a Mississippi Delta plantation recalled too many years later by a retired Methodist minister.

Sterling, Richard, 1812–1883.

Our own first reader; for the use of schools and families. By Richard Sterling ... and J. D. Campbell ... 2d ed. Greensboro, N. C., Sterling, Campbell & Albright; Richmond, Va., W. H. White, 1863.

iv, [5]–72 p. 17cm.

In addition to Southern attitudes, this volume reflects dwindling resources for Southern publishing by 1863.

Stiles, Joseph Clay, 1795–1875.

National rectitude the only true basis of national prosperity: an appeal to the Confederate States. Petersburg [Va.] Evangelical Tract Society, 1863.

(American culture series, 172: 11)

Microfilm copy (positive) made in 1961 by University Microfilms, Ann Arbor, Mich.

Collation of the original: 45 p.

A condemnation of the Southern demagogue and extortioner.

... The **Stranger's** guide and official directory for the city of Richmond ... v. 1, no. 1, October [1863] [Richmond] G. P. Evans & co., printers, 1863.

cover-title, 31 p. 16½cm.

Gives useful clues to the location and nature of governmental offices and businesses.

Swint, Henry Lee, *ed.*

Dear ones at home; letters from contraband camps. Selected and edited by Henry L. Swint. Nashville, Vanderbilt University Press, 1966.

274 p. map. 25 cm.

These letters, by two Quaker sisters who followed the Union armies and taught freedmen, add richly to the picture of life in the Confederacy.

[**Tardy,** *Mrs.* **Mary T**]

Southland writers. Biographical and critical sketches of the living female writers of the South. With extracts from their writings. By Ida Raymond [*pseud.*] ... Philadelphia, Claxton, Remsen & Haffelfinger, 1870.

2 v. 22cm.

A starting point for research into some of the Confederacy's valiant women.

Tharin, Robert Seymour Symmes, 1830–
Arbitrary arrests in the South; or, Scenes from the experience of an Alabama Unionist. By R. S. Tharin ... New York, J. Bradburn, 1863.
245 p. 16½ cm.

An emotionally unstable Unionist lawyer in Alabama, Tharin eventually gained the Federal lines; his account is a garrulous, excited narrative.

[**Thian, Raphael Prosper**]
Confederate note album, for a complete collection (with descriptive letter-press) of the various designs for face and back—selected by the Confederate treasury authorities for the currency of the Confederate States of America. 1861–1865. [Washington, R. P. Thain, 1876]
45, 88 p. 13½ x 24cm.

Describes the 88 designs selected by the C. S. Treasury for its currency.

Thornwell, James Henley, 1812–1862.
Our danger and our duty: by Rev. J. H. Thornwell, D. D. Columbia, S. C., Southern guardian steam-power press, 1862.
14 p. 20½cm.

The oft-repeated equation of the Confederate cause with the will of God.

Tichenor, Isaac Taylor, 1825–1902.
Fast-day sermon, by Rev. I. T. Tichenor, pastor of the First Baptist church of Montgomery; delivered before the General assembly of the state of Alabama, on Friday, Aug. 21st, 1863, and pub. by resolution of that body. Montgomery, Montgomery advertiser book and job printing office, 1863.
16 p. 21cm.

A sermon attributing the calamities suffered by the South to the covetousness of its people.

Todd, Richard Cecil.
Confederate finance. Athens, University of Georgia Press [1954]
x, 258 p. illus., ports. 25 cm.

A factual rather than interpretative study of the Confederate treasury department and its sources of revenue.

Tucker, John Randolph, 1823–1897.
The southern church justified in its support of the South in the present war: a lecture, delivered before the Young men's Christian association, of Richmond, on the 21st May, 1863; by Hon. John Randolph Tucker. Richmond, W. H. Clemmitt, printer, 1863.
35 p. 23cm.

God's will and the Southern cause become one and the same.

Underwood, John Levi.
The women of the Confederacy, in which is presented the heroism of the women of the Confederacy with accounts of their trials during the war and the period of reconstruction, with their ultimate triumph over adversity. Their motives and their achievements as told by writers and orators now preserved in permanent form. By Rev. J. L. Underwood ... New York and Washington, The Neale publishing company, 1906.
xvii, [19]–313 p. front. (port.) 23 cm.

Excerpts from a variety of sources recount the war work of Southern women; the whole is unbalanced and overly sentimental.

United Confederate veterans. *Arkansas division.*
Confederate women of Arkansas in the civil war, 1861–'65; memorial reminiscences. Published by the United Confederate veterans of Arkansas, November, 1907 ... Little Rock, Ark., H. G. Pugh ptg. co., 1907.
7 p. l., [17]–221 p. plates, ports. 24cm.

Useful though unbalanced monographs of a few of the thousands of women who sacrificed and suffered.

United daughters of the confederacy. *Arkansas division. Hiram L. Grinstead chapter, no. 575, Camden.*
The garden of memory; stories of the civil war as told by veterans and daughters of the confederacy; comp. by Mrs. M. A. Elliott, historian, H. L. Grinstead chapter, U. D. C., Camden, Arkansas ... Camden, Ark., Brown printing co. [1911]
3 p. l., 96 p., 2 l. incl. illus., ports. front. 25cm.

Too many stories in this potpourri are of doubtful authenticity and value.

United Daughters of the Confederacy. *Florida Division. Southern Cross Chapter No. 796, Miami.*
Memoirs & real Confederate receipts, by real daughters. Miami, 1960 [c1961]
67 p. 23 cm.

Another source for substitutes and ersatz in Confederate cooking.

United Daughters of the Confederacy. *Mississippi Division. Stephen D. Lee Chapter No. 34, Columbus.*

War reminiscences of Columbus, Mississippi, and elsewhere, 1861–1865. West Point, Miss., Printed by Sullivan's, ©1961.

33 p. illus. 23 cm.

Memories of social and economic conditions in small-town Mississippi.

United daughters of the confederacy. *Missouri division.*

Reminiscences of the women of Missouri during the sixties, gathered, compiled and published by Missouri division, United daughters of the confederacy ... [Jefferson City, The Hugh Stephens printing co., 192–?]

3 p. l., 3–311 p. 23cm.

A depiction of divided loyalties; includes the diary of a young woman banished to the South because of her Confederate sympathies.

United daughters of the confederacy. *North Carolina division. Pamlico chapter, no. 43, Washington, pub.*

The Confederate reveille, memorial edition. Published by the Pamlico chapter of the Daughters of the confederacy, Washington, N. C., May 10, 1898. Raleigh, Edwards & Broughton, printers, 1898.

162 p. incl. ports. front. 22½cm.

Another tribute to Confederate women, in this instance the heroines of the Tarheel State; some useful data will be found among the eulogies.

United daughters of the confederacy. *South Carolina division. Abbeville chapter.*

Confederate catechism of secession in Abbeville county, 1860–1865. [Abbeville? S. C., 193–?]

[8] p. 16cm.

A little book of questions and answers on conditions in the county.

United Daughters of the Confederacy. *South Carolina Division. Arthur Manigault Chapter, Georgetown.*

For love of a rebel. Georgetown, S. C. [©1964]

x, 212 p. illus. (part col.) 23 cm.

Useful for genealogy and military events; useless as social or economic history.

United daughters of the confederacy. *South Carolina division.*

South Carolina women in the confederacy. Records collected by Mrs. A. T. Smythe, Miss M. B. Poppenheim and Mrs. Thomas Taylor. Ed. and pub. by Mrs. Thomas Taylor, chairman, Mrs. Smythe, Mrs. August Kohn, Miss Poppenheim, Miss Martha B. Washington, state committee Daughters of the confederacy. Columbia, S. C., The State company, 1903–07.

2 v. pl., ports. (incl. fronts.) 24cm.

One of the better volumes in the U. D. C. series; contains excerpts from many good diaries and letters.

Virginia. State library, *Richmond.*

... Two Confederate items, ed. by W. W. Scott, law librarian. Richmond, D. Bottom, superintendent of public printing, 1927.

76 p. 23 cm.

Included in the pamphlet is the memoir of E. C. Moncure, a leading wartime Virginia jurist.

Virginia Central Rail Road Company.

Correspondence between the president of the Virginia Central Rail Road Company and the Postmaster General, in relation to postal service. Richmond, Printed by Ritchie & Dunnavant, 1864.

25 p. 23 cm.

A documentary source that shows Reagan's many problems in conducting the Postoffice Department within constitutional limits.

Waitt, Robert W 1920–

Confederate military hospitals in Richmond [by] Robert W. Waitt, Jr. Richmond, Richmond Civil War Centennial Committee, 1964.

40 p. illus., maps. 23 cm.

Popularly written, this pamphlet summarizes several hospitals and emphasizes the largest: Chimborazo.

Waitz, Julia Ellen (Le Grand) 1829–1881.

The journal of Julia Le Grand, New Orleans, 1862–1863; ed. by Kate Mason Rowland and Mrs. Morris L. Croxall. Richmond, Everett Waddey co., 1911.

318 p. front., ports. 20 cm.

Good accounts of conditions both before and after the occupation of the Gulf port.

Walker, Georgiana Freeman (Gholson) 1833–1904.
Private journal, 1862–1865, with selections from the post-war years, 1865–1876. Edited by Dwight Franklin Henderson. Tuscaloosa, Ala., Confederate Pub. Co., 1963.

148 p. port. 22 cm.

One chapter tells of Richmond in the early days of war; the work as a whole is a good introduction to blockade-running.

Walker, Jeanie Mort.
Life of Capt. Joseph Fry, the Cuban martyr. Being a faithful record of his remarkable career from childhood to the time of his heroic death at the hands of Spanish executioners; recounting his experience as an officer in the U. S. and Confederate navies, and revealing much of the inner history and secret marine service of the late civil war in America. By Jeanie Mort Walker ... Hartford, The J. B. Burr publishing co., 1875.

589 p. incl. front., plates, ports. 21 cm.

Although limited in information on blockade-running (in which Fry was involved), the book gives clues to other individuals involved in the activity.

[**Weeks, Stephen Beauregard**] 1865–1918.
... Confederate text-books. A preliminary bibliography. Washington, Govt. print. off., 1900.

cover-title, p. 1139–1155. 23cm.

This useful, annotated bibliography lists chronologically (by date of publication) all Confederate textbooks.

Western sanitary commission.
Report of the Western sanitary commission, on the white Union refugees of the South, their persecutions, sufferings, destitute condition, and the necessity of giving aid and relief on their coming to our military posts. St. Louis, Mo., Printed by R. P. Studley and co., 1864.

44 p. 22cm.

A source on the needs and suffering among both freedmen and refugees in the occupied South.

White, William Spottswood, 1800–1873.
Rev. William S. White, D. D., and his times. ⟨1800–1873⟩ An autobiography. Ed. by his son, Rev. H. M. White ... Richmond, Va., Presbyterian committee of publication, 1891.

284 p. front. (port.) 20cm.

One section of this Presbyterian minister's memoir describes life in wartime Lexington, Virginia.

Wiley, Bell Irvin, 1906–
Embattled Confederates; an illustrated history of Southerners at war. Illus. compiled by Hirst D. Milhollen. [1st ed.] New York, Harper & Row [1964]

ix, 290 p. illus., facsims., map, ports. 29 cm.

A first-rate synthesis of the best in modern scholarship on the Confederacy; exciting illustrations.

Wiley, Bell Irvin, 1906–
The plain people of the Confederacy [by] Bell Irvin Wiley. Baton Rouge, La., Louisiana state university press, 1943.

ix p., 2 l., 104 p. pl., ports. 21 cm.

Graphically describes living conditions, contributions of civilians to the war effort and waning morale as the war progressed.

Williams, Noble Calhoun, 1854–
Echoes from the battlefield; or, Southern life during the war. By Noble C. Williams ... Atlanta, Ga., The Franklin printing and publishing company, 1902.

ix, 94 p. 20½cm.

Informative on life in Atlanta, before and after Sherman's occupation of the city.

Windler, Penny Nichols.
Placid; a collection of authentic tales centering around Placid Plantation, Person and Cranville Counties, North Carolina, during the period 1861 through 1865. Sponsored by the Hampton Chapter of the United Daughters of the Confederacy. Warwick, Va., High-Iron Publishers [1961]

73 p. 22 cm.

Stories of life on a North Carolina plantation; told to a child and written down too many years later.

Wise, Jennings Cropper, 1881–
The military history of the Virginia military institute from 1839 to 1865, with appendix, maps, and illustrations, by Jennings C. Wise ... Lynchburg, Va., J. P. Bell company, inc., 1915.

576 p. front., plates, ports., maps (1 fold.) 23½ cm.

Has stood the test of time as a comprehensive, solid study of the South's most famous military school.

The **women** of the southern confederacy during the war 1861–5; original historic incidents of their heroism, suffering and devotion; published in "Our women in the war" supplements to leading newspapers in Tennessee and Mississippi, together with Arkansas memorial; clipped from original publications and arranged under direction of Gen'l C. Irvine Walker ... under whose general supervision, aiding the work for the memorials to the women of the confederacy, the various supplements were published ... Charleston, S. C. [1908]

[188] p. illus. (incl. ports.) 32 x 26½ cm.

The usual miscellany of such compilations, with little information not heretofore published.

Wood, Robert Crooke]

Confederate hand-book; a compilation of important data and other interesting and valuable matter relating to the war between the states, 1861–1865 ... [New Orleans, Graham press, ©1900]

126 p., 1 l. 1 illus., 2 col. pl. 22½ cm.

A rather disorganized collection of data on Confederate military and civilian personnel; now outdated.

Woodrow, James, 1828–1907.

Dr. James Woodrow ... Columbia, S. C., Printed by the R. L. Bryan company, 1909.

xix, 973 p. front. (port.) 23½ cm.

Character sketches by former students give some insight into this scientist who, during the war, headed a chemical laboratory at Columbia, S. C.

Wright, Louise (Wigfall) 1846–1915.

A Southern girl in '61; the war-time memories of a Confederate senator's daughter. Illustrated from contemporary ports. New York, Doubleday, Page, 1905.

xii, 258 p. illus., ports. 24 cm.

Contemporary family letters add to the usefulness of these memoirs of social and economic conditions.

THE CONFEDERACY

State and Local Studies

Thomas A. Belser, Jr.

Alabama. *Convention*, 1861.
Ordinances adopted by the people of the state of Alabama, in convention, at Montgomery, commencing on the seventh day of January, 1861. Andrew B. Moore, governor, William M. Brooks, president of the convention. Montgomery, Shorter & Reid, printers, 1861.
30, [1] p. 24½ cm.

Little more than a summary of what transpired; disappointing in many respects.

Alabama. *Laws, statutes, etc.*
Military code of the state of Alabama, revised and digested, with all amendments and additions to the end of the regular session of 1861. By P. H. Brittan, secretary of state. Montgomery, Ala., Montgomery advertiser, 1861.
95 p. 22½cm.

Regulations governing the state militia, as approved Dec. 10, 1861.

Alabama. *Convention*, 1861.
Ordinances and constitution of the state of Alabama, with the constitution of the provisional government and of the Confederate States of America. Montgomery, Barrett, Wimbish & co., printers, 1861.
152 p. 23 cm.

The ordinances indicate the legal changes necessary in the transition of the state from Union to Confederate. For debates, see W. R. Smith's work, cited later in this chapter.

Allen, V C
Rhea and Meigs Counties (Tennessee) in the Confederate War. [n. p., c1908]
126 p. col. front., ports. 19 cm.

Rosters and brief histories of thirteen infantry companies, plus biographical sketches of field and staff officers.

Amis, Moses Neal, 1849–

Historical Raleigh from its foundation in 1792; descriptive, biographical, educational, industrial, religious; reminiscences reviewed and carefully compiled ... By Moses N. Amis ... [Raleigh, Edwards & Broughton, printers] 1902.

1 p. l., [5]–230 p. incl. illus., port. 19½cm.

The most reliable study of the last capital to fall to Sherman's forces.

Andrews, Garnett.

Reminiscences of an old Georgia lawyer. By Garnett Andrews ... Atlanta, Ga., Franklin steam printing house, 1870.

vii, [9]–104 p. 22½cm.

The disappointingly thin recollections by a Unionist judge in northern Georgia--and the father of Eliza F. Andrews, who penned an even more famous and factual memoir.

Arkansas. *Adjutant-general's office.*

Report of the adjutant general of Arkansas, for the period of the late rebellion, and to November 1, 1866. Washington, Govt. print. off., 1867.

2 p. l., 278 p. 23½cm.

Concerned exclusively with Federal units raised in Arkansas; among the useful documents appended are those relating to the proposed 1864 evacuation of Fort Smith.

Arkansas. *Convention,* 1861.

Journal of both sessions of the Convention of the state of Arkansas, which were begun and held in the capitol, in the city of Little Rock. Published by authority. Little Rock, Johnson & Yerkes, state printers, 1861.

509 p. 22½cm.

The first session postpones action of secession; the second took the state out of the Union and laid down plans for defense.

Arnold, Richard Dennis, 1808–1876.

Letters of Richard D. Arnold, M. D., 1808–1876, mayor of Savannah, Georgia, first secretary of the American medical association. Edited by Richard H. Shryock ... [Durham, N. C., Duke university press, 1929]

178 p. port. 23 cm.

Particularly revealing correspondence by a learned physician and wartime mayor of Savannah.

Arthur, John Preston.

A history of Watauga County, North Carolina. With sketches of prominent families. By John Preston Arthur. Written at the request of Roy M. Brown, W. D. Farthing [and others] ... who guaranteed all costs of publication. Richmond, Everett Waddey co., 1915.

x, 364 p. front., plates, ports., coat of arms. 24cm.

A better-than-average county history; contains a good chapter on guerilla warfare in the Carolina mountain country.

Arthur, John Preston.

Western North Carolina; a history (from 1730 to 1913) by John Preston Arthur. Published by the Edward Buncombe chapter of the Daughters of the American revolution, of Asheville, N. C. Raleigh, N. C., Edwards & Broughton printing company, 1914.

710 p. incl. front. pl., ports. 23½cm.

One brief chapter sheds some light on civil and military affairs on this generally neglected region of the Confederacy.

Ashe, Samuel A'Court, 1840–

History of North Carolina, by Samuel A'Court Ashe ... Greensboro, N. C., C. L. Van Noppen, 1908–25.

2 v. front., plates, ports., maps, facsims. 24cm.

One of the better of the old multi-volume state histories; Vol. II, while dated, covers all aspects of the state's role in the conflict.

Avery, Isaac Wheeler, 1837–1897.

The history of the state of Georgia from 1850 to 1881, embracing the three important epochs: the decade before the war of 1861–5; the war; the period of reconstruction ... By I. W. Avery ... New York, Brown & Derby [c1881]

3 p. l., [vi]–x, 11–12 p., 1 l., [3]–754 p. front., ports., facsim., fold. map. 25cm.

Written by a gossipy newspaperman who was an ardent admirer of Joe Brown; handle accordingly the one-third of the work treating of the war period.

Bailey, James Henry.

Henrico home front, 1861–1865; a picture of life in Henrico County, Virginia from May, 1861, through April, 1865; based upon selections from the Minute books of the Henrico County Court. A project sponsored by the Henrico County Civil War Centennial Commission. [Richmond?] 1963.

xxiv, 275 p. illus., ports. 23 cm.

Confederate grass roots government at work; the editing is skillful and the notes are adequate.

Ball, Timothy Horton, 1826–

A glance into the great South-east; or, Clarke County, Alabama, and its surroundings, from 1540 to 1877. By Rev. T. H. Ball ... Grove Hill, Ala. [Chicago, Press of Knight & Leonard] 1882.

782 p. 20½cm.

One good chapter treats of the war in this southwestern Alabama county; contemporary letters, editorials and speeches make this work more valuable than the usual county chronicle.

Ball, William Watts, 1868–

The state that forgot: South Carolina's surrender to democracy, by William Watts Ball. Indianapolis, The Bobbs-Merrill company [c1932]

307 p. 22½ cm.

This well-researched study still remains popular because no one in a quarter-century has come forward with anything better.

Baptists. *Virginia. General association.*

Address of the Baptist general association of Virginia, June 4th, 1863 ... [n. p., 1863?]

8 p. 20cm.

A patriotic speech that blames the intransigence of Northern Christians for the war and calls upon all Southern brethern to trust in God and do their duty.

[**Barnard, Frederick Augustus Porter**] 1809–1889.

Letter to the President of the United States, by a refugee. Philadelphia, J. B. Lippincott & co., 1863.

32 p. 22½cm.

The president of the University of Mississippi bemoaned the plight of his school in wartime.

Barrett, John Gilchrist.

The Civil War in North Carolina. Chapel Hill, University of North Carolina Press [1963]

484 p. illus. 24 cm.

A detailed, scholarly account of action in North Carolina; well-written and admirably researched, it is the best study of the subject to date.

Barrett, John Gilchrist.

North Carolina as a Civil War battleground, 1861–1865. Raleigh, N. C., State Dept. of Archives and History, 1960.

99 p. illus. 23 cm.

This slim summary covers well the major military campaigns fought in the Tarheel State.

Barrett, Thomas.

The great hanging at Gainesville, Cooke county, Texas, October, A. D. 1862. By Thomas Barrett, one of the jurors empaneled to investigate and decide on what was to be done with those men, in which a story of that whole affair is given in detail with the consequences resulting from it. Gainesville, Tex., 1885.

2 p. l., 31 p. 19½cm.

A vivid--and hence chilling--account of vigilante justice in wartime; reprinted in 1961.

Bearss, Edwin C

Decision in Mississippi: Mississippi's important role in the War Between the States. [1st ed.] Jackson, Mississippi Commission on the War Between the States [1962]

xvi, 636 p. maps (part fold.) plans. 24 cm.

A minutely detailed, military study; Vicksburg is emphasized, Corinth is neglected, and the argument that Champion Hill was the turning point of the war in the West is unconvincing.

Bearss, Edwin C

Hardluck ironclad; the sinking and salvage of the Cairo, being a first-hand account of the discovery of the torpedoed Union gunboat and of operations to raise her from the bottom of the Yazoo, together with a description of artifacts found on board; including a history of the Western Flotilla of which she was a part, with numerous illustrations, and maps. By Edwin C. Bearss. [Baton Rouge] Louisiana State University Press, 1966.

xiii, 208 p. illus., maps, ports. 24 cm.

Bearrs's study is included in this catagory because the most moving sections of the book treat of efforts by Mississippians in the 1960's to raise the boat from the bottom of the Yazoo.

Bearss, Edwin C.

Steele's retreat from Camden and the Battle of Jenkin's Ferry, by Edwin C. Bearss. With an introd. by Lou Oberste. [Little Rock] Arkansas Civil War Centennial Commission [1967]

xiv, 190 p. plans, ports. 24 cm.

This military treatise, based almost entirely on the Official Records, casts little light on local affairs.

Belisle, John G.

History of Sabine parish, Louisiana, by John G. Belisle; from the first explorers and settlers to the present. [Many, La.] The Sabine banner press, 1912.

2 p. l., 3-319 p. illus. (incl. ports.) 22cm.

The one chapter on the war contains sketches of two companies in the 6th and 17th Louisiana, plus interesting recollections of the battles of Mansfield and Pleasant Hill.

Bettersworth, John Knox, 1909–

Confederate Mississippi, the people and policies of a cotton state in wartime, by John K. Bettersworth. University Station, Baton Rouge, La., Louisiana state university press, 1943.

xi, 386 p. front., plates, ports., map, 3 facsim. on 1 l. 23½cm.

An excellent, scholarly study; still the standard work on wartime Mississippi.

Bill, Alfred Hoyt, 1879–

The beleaguered city, Richmond, 1861–1865 ... by Alfred Hoyt Bill. New York, A. A. Knopf, 1946.

xiv p., 1 l., 313, xviii p., 1 l. front., plates, 2 port. on 1 l., fold. maps. 22 cm.

Interesting and colorful; yet the author was none too critical of his sources and frequently accepted rumor for fact.

Biographical and historical memoirs of eastern Arkansas, comprising a condensed history of the state, a number of biographies of distinguished citizens of the same, a brief descriptive history of each of the counties ... Chicago, St. Louis [etc.] The Goodspeed publishing co., 1890.

820 p. incl. ports. 28 x 22½cm.

Biographical and historical memoirs of northeast Arkansas, comprising a condensed history of the state ... biographies of distinguished citizens ... a brief descriptive history ... of the counties ... Chicago, Nashville and St. Louis, The Goodspeed publishing co., 1889.

981 p. ports. 28½ cm.

Biographical and historical memoirs of Pulaski, Jefferson, Lonoke, Faulkner, Grant, Saline, Perry, Garland and Hot Spring counties, Arkansas, comprising a condensed history of the state ... biographies of distinguished citizens ... [etc.] Chicago, St. Louis [etc.] The Goodspeed publishing co., 1889.

811 p. incl. pl., ports. 28 cm.

Biographical and historical memoirs of southern Arkansas, comprising a condensed history of the state ... biographies of its distinguished citizens, a brief descriptive history ... of the counties ... Chicago, St. Louis [etc.] The Goodspeed publishing company, 1890.

1088 p., 1 l. incl. ports. ports. 28½ x 23½cm.

Biographical and historical memoirs of western Arkansas, comprising a condensed history of the state ... biographies of distinguished citizens ... a brief ... history ... of the counties ... Chicago and Nashville, The Southern publishing company, 1891.

497 p. plates, port. 29cm.

The condensed histories in each volume are identical in format and but bare outlines. The principal value of the set for the historian lies in the excellent descriptions of the terrain of each county.

Birdsong, James Cook, 1843–

Brief sketches of the North Carolina state troops in the war between the states. Sketches include First, Second, Third, Fourth, Sixth, Seventh, Eleventh, Twelfth, Thirteenth, Fourteenth, Nineteenth, Twentieth, Twenty-eighth, Twenty-ninth, Thirtieth, Thirty-first, and Thirty-seventh regiments, together with First battalion of heavy artillery, Second battalion of light infantry, return of flag to Company I, Sixth regiment N. C. troops, General Lane's brigade, sketch of Henry L. Wyatt, first Confederate martyr, Lane's brigade corps of sharpshooters. Collected and comp. by James C. Birdsong ... Raleigh, N. C., J. Daniels, state printer, 1894.

213 p. 23 cm.

Sketches of the 22nd and 27th North Carolina contain interesting personal narratives; otherwise, the work has minimum usefulness.

Blackford, Charles Minor, 1833–

Campaign and battle of Lynchburg, Va. By Charles M. Blackford ... Delivered by request of the Garland-Rodes camp of Confederate veterans of Lynchburg, Virginia, June 18th, 1901. [Lynchburg, Va., Press of J. P. Bell company, 1901]

72 p. front. (port.) 19½cm.

A concise but accurate account of the repulse of Hunter's troops before Lynchburg; Blackford was not present, but he knew the participants and written record well.

Blease, Coleman Livingston, 1868–

... Destruction of property in Columbia, S. C., by Sherman's army. Speech of Hon. Cole. L. Blease, a senator from the state of South Carolina, delivered in the Senate May 15, 1930, relative to the destruction of property in Columbia, S. C., by Sherman's army. Washington, U. S. Govt. print. off., 1930.

ii, 112 p. 23cm.

A political effort, derived from both primary and secondary sources.

Bokum, Hermann, 1807–1878.

Wanderings north and south, by Hermann Bokum ... Philadelphia, King & Baird, printers, 1864.

2 p. l., 73 p. 22½cm.

Bokum's small and slanted account treats of persecutions he suffered while a refugee in East Tennessee, plus comments on a Philadelphia hospital.

Bond, Oliver James, 1865–1933.

The story of the Citadel, by Colonel O. J. Bond. Richmond, Garrett and Massie [c1936]

ix p., 1 l., 242 p. front., plates, port. 23½cm.

Much attention is given the war period in this story of one of the South's most famous military academies.

Booth, Edwin Gilliam, 1810–1886.

In war time. Two years in the confederacy and two years north. With many reminiscences of the days long before the war. By Edwin G. Booth. Philadelphia, J. D. Avil & co., 1885.

3 p. l., [3]–141, xii, 142–221 p. pl., ports. 22½cm.

The only connection between this thoroughly disorganized memoir and the Civil War is the title.

Bouligny, John Edmund, 1824–1864.

Remarks of Hon. J. E. Bouligny, on the secession of Louisiana. Delivered in the House of representatives, February 5, 1861. [n. p., 1861]

1 l. 22½cm.

A fervent plea for the Union, by the only Louisiana congressman who retained his seat after the secession of his state.

Bragg, Jefferson Davis.

Louisiana in the Confederacy, by Jefferson Davis Bragg ... Baton Rouge, La., Louisiana state university press [c1941]

ix, 341 p. 23½cm.

A good general account, with scant attention to military matters; a recent study by J. D. Winters emphasizes Bragg's inadequate research.

Brents, John A.

The patriots and guerillas of East Tennessee and Kentucky. The sufferings of the patriots. Also the experience of the author as an officer in the Union army. Including sketches of noted guerillas and distinguished patriots. By Major J. A. Brents. New York, J. A. Brents, 1863.

171 p. plates. 19cm.

An embittered commentary on an embittered section; Brents's own experiences are of some value.

Brevard, Caroline Mays, 1860–1920.

... A history of Florida from the treaty of 1763 to our own times, by Caroline Mays Brevard, edited by James Alexander Robertson. A posthumous work in two volumes published in memoriam of the author ...

Deland, Fla., The Florida state historical society, 1924–25.

2 v. fronts. (ports.) maps (1 double) 27cm.

Volume II contains six well-documented chapters on Florida's secession, organization of military forces, wartime finance, and military operations.

Brewer, Willis.

Alabama: her history, resources, war record, and public men. From 1540 to 1872. By W. Brewer ... Montgomery, Ala., Barrett & Brown, printers, 1872.

712 p. 23cm.

A useful reference work for regiments, battalions and batteries; occasionally inaccurate.

Brice, Marshall Moore.

Conquest of a valley. Charlottesville, University Press of Virginia [1965]

vii, 184 p. maps (part fold.) 24 cm.

This mistitled work treats solely and in detail of the June, 1864, engagement at Piedmont, Va.; an exhaustive study of the battle.

Bryan, Thomas Conn, 1905–

Confederate Georgia. Athens, University of Georgia Press [1953]

x, 299 p. 25 cm.

This concise but scholarly account emphasizes social and economic matters; analyses are left to the individual reader.

Butler, John Campbell, 1833–1911.

Historical record of Macon and central Georgia, containing many interesting and valuable reminiscences connected with the whole state, including numerous incidents and facts never before published and of great historic value. By John C. Butler. Macon, J. W. Burke & co., printers, 1879.

1 p. l., viii, [9]–351 p. front., illus. 19 cm.

Has one thin chapter on the war, with only casual mention of the local scene.

Cain, Cyril Edward, 1883– *ed.*

Four centuries on the Pascagoula. [State College? Miss., 1953–62]

2 v. illus. 24 cm.

Volume II includes a few worthwhile war letters, rosters of two companies in the 3rd and 27th Mississippi, notes on Ship Island prison, and a mass of genealogical data.

Cain, John Buford, 1892–

Methodism in the Mississippi conference, 1846–1870, by J. B. Cain ... Jackson, Miss., The Hawkins foundation, Mississippi conference historical society [©1939]

xx, 519 p. 19½cm.

A thoroughly reliable study that should be a model for others; heavy on the war period.

Campbell, Mary Emily (Robertson) 1905–

The attitude of Tennesseans toward the Union, 1847–1861. [1st ed.] New York, Vantage Press [1961]

308 p. illus. 21 cm.

Based on solid research, and possessed of a wealth of material, this work still suffers from poor editing and some erroneous statistics.

Capers, Ellison, *bp.*, 1837–1908.

South Carolina. By Brig.-Gen. Ellison Capers. [Atlanta, Confederate pub. co., 1899]

iv p., 1 l., 931 p. ports., 3 maps (2 double) 24cm.

Like all such volumes in the set "Confederate Military History," this one contains valuable biographical sketches at the end.

Capers, Gerald Mortimer, *jr.*

The biography of a river town; Memphis: its heroic age, by Gerald M. Capers, jr. Chapel Hill, The University of North Carolina press, 1939.

x p., 3 l., [3]–292 p. front., illus. (maps) plates, diagrs. 22½cm.

Ranked with--or against--McIlwaine's history as the best study of wartime Memphis; thoroughly researched.

Capers, Gerald Mortimer.

Occupied city; New Orleans under the Federals, 1862–1865 [by] Gerald M. Capers. [Lexington] University of Kentucky Press [1965]

ix, 248 p. maps. 23 cm.

The best study of a Southern city under wartime military occupation; rich in both social and economic data.

Cardozo, Jacob Newton.

Reminiscences of Charleston. By J. N. Cardozo. Charleston, J. Walker, printer, 1866.

144 p. 19 cm.

Over half of this little-known work treats of the author's wartime experiences.

Carse, Robert, 1903–

Department of the South; Hilton Head Island in the Civil War. Columbia, S. C., State Print. Co., 1961.

156 p. illus. 28 cm.

A highly illustrated survey of a coastal district attacked and occupied early in the war; overly heavy in military matters.

Caskey, Willie Malvin.

Secession and restoration by Louisiana, by Willie Malvin Caskey, with a foreword by Frank Lawrence Owsley. University, La., Louisiana state university press, 1938.

xi, [1], 318 p. 9 maps. 23½ cm.

A scholarly work that stresses economic and political aspects at the happy expense of military matters.

Cauthen, Charles Edward.

South Carolina goes to war, 1860–1865. Chapel Hill, University of North Carolina Press, 1950.

vii, 256 p. 23 cm.

Limited attention to social and economic problems in this political history of Confederate South Carolina.

Centennial news letter. v. 1–
Apr. 1959–
Richmond, Virginia Civil War Commission.

v. illus. 28 cm.

Has occasional items of note on the Confederate capital.

Chamberlayne, Edwin H *jr., comp.*

Record of the Richmond city and Henrico County, Virgina, troops, Confederate States army. (Series no. [1]–10) Comp. by E. H. Chamberlayne, jr., serg't "D" co., 1st Va. reg't infantry, C. S. A. Richmond, W. E. Jones, printer [etc.] 1879.

10 v. fold. tab. 23cm.

Contains service records of field and staff officers of the 1st Virginia, together with a detailed roster of the Richmond Grays, 1st--later 12th--Virginia.

Chandler, Greene Callier, 1829–1905.

Journal and speeches. With foreword by Walter Chandler. [Memphis? Tenn., 1954, °1953]

244 p. illus. 22 cm.

This journal is so badly mangled by editing as to be useless, yet it contains a number of wartime letters by family members.

Christian, William Asbury, 1866–1936.

Lynchburg and its people. By W. Asbury Christian. Lynchburg, J. P. Bell company, printers, 1900.

463 p. front., plates, ports. 20 cm.

Poorer than the author's study of Richmond; contains disappointingly little on this strategic city's role in the war.

Christian, William Asbury.

Richmond, her past and present, by W. Asbury Christian ... Richmond, Va., Manufactured by L. H. Jenkins, 1912.

3 p. l., [v]–vi p., 1 l., 618 p. col. front. (port.) plates (1 fold.) map. 24½cm.

One of the better histories of Richmond--though, like the others, its omissions equal its inclusions.

Claiborne, John Herbert, 1828–1905.

Seventy-five years in old Virginia; with some account of the life of the author and some history of the people amongst whom his lot was cast,—their character, their condition, and their conduct before the war, during the war and after the war, by John Herbert Claiborne ... New York and Washington, The Neale publishing company, 1904.

xvi, [17], 360 p. 2 port. (incl. front.) 22½cm.

Revealing for this observant physician's reminiscences of life in wartime Petersburg, Va.

Clapp, Theodore, 1792–1866.

Parson Clapp of the Strangers' Church of New Orleans, edited by John Duffy. Baton Rouge, Louisiana State University Press [1957]

ix, 191 p. illus., port., facsim. 24 cm.

Sketches and recollections by a likable minister who spent thirty-five years in New Orleans.

Clark, Richard H 1824–1896.

Memoirs of Judge Richard H. Clark, ed. by Lollie Belle Wylie. Atlanta, Ga., Franklin printing and publishing company, 1898.

xii, 407 p. front. (port.) 22½ cm.

A judge's recollections of Georgia politics; especially good for viewpoints on Joe Brown, A. H. Stephens and the Cobb brothers.

Clarke, H C *of Vicksburg, Miss.*

Diary of the war for separation, a daily chronicle of the principal events and history of the present revolution, to which is added notes and descriptions of all the great battles, including Walker's narrative of the battle of Shiloh. By H. C. Clarke ... [Augusta, Ga., Steam press of Chronicle & sentinel, 1862]

191 p. 20½cm.

The sometimes revealing and always interesting journal of Vicksburg's leading wartime printer.

Clewell, John Henry, 1855–

History of Wachovia in North Carolina; the Unitas fratrum or Moravian church in North Carolina during a century and a half, 1752–1902, from the original German and English manuscripts and records in the Wachovia archives, Salem, North Carolina, by John Henry Clewell, PH. D. New York, Doubleday, Page & company, 1902.

xiv, 365 p. front., illus. (incl. maps, plans) plates, ports. 23cm.

The original manuscripts and records of the Wachovia archives serve as the basis for the one chapter treating of the war period.

Clinton, Matthew William.

Tuscaloosa, Alabama: its early days, 1816–1865. Tuscaloosa, Zonta Club, 1958.

179 p. illus. 22 cm.

The final chapter is a good survey of wartime Tuscaloosa, its generals, hospitals, industries and citizens. The burning of the University of Alabama is adequately covered.

Coleman, Johnie W
Centennial in commemoration of the Civil War, Marietta, Cobb County & North Georgia: 1861–1865, 1961–1965. Marietta, Ga., ©1961.

unpaged. illus. 28 cm.

Local centennial froth; nothing for the scholar, serious or otherwise.

Conerly, Luke Ward, 1841–
Pike county, Mississippi, 1798–1876; pioneer families and Confederate soldiers, reconstruction and redemption, by Luke Ward Conerly. Nashville, Tenn., Brandon printing company, 1909.

368 p. incl. front., illus., ports. col. pl. 22½cm.

Has battle records and muster rolls for eleven county companies, plus biographical sketches of some officers and reminiscences of others; a good primary source.

The **Confederate** records of the state of Georgia, compiled and published under authority of the Legislature by Allen D. Candler ...
Atlanta, Ga., C. P. Byrd, state printer, 1909–

v. 26cm.

Extremely useful documents for Georgia's wartime economic problems; five volumes were printed; another--in manuscript form--is in the Georgia Archives.

Connelly, Thomas Lawrence.
Army of the heartland; the Army of Tennessee, 1861–1862. Baton Rouge, Louisiana State University Press [1967]

xii, 305 p. illus., maps. 25 cm.

Although this first of two planned volumes more aptly belongs under "Military Campaigns," it is included here because of the good light it throws on conditions in wartime Tennessee.

Conrad, August, 1842?–
The destruction of Columbia, S. C. A translation from the German by Wm. H. Pleasants, of 19th, 20th, 21st, and 22d chapters of "Lights and shadows in American life during the war of secession", by August Conrad. Published at Hanover, 1879. Roanoke, Va., The Stone printing and manufacturing company, 1902.

31 p. 23cm.

A German resident of the city related his personal experiences during the time of terror and blamed Federal troops for the destruction.

Corley, Florence Fleming.
Confederate City, Augusta, Georgia, 1860–1865. Columbia, University of South Carolina Press, 1960.

xiv, 130 p. illus., map. 29 cm.

An outgrowth of a master's thesis; contains a balanced narrative and excellent illustrations.

Couper, William, 1884–
One hundred years at V. M. I., by Colonel William Couper; with a foreword by General George C. Marshall ... Richmond, Va., Garrett and Massie, incorporated [©1939–

v. fronts., illus. (incl. plans) plates (part double) ports., facsims. (1 double) 23½ cm.

The definitive history of the academy; the whole of Vol. II and one third of Vol. III provide a wealth of data on the war years.

Dabney, Robert Lewis, 1820–1898.
A defence of Virginia, ⟨and through her, of the South,⟩ in recent and pending contests against the sectional party. By Prof. Robert L. Dabney ... New York, E. J. Hale & son, 1867.

356 p. 22cm.

A learned Presbyterian minister defended both slavery and Virginia's erstwhile support of it.

Davenport, Francis Garvin, 1905–
Cultural life in Nashville on the eve of the civil war, by F. Garvin Davenport ... Chapel Hill, The University of North Carolina press, 1941.

x p., 2 l., 232 p. front. 23½cm.

This superior work provides an excellent picture of life in a large Southern city at the outbreak of war.

Davis, Edwin Adams, 1904– *ed.*
Heritage of valor; the picture story of Louisiana in the Confederacy. Baton Rouge, Louisiana State Archives & Records Commission, 1964.

xv, 212 p. (chiefly illus., facsims., maps, plans, ports.) 28 cm.

Of limited effectiveness for social and economic history.

Davis, Edwin Adams, 1904–
Heroic years: Louisiana in the War for Southern Independence; WBRZ–TV 1964 lectures in Louisiana history. Baton Rouge, Bureau of Educational Materials and Research, College of Education, Louisiana State University [°1964]
xv, 130 p. illus. 24 cm.

A series of TV lectures slanted for local chauvinism and "students of Louisiana history."

Davis, Edwin Adams, 1904–
Louisiana, a narrative history. 2d ed. Baton Rouge, Claitor's Book Store, 1965.
xi, 394 p. illus. 27 cm.

A textbook-history naturally inferior to studies by Bragg and Winter; still, a good starting point.

Davis, Nora M *comp.*
Military and naval operations in South Carolina, 1860–1865: a chronological list, with references to sources of further information. With a foreword by W. Edwin Hemphill. Columbia, Published by the South Carolina Archives Dept. for the South Carolina Confederate War Centennial Commission, 1959.
[24] p. 23 cm.

Chronologically lists 227 operations, with references to appropriate volumes of the Official Records and/or other sources.

Davis, Reuben, 1813–1890.
Recollections of Mississippi and Mississippians, by Reuben Davis. Boston and New York, Houghton, Mifflin and company, 1889.
vi, 446 p. front. (port.) 22cm.

Revealing for state politics during the war period; fortunately, age had mellowed the fiery Davis when he penned these memoirs.

Davis, Thomas Frederick, 1877–
History of early Jacksonville, Florida; being an authentic record of events from the earliest times to and including the civil war, by Thomas Frederick Davis. Jacksonville, The H. & W. B. Drew company, 1911.
7 p. l., 190 p. 2 pl., group of ports., 2 plans. 21cm.

Contains some material not in Davis' better-known work (cited next) on local military units.

Davis, Thomas Frederick, 1877–
History of Jacksonville, Florida and vicinity, 1513 to 1924, by T. Frederick Davis ... [Jacksonville, Fla.] The Florida historical society, 1925.
2 p. l., 513 p. illus., plates (part double) maps (1 double) plans (part double) 23½cm.

More detailed than the previous work; Davis rightly deplored the resulting destruction of the city records, which he might otherwise have used to advantage.

Davis, Thomas Frederick, 1877–1946.
History of Jacksonville, Florida, and vicinity, 1513 to 1924. A facsim. reproduction of the 1925 ed. with introd. by Richard A. Martin. Gainesville, University of Florida Press, 1964.
xxxi, 513 p. illus., col. coat of arms, maps, plans, ports. 24 cm.

A facsimile reprint of the previous entry; sheds no additional light on Jacksonville during the war.

Davis, William Watson, 1884–
The civil war and reconstruction in Florida, by William Watson Davis ... New York, 1913.
2 p. l., vii–xxvi, 771 p. 24½cm.

Thanks to solid scholarship, this is still the basic work with which to begin any study of wartime Florida.

Davis, William Watson, 1884–1960.
The Civil War and Reconstruction in Florida. A facsim. reproduction of the 1913 ed. with introd. by Fletcher M. Green. Gainesville, University of Florida Press, 1964.
xlv, xxvi, 747, 20 p. col. coat of arms, ports. 22 cm.

A superb reprint of the previous entry; Fletcher Green's introduction should be "required reading" for all students of American history.

De Jarnette, Daniel C 1822–1881.
Secession of South Carolina. Speech of Hon. D. C. De Jarnette, of Virginia, in the House of representatives, January 10, 1861. [Washington, Printed at the office of the Congressional globe, 1861]
7 p. 24½cm.

A spirited, legalistic defense of the right of secession, culminating in a call for Virginia to stand with the South.

De Leon, Thomas Cooper, 1839–1914.

Four years in Rebel capitals; an inside view of life in the southern confederacy, from birth to death. From original notes, collated in the years 1861 to 1865, by T. C. De Leon ... Mobile, Ala., The Gossip printing co., 1890.

6, vii, 11–376 p. 22½cm.

Despite his journalistic style, De Leon showed perceptiveness and maturity of judgement. This is one of the most frequently cited of Confederate studies.

De Leon, Thomas Cooper, 1839–1914.

Four years in rebel capitals: an inside view of life in the Southern Confederacy, from birth to death. With a new introd. by E. B. Long. New York, Collier Books [1962]

416 p. 18 cm.

A paperback reprint of the previous entry; enhanced by the editor's sprightly biographical introduction.

[Demby, James William]

Mysteries and miseries of Arkansas; or, A defence of the loyalty of the state. By a refugee. St. Louis, The author, 1863.

88 p. 18½cm.

A bitter criticism of Federal policy in the Southwest, expecially toward Arkansas volunteers for the Union army; yet it contains passionate pleas for support of the Union cause.

Denman, Clarence Phillips, 1897–

The secession movement in Alabama, by Clarence Phillips Denman ... Montgomery, Alabama state department of archives and history, 1933.

xiii, 190 p. incl. front., illus. (maps) 19½ cm.

Still the standard study, but thin and dated; the emphasis is on the 1850's.

Denson, A Clark.

Westmoreland; or, Secession ferocity at the breaking out of the rebellion. Southern barbarism—minute men and citizens firing into the steamer Westmoreland, crowded with men, women and children, at Napoleon, Arkansas, in 1861. By A. C. Denson ... Saint Louis, P. M. Pinckard, printer, 1865.

48, [A]–K, [1], [A]–H p. 18cm.

This diatribe--a typical example of "waving the bloody shirt"--concerns the steamboat Westmoreland and events in and around Memphis, Tennessee.

The **Early** history of Bryan and the surrounding area. Narrative prepared by Joseph Milton Nance. [Bryan, Tex.] Hood's Brigade-Bryan Centennial Committee, 1962.

[64] p. illus., maps, ports. 28 cm.

Too cursory to be of high value, but a fairly reliable introduction to the wartime activities of one Texas county.

East, Charles.

Four Louisiana Civil War stories, by Charles East [and others] Baton Rouge, La., Louisiana Civil War Centennial Commission, 1961.

36 p. illus. 23 cm.

Mildly entertaining, but of no value to the serious student of the war.

East Tennessee relief association at Knoxville.

Report to the East Tennessee relief association at Knoxville; with tabular statements from the general agent, etc. by Thomas W. Humes, chairman of the committee. To which are appended the proceedings commemorative of the death of Edward Everett. Knoxville, Printed for the Association, 1865.

50 p. 23cm.

Lists the sources, kind, quantity, and value of food supplies purchased for the society; illustrates the work of Northern benevolent groups.

Elzas, Barnett Abraham, 1867–

Leaves from my historical scrap book, by Barnett A. Elzas ... Charleston, S. C., 1907.

[44] p. 21½cm.

Ten articles, originally published serially in a newspaper, provide insights into Jewish affairs in wartime Charleston.

Eno, Clara Bertha, 1854–

History of Crawford County, Arkansas. Van Buren, Press-Argus [1951]

499 p. illus., port. 24 cm.

Although published when the author was ninety-five, this study is by one of the better amateur historians; contains a number of personal reminiscences.

Everett, Edward, 1794–1865.
Account of the fund for the relief of east Tennessee; with a complete list of the contributors. By Edward Everett, chairman of the Committee. Boston, Little, Brown and company, 1864.
99 p. 22cm.

An unabridged copy of the stirring address condensed in the title two items previous.

Farber, James.
Fort Worth in the Civil War, as published in the Fort Worth Star-telegram. Belton, Tex., Peter Hansbrough Bell Press, 1960.
58 p. illus. 23 cm.

Another compilation that first appeared as a series of newspaper articles; more slanted for popular consumption than for scholarly use.

Farber, James.
Texas, C. S. A.; a spotlight on disaster. New York, Jackson Co. [1947]
xii, 265 p. front., map (on lining papers) 24 cm.

Superficial, opinionated and undocumented; intended for popular consumption.

Farmer, H H *M. D.*
Virginia before and during the war. By H. H. Farmer, M. D. Henderson, Ky., The author, 1892.
102 p. 22½cm.

Fiction purporting to be fact; replete with conversations incredible even for a 19th century volume.

Felton, *Mrs.* **Rebecca (Latimer) 1835–1930.**
"My memoirs of Georgia politics," written and published by Mrs. William H. Felton after she had reached her 75th birthday ... Atlanta, Ga., The Index printing company, 1911.
viii, [5]–680 p. illus., plates, ports. 23cm.

As contentious as it is biased; should be handled gingerly.

Ferguson, John Lewis, 1926– *ed.*
Arkansas and the Civil War, edited by John L. Ferguson. [Little Rock, Ark., Pioneer Press, 1965]
ix, 364 p. illus. (part col.) maps, ports. 24 cm.

Intended for teachers of Arkansas history, this work contains selections from printed sources, plus 43 pages of "facts and figures."

Fertig, James Walter.
... The secession and reconstruction of Tennessee ... By James Walter Fertig, A. M. Chicago, The University of Chicago press, 1898.
2 p. l., [7]–108 p. 23½cm.

Dated and somewhat limited in scope, this study contains useful data on the state's civil and military government.

Ficklen, John Rose, 1858–1907.
... History of reconstruction in Louisiana (through 1868) by John Rose Ficklen ... Baltimore, The Johns Hopkins press, 1910.
ix, 7–234 p. 25 cm.

A pioneer study, published posthumously from the author's notes; devotes five fact-filled chapters to wartime reconstruction.

Flanders, Bertram Holland, 1892-
Early Georgia magazines; literary periodicals to 1865, by Bertram Holland Flanders. Athens, The University of Georgia press, 1944.
xiv, 289 p. illus. (map) 22cm.

A simple bibliography that lists and rarely annotates; of use to those who research into the state's wartime history.

Fleming, Walter Lynwood, 1874–
Civil war and reconstruction in Alabama, by Walter L. Fleming ... New York, The Columbia university press, The Macmillan company, agents; [etc., etc.] 1905.
xxiii, 815 p. illus. (incl. maps) plates, ports., facsims. 23½cm.

Fleming's biased treatment of Reconstruction does not alter this work's status as the best study of Alabama suring the war years; probably the best of the "Dunning" studies.

Florida. *Board of state institutions.*

Soldiers of Florida in the Seminole Indian, civil and Spanish-American wars. Prepared and pub. under the supervision of the Board of state institutions, as authorized by chapter 2203, laws of Florida, approved May 14, 1903. ⌊Live Oak, Fla., Democrat print, 1903?⌋

368 p. 24½cm.

Brief histories and annotated muster rolls exist for the major units; also contains a list of medical officers and useful biographical sketches of 15 generals.

Florida. *Supreme Court.*

Cases adjudicated. v. 1-160; 1846/47-1948. Deland ⌊etc.⌋

161 v. 21-24 cm.

Florida justice proceeds as usual; Vol. IX covers 1861; Vol. X, 1862-1864; and Vol. XI, 1865.

Florida a hundred years ago. Dec. 1960–

⌊Coral Gables?⌋

v. 29 cm.

Samuel Proctor prepared the one volume printed; this chronology is useful as a starting point.

Folsom, James Madison, 1838–

Heroes and martyrs of Georgia. Georgia's record in the revolution of 1861. By James M. Folsom. Macon, Ga., Burke, Boykin & company, 1864.

164 p. 22 cm.

Brief histories of 17 Georgia units; written by officers of the units while under fire at Petersburg; the statistics are not as accurate as the historical summaries.

Fondé, Charles H.

An account of the great explosion of the United States ordnance stores, which occured ⌊!⌋ in Mobile, on the 25th day of May, 1865. Together with the proceedings of the principal sufferers ... and an appeal to the United States government for indemnity ... Written and compiled by Charles H. Fondé. Mobile, H. Farrow & co., printers, 1869.

12 p., 50 l., ⌊2⌋ p., 1 l. plans. 23 cm.

A detailed, accurate description of the property destroyed by an accidental explosion that gutted most of Mobile's business district.

Ford, John Salmon.

Rip Ford's Texas, John Salmon Ford. Edited with an introd. and commentary by Stephen B. Oates. Austin, University of Texas Press ⌊1963⌋

xlviii, 519 p. port., facsim. 24 cm.

A well-edited abridgement of this extraordinary Texan's voluminous manuscript memoirs.

Fortier, Alcée, 1856–1914.

A history of Louisiana, by Alcée Fortier ... ⌊Ed. de bibliophile⌋ New York, Goupil & co. of Paris, Manzi, Joyant & co., successors, 1904.

4 v. col. fronts., plates, ports., maps. 29cm.

The classic work in its day; now superseded by a number of studies.

Fortier, Alcée, 1856–1914.

Louisiana studies. Literature, customs and dialects, history and education. By Alcée Fortier ... New Orleans, F. F. Hansell & bro. ⌊1894⌋

vi, 307 p. 19½cm.

A potpourri of the five fields listed in the subtitle; somewhat vague on every subject.

Franklin, John Hope, 1915–

The militant South, 1800–1861. Cambridge, Belknap Press of Harvard University Press, 1956.

317 p. 22 cm.

Highly slanted background reading; the author comes extremely close to blaming Southern militancy for an inevitable conflict.

Friends, Society of. *North Carolina. Yearly meeting.*

An account of the sufferings of Friends of North Carolina Yearly meeting, in support of their testimony against war, from 1861 to 1865. Pub. by order of the representatives of North Carolina Yearly meeting of Friends. Baltimore, Press of W. K. Boyle, 1868.

28 p. 22½ cm.

Too self-pitying for the stern scholar, but a revealing commentary on how deeply war cut into all facets of life.

Fry, *Mrs.* **Anna M (Gayle)**

Memories of old Cahaba, by Anna M. Gayle Fry. Nashville, Tenn., Dallas, Tex., Printed for the author, Publiching house of the M. E. church, South, 1908.

128 p. illus., plates. 19½cm.

A good description of the city's wartime residences, businesses, churches and citizens, with several references as well to the 5th Alabama.

Gardner, Bettie Sue.

In memory of the Confederate veterans of Rockingham County, North Carolina. Reidsville, N. C., ©1961.

29 l. 31 cm.

Eulogies as superficial as they are cursory.

Garrett, Jill Knight.

The Civil War in Maury County, Tennessee, by Jill K. Garrett and Marise P. Lightfoot. [Columbia? Tenn., 1966]

265 p. ports. 28 cm.

A thick, mimeographed collection of soldiers' diaries, memoirs, muster rolls, newspaper items, etc.; the quality of the material ranges from excellent to useless.

Georgia. *Civil War Centennial Commission.*

The Civil War centennial; to commemorate the War Between the States, to honor our Confederate heroes, to tell the true story of Georgia's role in the conflict [and] to dramatize the great ideals that are the basis of our freedom and tradition. [Atlanta, 1960?]

35 p. illus. 20 cm.

One of many such publications that heralded the approaching Centennial.

Georgia. *Convention,* 1861.

Journal of the public and secret proceedings of the Convention of the people of Georgia, held in Milledgeville and Savannah in 1861. Together with the ordinances adopted. Pub. by order of the convention. (From state archives.)

(*In* The Confederate records of the state of Georgia. Atlanta, Ga., 1909. 26cm. v. 1, p. 212-773)

The source for the 1861 secession convention; similar works exist for the other Southern states.

Georgia. *Convention, 1861.*

Journal of the public and secret proceedings of the Convention of the people of Georgia, held in Milledgeville [Jan. 16–25] and Savannah [March 7–23] in 1861. Together with the Ordinances adopted. Pub. by order of the convention. Milledgeville, Ga., Boughton, Nisbet & Barnes, state printers, 1861.

416 p. 23 cm.

Motions, resolutions, ordinances proposed, ordinances adopted, votes of delegates, but no record of debate.

Georgia. *General assembly.*

Papers relative to the mission of Hon. T. Butler King to Europe. Milledgeville, Ga., Confederate union power press, 1863.

16 p. 22 cm.

Includes King's reports on his partially successful, 1861-1862 efforts to get European packet lines to Savannah; also contains his widely published letter to Lord John Russell.

Georgia. *General assembly.*

... Resolutions expressive of the determination of Georgia to prosecute the present war with the utmost vigor and energy. [Augusta, 1864]

2 p. 24½cm.

Georgia's assembly pledged in Jan., 1864, that the state would fight until Confederate independence was "unconditionally acknowledged" by Federal authorities.

Georgia. *Historical Commission.*

Georgia Civil War Historical markers. [Atlanta, 1964]

195 p. maps. 22 cm.

This useless listing contains both the location and the wording of Georgia's numerous highway markers; especially helpful for the tourist.

Georgia. *Soldier roster commission.*

Report. 1904–
[Atlanta, 1904–

v. 23cm.

Chairman Clement A. Evans reported to the General Assembly on the expenditures and progress made in collecting state muster rolls.

Georgia. *State Division of Confederate Pensions and Records.*
Roster of the Confederate soldiers of Georgia, 1861–1865 [compiled by] Lillian Henderson [director. Hapeville, Ga., Longino & Porter, 1959–
v. 24 cm.

The six volumes published to date provide detailed muster rolls of all Georgia infantry regiments; contains each man's service record and, where known, his postwar career.

Gibbes, James Guiguard, 1829–
Who burnt Columbia? By Col. James G. Gibbes. Newberry, S. C., E. H. Aull company, 1902.
137, iii p. front., ports. 23½cm.

A number of depositions of pro-Southern "witnesses" to the burning of the town, together with testimony "clearing" Sherman of any deliberate destruction.

Gold, Pleasant Daniel, 1876–
History of Duval County, Florida, by Pleasant Daniel Gold ... also biographies of men and women who have done their part in making Duval County, past and present. St. Augustine, Fla., The Record company, 1928.
693 p. incl. illus., ports. front., ports. 27½cm.

Three chapters are devoted to the war around Jacksonville, and are based on the Official Records; a trifle superior to the majority of county histories.

Govan, Gilbert Eaton, 1892–
The Chattanooga country, 1540–1951: from tomahawks to TVA, by Gilbert E. Govan and James W. Livingood. [1st ed.] New York, Dutton, 1952.
509 p. map (on lining papers) 22 cm.

A fair introduction to the subject; the wartime section is predominately social in content.

Graham, Henry Tucker, 1865–
An old manse [by] Henry Tucker Graham. 2d ed. Richmond, Va., Whittet & Shepperson, printers, 1916.
14 p. 16½ cm.

An informal but readable summary of "Stonewall" Jackson's famous headquarters in Winchester, Va.

Green, Juanita Whitaker, 1905–
The history of Union County, Arkansas. [Stephens? Ark.] ©1954.
201 l. illus. 26 cm.

Contains many wartime reminiscences by aged veterans and elderly civilians--all recorded in interviews held in the 1930's; some gold exists among the dross.

Greer, James Kimmins, 1896–
Louisiana politics, 1845–1861, by James K. Greer. Baton Rouge, La., Ramires-Jones printing co., 1930.
295 p. illus. (maps) 23cm.

The last chapter analyzes the struggle between cooperationists and secessionists prior to the secession convention; Greer relied heavily on contemporary newspapers.

Griffin, Clarence W 1904–
History of old Tryon and Rutherford counties, North Carolina, 1730–1936, by Clarence W. Griffin ... Asheville, N. C., The Miller printing company, 1937.
xv, 640 p. front., plates. 24cm.

Includes muster rolls with the names and service records of most of the 1,734 men these counties furnished to the Confederacy.

Grimsley, Daniel Amon, 1840–
Battles in Culpeper county, Virginia, 1861–1865. And other articles by Major Daniel A. Grimsley, of the sixth Virginia cavalry. Compiled and published by Raleigh Travers Green, Culpeper, Virginia. [Culpeper, Va., Exponent printing office] 1900.
2 p. l., 56 p. 22½cm.

With a keen memory and a flair for topographical description, Grimsley stressed the strategic importance of the county and recounted several actions in which he fought as a cavalry officer.

Guide to North Carolina historical highway markers.
Raleigh, 19
v. illus. 23 x 11 cm.

Markedly inferior to the Centennial publications of Georgia, Tennessee and Virginia; yet this is not the fault of the original compilers.

Hagan, Jane Gray.
The story of Danville. New York, Stratford House, 1950.
ix, 166 p. illus., ports. 24 cm.

Even though this is the most complete history of "The Last Capital of the Confederacy," sentimental statistics and loose organization render it of little use.

Hahn, George W 1842- *ed.*
The Catawba soldier of the civil war. A sketch of every soldier from Catawba County, North Carolina, with the photograph, biographical sketch, and reminiscence of many of them, together with a sketch of Catawba County from 1860 to 1911 ... Ed. and comp. by Prof. Geo. W. Hahn ... Hickory, N. C., Clay printing co., 1911.
2 p. l., [7]-385 p. illus. (incl. ports.) 23cm.

Lists almost 1,500 men who fought for the Confederacy, with biographical sketches and/or reminiscences of many.

[**Hale, Jonathan D**] *comp.*
... The bloody shirt ... Copyright secured by Dr. J. D. Hale. [Washington? D. C., 1888?]
cover-title, [1], 51 p. fold. facsim. (incl. port.) 16½cm.

Embittered over his failure to collect damages for property loss, Hale published this collection of "eyewitness" accounts of guerilla destruction hoping to gain support for his case.

Hale, Jonathan D.
Champ Furguson: a sketch of the war in East Tennessee detailing some of the awful murders on the border, and describing one of the leading spirits of the rebellion. Written by Dr. Hale. Cincinnati, 1862.
20 p. 19cm.

A Tennessee loyalist with obvious bias and a penchant for creating conversations gave his account of Confederate guerilla depredations perpetrated in the first year of the war.

Hamilton, Joseph Grégoire de Roulhac, 1878-
Reconstruction in North Carolina ... Raleigh, N. C., Presses of Edwards & Broughton [c1906]
264 p., 1 l. 22cm.

Hamilton's second chapter offers an unsympathetic treatment of the efforts in 1861-1863 to establish a Union government in eastern North Carolina.

Harris, D W
The history of Claiborne Parish, Louisiana, from its incorporation in 1828 to the close of the year 1885, with sketches of pioneer life in north Louisiana ... also the muster and death rolls of her sons in the late bloody war ... Comp. by D. W. Harris & B. M. Hulse. New Orleans, Press of W. B. Stansbury & co., 1886.
4 p. l., [7]-263, [1] p. 18 cm.

Emphasizes the 1828-1885 period; includes some useful data on the war period, plus the usual incomplete muster rolls.

Harris, W A.
The record of Fort Sumter, from its occupation by Major Anderson, to its reduction by South Carolina troops during the administration of Governor Pickens. Comp. by W. A. Harris ... Columbia, S. C., South Carolinian steam job printing office, 1862.
50 p. 23 cm.

A collection of letters, reports, speeches, etc., the whole giving the state's official view of the Sumter crisis; Confederate documents are conspicuously absent.

Hawkins, Rush Christopher, 1831-1920.
An account of the assassination of loyal citizens of North Carolina, for having served in the Union army, which took place at Kingston in the months of February and March, 1864. By Rush C. Hawkins. New York [J. H. Folan, printer] 1897.
46 p., 1 l. 22cm.

Solely military, this slanted narrative treats of a famous mass execution conducted by the Confederates at a critical period of the war.

Hayes, D J
Civil War military and naval engagements in the State of Texas. Houston, Tex., c1961.
8 p. illus. 22 cm.

Cursory accounts of seven actions (including three in Arizona-New Mexico), followed by an incomplete chronology gleaned from the Official Records.

Hays, Louise (Frederick) 1881-
History of Macon county, Georgia, by Louise Frederick Hays ... Atlanta, Ga., Stein printing company, 1933.
803, [21] p. front. (port.) illus. (incl. ports.) maps (1 mounted, fold.) 24cm.

Excerpts from soldiers' letters, grand jury presentments, notes on units and officers, and a few memoirs give this book some value.

Hempstead, Fay, 1847–

A pictorial history of Arkansas, from earliest times to the year 1890. A full and complete account, embracing the Indian tribes occupying the country; the early French and Spanish explorers and governors; the colonial period; the Louisiana purchase; the periods of the territory, the state, the civil war, and the subsequent period. Also, an extended history of each county in the order of formation, and of the principal cities and towns; together with biographical notices of distinguished and prominent citizens ... By Fay Hempstead. St. Louis and New York, N. D. Thompson publishing company, 1890.

xi, v–viii p., 1 l., 17–1240 p. front., illus. (incl. ports., maps.) fold. maps. 24cm.

One of the better of the older state histories; contains the usual: service records, notes on officers, etc., but slights wartime politics.

Henderson, Harry McCorry.

Texas in the Confederacy. San Antonio, Naylor Co. [1955]

166 p. 22 cm.

These brief histories and/or registers of famous Texas commands contain a number of factual errors and should be used with caution.

Herndon, Dallas Tabor, 1878–

Annals of Arkansas, 1947; a narrative historical edition, revising, reediting and continuing "A centennial history of Arkansas," preserving the record of the growth and development of the state and chronicling the genealogical and memorial records of its prominent families and personages. Hopkinsville, Ky., Historical Record Assn. [1947?]

4 v. (xxxix, 2000 p.) illus., ports. 27 cm.

A continuation of the work cited next, this set provides a fair amount of political, social and economic history.

Herndon, Dallas Tabor, 1878–

Centennial history of Arkansas, Dallas T. Herndon ... editor. Chicago, Little Rock, The S. J. Clarke publishing company, 1922.

3 v. front., illus., plates, ports. 27 cm.

Volume I has an accurate but all-too-brief survey of the state's military effort; it ignored political and economic history.

Hill, Daniel Harvey, 1859–1924.

Bethel to Sharpsburg, by Daniel Harvey Hill ... Raleigh, Edwards & Broughton company, 1926.

2 v. 23½cm.

Cut short by the death of the author, this set is based on the Official Records and treats of military affairs; J. G. de R. Hamilton contributed to Vol. I.

Hillman, Benjamin J

Monuments to memories; Virginia's Civil War heritage in bronze and stone, by Benjamin J. Hillman. [Richmond] Virginia Civil War Commission [1965]

48 p. illus., ports. 23 cm.

An excellent, profusely illustrated summary of the chief monuments in Virginia; includes backgrounds of the memorials and a glossary of the leading monuments.

Hillman, Benjamin J *ed.*

Virginia's decision; the story of the Secession Convention of 1861. Edited by Benjamin J. Hillman. [Richmond] Virginia Civil War Commission [1964]

23 p. illus., ports. 23 cm.

Written for the layman, this brief, factual account provides the necessary data needed for an understanding of what transpired.

Hills, Alfred C.

Macpherson, the Confederate philosopher. By Alfred C. Hills. New York, J. Miller, 1864.

209 p. 19½ cm.

A collection of satirical letters on wartime government and politics in Louisiana; Hills used the pseudonym "James B. Macpherson."

Hodgson, Joseph, 1838–

The cradle of the Confederacy; or, The times of Troup, Quitman, and Yancey. A sketch of southwestern political history from the formation of the federal government to A. D. 1861. By Joseph Hodgson ... Mobile, Printed at the Register publishing office, 1876.

4 p. l., [xiii]–xv, 528 p. 23 cm.

Hodgson, a Montgomery attorney, vividly recalled the excitement of the 1860 election and Alabama's secession; much data on W. L. Yancey.

Hoole, William Stanley, 1903–

A check-list and finding-list of Charleston periodicals, 1732–1864, by William Stanley Hoole. Durham, N. C., Duke university press, 1936.

xi, 84 p. 23½cm.

Useful for the reading material digested by embattled Charlestonians; now slightly in need of updating.

Huddleston, Edwin Glenn.
The Civil War in middle Tennessee, by Ed Huddleston. [Nashville] Nashville Banner, 1965.

159 p. illus. (part col.) facsims., maps, ports. 36 cm.

A Centennial potboiler, but the illustrations are good; covers the war from secession through the battle of Nashville.

Humes, Thomas William, 1815–1892.
The loyal mountaineers of Tennessee, by Thomas William Humes ... Knoxville, Tenn., Ogden brothers & co., 1888.

400 p. front., port. 22½cm.

An old story of Union loyalties, hardships and persecutions; includes descriptions of social and economic conditions in the area.

Hunnicutt, James W 1814–
The conspiracy unveiled. The South sacrificed; or, The horrors of secession. By Rev. James W. Hunnicutt, editor of the Fredericksburg (Va.) Christian banner ... Philadelphia, J. B. Lippincott & co., 1863.

xiv, 13–454 p. front. (port.) 18 cm.

A staunch Virginia Unionist (and former editor of the Fredericksburg Christian Banner) attacked secession, the Confederacy, and the war.

Hurlburt, J S.
History of the rebellion in Bradley County, East Tennessee. By J. S. Hurlburt. Indianapolis [Downey & Brouse, printers?] 1866.

viii, 9–280, 24 p. illus., fold. map. 21½cm.

In this mass of material, badly organized, are a few rich nuggets of material on sharply divided sentiments between neighbors.

Jackson, Walter Mahan.
The story of Selma. [Birmingham? Ala] 1954.

xii, 574 p. illus., ports., maps, facsims. 24 cm.

The one chapter on wartime Selma is inadequate but possessed of some worthwhile data on the operation of the arsenal and naval foundry there.

Jervey, Theodore Dehon, 1859–
Charleston during the civil war, by Theodore C. [!] Jervey ... Washington, 1915.

1 p. l., p. 167–176. 24½cm.

Jervey devoted practically all of this mistitled work to the subject of blockade-running.

Johns, John, *bp.*, 1796–1876.
A memoir of the life of the Right Rev. William Meade, D. D., bishop of the Protestant Episcopal church in the diocese of Virginia. By the Right Rev. J. Johns, D. D., with a memorial sermon by the Rev. William Sparrow, D. D. Baltimore, Innes & company, 1867.

vi p., 1 l., [v]–vi, [7]–537 p. 2 port. (incl. front.) 19½ cm.

Provides a host of insights into Virginia society; an Episcopal bishop's tribute to one of his most popular shepherds.

Johns, John Edwin.
Florida during the Civil War. Gainesville, University of Florida Press, 1963.

ix, 265 p. illus., ports., maps. 24 cm.

A good general history, despite some factual errors; Johns made extensive use of some sources unavailable to W. W. Davis, whose book this volume does not altogether supercede.

Johnson, Gerald White, 1890–
The secession of the southern states, by Gerald W. Johnson ... New York, G. P. Putnam's sons, 1933.

176 p. incl. front., illus. (incl. ports.) 19½cm.

Still a useful handbook, its popular style and lack of documentation notwithstanding.

Johnson, Sidney Smith, 1840–
Texans who wore the gray, by Sid S. Johnson, capt. 3rd Texas cavalry, Ross brigade, C. S. A., and brigadier general Texas brigade, Forrest's cavalry, U. C. V. ... [Tyler, Tex., ©1907–

v. illus., ports. 23 cm.

Only one volume of this cursory compilation ever appeared in print.

Jones, Charles Colcock, 1831–1893.

Georgians during the war between the states. An address delivered before the Confederate survivors' association, in Augusta, Georgia, on the occasion of its eleventh annual reunion on Memorial day, April 26, 1889, by Col: Charles C. Jones, jr. ... Printed by order of the association. Augusta, Ga., Chronicle pub. co., 1889,

34 p., 1 l.

A famous introduction to a subject more fully covered in a number of later works.

Jones, Charles Colcock, 1831–1893.

Memorial history of Augusta, Georgia; from its settlement in 1735 to the close of the eighteenth century, by Charles C. Jones, jr., LL. D. From the close of the eighteenth century to the present time by Salem Dutcher. Syracuse, D. Mason & co., 1890.

512, 57 p. ports. 26cm.

More a memorial than a history, but possessed of some worthwhile material.

Jones, Charles Edgeworth, 1867–

Georgia in the war, 1861–1865, by Chas. Edgeworth Jones ... [Atlanta, Ga., Printed by Foote & Davies co., ©1909]

167, [1] p. 17½cm.

A real hodgepodge that includes a thumbnail history, service records, various rosters, and some data on naval officers.

Jones, Walter Burgwyn, 1888–

Alabama secedes from the Union; an address by Judge Walter B. Jones before the Brannon historical society of the Womans college of Alabama, Montgomery. Montgomery, The Paragon press [192–?]

16 p. illus. 23cm.

More speculative than informative, but weak in both catagories.

Keating, John McLeod, 1830–1906.

History of the city of Memphis and Shelby County, Tennessee, with illustrations and biographical sketches of some of its prominent citizens, by J. M. Keating ... Syracuse, N. Y., D. Mason & co., 1888.

2 v. in 1. ports., maps (part double) 25 cm.

Too weak in content, and too superseded by the studies of Capers and McIlwaine, to be of significant value.

Kendall, John Smith, 1874–

History of New Orleans, by John Smith Kendall ... Chicago and New York, The Lewis publishing company, 1922.

3 v. front., illus. (incl. facsims.) ports., maps. 27cm.

The most voluminous history of the famous city, with strong attention paid to the war years.

Kennamer, John Robert, 1873–

History of Jackson county, by John Robert Kennamer ... Winchester, Tenn., Press of Southern printing and publishing co., ©1935.

3 p. l., 210 p. illus. (incl. port.) 22½cm.

This better-than-average county history describes major troop movements through Jackson, several skirmishes, the C. S. Nitre Bureau, and Federal boat-building on the Tennessee River.

Kilpatrick, Emmett.

The political history of Alabama during the war of secession ... par Emmett Kilpatrick ... Paris, E. de Boccard, 1924.

3 p. l., 161 p., 1 l. 25cm.

Shallow, inadequate and inaccurate; has more omissions than inclusions.

Kimball, William Joseph, 1922– *ed.*

Richmond in time of war. Boston, Houghton Mifflin [1960]

166 p. 24 cm.

This paperback source book for college students contains 223 documents and abstracts describing wartime Richmond; useful for the social scene.

Kimmel, Stanley Preston.

Mr. Davis's Richmond. New York, Coward-McCann [1958]

214 p. illus., ports., maps, facsims. 29 cm.

The text is a mishmash of misinformation and imagination, while some of the 200-plus "rare" illustrations are delightfully miscaptioned.

Knight, Lucian Lamar, 1868–1933.

A standard history of Georgia and Georgians, by Lucian Lamar Knight ... Chicago, New York, The Lewis publishing company, 1917.

6 v. fronts. (v. 1, 3) illus., pl., ports., double geneal. tab. 27½cm.

A basic source, but far from comprehensive; now showing age.

[Knight, Thomas Jefferson]

The life and activities of Captain Newton Knight and his company. [Ellisville, Miss., Printed by the Progress-item, ©1934]

cover-title, 90 p. illus. (incl. ports.) 18½cm.

A thin, highly unreliable booklet concerning the redoubtable Newt Knight and his war on the Confederacy from Jones County, Miss.; written by his son.

Lang, John H 1853–

History of Harrison county, Mississippi, by John H. Lang ... Gulfport, Miss., The Dixie press, 1936.

viii, 303 p. fold. map. 22cm.

Contains some rambling recollections of wartime by the octogenarian author, plus partial muster rolls for three companies in the 3rd and 20th Mississippi.

Langford, Ella Molloy.

Johnson County, Arkansas, the first hundred years [by] Ella Molloy Langford. [Clarksville, Ark., Ella M. Langford, 1921]

2 p. l., [7]–210 p. illus. (1 col.) plates. 23½cm.

One brief chapter contains worthwhile notes on the 26th Arkansas and 1st Arkansas Mounted Rifles; some attention was given to military events within the county.

Lawrence, Alexander A 1906–

A present for Mr. Lincoln, the story of Savannah from secession to Sherman. Macon [Ga.] Ardivan Press [1961]

321 p. illus. 22 cm.

Wherever possible, the author allowed "the people" (invaders included) to "speak for themselves;" judicious notes enhance an excellent study.

Lee, F D.

Historical record of the city of Savannah. By F. D. Lee and J. L. Agnew. Savannah, J. H. Estill, 1869.

xii, 200 p. fold. front., illus., fold. maps, plans. 19cm.

Long the basic source on Savannah, but the war period is now better covered in A. A. Lawrence's book.

Lefler, Hugh Talmage, 1901–

History of North Carolina. New York, Lewis Historical Pub. Co. [1956]

4 v. illus., ports. 28 cm.

The first three chapters of Vol. II adequately survey the state's course to secession, its war effort, and the impact of war upon it.

Lefler, Hugh Talmage, 1901– *ed.*

North Carolina history told by contemporaries. [2d ed., rev. and enl.] Chapel Hill, Univ. of North Carolina Press [1948]

xv, 502 p. 24 cm.

Selected documents in one chapter illustrate various aspects of the state's wartime struggle; each selection is preceded by a concise introduction.

Lindsley, John Berrien, 1822–1897, *ed.*

The military annals of Tennessee. Confederate. First series: embracing a review of military operations, with regimental histories and memorial rolls, compiled from original and official sources, and edited by John Berrien Lindsley ... Printed for subscribers. Nashville, J. M. Lindsley & co., 1886.

910 p. front., port. 25cm.

Has memorial rolls of most Confederate units; a brief--and sometimes inaccurate--history of the unit is usually included.

Lipscomb, William Lowndes, 1828–1908.

A history of Columbus, Mississippi, during the 19th century, by Dr. W. L. Lipscomb. Pub. by the S. D. Lee chapter of the Daughters of the confederacy; Mrs. Georgia P. Young, historian ... of the chapter ... editor. Birmingham, Ala., Press of Dispatch printing co., 1909.

167 p. front., plates, ports. 24 cm.

Lists Loundes County units in Confederate service and contains three company muster rolls; the chief attraction is a Memorial Day address by Stephen D. Lee.

Long, *Mrs.* **Ellen Call.**

Florida breezes; or, Florida, new and old, by Ellen Call Long. Jacksonville, Fla., Ashmead bros., 1882.

vi, 401 p., 1 l. 22½cm.

Of uneven quality and poorly proofed, this book by the strong-minded daughter of Richard Keith Call presents much material not found elsewhere.

Long, Ellen Call.

Florida breezes; or, Florida, new and old. A facsimile reproduction of the 1883 ed., with introd. by Margaret Louise Chapman. Gainesville, University of Florida press, 1962.

xxiii, facsim. (vi, 401 p.), 8 p. 23 cm.

One of the handsome Florida Quadracentennial reprints; enhanced by an excellent introductory essay.

Loudoun Co., *Va.* ***Civil War Centennial Commission.***

Loudoun County and the Civil War; a history and guide. Text by John Divine [and others] Edited by Fitzhugh Turner, with a foreword by George A. Horkan, Jr. With end-paper and battle maps by H. Garver Miller. [Leesburg, 1961]

80 p. illus. 24 cm.

A concise and accurate account of the county in wartime; Ball's Bluff and Mosby's Confederacy are the major subjects.

Louisiana. ***Civil War Centennial Commission.***

Louisiana in the Civil War, a bibliography. [Baton Rouge, 1961]

unpaged. 23 cm.

This short listing is of use to the beginning student, but hardly a bibliography in the exhaustive sense of the word.

Louisiana. *Commissioner of military records.*

Records of Louisiana Confederate soldiers and Louisiana Confederate commands ... Compiled by Andrew B. Booth, commissioner Louisiana military records ... New Orleans, La., 1920.

3 v. in 4. 26 cm.

A register of 900 military organizations, an alphabetical listing of engagements in Louisiana, and an alphabetical roll of more than 50,000 soldiers--with the war services of most and the physical descriptions of some.

Louisiana. *Constitutional convention,* 1864.

Debates in the Convention for the revision and amendment of the constitution of the state of Louisiana. Assembled at Liberty hall, New Orleans, April 6, 1864. By Albert P. Bennett, official reporter ... New Orleans, W. R. Fish, printer to the Convention, 1864.

643 (*i. e.* 644) p. 23cm.

This convention was called to reestablish Union government by revising the state constitution. The journal records motions, resolutions, actions and the text of the new constitution.

Louisiana. *Constitutional convention,* 1864.

Official journal of the proceedings of the Convention for the revision and amendment of the constitution of the state of Louisiana. By authority. New Orleans, W. R. Fish. printer to the Convention, 1864.

148 p., 1 l., x p. 23 cm.

The debates are full and frequently colorful.

Louisiana. *Convention,* 1861.

Official journal of the proceedings of the Convention of the state of Louisiana. By authority. New Orleans, J. O. Nixon, printer to the State convention, 1861.

330 p. 24½cm.

Gives the text of ordinances and resolutions introduced and the action taken; does not include debates.

Louisiana. *Governor, 1864–1865* (*Allen*)

Inaugural address to the Legislature of the State of Louisiana. Delivered at Shreveport Jan. 25, 1864. [n. p., 1864]

9 p. 24 cm.

In this long, impassioned address, Allen sought to restore confidence in his people and called upon the legislature for many special measures to meet the exigencies of the times.

Louisiana historical association.

Calendar of the Jefferson Davis postwar manuscripts in the Louisiana historical association collection, Confederate memorial hall, New Orleans, Louisiana. [New Orleans] 1943.

1 p. l., ii numb. l., [2], 325 p. 27½cm.

A fine descriptive calendar that condenses and paraphrases each of the 586 manuscript items in the collection. Most of the letters treat of the war years.

Louisiana. *Legislature.*

... Joint resolutions of the Legislature of Louisiana in relation to the further prosecution of the war ... [Richmond, 1864]

1 l. 24cm.

Charged the North with ruthless barbarity and utter disregard of the rules of civilized warfare; repledged the state to an unrelenting war.

Louisiana soldiers' relief association, *Richmond, Va.*

Louisiana soldiers' relief association, and hospital, in the city of Richmond, Virginia ... Richmond, Enquirer book and job press. Tyler, Wise, Allegre & Smith, 1862.

38 p. 21½cm.

Revealing for the drama and pathos in one of Richmond's hospitals.

McArthur, Henry Clay, 1838–

The capture and destruction of Columbia, South Carolina, February 17, 1865; personal experiences and recollections of Major H. C. McArthur, fifteenth Iowa infantry volunteers, a. d. c. to General W. W. Belknap, commanding Crocker's Iowa brigade, seventeenth army corps. [Washington, 1911]

cover-title, 16 p. illus. 22½cm.

This officer in the 15th Iowa offered "eyewitness" testimony that Confederate troops caused the conflagration that destroyed much of the city.

McConnell, Joseph Carroll, 1892–

The west Texas frontier; or, A descriptive history of early times in western Texas; containing an accurate account of much hitherto unpublished history ... By Joseph Carroll McConnell. [Jacksboro, Tex., Gazette print, ©1933–39]

2 v. plates, ports. 23½ cm.

Contains many insights on the war's effect at the edge of American society.

McCormick, Edgar Lindsley, 1914– *ed.*

Sherman in Georgia; selected source materials for college research papers. Edited by Edgar L. McCormick, Edward G. McGehee, and Mary Strahl. Boston, Heath [1961]

114 p. illus. 24 cm.

A well-balanced selection of primary source materials to aid the beginning student in the writing of historical research papers.

McCormick, John Gilchrist.

... Personnel of the convention of 1861, by John Gilchrist McCormick, A. B. Legislation of the convention of 1861, by Kemp Plummer Battle, LL. D. Chapel Hill, N. C. [University press] 1900.

144 p. 22cm.

Short biographical sketches of the delegates to the N. C. secession convention, together with a concise history of the convention's four sessions; a basic study.

McGill, Samuel Davis, 1819–1896.

Narrative of reminiscences in Williamsburg county, by Samuel D. McGill ... Columbia, S. C., The Bryan printing co., 1897.

vii, 304 p. 23 cm.

Of limited value except for pages listing prices of commodities seldom found in advertisements--pencils, thread, horn buttons, yarn, etc.

McGregor, James Clyde, 1883–

The disruption of Virginia, by James C. McGregor, PH. D. New York, The Macmillan company, 1922.

xiv p., 1 l., 328 p. fold. map. 19½ cm.

An old and little-known work, overshadowed by the studies of Munford and Shanks; contains some data not found elsewhere.

McIlwaine, Shields, 1902–

Memphis down in Dixie. [1st ed.] New York, E. P. Dutton [1948]

400 p. port., map (on lining-papers) 22 cm.

Still the best study of the city, though the Civil War chapters are disappointingly thin.

McKinnon, John Love, 1840–

History of Walton County, by John L. McKinnon. Atlanta, Ga., The Byrd printing co., 1911.

389 p. ports. 23 cm.

The story of an anti-secessionist, Scotch-Irish community of west Florida; included are memoirs by the keenly observant McKinnon of service in the 1st Florida.

McLure, Mary Lilla.
History of Shreveport and Shreveport builders, by Lilla McLure and J. Ed Howe. Shreveport, La. [Journal printing company] 1937.

463, [1] p. illus. (incl. ports.) 23½cm.

Has a brief but informative chapter on wartime Caddo Parish and Shreveport, the state's capital in the 1863-1865 period.

McMillan, Malcolm Cook, 1910– *ed.*
The Alabama Confederate reader. [University, Ala.] University of Alabama Press, 1963.

468 p. illus. 24 cm.

This anthology of judiciously selected contemporary writings examines every facet of the state's wartime history; the introduction and historical notes are excellent.

McRaven, William Henry.
Nashville, Athens of the South. Chapel Hill, Published for the Tennessee Book Co. by Scheer & Jervis, 1949.

xii, 303 p. illus. 24 cm.

The basic source, though the Civil War does not receive unusual treatment.

Marchand, Sidney Albert, 1887–
Forgotten fighters, 1861–1865, Ascension Parish, Louisiana [by] Sidney A. Marchand. [Donaldsonville? La., 1966]

172 p. illus., ports. 23 cm.

A recently published roster of soldiers from one Louisiana parish; such compilations, plentiful for the Northern side, are rare in Southern annals.

Martin, John H *comp.*
Columbus, Geo., from its selection as a "trading town" in 1827, to its partial destruction by Wilson's raid, in 1865. History—incident—personality ... Compiled by John H. Martin. Columbus, Ga., T. Gilbert, 1874–75.

2 v. in 1. 20cm.

A year-by-year compilation of important political and military events, local incidents, personal items, etc.; gleaned from primary sources, this is an excellent study.

Martin, Thomas H.
Atlanta and its builders, a comprehensive history of the Gate city of the South, by Thomas H. Martin ... [Atlanta] Century memorial publishing company, 1902.

2 v. plates, ports. 26½cm.

Two-thirds of Vol. I is devoted to the war period and includes a lengthy account of the Atlanta campaign based on the Official Records; the whole work is now outdated.

Mathes, James Harvey.
The old guard in gray. Researches in the annals of the Confederate historical association. Sketches of Memphis veterans who upheld her standard in the war, and of other Confederate worthies ... By J. Harvey Mathes. [Memphis, Press of S. C. Toof & co., 1897]

3 p. l., 11–292 p. front. (port.) illus. 23½cm.

Biographical sketches of 458 Confederate veterans; these provide an interesting key to postwar occupations of a sample group.

May, John Amasa.
South Carolina secedes, by John Amasa May and Joan Reynolds Faunt. With biographical sketches of members of South Carolina's Secession Convention, compiled by Joan Reynolds Faunt. Columbia, University of South Carolina Press, 1960.

231 p. illus. 24 cm.

A skillful abridgement of the journals of the S. C. Conventions, together with declarations, addresses, and biographical sketches.

Mayo, Joseph.
Virginia abstractions. An address before the society of alumni of the Virginia military institute. Delivered July 3, 1873. By Col. Joseph Mayo ... Richmond, Clemmitt & Jones, book and job printers, 1873.

20 p. 23½cm.

In reply to Northern assertions that Virginia arguments of justification were "abstractions," Mayo vigorously defended the rightness and legality of the Southern cause.

Meynardie, Elias James.
The siege of Charleston; its history and progress. A discourse delivered in Bethel church, Charleston, S. C., November 19, 1863, (Thansgiving day.) By Rev. E. J. Meynardie ... Columbia, Steam-power press of Evans & Cogswell, 1864.

15 p. 22½ cm.

More sermonistic than informative, but useful as an illustration of the emotions of that day

Mississippi. *Commission on the War Between the States.*
Mississippi in the War Between the States; a booklet of facts for the information of Mississippians in connection with the observance of the Civil War Centennial, 1961–1965. [Jackson, 1960]
36 p. 28 cm.

A handy collection of documents, facts, and figures on wartime Mississippi; one of the best of the state Centennial publications.

Mississippi. *Convention*, 1861.
Journal of the State convention and Ordinances and resolutions adopted in January, 1861, with an Appendix. Pub. by order of the Convention. Jackson, Miss., E. Barksdale, state printer, 1861.
256 p., 1 l. fold. tab. 21cm.

Includes motions, resolutions, ordinances, and votes of the delegates, plus executive correspondence and the Adjutant General's 1860 report.

Mississippi in the Confederacy. [Baton Rouge] Published for the Mississippi Dept. of Archives and History, Jackson, by Louisiana State University Press [1961]
2 v. illus., ports., maps. 25 cm.

Volume I contains 200 selections that tell Mississippi's wartime story as contemporaries saw it; Vol. II contains as many excerpts by later writers.

Mississippi. *Jefferson Davis memorial commission.*
The Jefferson Davis memorial in the Vicksburg national military park. [Vicksburg, Press of the Mississippi printing company, 1927]
cover-title, 28 p. incl. pl. 23½cm.

A proud state honors its most famous wartime son.

Mississippi. *Laws, statutes, etc.*
Laws of the state of Mississippi; appropriations, general legislation and resolutions passed at a ... session of the Mississippi Legislature ...

[Jackson, etc.] 18
v. 20–24cm.

Acts of the Dec., 1862, called session relate to war matters; those of the regular session were concerned with routine state business.

Mississippi. *Legislature.*
... Resolutions of the Legislature of the state of Mississippi in relation to the recent act of the Congress of the Confederate States suspending the privilege of the writ of habeas corpus. [Richmond, 1864]
2 p. 23½cm.

Mississippi's congressional delegation was instructed to work for a repeal of the Feb., 1864, suspension act, which the resolution condemned as dangerous and unconstitutional.

Montague, Ludwell Lee, 1907–
Gloucester County in the Civil War. Gloucester, Va., DeHardit Press, 1965.
ix, 97 p. illus., maps, ports. 28 cm.

Based on reminiscences, county records and neglected manuscripts, these 57 newspaper articles are a superb testimonial to one Virginia region.

Moore, Louis Toomer, 1885–
Stories old and new of the Cape Fear region. Wilmington, N. C., 1956.
261 p. illus. 24 cm.

A collection of stories, largely anecdotes, of wartime life around the Wilmington, N. C., region.

Moore, W D.
The life and works of Col. Henry Hughes; a funeral sermon, preached in the Methodist Episcopal church, Port Gibson, Miss., October 26th, 1862. By Rev. W. D. Moore. Mobile, Farrow & Dennett, printers, 1863.
40 p. 22½cm.

An Englishman's eulogy to a Mississippi white supremist; especially good for state scenes in wartime.

Morton, Oren Frederic, 1857–1926.
A history of Rockbridge County, Virginia, by Oren F. Morton ... Staunton, Va., The McClure co., inc., 1920.
4 p. l., 574 p. front., plates, ports. 26½ cm.

The one chapter on the war is superficial, though possessed of material from the Lexington Gazette; contains an original roster of the Rockbridge Artillery.

Morton, Oren Frederic, 1857–1926.

The story of Winchester in Virginia, the oldest town in the Shenandoah Valley, by Frederic Morton ... Strasburg, Va., Shenandoah publishing house, 1925.

336 p. incl. front. pl., ports. 24cm.

In spite of several glaring weaknesses, this remains the best study of the Shenandoah Valley's pivotal city; weak on the war period.

Mulvihill, Michael J *comp.*

Vicksburg and Warren county, Mississippi, Tunica Indians, Quebec missionaries, civil war veterans, designed and compiled by M. J. Mulvihill, sr., 1931. Published by authority of the Mayor and Aldermen of the city of Vicksburg and the Board of supervisors of Warren county, Mississippi. [Vicksburg, Miss., Printed by Van Norman printing co., 1931]

80 p. incl. illus., plates. 23 cm.

Odds and ends of local history, loosely tossed together; those relative to the war were lifted from the Official Records.

Munford, Beverley Bland, 1856–

Virginia's attitude toward slavery and secession, by Beverley B. Munford ... New York [etc.] Longmans, Green, and co., 1909.

xiii p., 1 l., 329 p. 22 cm.

Munford's treatment will continue to be the standard source until some historian undertakes a new and updated work.

Murphy, William M.

Notes from the history of Madison Parish, Louisiana, by William M. Murphy of the Louisiana bar. [Ruston, La.] Louisiana polytechnic institute, Department of printing, 1927.

25 p. 23cm.

Although Milliken's Bend was located in this parish, Murphy devoted to it only seven worthless pages.

National War Committee of the Citizens of New York.

Report of the committee who visited Washington on the affairs of western Texas. [New York, 1862]

15 p. 23 cm.

Accompanied by A. J. Hamilton, the committee assured Lincoln that an invasion by 5,000 Federal troops would be supported by 10,000 Texas loyalists.

Neal, John Randolph, 1874–

Disunion and restoration in Tennessee, by John Randolph Neal ... New York, The Knickerbocker press, 1899.

2 p. l., 80 p. 24½cm.

Only thirty pages of this early doctoral dissertation treat of the war period; Neal argued that most Tennesseans favored secession.

Neale, Walter, 1873–

The sovereignty of the states, an oration; address to the survivors of the Eighth Virginia regiment, while they were gathered about the graves of their fallen comrades, on the battle-ground of Manassas, July 21, 1910, by Walter Neale. New York and Washington, The Neale publishing company, 1910.

4 p. l., 143 p. 19cm.

In this lengthy address (to veterans of the 8th Virginia), Neale reaffirmed everything for which the Southern states had stood.

New Orleans. *Mayor -1862 (John T. Monroe)*

Correspondence between the mayor and federal authorities relative to the occupation of New Orleans, together with the proceedings of the Common council. New Orleans, Printed at the Bulletin book and job office, 1862.

29 p. 24 cm.

Mayor John T. Monroe and Federal naval officers negotiate the surrender of the city, while the council continues on a business-as-usual basis until May 4, 1862.

Nicholson, James William, 1844–1917.

Stories of Dixie, by James W. Nicholson ... New York, Cincinnati [etc.] American book company [c1915]

242 p. incl. front., illus. pl., ports. 19 cm.

An attempt to depict "life as it was" by means of a semi-fictionalized autobiography.

Nicholson, James William, 1844–1917.

Stories of Dixie. [Rev. ed.] Baton Rouge, Claitor's Book Store, 1966.

247 p. illus., map, ports. 20 cm.

Of no more value than the original edition; Nicholson's statement that the book was intended for young people is all too true.

North Carolina.
Public documents. 18 –1919 session.
Raleigh.
v. in 24 cm.

Includes reports of commissioners to other states; comments by State Salt Commissioners, and valuable data on goods received from blockade runners.

North Carolina. *Confederate Centennial Commission.*
A guide to military organizations and installations, North Carolina, 1861–1865, compiled by Louis H. Manarin. [Raleigh, 1961]
1 v. 28 cm.

Published from preliminary research (hence incomplete), this is a fine introduction to the state's many military units.

North Carolina. *Confederate Centennial Commission.*
North Carolina at Gettysburg. Published ... on the occasion of the rededication of the North Carolina Monument at Gettysburg National Military Park, July 1, 1963. [Raleigh, 1963]
27 p. illus., ports. 15 x 21 cm.

Eulogies to the past and reaffirmations of nationalism for the future comprise this booklet issued as a part of the Centennial.

North Carolina. *Convention,* **1861–1862.**
Journal of the Convention of the people of North Carolina ... Raleigh, J. W. Syme, printer to the Convention, 1862.
4 v. in 1. 22cm.

Records, petitions, motions, resolutions, ordinances, and votes of individual delegates; debates are not given.

North Carolina. *General assembly.*
... Resolutions against the policy of arming slaves. [Richmond? 1865]
1 l. 25cm.

These resolutions of Mar. 4, 1865, deny the constitutional power of the Confederate government to impress and arm slaves.

North Carolina. *General assembly.*
Roster of North Carolina troops in the war between the states. Prepared, by order of legislature of 1881, by John W. Moore ... Raleigh, Ash & Gatling, state printers, 1882.
4 v. 23cm.

Moore's volumes contain the names of 104,498 men who served in Confederate armies; this work is now being superseded by the Manarin compilation.

North Carolina. *General Assembly. House of Representatives.*
Journal. 1778–
[Raleigh, etc.]
v. in 23–37 cm.

Usually bound with state journals, and covering regular and extraordinary sessions, these volumes constitute a record of the state's wartime legislation.

North Carolina. ***State Dept. of Archives and History.***
Civil War pictures, by D. L. Corbitt and Elizabeth W. Wilborn. Raleigh, 1961.
viii, 89, [2] p. illus., fold. map, ports. 23 cm.

An enlarged and improved edition of a booklet first published in 1958; useful for illustrations of local scenes.

North Carolina. State literary and historical association.
... Five points in the record of North Carolina in the great war of 1861–5. Report of the committee appointed by the North Carolina literary and historical society—1904. Goldsboro, N. C., Nash brothers, printers, 1904.
79 p. maps (4 double) 23cm.

A broadcasted synopsis for Clark's famous 5-volume work on North Carolina units.

Oates, John Alexander, 1870–
The story of Fayetteville and the upper Cape Fear. [Fayetteville? N. C., 1950]
xxxii, 868 p. illus., ports., maps, facsims. 24 cm.

Especially revealing for the capture and occupation of the city by Sherman.

Oates, Stephen B
Confederate Cavalry west of the river. Austin, University of Texas Press [1961]

xviii, 234 p. illus., ports., maps (1 fold.) 24 cm.

This interesting study emphasizes logistics as well as engagements; M. A. theses need not be dull, as this revised work demonstrates.

O'Connor, Michael Patrick, 1831–1881.
The life and letters of M. P. O'Connor. Written and ed. by his daughter, Mary Doline O'Connor. New York, Dempsey & Carroll, 1893.

xi, 561 p. front. (port.) 23½ cm.

An excellent source for insights into one of South Carolina's most forceful secessionists; also reveals much of the 1861 war spirit.

Parramore, Thomas C *ed.*
Before the Rebel flag fell; five viewpoints of the Civil War. Collected and edited by Thomas C. Parramore, F. Roy Johnson, [and] E. Frank Stephenson, Jr. Murfreesboro, N. C., Johnson Pub. Co. [1965]

A–N, 132 p. 22 cm.

Short excerpts from the reminiscences of five soldiers and civilians; none are of outstanding value, and each varies in interest.

Patrick, Rembert Wallace, 1909–
Florida under five flags [by] Rembert W. Patrick ... Gainesville, University of Florida press, 1945.

xiv, 140 p. incl. front., illus. (incl. ports., maps, facsims.) 28½ cm.

Provides a concise and readable introduction to a story exhaustively covered by the Johns volume.

Patton, James Welch, 1900–
Unionism and reconstruction in Tennessee, 1860–1869, by James Welch Patton ... Chapel Hill, The University of North Carolina press, 1934.

xii, 267 p. front. (port.) plates, facsim. 23½cm.

A scholarly though now outdated political history, with "Parson" Brownlow the central figure; social and economic forces are slighted; reissued in 1966.

Perrin, William Henry, *d.* 1892? *ed.*
Southwest Louisiana, biographical and historical; ed. by William Henry Perrin ... New Orleans, The Gulf publishing company, 1891.

404, 398 p. incl. ports. pl., ports. 26 x 20cm.

An all-too-typical example of the "subscription" biographical compendium, this work is practically worthless to the historian.

Phillips, Edward Hamilton, 1910–
The Shenandoah Valley in 1864, an episode in the history of warfare, by Edward H. Phillips. Charleston, The Citadel, the Military College of South Carolina, 1965.

36 p. 23 cm.

Entirely military in content, this is nevertheless a skillfully written summary of the Second Valley Campaign.

[**Phillips, Edwin D**] 1827–1864.
Texas and its late military occupation and evacuation. By an officer of the army. New York, D. Van Nostrand, 1862.

35 p. 23cm.

A hasty, defensive memoir of a Federal officer who made unsuccessful efforts to save government stores when Texas state forces in 1861 seized all Federal property.

Phillips, Ulrich Bonnell, 1877–1934.
... Georgia and state rights. A study of the political history of Georgia from the revolution to the civil war, with particular regard to federal relations ... By Ulrich Bonnell Phillips ... Washington, Govt. print. off., 1902.

224 p. xii pl. (1 fold.; maps, charts) 23½ cm.

Scholarly, colorless and venerable; the last chapter treats of secession, and the focus is on the Toombs-Stephens struggle.

Pillar, James L
The Catholic Church in Mississippi, 1837–65. New Orleans, Hauser Press [1964]

xviii, 380 p. illus., ports., maps. 24 cm.

Approximately half of this well-researched book treats of Catholic activities in wartime Mississippi.

Poe, Orlando Metcalfe, 1832–1895.

Personal recollections of the occupation of East Tennessee and the defense of Knoxville. A paper read before Michigan commandery of the Military order of the loyal legion of the United States, December 5th, 1888, by companion Orlando M. Poe ... Detroit, Ostler printing company, 1889.

48 p. maps. 23 cm.

A good, brief account of the 1863 East Tennessee campaign; written by the Army of the Ohio's chief engineer, who designed Knoxville's fortifications.

Porter, James Davis, 1828–1912.

... An address delivered at the unveiling of the Henry County confederate monument, Paris, Tennessee, Saturday, October 13, 1900. By ex-Governor James D. Porter. Paris, Tenn., Post-Intelligencer job print., 1900.

24 p. incl. front. (port.) pl. 19cm.

Eulogies to the brave warriors of Paris, Tenn.

Porter, John W H.

A record of events in Norfolk county, Virginia, from April 19th, 1861, to May 10th, 1862, with a history of the soldiers and sailors of Norfolk county, Norfolk city and Portsmouth, who served in the Confederate States army or navy. By John W. H. Porter ... Portsmouth, Va., W. A. Fiske, printer, 1892.

366 p. illus. 24cm.

Included in this useful volume are unit histories, biographical sketches, a chapter on the C. S. S. Virginia, and another on the battle of Hampton Roads.

[Powe, James Harrington] 1835–1898.

Reminiscences & sketches of Confederate times by one who lived through them; ed. by Harriet Powe Lynch ... Columbia, S. C., The R. L. Bryan company, 1909.

44 p. 23 cm.

Chauvinistic comments on Forts Wagner and Sumter; of limited use only.

Powhatan, Va. Citizens.

... Resolutions adopted by a meeting of the people of Powhatan, held in the Courthouse on February court day, 1865 [pledging loyalty to the cause of the Confederacy] [Richmond, 1865]

1 l. 25cm.

When efforts to secure peace failed, these citizens rededicated themselves to the war effort and reassured the troops in the field.

Proctor, Samuel.

Florida commemorates the Civil War centennial, 1961–1965; a manual for the observance of the Civil War in the counties and cities of the State of Florida. [Coral Gables, Florida Civil War Centennial Commission, 1962?]

24 p. fold. map. 23 cm.

A helpful guide for those interested in commemorating the Centennial.

Pulliam, David Loyd, 1857–

The constitutional conventions of Virginia from the foundation of the commonwealth to the present time, by David L. Pulliam ... Richmond, J. T. West, 1901.

180 p. 23½ cm.

Gives due attention to the secession conventions, yet somewhat biased.

Rains, George Washington, 1817–1898.

History of the Confederate powder works, by Col. (General) Geo. W. Rains ... An address delivered by invitation before the Confederate survivors' association, at its fourth annual meeting, on Memorial day, April 26th, 1882. Augusta, Ga., Chronicle & constitutionalist print, 1882.

30 p. 22cm.

A detailed and highly technical account of the Augusta arsenal; written by the South's foremost gunpowder expert.

Rainwater, Percy Lee, 1888–

Mississippi, storm center of secession, 1856–1861, by Percy Lee Rainwater ... Baton Rouge, La., O. Claitor, 1938.

xi, [1], 248 p. illus. (incl. maps) 23½ cm.

The standard scholarly study, based on extensive research; particularly good for views on public opinion.

Reed, Emily Hazen.

Life of A. P. Dostie; or, The conflict of New Orleans. By Emily Hazen Reed ... New York, W. P. Tomlinson, 1868.

xi, [13]–374 p., 1 l. front. (port.) 20 cm.

A primary source for Louisiana's reconstruction government; Dostie, a dentist and leading Radical, was state auditor during the Hahn regime.

Rerick, Rowland H.

Memoirs of Florida; embracing a general history of the province, territory and state; and special chapters devoted to finances and banking, the bench and bar, medical profession, railways and navigation, and industrial interests, by Rowland H. Rerick; ed. by Francis P. Fleming ... including personal memoirs of many citizens of the state. Atlanta, Ga., The Southern historical association, 1902.

2 v. port. 26½cm.

Volume I contains a remarkably good survey of events in wartime Florida, and of Florida units in Confederate armies.

[Reynolds, Bernard]

Sketches of Mobile. From 1814 to the present time. Incidents connected with the occupation of the town. Anecdotes of old citizens, etc., etc. Mobile, Ala., B. H. Richardson, 1868.

1 p. l., 79, [1] p. 22cm.

Composed for the most part of gossip and anecdotes; like all such works, it must be handled with extreme care.

Richardson, Simon Peter, 1818–1899.

The lights and shadows of itinerant life: an autobiography of Rev. Simon Peter Richardson ... with an introduction by Rev. John B. Robins, D. D. Nashville, Tenn., Dallas, Tex., Barbee & Smith, 1901.

xix, 288 p. ports. 19cm.

Sentimental recollections by a pious Floridian who served as chaplain of state troops.

Richmond. *City Council.*

Richmond at war; the minutes of the City Council, 1861–1865. Edited by Louis H. Manarin. Chapel Hill, University of North Carolina Press [1966]

645 p. illus., maps, ports. 28 cm.

Indispensable to any study of the dual capital; contains a wealth of material other than the minutes; skillfully edited.

Richmond. *Civil War Centennial Committee.*

Troop movements at the Battle of Cold Harbor, 1864. [Richmond, 1964]

16 l. of maps. 32 x 47 cm.

This atlas of easy-to-read maps is indicative of the superb publications issued by one Southern city's Centennial agency.

Richmond. Battle abbey.

Biographic catalogue of the portraits in the Confederate memorial institute "The Battle abbey". Richmond, Va., R. E. Lee camp, no. 1, Confederate veterans, 1929.

cover-title, 46 p. illus. (1 col., incl. port.) 23cm.

Biographical sketches, some containing flagrant errors, of 182 soldiers whose portraits hang in the Abbey.

Riley, Benjamin Franklin, 1849–

History of Conecuh County, Alabama. Embracing a detailed record of events from the earliest period to the present; biographical sketches of those who have been most conspicuous in the annals of the county; a complete list of the officials of Conecuh, besides much valuable information relative to the internal resources of the county. By Rev. B. F. Riley ... Columbus, Ga., T. Gilbert, printer, 1881.

xi, [13]–233 p. 19cm.

One chapter highlights the 1865 cavalry raid into this south Alabama county; a company roster for the 4th Alabama is appended.

Riley, Benjamin Franklin, 1849–1925.

History of Conecuh County, Alabama. A reprint of the 1881 ed., to which has been added a picture and biographical sketch of the author and an index, compiled by J. Vernon Brantley. Blue Hill, Me., Printed by the Weekly Packet [1964]

246 p. port. 19 cm.

The addition of an introduction about the author, plus a fairly complete index, make this reprinting of more value than the original edition.

Rivers, William James, 1822–

Rivers' account of the raising of troops in South Carolina for state and confederate service 1861–1865. Pub. for revision and amendment. Columbia, S. C., The Bryan printing co., state printers, 1899.

44 p. 23cm.

A summary of manpower contributions; by the South Carolina professor who began the roster of troops later continued by A. S. Salley.

Roberts, Walter Adolphe, 1886–

Lake Pontchartrain [by] W. Adolphe Roberts. [Indianapolis, The Bobbs-Merrill company, 1946]

376 p. plates, ports. 22 cm.

The brief section on the war period is worthless.

Robertson, James I
Virginia, 1861–1865: iron gate to the Confederacy. Official publication: Virginia Civil War Commission. [Richmond, 1961]

64 p. illus. 23 cm.

A well-written booklet that admirably serves its purpose in introducing the general public to the war fought in Virginia.

Rogers, William Warren.
Thomas County during the Civil War. Tallahassee, Florida State University, 1964.

xv, 112 p. illus., map, ports. 24 cm.

Covering every aspect of the war on a county level, this study might well serve as a model for the writing of local history.

Rowland, Dunbar, 1864– *ed.*
Mississippi; comprising sketches of counties, towns, events, institutions, and persons, arranged in cyclopedic form, planned and ed. by Dunbar Rowland ... Atlanta, Southern historical publishing association, 1907.

3 v. fronts. (v. 1-2, v. 1: port.) illus. (ports.) $26\frac{1}{2}^{cm}$.

The fullest study of the state, but now ranked at least third for a scholarly account of the Civil War period.

Ryder, Charles Jackson, 1848–
... The debt of our country to the American highlanders during the war. By Secretary C. J. Ryder. New York, N. Y. [190–?]

cover-title, 8 p. illus. $23\frac{1}{2}^{cm}$.

Published by the American Missionary Assn., this tract dips the flag to Unionists in East Tennessee.

St. Landry Parish, *La.*
An ordinance organizing and establishing patrols for the police of slaves in the parish of St. Landry. Opelousas [La.] Printed at the office of the Opelousas patriot, 1863.

29 p. $19\frac{1}{2}^{cm}$.

Provided for the establishment of a wartime slave patrol and defines its duties and powers.

Salley, Alexander Samuel, 1871– *ed.*
Tentative roster of the Third regiment, South Carolina volunteers, Confederate States provisional army. Ed. by A. S. Salley, jr. ... Columbia, Printed by the State co., 1908.

129 p. $23\frac{1}{2}^{cm}$.

Admittedly inaccurate and incomplete, this compilation was published in the hope of stimulating veterans to supply data and make corrections.

Saucier, Corinne L
History of Avoyelles parish, Louisiana, by Corinne L. Saucier ... New Orleans, Pelican publishing company [©1943]

8 p. l., 542, [19] p. front., illus., plates, ports., maps (part fold.) facsims., diagr. $23\frac{1}{2}^{cm}$.

A typical county history, this work has the usual summaries, plus a list of the parish's principal slaveholders and the number of slaves held by each at the time of secession.

Selby, Julian A 1833–
Memorabilia and anecdotal reminiscences of Columbia, S. C., and incidents connected therewith. By Julian A. Selby. Columbia, S. C., The R. L. Bryan company, 1905.

200 p. front. (port.) 24 cm.

Too sketchy and seemingly manufactured for a truly reliable work.

Sellers, William W 1818–1902.
A history of Marion county, South Carolina, from its earliest times to the present, 1901. By W. W. Sellers, esq., of the Marion bar. Columbia, The R. L. Bryan company, 1902.

ix, 647 p. front. (port.) 25 cm.

Unusually heavy in its treatment of the Civil War; 74 pages of muster rolls are included.

Scott, Edwin J *b.* 1803.
Random recollections of a long life, 1806 to 1876. By Edwin J. Scott ... Columbia, S. C., C. A. Calvo, jr., printer, 1884.

1 p. l., vi, [3]-216 p. $19\frac{1}{2}^{cm}$.

Of minimal value for observations of wartime Columbia and Lexington, S. C.

Shanks, Henry Thomas.

The secession movement in Virginia, 1847–1861, by Henry T. Shanks ... Richmond, Garrett and Massie [c1934]

xi p., 1 l., 296 p. incl. front., maps. 23½ cm.

Perhaps the best of the state secession studies; a model for scholarship and comprehensiveness.

Sherman, Andrew Magoun, 1844–1921.

In the lowlands of Louisiana in 1863; an address delivered by Rev. Andrew M. Sherman, at the forty-second annual reunion of the Twenty-third Conn. regimental association, held at Steeplechase island, Bridgeport, Connecticut, on Thursday, August 20, 1908 ... [Morristown, N. J., The Howard publishing company, 1908?]

40 p. front. (port.) 23cm.

Despite the passage of time, Sherman's memoirs of a journey to Ship Island, Berwick Bay and Brashear City remain vivid and generally trustworthy.

Sherrill, William Lander, 1860–

Annals of Lincoln county, North Carolina; containing interesting and authentic facts of Lincoln county history through the years 1749 to 1937, by William L. Sherrill ... Charlotte, N. C. [The Observer printing house, inc.] 1937.

6 p. l., [7]–536 p. plates, ports., facsims. 23½ cm.

Cursory vignettes that originally appeared as newspaper articles; of interest primarily to genealogists.

Shugg, Roger Wallace.

Origins of class struggle in Louisiana; a social history of white farmers and laborers during slavery and after, 1840–1875, by Roger W. Shugg. University, La., Louisiana state university press. 1939.

x p., 1 l., 372 p. 23½ cm.

This authoritative and well-documented study asserts that not even civil war altered the social structure of the South.

Sillers, Florence (Warfield) ***comp.***

History of Bolivar County, Mississippi; compiled by Florence Warfield Sillers and members of Mississippi Delta Chapter, Daughters of the American Revolution, and the County History Committee. Edited by Wirt A. Williams. Jackson, Printed by Hederman Bros. [c1948]

ix, 634 p. illus., ports. 27 cm.

This study sags a bit from chauvinism, yet it contains some data not found elsewhere.

[**Simms, William Gilmore**] 1806–1870.

Sack and destruction of the city of Columbia, S. C. To which is added a list of the property destroyed. Columbia, S. C., Power press of Daily phœnix, 1865.

76 p. 20½ cm.

This is one of the better-known works on the burning of Columbia, primarily because of Simms's status in American letters; a highly imaginative piece.

Simms, William Gilmore, 1806–1870.

Sack and destruction of the city of Columbia, S. C. By Wm. Gilmore Simms. 2d ed., edited with notes by A. S. Salley. [Atlanta] Oglethorpe university press, 1937.

2 p. l., vii–xx, [2], 25–106 p. 23½ cm.

Salley's biographical sketch of Simms defends his fellow Carolinian's literary stature but adds nothing to the story of Columbia.

Simpson, Harold B.

The Marshall Guards; Harrison County's contribution to Hood's Texas Brigade, by Harold B. Simpson. Marshall, Tex., Port Caddo Press [1967]

viii, 26 p. port. 23 cm.

A roster of Co. E, 1st Texas Infantry, with some bibliographical references to Harrison County.

Sitterson, Joseph Carlyle, 1911–

The secession movement in North Carolina, by Joseph Carlyle Sitterson ... Chapel Hill, The University of North Carolina press, 1939.

vii p., 2 l., 3–285 p. illus. (maps) 23cm.

The standard work on the subject, and second only to Shank's study in the field; reliable and readable.

Smartt, *Mrs.* **Eugenia (Persons)**

History of Eufaula, Alabama, by Eugenia Persons Smartt ... [Birmingham, Ala., Roberts & son, printers, c1933]

1 p. l., v–ix, [1], [11]–297, [2] p., 1 l. illus. (incl. ports.) 23½cm.

Offers some useful information on local militia prior to the outbreak of civil war; a few wartime documents are included.

Smith, George Gilman, *b.* 1836.

The history of Georgia Methodism from 1786 to 1866, by Rev. George G. Smith, D. D. Atlanta, Ga., A. B. Caldwell, 1913.

430 p. incl. plates, ports. port. 24cm.

An old and standard work; to be used as a starting point for any new treatment of the subject.

Smith, Ralph J 1840–

Reminisences [!] of the civil war, and other sketches; by Ralph J. Smith. [San Marcos? Tex., 1911]

cover-title, 26 p. port. 23cm.

This too-brief memoir treats largely of the author's experiences in the 2nd Texas Infantry.

Smith, Sidney Adair, *ed.*

Mobile: 1861–1865; notes and a bibliography. Edited by Sidney Adair Smith and C. Carter Smith, Jr. Chicago, Wyvern Press of S. F. E., inc. [c1964]

v, 52 p. illus., facsims. 25 cm.

Manuscript excerpts, supplemented by extracts from well-known sources, present a clear picture of wartime Mobile; more compilations such as this are needed.

Smith, William Russell, 1815–1896.

The history and debates of the Convention of the people of Alabama, begun and held in the city of Montgomery, on the seventh day of January, 1861; in which is preserved the speeches of the secret sessions and many valuable state papers. By William R. Smith, one of the delegates from Tuscaloosa. Montgomery, White, Pfister & co.; Atlanta, Wood, Hanleiter, Rice & co.; [etc., etc.] 1861.

v p., 1 l., [9]–464, xii p. 22½ cm.

While some speeches are omitted, and all those included are abridged, this remains the best single source for what was said at Alabama's secession convention.

Sons of Confederate veterans.

Minutes of the annual reunion.

[Waco, Tex.,

v. ports. 23½cm.

The volume for the 13th annual reunion includes historical papers as well as the usual florid oratory; Vol. XIII has an interesting defense of Gen. Lucius Northrop.

South Carolina. *Archives dept.*

South Carolina troops in Confederate service. Vol. 1– Comp. by A. S. Salley, jr., secretary of the Historical commission of South Carolina. Columbia, S. C., The R. L. Bryan company, 1913–

v. 24½ cm.

One of the weaker state rosters; only three volumes were published, and they contain disappointingly little data on individual soldiers.

South Carolina. *Chickamauga commission.*

Ceremonies at the unveiling of the South Carolina monument on the Chickamauga battlefield, May 27th, 1901. Together with a record of the commission who suggested and were instrumental in securing and erecting the monument, etc. [n. p., 1901]

50 p. 2 pl. 22cm.

Expected and deserved eulogies comprise the bulk of this work.

South Carolina. *Comptroller general's office.*

Report of the comptroller general.

Columbia, S. C. [18

v. in tables (part fold.) 23½cm.

The 1861 report has a wealth of material on the financial conditions of railroads, banks and the tax situation.

South Carolina. *Confederate War Centennial Commission.*

South Carolina speaks ... addresses of prominent South Carolinians speaking on South Carolina's participation in the centennial of the Confederacy. Columbia [1961]

43 p. 23 cm.

Observations by many on why the Centennial should be noted.

South Carolina. *Convention,* 1860–1862.

The address of the people of South Carolina assembled in convention, to the people of the slaveholding states of the United States. Printed by order of the Convention. Charleston, Evans & Cogswell, printers to the Convention, 1860.

16 p. 24 cm.

Speaking to the people of the other slave states, the Convention again justified secession and urged the formation of a Southern nation.

South Carolina. *Convention*, 1860–1862.
Journal of the Convention of the people of South Carolina, held in 1860–61. Together with the reports, resolutions, &c. Pub. by order of the Convention. Charleston, Evans & Cogswell, printers to the Convention, 1861.
420, [1], 96 p. 23cm.

The bare-bones record of South Carolina's convention at work.

South Carolina. *Convention*, 1860–1862.
Journal of the Convention of the people of South Carolina, held in 1860, 1861 and 1862, together with the ordinances, reports, resolutions, etc. Pub. by order of the Convention. Columbia, S. C., R. W. Gibbes, printer to the Convention, 1862.
873 p. 23½cm.

One of the fuller journals by a Southern state--and one of the most valuable.

South Carolina. *Convention, 1860–1862.*
Report of the Special Committee of Twenty-one on the Communication of His Excellency Governor Pickens, together with the reports of heads of departments, and other papers. Columbia, R. W. Gibbes, printer to the Convention, 1862.
7 p. 25 cm.

Prime source material; an excellent summary of the state's war effort, as viewed by state officials, through July, 1862.

South Carolina. *Executive Council.*
Journals of the South Carolina Executive Councils of 1861 and 1862; edited by Charles E. Cauthen. Columbia, South Carolina Archives Dept., 1956.
xv, 336 p. facsim. 28 cm.

These journals, skillfully edited, record the daily meetings of both councils; the 1861 agency was essentially advisory; that of 1862 wielded extensive executive power.

South Carolina. *Governor, 1860–1862 (F. W. Pickens)*
... Correspondence and other papers, relating to Fort Sumter. Including correspondence of Hon. Isaac W. Hayne with the President. 2d ed. Charleston, Presses of Evans & Cogswell, 1861.
43 p. 23cm.

A basic source for the guarded exchange of correspondence between Columbia and Washington.

South Carolina. *Historian of Confederate records.*
Report of the historian of the Confederate records to the General assembly of South Carolina. –1899. Columbia, S. C., The Bryan printing co., state printers [etc.] 18 –1900.
v. tables. 23cm.

The 1898 report is a checklist of document collections in the archives, together with admittedly incomplete statistics on troops.

South Carolina. *State Auditor.*
Report.
Columbia, C. P. Pelham.
v. 22 cm.

The 1863 report provided a clear summary of manufacturing activities, as well as military expenditures by the state government.

South Carolina. University.
War records. [Columbia, 1907–08]
2 v. 21 cm.

A starting point only for a subject badly in need of fuller study.

Spencer, Cornelia (Phillips) 1825–1908.
The last ninety days of the war in North Carolina. By Cornelia Phillips Spencer. 2d thousand. New York, Watchman publishing company, 1866.
287 p. 18 cm.

Useful observations by an intelligent and discerning woman.

Sprague, John Titcomb, 1810–1878.
The treachery in Texas, the secession of Texas, and the arrest of the United States officers and soldiers serving in Texas. Read before the New-York historical society, June 25, 1861. By Major J. T. Sprague, U. S. A. New-York, Printed for the Society, 1862.
1 p. l., p. [109]–142. 25½ cm.

An officer seized and paroled in 1861 by Texas State forces charged his oppressors with deliberate treason and marshalled many documents to support his accusations.

Sprunt, James.
... Tales of the Cape Fear blockade. By James Sprunt ... Raleigh, Capital printing company, 1902.
112 p. pl. 18 x 15cm.

While concentrating on the blockade, this study (reissued in 1960) is also a reliable source for wartime life in and around Wilmington, N. C.

Squires, William Henry Tappey, 1875–
The land of decision ... by W. H. T. Squires ... Portsmouth, Va., Printcraft press, inc., 1931.
xiv p., 1 l., 402 p. incl. front. plates, ports., maps. 24½cm.

A collection of miscellaneous sketches, mostly of men and events in wartime Virginia; disorganized, overwritten and inaccurate

Standard, Diffee William.
Columbus, Georgia, in the Confederacy; the social and industrial life of the Chattahoochee River port. New York, William-Frederick Press, 1954.
77 p. 22 cm.

A brief but useful booklet that emphasizes the importance to the Confederacy of this war-stimulated manufacturing center.

Stanley, J Randall.
History of Jackson County. Published under the auspices [of the] Jackson County Historical Society. [Marianna? Fla., ©1950]
281 p. illus. 24 cm.

Included are sketches of this Florida county's delegates to the secession convention, brief histories of military units, and a partial roster of those who served in the armies.

Staples, Thomas Starling, 1879–
Reconstruction in Arkansas, 1862–1874, by Thomas S. Staples ... New York, 1923.
451 p. 23 cm.

Contains a useful account of the establishment and administration of Union government, military and civil, in Arkansas, 1862-1865.

Stegeman, John F
These men she gave; Civil War diary of Athens, Georgia. Athens, University of Georgia Press [1964]
viii, 179 p. illus., ports., maps. 23 cm.

More a lively study of Athens units and the Cobb brothers, Howell and Thomas; based on wide use of newspapers and unpublished manuscripts.

Stick, David, 1919–
The Outer Banks of North Carolina, 1584–1958. Illustrated by Frank Stick. Chapel Hill, University of North Carolina Press [1958]
xii, 352 p. illus., maps. 24 cm.

Two lively but superficial chapters recount Federal amphibious operations and Union occupation of the area in question.

Stockard, Sallie W[alker]
The history of Guilford County, North Carolina. By Sallie W. Stockard ... Knoxville, Tenn., Gaut-Ogden co., printers, 1902.
197 p. front., plates, ports. 21cm.

An example of the poorest type of county history; a single three-page "chapter" covered the Civil War years.

Struggle for Vicksburg; the battles & siege that decided the Civil War, from the editors of Civil War times illustrated. Harrisburg, Pa., Stackpole Books [1967]
66 p. illus. (part col.), maps (part col.), ports. (part col.) 29 cm.

A reprint in hardcover of the July, 1967, issue of Civil War Times Illustrated; popularly written and profusely illustrated; a good summary of the campaign for the river city.

Teasdale, Thomas Cox, 1808–1891.
Reminiscences and incidents of a long life, by Rev. Thos. C. Teasdale, D. D., with a brief introduction by Rev. C. E. W. Dobbs ... 1st ed. St. Louis, Mo., National Baptist publishing co., 1887.
xiii, 385 p. front. (port.) 19½cm.

Recounts the unique wartime benevolences of a Baptist clergyman at Lauderdale Springs, Miss.

Temple, Oliver Perry, 1820–1907.
East Tennessee and the civil war, by Oliver P. Temple ... Cincinnati, The R. Clarke company, 1899.

xvi, 588 p. ports., fold. map. 24 cm.

A vindication of Unionism; Temple expounded on social, economic and political considerations behind the Unionist preference on the part of many Tennesseeans.

Tennessee.
State of Tennessee and the United States. Extracts from records, journals and documents, for use in the matters of controversy referred to in House joint resolution no. 25, acts of Tennessee, page 498, compiled September 24, 1895. Nashville, Tenn., Brandon printing company [1895]

cover-title, 230 p. 22½cm.

Contains much useful data on the principal railroads operative in the state at the outset of war; also shows damage to each by the conflict.

Tennessee. *Adjutant-general's office.*
Report of the adjutant general of the state of Tennessee, of the military forces of the state, from 1861 to 1866. Nashville, S. C. Mercer, printer to the state, 1866.

695, xii, ii p. 23cm.

Has incomplete muster rolls for 33 Federal regiments; Negro units were not included.

Tennessee. *Civil War Centennial Commission.*
Directory of Civil War monuments and memorials in Tennessee. Nashville, 1963.

93 p. illus. 28 cm.

A listing--with illustrations--of the many stone monuments erected in the Volunteer State to honor its Civil War individuals and units.

Tennessee. *Civil War Centennial Commission.*
Guide to the Civil War in Tennessee. 1st ed. Nashville, Division of Information, Dept. of Conservation, 1960.

32 p. illus. 28 cm.

A thumbnail history for tourists; gives a chronological synopsis of major events and a descriptive list of highway markers and monuments.

Tennessee. *Civil War Centennial Commission.*
Outline of unit of work on the Civil War. Prepared jointly by the Tennessee Civil War Centennial Commission and the Tennessee State Dept. of Education. [Nashville] State Dept. of Education, 1960.

6 l., 10 p. 28 cm.

A proposed Civil War unit study for upper grades in public schools; includes a brief annotated bibliography and a checklist of films and recordings.

Tennessee. *Civil War Centennial Commission.*
Tennesseans in the Civil War; a military history of Confederate and Union units with available rosters of personnel. Nashville, 1964–

v. 28 cm.

One of the best compilations of the Centennial; Vol. I contains capsule summaries of the units; Vol. II is an alphabetical roster (with unit) of every Tennessee soldier.

Tennessee. State Library and Archives, *Nashville.*
Index to Tennessee Confederate pension applications. [Nashville, 1964?]

viii, 323 p. 30 cm.

A rainbow to genealogists; of restricted value to the scholar and layman.

Tennessee. State Library and Archives, ***Nashville. Manuscript Section.***
Index to questionnaires of Civil War veterans. Nashville, 1962.

33 p. 28 cm.

An alphabetical listing of the names and home counties of 1,466 Confederate and 1,157 Federal veterans living in Tennessee; the questionnaires went out in 1914, 1915 and 1920.

Texas. *Comptroller's office.*
Condensed statements of the acting provisional comptroller's report, comprising statements from August 31, 1863, to June 8, 1865; also, from October 13, 1865, to August 13, 1866. Austin, Printed at the office of the "State gazette," 1866.

18, 9, 12, 10, [3] p. 21½cm.

Useful documents for a clearer understanding of the state's financial problems during the war.

Texas. *Convention, 1861.*
... Journal of the Secession convention of Texas, 1861. Ed. from the original in the Department of state by Ernest William Winkler, state librarian. [Austin] Austin printing company, 1912.
469, [1] p. fold. facsim. 23 cm.

In addition to the ordinary record of proceedings, the journal includes key addresses, committee reports, vote talleys and much correspondence.

Texas. *Convention, 1861. Committee on public safety.*
Reports of the Committee on public safety to the Convention of the people of the state of Texas, which assembled at Austin, the 28th January, 1861, and re-assembled on the 2d day of March, 1861: containing the missions to San Antonio, to the Rio Grande, and to the N. W. frontier. Gen'l Roger's mission to Louisiana, to procure arms, and the conference of the sub-committee with the late Governor Houston, with accompanying documents. Austin, J. Marshall, state printer, 1861.
173 p. 20cm.

The official collection of documents and correspondence relative to the confiscation of Federal property in 1861; bound with other useful state documents.

Texas. *Legislature.*
... Joint resolutions of the state of Texas. [Richmond? 1864]
1 l. 23½cm.

A typical legislative expression of determination to fight to the bitter end, but atypical in its expression of confidence in Jefferson Davis.

Texas. *Treasury dept.*
Report of the treasurer ...
Austin [etc.] 18
v. 22–23cm.

The 1861 report vividly reveals--through statistics--the disrupted school system caused by war.

Texas almanac. 1857–
[Dallas, etc.] A. H. Belo Corp. [etc.]
v. illus., ports., maps (part fold., part col.) 19–22 cm.

Issued for each year of the war, these almanacs provide interesting data on economic and political affairs.

Thomas, David Yancey, 1872–
Arkansas in war and reconstruction 1861–1874, by David Y. Thomas ... Little Rock, Arkansas division, United daughters of the confederacy, 1926.
6 p. l., 446 p. front., plates, port. 19½cm.

Based largely on the Official Records, and full of gaps, this still remains the most reliable treatment of the war in Arkansas.

Thomas, Edward J 1840–
Memoirs of a southerner, 1840–1923, by Edward J. Thomas. Savannah, Ga., 1923.
2 p. l., [7]–64 p. 18½cm.

Possesses a few glimpses of wartime Savannah.

Thomas, John Peyre, 1833–1912.
The history of the South Carolina military academy, with appendixes. By John Peyre Thomas. Charleston, S. C., Walker, Evans & Cogswell co., 1893.
xii, 579 p. front., plates, ports. 24cm.

This old but fact-filled volume contains much data on the role of the Citadel in the war.

Thorpe, John Houston, 1840–
Roster of Nash county confederate soldiers, by John H. Thorpe; and copy of Edgecombe county roster. Raleigh, Edwards & Broughton printing company, 1925.
135 p. 19 cm.

The alphabetical roster gives enlistment date, company, regiment, and service record of each soldier; the roster for Edgecombe County is much less detailed.

Tompkins, Daniel Augustus, 1852–1914.
History of Mecklenburg County and the city of Charlotte, from 1740 to 1903. By D. A. Tompkins ... Charlotte, N. C., Observer printing house, 1903.
2 v. fronts. (1 col.) plates (part col.) ports. (1 col.) maps, facsims., diagr. 24cm.

Includes the rosters of 21 companies, totaling 2, 735 men.

Trezevant, D H
The burning of Columbia, S. C. A review of northern assertions and southern facts. By Dr. D. H. Trezevant. Columbia, South Carolinian power press, 1866.

31 p. 21½ cm.

A straightforward, if impassioned, account by a distinguished eyewitness; Trezevant was highly critical of Sherman's explanations.

Tucker, Glenn.
Front rank. Written for the North Carolina Confederate Centennial Commission. With illus. by Bill Ballard. Raleigh, North Carolina Confederate Centennial Commission [©1962]

83 p. illus. 29 cm.

A well-written but cursory treatment of North Carolina's military contributions.

Turner, Benjamin Sterling, 1825–
Public buildings in Selma, Alabama—The refunding of the cotton tax. Remarks of Hon. Benjamin S. Turner, of Alabama, in the House of representatives, May 30 and 31, 1872 ... [Washington, Printed at the Congressional globe office, 1872]

4 p. 23½cm.

One of Alabama's three Negro congressmen, Turner pled eloquently for Federal construction as partial compensation for Selma's extensive war damage.

Turner, Joseph Kelly.
History of Edgecombe county, North Carolina, by J. Kelly Turner and Jno. L. Bridgers, jr. Raleigh, Edwards & Broughton printing co., 1920.

486 p. plates, ports., map, plans, facsims. 23½cm.

One long, solid chapter on the war stresses military contributions (including Dorsey Pender); yet it gives attention to political and economic affairs.

U. S. *National park service.*
Manassas to Appomattox; national battlefield parks tour in Virginia. [Washington, U. S. Govt. print. off., 1939]

31, [1] p. illus. (incl. maps) 27cm.

An excellent and useful little guide in its day; because of many Centennial activities in Virginia, the booklet now needs heavy revision.

Van Deusen, John George, 1890–
Economic bases of disunion in South Carolina, by John G. Van Deusen, PH. D. New York, Columbia university press; London, P. S. King & son, ltd., 1928.

360 p. front. (fold. map) 23cm.

A scholarly study in the Beardian tradition; argues that soil exhaustion, inadequate finances, etc. were more important in creating sectionalism and secession than was slavery.

Virginia. *Civil War Commission.*
The Civil War centennial; an opportunity for all Virginians ... [Richmond, 1960]

44 p. form. 20 cm.

A guide to local areas and agencies on how to honor their past; designed for the uninformed layman.

Virginia. *Civil War Commission.*
A register of military events in Virginia, 1861–1865. Compiled by N. E. Warinner. [Richmond] 1959.

79 p. 23 x 10 cm.

This handy reference work lists alphabetically, by year, more than 1,000 battles and skirmishes, and for each directs the reader to the appropriate volumes of the Official Records.

Virginia. *Civil War Commission.*
Selected Civil War State historical markers, Virginia. [Richmond, 1961]

48 p. 19 cm.

Somewhat inferior to a comparable publication for Georgia, but nevertheless useful and informative.

Virginia. *Civil War Commission.*
Virginia joins the Confederacy; chronology of events, November, 1860 through June, 1861. Richmond [1961]

18 p. 19 cm.

A brief chronology to a chain of events covered by the works of Munford and Shanks.

Virginia. *Convention, Richmond,* 1861.
Addresses delivered before the Virginia state convention by Hon. Fulton Anderson, commissioner from Mississippi, Hon. Henry L. Benning, commissioner from Georgia, and Hon. John S. Preston, commisioner from South Carolina, February, 1861. Richmond, W. M. Elliott, printer, 1861.
64 p. 22cm.

Fervent pleas that the Old Dominion cast her lot with her Southern sisters.

Virginia. *Convention, Richmond, 1861.*
Journals and papers of the Virginia State Convention of 1861. Richmond, Virginia State Library, 1966.
3 v. 23 cm.

Superior in two respects to the recently published Proceedings: this work was compiled by Wyatt M. Elliot, the official printer, and it contains minutes of secret sessions.

Virginia. *Convention, Richmond, 1861.*
Proceedings of the Virginia State Convention of 1861, February 13–May 1. George H. Reese, editor. Richmond, Virginia State Library [Historical Publications Division] 1965.
4 v. 24 cm.

Reproduces accounts of proceedings from the Richmond Enquirer; much rhetoric and local data included.

Virginia. *General assembly.*
... Preamble and resolutions asserting the jurisdiction and sovereignty of the state of Virginia over her ancient boundaries. Adopted October 8, 1863. [Richmond, 1864]
2 p. 23½cm.

The Old Dominion emphatically denied West Virginia's assertion of independence.

The **Virginia** highway historical markers; the tourist guide book of Virginia, featuring the inscriptions on the official markers along the historic and romantic highways of the Mother state ... Strasburg, Va., Shenandoah publishing house, inc., ©1930.
224 p. illus. (incl. maps) 27cm.

A guide to Virginia's markers, many of them error-filled, and most of them written by H. J. Eckenrode; the Virginia Centennial Commission's brochure is more reliable.

Virginia. *Laws, statutes, etc.*
Acts of the General assembly of the state of Virginia, passed in 1861, in the eighty-fifth year of the commonwealth. Richmond, W. F. Ritchie, public printer, 1861.
379, 73 p., 1 l. 23½cm.

This and subsequent collections of the Assembly provide much data on social and economic adjustments made necessary by the war.

Virginia. Military Institute, *Lexington.*
The Lieutenant Willis Jefferson Dance, Junior, memorial lectures delivered at the Virginia Military Institute, Lexington, Virginia, 1952–1963. Lexington, V. M. I. Foundation [1965]
viii, 192 l. illus., ports. 29 cm.

Subjects included in these lectures range from Lee and Jackson to the 1862 Valley Campaign and the 1864 battle of New Market.

Virginia. *Secretary of Virginia military records.*
Report.
Richmond, 1910–
v. 23cm.

The 1909 volume is a progress report on the modestly successful attempt to collect Virginia's Confederate records.

Waddel, John Newton, 1812–1895.
Memorials of academic life: being an historical sketch of the Waddel family, identified through three generations with the history of the higher education in the South and Southwest. By John N. Waddel ... Richmond, Va., Presbyterian committee of publication, 1891.
583 p. front. (port.) 20½cm.

Diary-like passages that are quite revealing for Mississippi wartime society; Waddel served as chief of chaplains in the Army of Tennessee.

Waddell, Alfred Moore, 1834–1912.
The last year of the war in North Carolina, including Plymouth, Fort Fisher and Bentonsville. An address before the Association army of northern Virginia, delivered in the hall of the House of delegates, Richmond, Va., October 28, 1887, by Hon. A. M. Waddell ... Printed by order of the Association. Richmond, W. E. Jones, printer, 1888.
31 p. 24cm.

This work has long been superseded by better, if not more honest, scholarship.

Waddell, James D *ed.*

Biographical sketch of Linton Stephens, (late associate justice of the Supreme court of Georgia,) containing a selection of his letters, speeches, state papers, etc. Ed. by James D. Waddell ... Atlanta, Ga., Dodson & Scott, 1877.

3 p. l., 434 p. front. (port.) 23cm.

Mostly a collection of extracts from the letters of Linton Stephens to his half brother, Alexander; disappointing in content for the war years.

Waddell, Joseph Addison.

Annals of Augusta county, Virginia, with reminiscences illustrative of the vicissitudes of its pioneer settlers; biographical sketches ... a diary of the war, 1861–'5, and a chapter on reconstruction, by Jos. A. Waddell ... Richmond, W. E. Jones, 1886.

vii, 374 p. 2 maps (incl. front.) 25½cm.

Reliable and detailed, in spite of its age; contains much data on Staunton, Va., and the 5th Virginia.

Walker, Anne Kendrick.

Backtracking in Barbour county, a narrative of the last Alabama frontier, by Anne Kendrick Walker ... Richmond, Va., The Dietz press, 1941.

3 p. l., [v]–xxvii, 353 p. front., plates, ports., maps, facsims. 23½ cm.

Good local history; five chapters cover the war in this southeastern Alabama county, with emphasis on the home front and Eufaula.

Walker, Anne Kendrick.

Russell County in retrospect; an epic of the far southeast. Richmond, Dietz Press, 1950.

xxii, 423 p. illus., map, ports. 24 cm.

The two chapters devoted to the war years in this east Alabama county include muster rolls and service records, plus a fine account of Wilson's 1865 raid on Columbus, Ga.

Walker, Charles Duy, 1849?–1877.

Memorial, Virginia military institute. Biographical sketches of the graduates and élèves of the Virginia military institute who fell during the war between the states. By Charles D. Walker ... Philadelphia, J. B. Lippincott & co., 1875.

585 p. 23 cm.

An extremely valuable collection of biographical sketches; many contain lengthy excerpts from wartime letters by former cadets who gained prominence in the Confederacy.

Walker, Peter Franklin.

Vicksburg; a people at war, 1860–1865. Chapel Hill, University of North Carolina Press [1960]

xvi, 235 p. illus., map. 24 cm.

Probably the most authoritative study on this critical Mississippi city.

Wallace, David Duncan, 1874–

The history of South Carolina, by David Duncan Wallace ... New York, The American historical society, inc., 1934.

4 v. fronts., illus., plates, ports., maps. 27½cm.

Volume III contains a worthwhile survey of the war years.

Wallace, Ernest.

Texas in turmoil, 1849–1875. Illustrated by Warren Hunter. Austin, Tex., Steck-Vaughn Co. [1965]

vii, 293 p. illus., maps, ports. 22 cm.

Marred by so many weaknesses as to be of limited value even for the popular reader.

Wallace, Lee A

A guide to Virginia military organizations, 1861–1865. Compiled by Lee A. Wallace, Jr. Richmond, Virginia Civil War Commission, 1964.

348 p. illus., ports. 28 cm.

An indispensable volume for Virginia units; a brief introduction to the work's various sections, and notes on unit organizations, increase the overall value.

Warmoth, Henry Clay, 1842–1931.

War, politics and reconstruction; stormy days in Louisiana, By Henry Clay Warmoth. New York, The Macmillan company, 1930.

xiii p., 1 l., 285 p. front., ports. 22½cm.

Far more politics and reconstruction than war comprise this now-dated study.

Wayland, John Walter, 1872–
A history of Rockingham county, Virginia, by John W. Wayland ... Dayton, Va., Ruebush-Elkins company, 1912.

4 p. l., v–vii, [2], 10–466, [7] p. front., 1 illus., plates, ports., maps (part fold.) facsims. 23cm.

A better one-chapter summary of the war than the usual county history contains; has much statistical data, with many references to the 10th Virginia Infantry.

Wayland, John Walter, 1872–1962.
A history of Shenandoah county, Virginia, by John W. Wayland ... Strasburg, Va., Shenandoah publishing house, 1927.

874 p. illus. (incl. ports., maps, plan) 23½ cm.

Wayland again utilized contemporary newspapers, diaries and reminiscences--but not as successfully as in his Rockingham County study.

Wayland, John Walter, 1872–
Stonewall Jackson's way; route, method, achievement, by John W. Wayland. Staunton, Va., The McClure company, inc., 1940.

2 p. l., vii–xv, 244 p. illus. (incl. ports., maps) 31½cm.

Photographs and maps enhance a superb text that recounts Jackson's exploits in the Valley; reprinted with minimum changes in 1956.

Wayland, John Walter, 1872–1962, *ed.*
Virginia Valley records; genealogical and historical materials of Rockingham county, Virginia, and related regions (with map) by John W. Wayland ... Special contributors: David A. Heatwole ... Rev. J. R. Ellis ... Joseph K. Ruebush ... [and others] Strasburg, Va., Printed by Shenandoah publishing house, inc., 1930.
4 p. l., [7]–491 p. fold. map. 23½ cm.

A hodgepodge of local lore and legal records, mainly of genealogical interest; the best section are the letters and notes of Capt. John Q. Winfield, 7th Virginia Cavalry.

Weeks, Stephen Beauregard, 1865–1918.
"The University of North Carolina in the civil war." An address delivered at the centennial celebration of the opening of the institution, June 5th, 1895, by Stephen Beauregard Weeks ... Richmond, W. E. Jones, printer, 1896.

1 p. l., 38 p. 23cm.

A bare introduction to a subject deserving greater study.

Weitzel, Godfrey, 1835–1884.
Richmond occupied. Entry of the United States forces into Richmond, Va., April 3, 1865; calling together of the Virginia Legislature and revocation of the same. Edited with an introd. by Louis H. Manarin. [Richmond, Richmond Civil War Centennial Committee, 1965]

65 p. illus. (1 fold.) fold. map, ports. 23 cm.

The unique and revealing diary of the Federal commander whose XXV Corps occupied the city; skillfully edited.

Wellman, Manly Wade, 1905–
The county of Warren, North Carolina, 1586–1917. Chapel Hill, University of North Carolina Press [1959]

282 p. illus. 24 cm.

Contains a lively account of the county at war, with emphasis on the local scenes; enhanced by quotations from contemporary sources.

Whitt, Jane Chapman.
Elephants and Quaker guns; a history of Civil War and circus days. [1st ed.] New York, Vantage Press [1966]

103 p. illus., facsims, maps. 21 cm.

Casts a very pale light on wartime events in Fairfax County, Va.

Williams, R H 1831–
With the border ruffians; memories of the far West, 1852–1868, by R. H. Williams, sometime lieutenant in the Kansas rangers and afterwards captain in the Texan rangers; ed. by E. W. Williams ... New York, E. P. Dutton and company, 1907.

xiv p., 1 l., xv–xviii, 478 p. 4 pl., 2 port. (incl. front.) 22½cm.

Useful for insights of wartime prices and problems in Texas.

Williams, Thomas Harry, 1909–
The Civil War in Louisiana; a chronology by T. Harry Williams and A. Otis Hébert, Jr. [Baton Rouge, Louisiana Civil War Centennial Commission, 1961?]

29 p. illus. 24 cm.

In addition to the chronology of principal civil and military events, this work lists 269 engagements, 23 historical markers, and 20 gravesites of Confederate generals.

Williams, Thomas Harry, 1909–
Louisiana commemorates the Civil War. [Baton Rouge, Louisiana Civil War Centennial Commission, 196–?]
iii, 15 p. illus. 23 cm.

Paragraph summaries designed to whet the appetite.

Winston, E T.
Story of Pontotoc, part I[–III] ... [by] E. T. Winston. [Pontotoc, Miss.] Pontotoc progress print, 1931.
2 p. l., 192, [6], 203–319, [4] p. incl. illus., plates. 22½cm.

Contains a good description of the mustering of an infantry company from one Mississippi county.

Winters, John D
The Civil War in Louisiana. [Baton Rouge] Louisiana State University Press [1963]
xiv, 534 p. illus., ports., maps, plans. 25 cm.

By far the best military history of the war in Louisiana; compliments Bragg's older work, which stressed political and economic factors.

Woldert, Albert, 1867–
A history of Tyler and Smith County, Texas. San Antonio, Naylor Co. [1948]
xi, 165 p. illus., port., map. 21 cm.

Of limited usefulness for data on Camp Ford prison.

Wooten, Dudley Goodall, *ed.*
A comprehensive history of Texas, 1685–1897, ed. by Dudley G. Wooten ... Dallas, W. G. Scarff, 1898.
2 v. fronts., illus. (incl. plan) plates (1 col.) ports., maps, facsims., tables. 26cm.

Volume II contains a potpourri of data on Texas' wartime history.

Wright, Marcus Joseph, 1831–1922.
Arkansas in the War 1861–1865. Batesville, Ark., Independence County Historical Society [1963]
104 p. illus. 23 cm.

Recently published from a manuscript long buried in a private collection; contains a host of tables, rosters and statistics.

Wright, Marcus Joseph, 1831–1922.
Tennessee in the war, 1861–1865; lists of military organizations and officers from Tennessee in both the Confederate and Union armies; general and staff officers of the provisional army of Tennessee, appointed by Governor Isham G. Harris ... comp. and prepared by General Marcus J. Wright. Williamsbridge, New York city, A. Lee publishing company [c1908]
228 p. 21cm.

Composed of service records of Confederate and Federal generals, notes on other officers, numerical lists of Southern units, and an alphabetical roster of engagements.

Wright, Marcus Joseph, 1831–1922.
Texas in the War, 1861–1865. Edited and notes by Harold B. Simpson. [1st ed. Hillsboro, Tex.] Hill Junior College Press [1965]
xx, 246 p. ports. 24 cm.

Greatly enhanced by Col. Simpson's excellent notes and appendices, this is by all odds the most useful of the Wright state compendiums.

Yeary, Mamie, 1876– *comp.*
Reminiscences of the boys in gray, 1861–1865, comp. by Miss Mamie Yeary ... Dallas, Tex., For the author by Smith & Lamar, publishing house M. E. church, South [c1912]
3 p. l., 904 p. front., plates (1 col.) ports. 25½cm.

Recollections of dozens of Confederate veterans living in Texas in the early 1900's; the accounts are generally brief, frequently hazy, but occasionally sharp and worthwhile.

CUMULATIVE INDEX

Compiled by James I. Robertson, Jr.